Lawrence Erlbaum Associates, Inc., Publishers
365 Broadway
Hillsdale, New Jersey 07642

**Library of Congress Cataloging in Publication Data**

Main entry under title:

Information integration by children.

"This book is based on a conference held in June
1977 in Kassel, Germany."
Bibliography: p.
Includes indexes.
1. Cognition in children—Congresses. 2. Human
information processing—Congresses. I. Wilkening,
Friedrich. II. Becker, Johannes. III. Trabasso, Tom.
BF723.C5I53      155.4'13      79-24289
ISBN 0-89859-015-9

Printed in the United States of America

# Contents

**Preface**    vii

## PART I: INTEGRATION THEORY AND APPLICATIONS

1. Information Integration Theory in Developmental Psychology
   *Norman H. Anderson*    *1*

2. Development of Dimensional Integration in Children's Perceptual
   Judgment: Experiments with Area, Volume, and Velocity
   *Friedrich Wilkening*    *47*

3. Integration of Intent and Consequence Information
   in Children's Moral Judgments
   *Manuel Leon*    *71*

4. Information Processing in Children's Choices Among Bets
   *Wilfried Hommers*    *99*

## PART II: STIMULUS ANALYSIS AND INTEGRATION

5. The Relation of Stimulus Structure to Perceptual and Cognitive
   Development: Further Tests of a Separability Hypothesis
   *Bryan E. Shepp, Barbara Burns, and Dorothy McDonough*    *113*

v

6. Where Does One Part End and Another Begin? A Developmental Study
   *Stephen M. Kosslyn, Karen H. Heldmeyer, and Arnold L. Glass*      *147*

7. Integrating and Disintegrating Information: The Role of
   Perception and Conception in the Development of Problem Solving
   *Richard D. Odom and Joseph G. Cunningham*      *169*

8. Information Integration Through Structural Abstraction in
   Discrimination Learning
   *Richard S. Bogartz*      *183*

**PART III: INTEGRATION OF EVENTS IN DISCOURSE PROCESSING**

9. Memory and Inferences in the Comprehension of Narratives
   *Tom Trabasso and David W. Nicholas*      *215*

10. Toward a Taxonomy of Inferences for Story Comprehension
    *David W. Nicholas and Tom Trabasso*      *243*

11. Children's Understanding of Stories: Assimilation by a General
    Schema for Actions or Coordination of Temporal Relations?
    *Heinz Wimmer*      *267*

**Author Index**      **291**

**Subject Index**      **297**

# Preface

This book is based on a conference held in June 1977 in Kassel, Germany. The conference was part of a broad program for the advancement of developmental psychology in Germany being sponsored by the Volkswagen Foundation. One main aim of this program was to improve the scientific interchange between developmental psychologists, both within Germany and with other countries. The publication of this book is one step in that direction.

The conference was planned and organized by the first two editors of this book. The topic of *information integration by children* attracted us for several reasons. First, there was promising research in Germany that could be subsumed under this general theme, the single attempts, however, being scattered over different laboratories with little or no contact among each other. Second, there were interesting new developments in this area in the United States that we thought should be made known to the German audience without the usual transatlantic lag. Third, we hoped that it would be interesting in itself to bring together the diverse American approaches to the study of information integration by children.

In inviting the speakers for the conference, we attempted to have a broad coverage. Fortunately, all six American researchers whom we asked accepted our invitation. The other participants at the conference were about twenty psychologists from the German-speaking countries. Of this group, four each presented a paper. In addition to those contained in this book, Eva and Michael Dreher (University of Augsburg) talked about "Information processing strategies of children and adolescents in tasks of different levels of complexity," and Peter Heymans (University of Nijmegen) presented a paper entitled "Social-cognitive development: Formalization of some aspects with both information about the whole configuration of an object and about its particular parts, which may be integrated into the global shape. In their chapter, Kosslyn et al. examine how such a way of processing could have developed. In a series of experiments, they attempt to determine what kinds of stimulus properties serve to delineate part boundaries at different ages, the main stimulus variables under investigation being contour, color, and texture changes. Contour changes turned out to be relatively important for very young children, whereas they less often than older children and adults organized figures according to changes in color and texture. On the whole, however, the differences in the effectiveness of the different stimulus dimensions over age appeared to reflect gradual rather than qualitative changes. The authors conclude, therefore, that the Kosslyn and Shwartz model may, at least in principle, also hold for children.

In Chapter 7, Odom and Cunningham examine integration and disintegration of information in children's problem solving. To study this issue, Odom and Cunningham use matrix tasks that, for problem solution, require either the combination (integration) or the analysis (disintegration) of information given on the perceptual dimensions involved, for example form, color, and position. The salience of these dimensions, which was individually assessed before each experiment, was systematically varied. Children as young as 5 years showed an ability to both analyze and integrate the information, provided the dimensions relevant for problem solution were high in salience. On the basis of these results, Odom and Cunningham criticize conceptual-change theories like the Piagetian or the "selective attention" approach. They conclude that more emphasis should be given to the perceptual characteristics of the information if the development of integration and disintegration processes is to be understood.

Bogartz, in Chapter 8, examines children's information integration in discrimination learning. The solutions of the tasks he uses require either a combination of stimulus attributes (conditional discrimination problems) or a combination of stimuli (transverse patterning problems). Most of the children at all age levels from 6 to 10 years solved the conditional discrimination problems. Of particular interest in the present context is how these children arrived at their solution. They appeared to integrate the information by assimilation of specific content to abstract structures that could then be applied to new situations. Bogartz presents further evidence of learning through structural abstraction in his experiment on the transverse patterning problem, which has often been reported as being too difficult for children and even for many adults. Bogartz shows that children as young as 9 years are able to solve this problem when they are presented with a structural analogue, namely the well-known paper-rock-scissors game.

In Part III, the analysis of integration of information is extended to a different and more complex content, namely language. In Chapter 9,

Trabasso and Nicholas review the evidence on children's ability to construct representations of related sentences that reduce the original prose into integrated, meaning units. In the first part of their chapter, they critically examine the constructivist position of Paris who derived his false-recognition procedures from the seminal work of Bransford and Franks. Following this, they review Trabasso and his colleagues' studies on how children construct linear orders from premises in transitive reasoning tasks. The primary findings discussed in their review are that children as young as 4 years of age do integrate linguistic information into semantic or linear representations in memory to recognize probes or answer inferential questions. The ability to construct such representations, however, is constrained by limits of memory and semantic development.

In Chapter 10, Nicholas and Trabasso address directly a shortcoming in the work on integrating information across sentences, namely, the absence of any systematic taxonomy of what kinds of integration can occur. Conceptualizing the making of inferences as either connecting sentences or filling in missing events, the child, as comprehender, is viewed as one who constructs an event chain while reading or hearing text. The kinds of causes or consequences predicted by the child as well as other forms or means of making the links in the chain are discussed. This taxonomic approach paves the way for more systematic questioning of the child's ability to integrate information across sentence units in narratives.

In Chapter 11, Wimmer describes how children can use higher order schema to assimilate new information in the comprehension of stories. These action-based schema allow the child to construct a representation of the story through the use of existing structures, and they take advantage of the regular organization that exists in folktales, myths, and children's stories. Wimmer shows how deviations from the schema in the story disrupt comprehension and affect recall of the stories. On the positive side, he shows how story schema allow the child to remember main or central events, their temporal order and causal relations.

From all chapters, a general result emerges: Children can integrate information. This has been shown for children down to the age of 3 years and for various contents: perceptual judgment, moral and social judgment, decision making, problem solving, discrimination learning, story comprehension, and discourse processing. For some researchers, the general result that children can and do integrate information may seem trivial. It has to be emphasized, however, that the field of developmental psychology is still pervaded by Piaget's notion that cognition in young children is characterized by "centration" and that they are unable to coordinate information from different dimensions.

The finding that children can and do integrate information was to a large extent made possible by new methodological approaches in developmental

# INTEGRATION THEORY AND APPLICATIONS

# 1 Information Integration Theory in Developmental Psychology

Norman H. Anderson
*University of California, San Diego*


Virtually all thought and behavior has multiple causes. Seldom does an external stimulus or internal force act alone without being conditioned by the simultaneous operation of other forces. This basic fact of multiple causation is well known in every area of psychology, from perceptual judgments of size and distance to social judgments of attractiveness or fairness.

But multiple causation is hard to study. Although innumerable investigators have been concerned with specific problems of stimulus integration and interaction, attempts at general theory have been rare. The reason is simple. When diverse causal forces are at work, each pushing in its own direction, the net resultant is difficult to predict and difficult to analyze. To pursue the analysis requires a quantitative theory of stimulus integration. That in turn requires a capability for measuring the subjective, psychological values of the stimuli. Lack of such a measurement capability has held back the study of stimulus integration.

Information integration theory has provided a successful approach to the general analysis of stimulus integration. The success of this approach rests in considerable part on the discovery that much of thought and judgment is governed by simple algebraic models. Algebraic models have been considered by many investigators in many areas but, without a measurement capability, these models have remained pseudoequations without mathematical content.

The success of the integration–theoretical approach became possible by reversing the traditional idea that measurement was a methodological preliminary to substantive inquiry. Instead, measurement was made an organic component of substantive theory. The algebraic models thus became the base and frame for measurement. Useful contributions have been made in almost every area of psychology (Anderson, 1974a, 1974b, 1974c, 1978, 1980). This work is a promising beginning to a unified, general theory of judgment and decision.

This chapter discusses applications of integration theory to developmental psychology. Although these developmental studies have only recently begun, they have produced exciting results as well as some useful suggestions for further work.

## OVERVIEW OF THEORY AND METHOD

### Basic Ideas

The nature of integration theory can be illustrated in terms of the functional measurement diagram of Fig. 1.1. Physical stimuli, $S_1, S_2, \ldots$ impinge on the organism and are processed by the valuation function $V$ to become psychological representations, $s_1, s_2, \ldots$. These psychological stimuli are combined by the integration function $I$ into an implicit or covert response, $r$. Finally, this implicit response is transformed by the output function $M$ to become the overt, observed response $R$. Thus, the diagram portrays a chain of three basic operations that lead from the observable stimulus to the observable response.

The valuation function $V$ is the first basic operation. For simple psychophysical stimuli, $V$ is commonly known as the psychophysical law that relates physical intensity to psychological sensation. However, the concept of valuation also applies to verbal stimuli or perceptual patterns that lack a physical metric.

FUNCTIONAL   MEASUREMENT   DIAGRAM

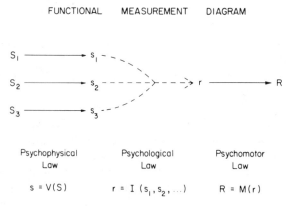

Psychophysical Law  
Psychological Law  
Psychomotor Law

$$s = V(S) \qquad r = I(s_1, s_2, \ldots) \qquad R = M(r)$$

FIG. 1.1.   Functional measurement diagram.

The most important operation in the chain of Fig. 1.1 is the integration function $I$. This is also called the psychological law because it relates stimuli and response at the psychological level. This point deserves emphasis for it is with these internal, psychological processes that the theory is concerned.

Finally, the response function $M$ mediates between the implicit response and the more or less arbitrary constraints of the measuring apparatus employed by the investigator. If $M$ is a linear function, so that $R$ is a linear function of $r$, then $R$ is said to be a linear or "equal-interval" scale.

The functional measurement diagram shows a chain of three conceptually distinct functions. Two of these are associated with problems of measurement: $V$ with stimulus measurement, $M$ with response measurement. However, it is the integration function $I$ that has the fundamental role. It provides the base and frame for solving the two problems of measurement as will be illustrated by the parallelism theorem below. These measurement problems, however, are in one sense only incidental to determining the function $I$ that governs stimulus integration. It is the integration processes that have primary importance.

The next subsections illustrate this integration-theoretical approach in a simple experiment on toy preferences and discuss some of the associated problems of method and procedure.

## The Averaging Hypothesis

Theory and method can be simply illustrated by an initial experiment on judgments of toys. The child is shown two toys at a time and asked how much he would like to play with this pair of toys. Each toy has a certain attractiveness to the child, and the question is how the attractiveness values of the separate toys are integrated to produce the overall response to the pair (Butzin & Anderson, 1973).

Of course, younger children might not yet be able to integrate. For example, they might consider only the more attractive toy and ignore the less attractive toy. However, the theoretical hypothesis in this experiment was that the child would integrate and, moreover, that this integration would obey an averaging rule. That is, the attractiveness of the pair would equal the average attractiveness value of the separate toys.

But this averaging hypothesis involves a long-standing problem, namely, the problem of psychological measurement. There is no physical measure of attractiveness. A test of the averaging model must allow for the subjective, psychological attractiveness values of the toys. Some way must be found, therefore, to measure subjective values on valid linear ("interval") scales.

The theory of functional measurement, which was developed as part of information integration theory, provides a way to measure subjective values.

This measurement methodology is basically simple and it has been successful. How it works will be brought out in the further discussion of the toy experiment.

## Two Aspects of Method

Two key features of experimental method that are typical in integration–theoretical studies appear in the toy experiment. The first is the use of factorial design. This kind of design provides the necessary constraints to test the hypothesized model in a simple way.

The design was a 3 × 3, row × column factorial and is illustrated in Table 1.1. Three toys were selected, Low, Medium, and High in attractiveness value, and these formed the row factor in the design. Three other toys were selected similarly for the column factor. Thus, each cell of the design represents a pairing of one row toy and one column toy. Each child judged all nine of these toy pairs.

The second key feature of method is the use of a numerical response. In this toy experiment, the response scale consisted of a row of seven schematic faces, graded successively from a deep frown to a big smile. The child pointed to one face to indicate how happy he would be with each toy combination. These faces were numbered 1 to 7 and these numbers were used in the analysis. The entries in Table 1.1 are the mean ratings for the group of 30 children.

These data provide a simple test of the averaging hypothesis if a special condition is fulfilled. The condition is that the rating scale is a linear ("equal–interval") scale. This means that the observable response numbers are a linear function of the subjective attractiveness values. Of course, this condition may seem untestable because the subjective values are unobservable. The long-continued controversies in measurement theory stem from just this difficulty.

Actually, the problem of the linear scale has a simple solution. It is easy to test whether the child is using the ratings in a linear way, which fortunately,

TABLE 1.1
Mean Attractiveness Judgments of Combinations of Two Toys

|           | Column Toy | | |
|-----------|------|--------|------|
| Row Toy   | High | Medium | Low  |
| High      | 6.53 | 5.67   | 3.92 |
| Medium    | 5.83 | 4.57   | 3.03 |
| Low       | 4.62 | 3.53   | 1.98 |

*Note:* Data from Butzin and Anderson, 1973.

turns out to be true. This outcome is so important that the measurement logic deserves explicit discussion.

## Parallelism Theorem

The parallelism theorem provides a very simple analysis of adding-type models. To illustrate, consider the data from the toy experiment in Table 1.1. The theoretical question in this experiment concerned the rule for integration. If an adding-type rule holds, then the factorial plot of these data should exhibit parallelism. A more precise statement, which applies to data from any factorial design, is as follows.

Parallelism theorem: *Suppose that (1) the integration process follows an adding-type model; (2) the overt, measured response is a linear scale. Then (1) the factorial plot of the data will be a set of parallel curves; (2) the row (column) means of the data table will be linear scales of the subjective values of the row (column) stimuli.*

Proof and discussion of this theorem have been given elsewhere (e.g., Anderson, 1974c, 1976c; Anderson & Cuneo, 1978a; Butzin & Anderson, 1973). Here it may be noted that both assumptions of the theorem are necessary for parallelism. If one was wrong, then parallelism would not, in general, obtain. It follows, therefore, that observed parallelism provides support not only for the model, but also for the linearity of the response scale.

To apply the parallelism theorem to the toy experiment, the data from Table 1.1 were plotted in factorial form in Fig. 1.2. The three curves appear reasonably parallel and the statistical test showed nonsignificant deviations from parallelism. Much the same pattern was observed for the 5-7 year

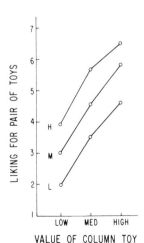

FIG. 1.2. Attractiveness judgments of pairs of toys from Table 1.1. (After Butzin & Anderson, 1973.)

subgroup and the 8–13 year subgroup. As far as one experiment may go, therefore, this one accomplishes three simultaneous goals.

1. It supports the adding-type model for toy integration.
2. It supports the linearity of the response scale.
3. It provides linear scales of the subjective values of the toys.

The directness and simplicity of this analysis are notable. Little more is needed than to run the experiment and plot the data. The graph speaks directly to the theoretical hypothesis.

## Stimulus Scaling

The parallelism test of the toy averaging hypothesis did not require or use separate scale values for the individual toys. This test relies only on the judgments about pairs of toys. Once the model has passed this test of fit, the marginal means provide functional scales of toy value as stated in the theorem.

It may seem odd not to use the ratings of the single toys as scale values in the model test. Actually, that could be a serious mistake (Butzin & Anderson, 1973, p. 535). If done in the usual way, it would only increase error variability and thereby decrease the power of the test. It can also potentiate regression artifacts when the separate ratings are not obtained within the very same situation. Thus, the conclusion of Hendrick, Franz, and Hoving (1975), that children average personality traits in judgments of persons, is not warranted because of the probable regression artifacts.

It should be noted that stimulus values can be obtained for each child separately. This is clearly necessary. A doll, for example, would have different values for boys or girls, or even for girls at different ages. The model can hardly be tested for one child using the values of another child. In fact, the statistical test of the model, although made for the group data, actually employs individual values for each child. If desired, functional scaling could be used to assess value systems at the individual level.

## Averaging Model

A natural reaction to the parallelism theorem is to ask whether there is more than one integration model that could produce parallelism. In fact, two quite different processes, adding and averaging, can produce parallelism. This issue has both theoretical and methodological importance.

The toy experiment illustrates the critical test that has been used to distinguish between the adding and averaging models. In Fig. 1.3., the open-circle curve gives the response to the column toy when presented alone. The

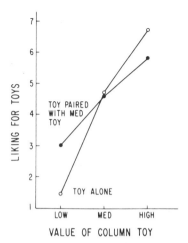

FIG. 1.3.   Critical test of averaging versus adding. (After Butzin & Anderson, 1973.)

filled-circle curve gives the response to this same column toy when paired with the medium value row toy. The crossover of these two curves eliminates the adding model but supports the averaging model.

The logic of this critical test is straightforward. According to the adding model, when the medium row toy is paired with the column toy, the value of this combination should be greater than the value of the column toy alone. Hence, the filled-circle curve must lie above the open-circle curve at every point. This prediction is robust for it holds even if the response scale is only monotone (ordinal) and even if the adding model is not exact but only directional. In other words, the crossover is a qualitative test that eliminates an entire class of adding models.

The averaging model predicts the crossover. The average value of the medium row toy and the low column toy is higher than the value of the low column toy alone; the average value of the medium row toy and the high column toy is lower than the value of the high column toy alone. This agrees exactly with the data.

Taken together, the parallelism in Fig. 1.2. and the crossover in Fig. 1.3. provide strong support for the averaging model. The parallelism indicates the operation of one of two simple models, adding or averaging. The crossover diagnoses between these two models.

This experiment is one of many that have supported the averaging model. Although most of these experiments have been with adults, the evidence from the available developmental studies seems to agree. Collectively, these studies point to a pervasive averaging tendency in human judgment. This fact has extensive theoretical ramifications.

One methodological implication of the averaging hypothesis deserves mention. Detailed analysis shows that the averaging model predicts parallelism only under the special condition of equal weighting. All the row (or column) stimuli must have equal importance or weight among themselves. This condition should be kept in mind when designing experiments. The simplicity of the parallelism analysis suggests the desirability of trying to ensure equal weighting. If equal weighting seems uncertain, then auxiliary information about the weights may account for systematic discrepancies from parallelism.

## Other Integration Models

Other algebraic models for information integration have also been studied. In some situations, it appears that the stimulus information should be multiplied. Expected value in a game of chance, for example, is the value of the prize times the probability of winning it (see following). Multiplying models have a simple analysis, provided by the linear fan theorem whose statement and logic are much like the parallelism theorem.

Linear Fan Theorem: *Suppose that (1) the integration process follows a multiplying model; (2) the overt, measured response is a linear scale. Then (1) the appropriate factorial plot of the data will form a linear fan of diverging straight lines; (2) the row (column) means of the data table will be linear scales of the subjective values of the row (column) stimuli.*

In addition, there is a group of nonlinear models that do not have simple graphical analyses. For example, the ratio model for two competing responses takes the response as $X_1/(X_1 + X_2)$, where $X_1$ and $X_2$ are the strengths of the two forces. This model has arisen in decision theory, psycholinguistics, speech identification, and group bargaining. General methods of analysis are illustrated in Leon and Anderson (1974), Oden (1977), and Anderson (1977).

## Statistical Analysis

Problems of statistical analysis have been considered in the various experimental reports and will not be discussed in any detail here. These problems are quite important, however, and deserve careful attention. Accordingly, a few general points may be noted.

Analysis of variance constitutes the main statistical tool and, indeed, is ideally suited to the kinds of questions that arise. For example, the graphical test of parallelism is equivalent to the test of the row × column interaction term in the analysis of variance. If the model is true, then this term is zero in principle and so should be nonsignificant in practice. This test is a normal supplement to the graphical test. Analogous tests are available for the other algebraic models. These methods can, of course, be readily generalized to experiments with more than two pieces of information.

Row and column main effects are typically trivial in these judgmental tasks. They are virtually guaranteed by the choice of stimuli and in general do not deserve to reported. However, main effects can become important in the study of limited capacity processing as noted below.

## Rating Scale Methodology

The functional measurement analyses are quite simple when the ratings form a linear scale. Response linearity is not merely an assumption, of course, because it receives validating support from the observed parallelism. If the response scale was not linear, then the model would not, in general, produce parallelism as noted above.

It may seem surprising that so simple and straightforward a methodology was so long in being recognized. In fact, the rating method has been almost universally condemned and shunned by writers in measurement theory. There was some reason for this because ratings are subject to various well known biases. Fortunately, it appears that only a few modest experimental precautions are needed to eliminate these biases (Anderson; 1974a, p. 231; 1974c, p. 245; 1980).

The most important procedural detail concerns establishing the frame of reference. The rating of any one stimulus is always relative to what other stimuli are being rated. A 6-cm square, for example, could be the largest or the smallest of the group and cannot be meaningfully rated until the frame of reference has been established.

The standard device for setting up the frame of reference has been stimulus end anchors. These are stimuli that are just noticeably more extreme, lower or higher, than the regular experimental stimuli. The subject is presented with these end anchors in the instruction–practice phase and, if appropriate, is told directly that these are the smallest and largest stimuli that will be given and that they correspond to the end responses on the rating scale. These end anchors define the stimulus range and help the subject set up a frame of reference for using the rating scale (see, e.g., Anderson & Cuneo, 1978a).

When feasible, the end anchors may be left in sight throughout the experiment. In the rectangle experiment of Fig. 1.4., for example, the end achors were 5 × 5 and 13 × 13 squares that were placed at the ends of the graphic response scale. In other experiments, the end anchors may be presented along with the regular experimental stimuli in order to maintain the frame of reference.

In addition, the end anchors have another function. They are intended to tie down the end responses so that the responses to the regular experimental stimuli come from the interior of the scale. This helps avoid end effects, such as the so-called floor and ceiling effects.

FIG. 1.4. Graphic happiness rating scale. Copyright 1978 by the American Psychological Association. Reprinted by permission.

With adults, either a numerical or a graphical rating scale may be used. Numerical ratings are convenient and seem adequate for most purposes. However, there is some evidence that graphic scales may avoid local number preferences and scale lumping that can occur with numerical scales.

With children, only the graphic scale has been used. Most applications to date have relied on the face happiness scale, which seems well designed to tap into the child's conception of a graded continuum. However, the face scale sometimes entails an indirect judgment. In one experiment on rectangle area, for example, the rectangle was a facsimile cookie, and the judgment was how happy a hungry little child would be to have that cookie. This instruction is more motivating than judging area and it seems to give the same results (Anderson & Cuneo, 1978a).

The optimal number of steps to use in the rating scale is uncertain. The above toy experiment used a seven-step scale. Seven steps seem uncomfortably few when a linear scale is desired. Indeed, some suggestion of a ceiling effect can be seen in Fig.1.2, and this was even more pronounced in the younger age range, from 5 to 7 years. At the time, it was feared that using more steps would cause lumping into, say, small, medium, and large responses. This fear seems to have been unfounded. Much current work uses the happiness scale of Fig. 1.4. The child points to one of the 19 1/2-cm white circles to express amount of happiness.

In the initial work, 5 years had seemed to be the earliest age at which children could use the rating scale. However, recent work has been able to push this age limit back almost to 3 years. One factor that may be important in this respect is the use of visual stimuli. Thus, even in the need and deed experiments of Fig. 1.9, this abstract information was presented in picture form. This reduction in the lower age limit allows a powerful methodology to be used in exploring an important developmental period.

An unresolved problem is that of reducing the response variability at the younger ages. Although even the 3-year-olds seem to use the scale in a linear way, there is a steady increase in response variability below age 6. Because the younger children clearly must have the cognitive structures required to employ the rating response, it would seem possible to decrease the response variability. As yet, however, no information on this matter has turned up.

It deserves emphasis, incidentally, that the very capacity to use a rating scale presents a fundamental but little studied problem in cognitive psychology. Some aspects of this problem are considered in range–frequency theory of category judgment (Anderson, 1974a, 1975; Parducci, 1974).

It should be emphasized that the rating scale methodology is not a finished product but needs continued development. The procedures that have been outlined appear to give good results but they can undoubtedly be improved. Methods that decrease response variability at the younger ages are especially desirable. Moreover, different procedures might be more appropriate for different tasks. Comparative studies of different procedures would thus be desirable for the continuing improvement of this response methodology.

## Individual Child Analyses

A special advantage of the integration–theoretical aproach is that it allows and encourages analyses for individual children. This capability for individual analysis has yielded cogent results on issues of centration and integrational capacity (Anderson & Butzin, 1978; Anderson & Cuneo, 1978a; Leon, 1976, 1977; Wilkening, 1979). Furthermore, this capability is important, if not necessary, to take adequate cognizance of individual differences in value.

A single session, it should be noted, may not provide enough data for a completely satisfactory test of the integration rule at the individual level. Attention therefore needs to be given to development of tasks and procedures that can hold the child's interest over extended sessions. This goal is particularly important for longitudinal studies and in applications of the ergodic heuristic that is discussed in a later section.

## EXPERIMENTAL APPLICATIONS

A number of experimental applications of the integration–theoretical approach will be summarized in this section. Most of the applications have been to various problems of social judgment. However, the same methods can be used to study perceptual judgment and some interesting results have been obtained, as illustrated in the first application.

### The Height + Width Rule

Judgment of area seems to be a simple perceptual task. The child is shown a rectangular cookie, say, and asked to judge "how much" cookie there is. Even if the child is not very good at this, his judgments should correspond roughly to the actual physical area. Physical area obeys a Height × Width rule, and so the child's judgments should conform to a multiplying model.

A simple graphical test of the Height × Width rule is provided by the linear fan theorem noted previously. By virtue of this theorem, the factorial plot of the data should form a diverging fan of straight lines. This linear fan pattern has been obtained with adults (Anderson, 1974a, Figure 8) and it was expected that children would exhibit the same Height × Width rule.

It came as a shock, therefore, to find that 5-year-olds followed a Height + Width rule, as though their judgment of area was obtained by adding the lengths of the sides. This adding pattern can be seen in the experiment of Fig. 1.5, in which height and width of the cookie were varied in a 3 × 3 factorial design. The curves are essentially parallel. By virtue of the above parallelism theorem, these curves demonstrate that the child follows an adding-type, Height + Width rule (Anderson & Cuneo, 1978a).

The natural reaction to such a result is that something is wrong. Some possibilities may be noted briefly.

1. The observed parallelism is a statistical fluke, or perhaps some peculiarity of the particular experimental conditions.

This possibility can be definitely ruled out. The same Height + Width pattern was obtained in seven different experiments with varied conditions, as well as considerable unreported pilot work conducted over a two-year period. Furthermore, independent discovery of this same Height + Width pattern was made by Wilkening (1979) using somewhat different procedures.

2. The 5-year-olds really follow the multiplying model, but the linear fan pattern does not attain statistical significance because reponse variability is substantial at this age.

This response variability argument can also be definitely ruled out. If the true response pattern was a linear fan, then the observed means would be

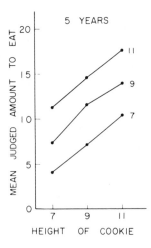

FIG. 1.5.  Judged area of rectangles obeys the adding rule, Height + Width. (After Anderson & Cuneo, 1978a, Experiment 1.)

1. INFORMATION INTEGRATION THEORY 13

expected to exhibit this shape even though it might not attain significance. But across seven different experiments, no visible trace of this linear fan shape appeared (cf. Anderson & Cuneo, 1978b; Bogartz, 1978).

3. The effect is peculiar to rectangles.

This is a real possibility. The same Height + Width pattern was obtained with isosceles triangles and with wax cylinders, but even these could be argued to be essentially rectangular.

4. Something is wrong with the response scale.

This is a natural initial reaction. However, there are several considerations that provide solid support for the response scale. One is the very neatness of the parallelism. Another is the fact that 5-year-olds have also exhibited parallelism in a variety of other tasks in which adding-type models seem sensible on a priori grounds. It might be argued that 5-year-olds employ a general purpose adding strategy, but that is not an objection to the response scale.

An interesting variant of this objection argues that the child really estimates the area, but that the response is a logarithmic function of this estimate. Then the observed data would follow an adding pattern because log (Height × Width) = log Height + log Width. However, this objection appears to be ruled out by data in which the child judged "how much" for pairs of rectangles. The logarithmic objection would imply that these data would not be parallel, whereas in fact they were (Anderson & Cuneo, 1978a, Experiment 6).

5. The child has limited attention and responds on some trials to Height, on other trials to Width. This mode of response would produce parallel curves even though the child does not actually integrate.

This attentional interpretation is more plausible because these same 5-year-olds judged liquid quantity using a Height-only rule, ignoring glass Width (Anderson & Cuneo, 1978a, Experiment 1). With rectangles, in contrast to glasses, Height would be no more salient than Width.

The elimination of this objection provides a nice illustration of the analytical power of the integration–theoretical approach. If this objection was correct, then the within-child response variability should be much less for the 7 × 7 square than for the 7 × 11 rectangle. This follows because the response to the square would be the same regardless of whether the child responds to Height or to Width. For the rectangle, however, the response would be quite different in the two cases, and that would markedly raise the within-child variability. Because the data showed no trace of this difference in variability, the limited attention explanation can be eliminated.

Overall, therefore, the Height + Width pattern seems to be empirically solid. Accordingly, attention may be turned to its theoretical interpretation.

## Theoretical Interpretation of
## the Height + Width Rule

The Height + Width rule is surprising in more than one respect. From an adult view, the child need only look to see how much cookie there is : Simple perception of the size of the cookie would produce the physically correct Height × Width rule without any actual multiplication. Not only does the child not do what seems perceptually simple, but instead appears to do something that is cognitively complex.

The theoretical interpretation given by Anderson and Cuneo (1978a) may be summarized briefly as follows. The young child possesses a general purpose metric sense, that is, a single, internal scale on which diverse quantities are measured. However, the young child does not possess adult concepts of certain quantities such as area. When called upon to make such judgments, the child understands that some quantitative judgment is wanted and seizes on salient cues that seem to be relevant. For the cookie task, in particular, both Height and Width are salient to the young child. These salient cues are then integrated by a general purpose, adding-type rule.

The assumption of a general metric sense rests, in part, on the child's ability to use the graphic rating scale in many different tasks. It is a reasonable speculation that the general metric sense is an internalized length scale, developed from reaching movements and similar activity.

The assumption of a general purpose adding-type rule is conjectural. If true, however, then it should appear in other unexpected places. Cuneo's (1978) Length + Density rule and the Probability + Value rule discussed later thus provide important support for the general purpose adding-type rule in young children.

## Other Work on Judgments of Area[1]

Independently from the above work on the Height + Width rule, two other investigators have applied integration theory to study children's judgments of area. Wilkening (1979) replicated the Height + Width rule using somewhat

---

[1]The chapter by Shepp, Burns and McDonough presents a thoughtful, judicious comparison and contrast between their results on perception of rectangles and the Height + Width rule obtained by Anderson and Cuneo and by Wilkening cited above. Their chapter arrived after the present chapter had been completed, however, and only two brief comments can be added here.

First, the criticism that the Height + Width interpretation "assumes" that height and width are independent does not seem appropriate. The Height + Width rule is not an assumption but a deduction. If area or shape contributed to the judgment, as Shepp et al. suggest, then parallelism would not in general be obtained. The fact that the Height + Width rule was also obtained for both right and isoceles triangles also supports the argument against area and shape effects.

Second, although Shepp et. al. are certainly correct in stressing the importance of perceived stimulus structure for the study of combination rules, it is important to recognize that these rules

different procedures and, of special interest, a larger range of height and width than in Fig.1.5. In contrast, a Height × Width rule was found by Verge and Bogartz (1978), who used a production response in which the child adjusted a variable square to equal the area of a given rectangle.

This difference in outcome may result from the difference in response mode between the one-dimensional graphic rating scale used by Anderson and Cuneo, and by Wilkening, and the two-dimensional area production used by Verge and Bogartz. Bogartz (1978) questioned whether the experiments by Anderson and Cuneo (1978a) had sufficient statistical power to detect the operation of a multiplying rule, but further analyses showed extremely high power (Anderson & Cuneo, 1978b). The area production response may seem more natural than the graphic rating, but it has the geometrical peculiarity of making an actual Height + Width rule appear like a Height × Width rule (Anderson & Cuneo, 1978b). The graphic rating method has the advantage of being congruent to the concept of a general metric sense and of being usable in many other tasks. However, the area production response has considerable interest in its own right, for example, in the study of the one-dimensional side matching response strategy that Verge and Bogartz observed in many of their younger children.

## The Length + Density Rule

Cuneo (1978) has applied integration theory to obtain fundamental results on children's judgments of numerical quantity. The children were told about a story child who wanted to make a bead necklace for mother. They were shown a single row of beads and used the happiness scale of Fig. 1.4 to rate how happy the story child would be with that many beads. Counting was not allowed so that judgments had to be made on an intuitive–perceptual basis. Stimulus end anchors were used to define the frown and smile and the children used the intermediate steps to judge the experimental stimuli. These

---

can help delineate and validate the effective stimulus structure. The Height + Width rule provides a good example of this. The study of combination rules may be especially helpful with semantic stimuli or with symbolic stimuli such as schematic faces for which stimulus structure cannot adequately be defined at the physical level but is intimately bound up with cognitive structure and response structure.

A similar issue arose in measurement theory in which the traditional assumption was that stimulus scaling had to precede study of combination rules. Functional measurement succeeded by reversing the traditional orientation, making the scales derivative from the combination rules. A similar approach to structure analysis may be helpful, for structure may be viewed as qualitative measurement.

Inconsistencies between the implications of two different experimental approaches can be the most valuable kind of clue to progress. Shepp et al. perform a useful service by bringing under scrutiny the apparent inconsistency between the implications of the classification tasks and the present integration rules.

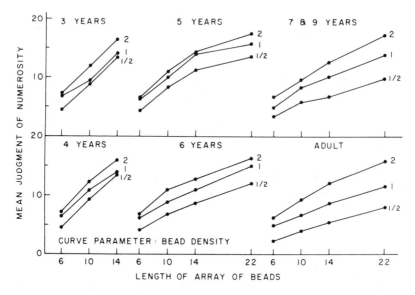

FIG. 1.6.   Mean judgment of numerosity of row of beads as a function of its length and density for six age groups. (After Cuneo, 1978.)

stimuli were constructed from the length × density factorial design indicated in Fig. 1.6.

The theoretical interpretation is clear from the factorial patterns of Fig. 1.6. The parallelism in the left panels implies that the 3- and 4-year-olds integrate by an adding-type, Length + Density rule. The linear fan pattern in the two right panels implies that older children and adults follow the normative, physically correct Length × Density rule. The mild divergence in the two center panels points to a transition from adding to multiplying around 5 to 6 years of age. Independent work by Pringle, Andrews, and Shanteau (in press) has obtained analogous results for judgments of numerosity of square arrays of dots by 5-6-year-olds.

The results from the 3-4-year-olds are theoretically most important and several points deserve emphasis. First, these data provide cogent support for the concept of a general-purpose adding rule mentioned above. Under this interpretation, these children cannot judge number per se but they utilize the general-purpose adding rule to integrate the two salient cues of length and density. Second, the vertical separation of the three curves in the left panels provides the first clear evidence that the youngest children are sensitive to density; methods used in previous work have been inadequate to demonstrate density effects. Third, no centration was found even at the youngest ages. Fourth, children as young as 3 years can use the face happiness scale in a true linear way. Cuneo's (1978) thesis gives further results and follow-up

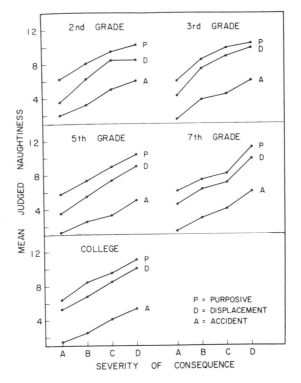

FIG. 1.7.  Judged badness of story children as a function of consequences (on horizontal axis) and intent (curve parameter). (After Leon, 1976, 1977.)

and the vertical separation of the three curves reflects the intent information. It appears that the children do integrate the intent and damage information, a conclusion that was supported by the individual analyses. No less important, the parallelism indicates that the integration follows an adding-type rule across all five age levels.

However, Fig. 1.7 is only one part of a complex experiment. A substantial minority of subjects employed alternative integration rules. The most common was the accident–configural rule that was followed by a number of subjects scattered across all age levels. In this rule, the damage was ignored when it was accidental; otherwise, parallelism was obtained as with the main group of subjects in Fig. 1.7. This accident–configural rule is also clear evidence that even the younger children integrate the intent information.

Two other integration rules were the damage-only and intent-only rules, used respectively by eight and six of the 51 5- and 6-year-old children. These rules, in which one of the two pieces of information was systematically ignored, may be called limited attention rules. This attentional interpretation is supported by the fact that the same children made sensible, graded judgments to the ignored information when it was presented alone.

experiments, including a clever method for validating the
response scale at the youngest ages.

## Moral Judgment

In one of the Piagetian choice tasks, the child is to say which
characters is naughtier, one who did a great deal of damage with
to, or one who had bad intent but did only a little damage. "We o
following result. Up to the age of 10, two types of answers exist side
one type actions are evaluated in terms of the material r
independently of motives; according to the other type of answe
alone are what counts" (Piaget, 1932/1965, pp. 123–124).

Piaget thus denies that children under 10 years integrate the two
given information about intent and consequence. Instead there a
distinct moral attitudes, objective and subjective." A child may exhibi
the other attitude, depending on the particular story, but the two attitu
not act together (p. 133), a moral centration.

Unfortunately, Piaget's discussion has been almost unif
misinterpreted. The position attributed to him in the literature has n
always been that younger children judge solely on the basis of outcome
are insensitive to intent. Much effort has therefore gone into showing
younger children can utilize intent information (e.g., Buchanan & Thomps
1973; Costanzo, Coie, Grumet, & Farnill, 1973; Hebble, 1971; see a
Keasey, 1978). But Piaget explicitly denied a stage theory, and explici
noted that younger children could and did make some intent-based choic
(p. 124).

In the prevailing concern to show that younger children can use inten
information, Piaget's striking claim about moral centration has received little
attention. The three studies cited above showed main effects for both factors
of intent × damage designs, an outcome that tends to support the integration
hypothesis. However, the same outcome is predicted by Piaget's centration
hypothesis—as an artifact of averaging over children, some of whom center
on one piece of information, some on the other (see previous discussion of
Height + Width rule). Clear evidence for the integration hypothesis requires
analysis at the individual level. This approach was pursued in basic work by
Leon (1976, 1977), who went further to study the exact form of the integration
rule (see also Chapter 3 by Leon in this volume).

One part of Leon's results in shown in Fig. 1.7. The child judged how much
punishment a story character should get when his intent and the damage he
caused were explicitly specified. The factorial design was based on three
degrees of intent, from Accident to Purposive, and four graded degrees of
damage as listed on the horizontal axis.

The separate panels for the five age groups in Fig. 1.7 all tell the same story.
The upward slope of the curves reflects the effect of the damage information,

One other aspect of Leon's work is notable for its bearing on the general problem of attributional inference. In some of the stories, only the intent or only the damage information was presented. Now harmful intent creates some likelihood of damage; damage creates some suspicion of harmful intent. It may be hypothesized, therefore, that the child will make inferences about the missing information and integrate this inferred information in with the given information.

A striking aspect of Leon's work is evidence for the operation of these implicit inferences. The general trend was toward more inference at older ages, although the interpretation of the results was somewhat complicated by possible transfer effects. Despite this ambiguity, Leon's analyses illustrate the power of the integration–theoretical approach to diagnose the nature of the information processing. Also notable is a study by Surber (1977), which showed that the absolute importance of intent information was constant across age.[2]

## Deservingness

Ideas of fairness and deservingness are pervasive in social life and play a prominent role in moral development. Many different factors can affect judgments of deservingness. These include how hard the person tried, how much he accomplished relative to his ability, his neediness, and various personal factors such as age, physical appearance, and likableness. Basic developmental questions are concerned with what factors the child is sensitive to and how those factors are integrated. A series of three experiments applying information integration theory to these questions (Anderson & Butzin, 1978) will be briefly summarized here.

Fig. 1.8 presents judgments about deservingness of boys who were described by two pieces of information, how hard they worked cleaning up the campground in the afternoon (listed on the horizontal axis) and how hard they worked in the morning (listed as curve parameters). The child's task was to indicate how many pieces of candy the boys should get.

The graph indicates that the children took account of both pieces of information and made fairly fine graded judgments. Every individual child showed the same general pattern of graded response to the two pieces of information.

---

[2]This important paper by Surber (1977) appeared after this chapter was written but deserves special mention. Surber tested the averaging hypothesis for intent–consequence integration with good results and went on to use the averaging model to estimate the weight or importance parameters. The main developmental trend was a decrease in the absolute weight of consequence information, by a factor of 10 to 1 or more, from kindergarten to adult. In contrast, the absolute weight of intent information remained approximately constant across age levels. The model analysis thus provided information about significant developmental parameters that cannot generally be obtained with other methods.

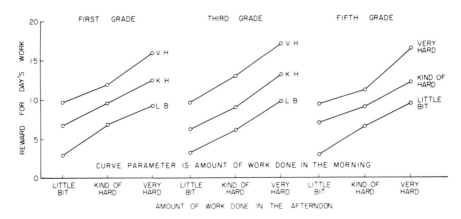

FIG. 1.8.   Judged deservingness of story children as a function of how hard they worked and how much they accomplished in the morning (curve parameter) and in the afternoon (listed on horizontal). (From Anderson & Butzin, 1978.) (Copyright 1968 by the American Psychological Association. Reprinted by permission.)

The graph also suggests the operation of an averaging rule. At each age level, the three curves are roughly parallel. The oldest group does exhibit a moderate deviation from parallelism, but this pattern did not reappear in the later experiments. Over all three experiments, the data provided good support for the integration model.

A second task was also used. Information was presented about deservingness of each of two boys, and the child was to play Santa Claus and divide a fixed number of toys between them in a fair manner. Two steps were taken in an effort to obtain developmental trends. The age range was lowered to include 4-, 5-, 6-, and 8-year-olds; and the number of pieces of stimulus information was increased to four. Thus, each of the two boys was described by two pieces of information, about how hard he worked (indicated by pictures showing how many dishes he had washed for his mother), and about his need (indicated by a picture showing how many toys he already had). It was expected that the younger children would place greater weight on the objective information about achievement, less weight on the subjective factor of need (Piaget, 1932/1965).

The overall mean data are in Fig. 1.9. The response measure is the number of toys apportioned as first boy's share. This response increased directly with first boy's need and achievement (listed on the horizontal axis). And of course, the response varied inversely with the need and achievement of second boy (listed as curve parameter).

These data suggest that need has at least as much importance as deed. Thus, the relative height of the two middle points on each curve indicates that first boy was considered more deserving for High Need–Low Deed than for Low Need–High Deed. Surprisingly, there was no developmental trend; all four age groups from 4 to 8 showed essentially the same pattern. These data provide no support for Piaget's (1932/1965) claim of a developmental trend from reliance on objective factors in younger children to reliance on subjective factors in older children. Even the 4-year-olds exhibit a well developed sensitivity to the needs of others.

Also of interest was the appearance of the same cognitive algebra of equity as has been found with adults (Anderson, 1976a). A simple ratio model derived from integration theory was generally supported in all three experiments in this article. Furthermore, integration of multidimensional input information, as in the experiment of Fig. 1.8, obeyed the rule of equity integration and infirmed the rule of input integration that had previously been standard in equity theory (see also below).

### Integrational Capacity

Integrational capacity would be expected to increase with age so that older children would be able to attend to and integrate a larger informational field. However, assessment of integrational capacity presents difficulties. An application of present methods to this problem can be illustrated with the equity experiment of Fig. 1.9.

In that experiment, the design was a four-way factorial since two pieces of information were given about each boy in the story. What information the children took account of can be determined by looking at the main effects of the factorial design. Since each child judged two replications of the complete design, the main effects can be tested for each of the 10 individual children at each age group.

All 10 of the 8-year-olds showed highly significant main effects for all four stimulus factors. This shows that these children attended to and integrated all four pieces of stimulus information in making their judgment. Integrational

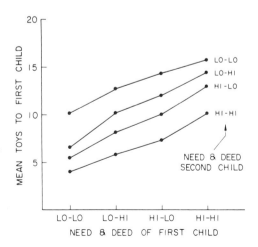

FIG. 1.9. Equity division of 20 toys between two children, each characterized by their need and accomplishment. (From Anderson & Butzin, 1978.) (Copyright 1968 by the American Psychological Association. Reprinted by permission.)

capacity showed a steady development trend that can be most simply summarized by noting that 7 of the 6-year-olds, 5 of the 5-year-olds, and 4 of the 4-year-olds showed at least three significant main effects. Even in the youngest age group, therefore, a substantial proportion of the subjects turned in a very creditable performance.

This deservingness experiment was not designed primarily to study integrational capacity. For that purpose it would probably be desirable to make the stimulus factors more homogeneous and to vary systematically the number of pieces of information given for each judgment on a within-child basis.

A group deservingness scenario presents attractive possibilities as an experimental task for studying integrational capacity. Each member of the group would be characterized by the size of his or her contribution, and the subject would judge the deservingness of the group. All information would thus be homogeneous, and the number of pieces could readily be varied. Of course, heterogeneous information could also be used, with different group members described by actions, need, and so forth. Various kinds of groups, from playground to family, could also be employed. This scenario appears to have the flexibility needed for assessing integrational capacity.

## Perception of Groups

Important work by Singh and his associates has begun to explore how children integrate information about groups. In judgments of playgroups (Singh, Sidana, & Saluja, 1978), the group attributes were the personal attractiveness of the members of the group and the number of toys that the group had to play with. These were varied in factorial design, and the children judged the attractiveness of each of the playgroups. The resulting parallelism provided support for an adding-type model. A supplementary critical test ruled out the adding hypothesis and ruled in the averaging hypothesis in accord with the logic of Fig. 1.3. Quite similar results were obtained by Singh, Sidana, and Srivastava (1978) for judgments of parental groups as a function of the personal characteristics of the mother and father. These results from India provide notable cross-cultural support for integration theory.

Numerous other information variables deserve study. These include the size of the group, the attractiveness, both social and physical (Dion & Berscheid, 1974) of the group members, the numerous incentives and activities that the group can provide, special status roles or niches such as leader, clown, or scapegoat (Anderson, Lindner, & Lopes, 1973). These and other group variables lend themselves naturally to the present approach, which considers judgments about groups to be an integrated resultant of information about the positive and negative attributes of the group.

Hartup's (1970, p. 364) review notes with regret the post-World War II decline in studies of children's groups. This decline may result from "preoccupation with a relatively narrow range of methods," Hartup comments, noting that "the most widely used weapon in this field is the correlation coefficient" (p. 437). These correlations reflect the prevalence of differential studies with their emphasis on personality correlates. Hartup suggests that a shift from correlational analysis to experimental analysis could provide a more effective attack on many problems of children's perception of groups. For this purpose, information integration theory has many advantages, both methodological and conceptual (Anderson, 1976d, Section 7.5).

## Ulterior Motives

Butzin (1978) has discovered a fascinating developmental trend in the way that information about ulterior motives is processed. Children judged goodness of a story child who helped mother make cookies. They were told how much money mother had promised the child for helping and how much the child had helped. These two variables were varied in the 3 × 3 design indicated in Fig. 1.10.

The 9-year-olds in the right panel of Fig. 1.10 exhibit an adult pattern. Judged goodness is a direct function of amount of help (listed on the horizontal axis) and an inverse function of amount paid (listed as curve parameter). The rationale for the inverse relation is simple: The more the

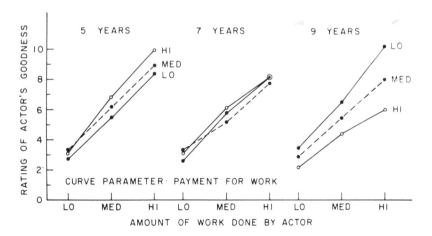

FIG. 1.10.   Mean judgment of actor's goodness as a function of how much he helped his mother, and how much she paid him to help, for three age groups. (After Butzin, 1978.)

child is paid, the greater is the presumption that its work resulted from the ulterior, selfish money motive rather than from a true wish to help.

The remarkable aspect of these data appears in the left panel for the 5-year-olds. Here, goodness is a direct function of amount paid; this variable has the opposite directional effects at the youngest and oldest age groups. Butzin's further thesis experiments studied why the 5-year-olds employed this unusual integration rule as well as the nature of the transition stage visible in the center graph for the 7-year-olds.

## Moral Extenuation

In other work on moral judgment, Butzin (1977) has examined the role of extenuation in retaliatory acts. Children of 4, 6, and 8 years of age were shown a playmate-doll who went to play at the house of an actor-doll. The playmate purposefully broke some of the actor's toys (provocation) whereupon the actor went to the playmate's house and broke some of her toys (retaliation). Provocation and retaliation were varied in a 3 × 3 design in terms of number of toys broken.

The main result was that provocation had an inverse, extenuating effect at all ages. Even the 4-year-olds judged the actor as less bad when her playmate had broken more of her toys. At this age, "getting even" seems already well established as a proper social motivation.

The magnitude of the extenuation effect seemed about as large at 4 years as at 8 years. However, an apparent trend did appear in the integration rule. The data for the 4-year-olds exhibited parallelism, which suggests that they may have integrated provocation and retaliation by the general-purpose adding rule mentioned above.

The 6- and 8-year-olds appeared to show a different pattern, one in which the effect of provocation was least when the level of retaliation was low and increased as level of retaliation increased. This pattern agrees with the commonsense hypothesis that extenuation should act indirectly as a proportionate multiplier of the retaliatory act. Further work on these questions is in progress.

## Social Attribution

In social interaction, people frequently attribute various characteristics to others, especially in regard to the causes behind their actions. The basic question about how causal attribution rules develop was studied by Kun, Parsons, and Ruble (1974), who obtained judgments about the expected performance of a story character as a function of information given about motivation and ability. The results pointed toward a change from an adding-type rule,

Performance = Motivation + Ability,

for the younger children, to a multiplying rule,

Performance = **Motivation** × Ability,

for older children. A similar rule development has been found in judgments of area (Anderson & Cuneo, 1978a) and numerosity (Cuneo, 1978). These results suggest that the younger children have an adding-type rule that is used as a general purpose integration strategy.

Kun (1977) gives an instructive analysis of the development of integration rules that has special value and interest for its focus on qualitative rather than quantitative aspects. In one experiment, subjects received information about performance and either ability or effort; they made judgments of either effort or ability. Both judgments were direct functions of performance, as expected, and this dependence showed little or no trend from 6 to 12 years of age.

However, each judgment is also a function of a second variable besides performance, and these functional dependencies were quite interesting. For the older children, judgments of effort were inversely related to ability, the same rule that characterizes adult judgment. The younger children, however, showed a direct relation. Thus, the developmental trend is from a halo-type rule, in which the person with more ability is said to have tried harder, to the inverse compensation rule of adult thought.

Moreover, there was an ability-effort asymmetry, presumably arising because ability is a more abstract concept than effort. Judgments of ability showed a mild, overall halo-type effect with little developmental trend. These conclusions were supported and extended in a second experiment in which information about task difficulty was also included.

Kun's results provide basic information about developmental aspects of both valuation and integration processes, especially about the qualitative structure of the integration rules. Further work is desirable with other judgmental tasks to assess how far the above trends depend on learned aspects of the given task. With judgments of quantity, for instance, the inverse compensation rule might appear at an earlier age.

Three other reports may be briefly noted. Suls and Gutkin (1976) read children stories that contained two pieces of information about parents' evaluation of a boy's action of helping a friend deliver papers on a rainy day. The expectancy information specified that the boy expected his parents either to give him some extra allowance for his actions or to be angry at him for going out on a rainy day. The consequence information specified whether the parents in fact rewarded or punished the boy for his action. The children rated the boy on likableness. Although Suls and Gutkin employed a different theoretical perspective, reconsideraton of their data shows three aspects that bear on the cognitive algebra of children's judgments. First, the boy was liked more when he helped his friend despite his parents' expected disapproval. This result is consistent with an additive force model for attribution (Anderson, 1974b), the boy's action being taken to signal a stronger dispostion to help when performed against force of parental opposition. Second, the data from the 2 × 2 design were approximately parallel, and the interaction did not approach significance. This suggests that the information was integrated by an adding-type rule to determine the likableness response. Third, collateral data on moral judgment also obeyed an adding-type, intent + consequence rule. These data thus provide more evidence for a general cognitive algebra in children's judgments.

The report by McArthur and Eisen (1976), although not strictly an attributional study, deserves mention for its importance. Children were read a short story in which two characters, a boy and a girl, exhibited differential achievement behavior. The children's persistence in a subsequent achievement task was substantially influenced by the achievement role of the same-sex character in the story. McArthur was primarily concerned with sex stereotyping and the effects of children's storybooks on the development of the self-concept. Her view is congenial to the present approach in which the self-concept would be considered as the ongoing resultant of a continuing process of information integration (Anderson, 1976d, 1979).

Ruble and Feldman (1976) found that the order of presenting information about consensus, distinctiveness, and consistency had a substantial effect on the attributional responses. Their work is important, both methodologically and theoretically. It could have been more informative, however, had numerical response measures been employed instead of choice data, as was suggested for the earlier prototype experiment by McArthur (1972) (see Anderson, 1974b, p. 33–37).

## Limited Attention Processing

When both row and column factors have significant effects, the natural interpretation is that the subject pays attention to both pieces of information and integrates both to arrive at his judgment. For many purposes, this conclusion is all that is desired, regardless of the exact nature of the integration rule.

Unfortunately, this conclusion does not strictly follow from group data. Suppose that some subjects used only the row information in their judgments, while others used only the column information. Then both row and column factors would still generally have significant effects. Moreover, the graph of the group means would actually be parallel. Some caution is therefore necessary because group averages may mask limited attention processing by individual subjects.

This interpretational problem can sometimes be resolved from design considerations. In the toy experiment of Fig 1.1, for example, the question arose whether the younger children were "centering," so that their judgment depended on only one of the two toys. In this case, row and column factors were alike and not distinguishable as such to the subject. Any concentration of attention would presumably favor the more attractive toy, and this would produce systematic deviations from parallelism. In this case, therefore, the data indicate that the children integrated both pieces of information.

More generally, this interpretational problem can be attacked with individual child analyses. If the complete factorial design is presented to each child two or more times, then an analysis of variance can be performed for each child. The F ratio for each main effect tests the null hypothesis that the child ignored the corresponding stimulus information. That avoids the problems with group averages.

It should be recognized, however, that the statistical power of these individual analyses will be low when the design is small and/or when the number of replications is small. In that case, a nonsignificant main effect does not warrant acceptance of the null hypothesis that the child did not take account of the corresponding stimulus information. Use of confidence intervals (e.g., Anderson, 1977, p. 208) may provide guidance in this respect.

A number of analyses of this kind have been conducted (e.g., Anderson & Butzin, 1978; Anderson & Cuneo, 1978b; Leon, 1976, 1977, Chapter 3, this volume; Kun, Parsons, & Ruble, 1974; Wilkening, 1979, Chapter 2, this volume). In general, the individual analyses have supported and confirmed the group analysis to the extent that most subjects attend to and integrate all the given information. Of course, these group averages may mask a small number of individuals who use limited attention processing. Leon's intent-only and damage-only rules discussed previously illustrate this. In addition, limited attention processing in younger children has been observed when four pieces of stimulus information were used in an equity experiment as noted above.

The problem of limited attention can pushed one final step to the level of the individual child. If the individual child systematically ignores one piece of information, it will be seen directly in the corresponding main effect of the design. However, even if all main effects are significant, it could still be argued that the child uses variable limited attention processing. That is, the child attends on some trials to the row information, on some trials to the column information, but only to one or the other on any given trial. Both row and column factors would still generally have significant effects. Moreover, the graph for the means over trials for the individual child would show parallelism. This situation is exactly analogous to that above for group averages. Some caution is therefore necessary even with individual child analyses because trial means can mask variable limited attention processing on individual trials.

Fortunately, even this interpretational problem can be handled by present methods. The essential idea is simple. If the subject uses variable limited attention processing, then the within-cell variance will be greater as the difference between the row and column stimulus information is greater. On the other hand, if the child attends to and integrates all the given information on each trial, then no such systematic variance pattern would be produced. The within-cell variances can be thus used to test for variable limited attention processing. The one application of this approach, for the Height + Width data of Fig. 1.5, found no evidence for variable limited attention processing (Anderson & Cuneo, 1978a).

Limited attention processing may seem like a methodological problem, but it is really an opportunity. As the field of stimulus information is made larger or more complex, capacity limitations will become increasingly important. Developmental trends in attention and capacity limitations have special interest and present methods provide simple ways to study these trends.

## RESEARCH PROSPECTS IN
## PERCEPTUAL JUDGMENT

This section considers a variety of problems in perceptual judgment that involve stimulus integration. Most of these applications build upon fascinating and fundamental contributions of Piaget. However, the Piagetian approach to these problems has been dominated by a concern with operational thinking. Perceptual aspects have been segregated theoretically (Flavell, 1963; Wohlwill, 1962) and largely ignored experimentally. The perceptual judgment approach thus provides a proper complement to the operational approach, especially with regard to stimulus integration. The present applications may thus help restore a better balance of theoretical focus and also help lead to unified approach that includes both judgmental and operational thinking (Anderson & Cuneo, 1978a,b).

### Length

According to Piaget, Inhelder, and Szeminska (1960), younger children will say that straight and curved strings have equal length when their endpoints are aligned in one-to-one correspondence. Although this claim may reflect the proclivity of Piagetian methods to reach all-or-none conclusions, it does indicate that the straight line distance between endpoints is used as a judgmental cue about length. This implication can be made a tool for developmental analysis.

An integrational hypothesis would consider judged length to be the resultant of two pieces of information, actual length, and endpoint distance. The integration would then obey the generalized rule

Judged Length = String Length $\circledast$ Endpoint Distance

where $\circledast$ is a generalized integration operation. This hypothesis may be evaluated by varying the two stimulus variables in factorial design.

It would be expected that children who judge the two strings to have equal length in Piaget's choice task would nevertheless utilize string length in the present task of judging the length of single strings. If so, string length will have a main effect in the analysis of the factorial design. This main effect provides a direct measure and test of the integrational hypothesis.

The potential of this approach lies in its possibilities as a method for developmental analysis. The main effect of string length can be considered as a developmental parameter. It measures the degree of development to the demands of the task. Thus, it would become possible to trace out the course of development in a continuous manner.

Of special interest is the possibility that the integration will obey a simple adding-type model. In that case, the functional scales of the two stimulus variables would provide more incisive developmental parameters. These could be useful in the study of attentional variables, offsetting the alignment of the endpoints, for example, or as sensitive indices of various kinds of training.

## Density

Judgments of density do not seem to have received systematic study. Most reports find no clear evidence that density is an effective cue in judgments of numerousness (Gelman, 1972; Mehler & Bever, 1967). Piaget (1968) and Pufall and Shaw (1972) have claimed that very young children are sensitive to density but their evidence is not satisfactory (Anderson & Cuneo, 1977, p. 77).

Direct judgments of density could be obtained by presenting arrays of equally spaced objects and asking for judgments of "how close together" the objects are. Such judgments would presumably be largely independent of length and so validate the conception of density as a local metric cue in judgments of the numerousness of the objects.

An alternative approach used by Cuneo (1978) asks for judgments of numerosity of rows of objects. Length of row and density of objects were varied in factorial design. The appearance of a Length + Density rule in 3-, 4-, and 5-year-olds provides the first clear evidence that these age groups are sensitive to density and integrate it into their judgment.

Arrays in which the objects are unequally spaced are also of interest. For example, the array could consist of two or more collinear, constant density arrays, each varied separately in factorial design. Judgment of density in such variable density arrays evidently requires some kind of scanning integration. The normative, physical rule is a weighted average, and the psychological rule would be expected to be the same, but with weights determined by attentional factors and integrational capacity. The serial integration model (Anderson, 1974c, Section 6, 1980) could then be used to dissect the effects of the separate segments.

## Velocity

The integration–theoretical approach may be helpful in following up the many interesting observations of Piaget (1971) on the development of concepts of speed. Around 5 years of age, for example, children will claim that two trains travelling through tunnels of different length have travelled at the same speed when they enter and exit the tunnels at the same time. From such observations, Piaget concludes that the child's intuitive conception of speed is limited to perception of overtaking and is not the result of correlating time and distance travelled (pp. 139, 163). Direct supporting evidence was obtained from tests with "certain fully visible movements of different speeds where overtaking is absent" (p. 148).

Piaget's theory thus implies that the child could not judge the speed of a single moving object for then there is no overtaking. Yet it seems hard to believe that children cannot judge fast or slow of single moving objects. As an alternative to Piaget's view, therefore, it may be conjectured that young children possess an intuition of speed that is fairly primitive perceptually. On this view, children should be able to make graded judgments of speed as soon as they are capable of quantitative judgments.

This proposition could easily be tested by asking for judgments of speed of a single visible object that travelled a certain distance at a certain speed. Both perceived local speed and total distance are assumed to act as effective cues, being integrated by the generalized rule

Local Speed $\circledast$ Distance.

The terms in this expression represent the subjective values of the two stimulus variables. Rationally, the effect of the distance cue should be zero, but even adults show a perceptual effect of distance (e.g., Rachlin, 1966).

An interesting extension of this task concerns variable speed objects. An overall judgment of speed must be some average of the speed in the successive segments of the total path. The serial curve (Anderson, 1974c, p. 262) of weight parameters for successive path segments could yield important developmental information about children's integrational capacities. Numerous related integration tasks are possible. An independent application of integration theory to these problems is given in the chapter by Wilkening who presents some additional theoretical and experimental results.

There is no doubt about the great interest and importance of Piaget's observations on children's concepts of speed. When the tunnel hides the train, a judgment of its speed evidently requires a supraperceptual, cognitive operation that coordinates distance and time. Indeed, this coordination should follow the cognitive algebra:

Judged Speed = Distance ÷ Time

This rule also may be readily studied with present methods (see also Svenson, 1970). As this example illustrates, the integration–theoretical approach can work harmoniously with the Piagetian operational approach and can provide useful complementary information on developmental trends.

## Subjective Probability

Development of probability concepts was studied in a preliminary experiment with the following simple task. Children were told a story about a thirsty boy who wanted some Kool-Aid. To get the Kool-Aid, he had to spin an arrow spinner mounted at the center of a circular disk with red and white sectors. Only if the spinner stopped in the red sector of the disk would the story boy get the Kool-Aid. A 3 × 2 factorial design was used in which the proportionate size of the red sector was .2, .5, and .8 of the full circle (72, 180, and 288 degrees of arc, respectively), and the Kool-Aid was either at a low or a high level in a glass. The children used the face scale of Fig. 1.4 to judge how happy the story boy would be with each of these six stimulus combinations.

The size of the red sector governs the probability that the story boy will get the Kool-Aid. The theoretical question concerns the integration of this probability information with amount of Kool-Aid. A normative, physicalistic integration rule is suggested by statistical theory and states that the expected value of a chance event equals the probability of success times the value of a successful outcome. It is an interesting speculation of long standing that human judgment may obey an analogous model, but with the objective values replaced by their subjective counterparts. This hypothetical integration model may be written

$$\text{Subjective Expected Value} = \text{Subjective Probability} \times \text{Subjective Value}$$
$$SEV = SP \times SV.$$

Although this equation has been a central concern of psychological decision theory, it has not been testable because of lack of a capability for simultaneous measurement of subjective probability and value. This measurement problem was solved with the development of the linear fan theorem by Anderson and Shanteau (1970). This functional measurement analysis can transform the above verbal statement into an exact mathematical equation in subjective value. Adults do indeed follow this multiplying *SEV* model.

Present concern is with children's sensitivity to the probability cue and their use of this cue in the integration task. The child may recognize that it is "harder" for the spinner to stop in a smaller red sector without being able to integrate this information into the happiness judgment. Younger children, moreover, would be expected to utilize the general-purpose adding rule discussed previously.

The results are in Fig. 1.11. The 4-year-olds exhibit the parallelism expected from the general-purpose adding rule. The multiplying rule, however, is already present at age 5, as shown by the linear fan pattern. Its development appears to be rapid because little change appears at older ages.

The linear fan pattern demonstrates that 5-year-olds have a functional concept of probability. The 4-year-olds understand that the red sector is a relevant, quantitative cue but may not understand its probabilistic nature. Only when this probabilistic aspect is understood can the multiplying rule appear. Beyond its intrinsic interest, this result illustrates a potential of present methods for studying cognitive development.

Several extensions of the spinner task deserve mention. For example, two red sectors could be used instead of only one, and the child would be rewarded

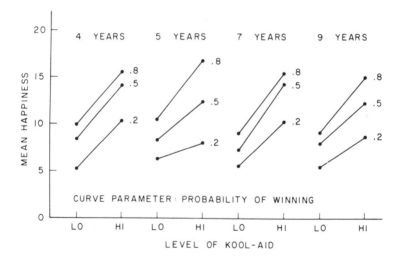

FIG. 1.11.   Mean happiness as a function of amount to win and probability of winning. (N. H. Anderson, unpublished experiment, November, 1977.)

if the spinner stopped in either sector. The rational model for this more complex integration task is

$$SEV = (SP_1 + SP_2) \times SV,$$

where $SP_1$ and $SP_2$ represent the subjective probabilities of stopping in the two respective sectors. Similarly, separate rewards could be given for each sector, leading to the model

$$SEV = SP_1 \times SV_1 + SP_2 \times SV_2.$$

Also of interest are the multiplication rules for probabilities that could be studied using two spinners. For example, the child could be told that the boy would have to spin both spinners and that both would have to stop in the red to win the Kool-Aid. Here the normative model is

$$SEV = (SP_1 \times SP_2) \times SV.$$

This task might also be used with two children, each spinning one of the spinners in a group effort to get the Kool-Aid. This setting might make the structure of the task more meaningful and it would also have interest for studies of egocentrism and cooperation. In addition, these more complex tasks appear to involve elements both of perceptual judgment and of the kind of operations studied by Piaget. Accordingly, such tasks could form a basis for the joint study of these two kinds of processes.

## Definition and Measurement of Conservation

In the present theoretical approach, conservation is considered as an expectation that some property of an object will remain constant across transformations of the object. This expectation will influence judgments of the object after transformation; it will be integrated in with the other cues and that allows it to be measured and traced out developmentally.

The essential idea can be illustrated for conservation of number. Let $A$ and $A'$ be two arrays with equally many objects, each of which can be transformed into the other by some rearrangement. Let $N(A)$ denote judged numerosity of $A$ when it is presented alone, and similarly for $N(A')$. Let $X$ denote judged numerosity of $A$ after it has been presented and then transformed into $A'$. If no conservation tendency is present, then $X$ will depend only on the appearance of the array after transformation: $X = N(A')$. To the extent that a conservation tendency is present and operative, $X$ will depend on the appearance before transformation. In general, therefore, $X$ may be represented as an average of the pre- and post-transformation judgments:

$$X = wN(A) + (1-w)N(A').$$

Because $w$ is the only unknown in this equation, it may be evaluated directly from the judgments.

The value of $w$ is a measure of the strength of the conservation tendency, ranging from 0 when conservation is entirely absent to 1 when conservation is complete. By measuring $w$ as a function of age, the development of conservation may be traced out directly at an empirical level. By measuring $w$ as a function of training condition, a sensitive index of training effectiveness becomes available. And by measuring $w$ for very small numbers, the development of conservation can presumably be traced back at least to age 3. Further discussion is given in Anderson and Cuneo (1978a).

## RESEARCH PROSPECTS IN SOCIAL JUDGMENT

This section considers a variety of problems in social judgment in which information integration plays an important role. The first several problems have been studied using adults and have yielded considerable support for a cognitive algebra of social judgment. Initial studies suggest that much the same cognitive algebra is present at fairly early ages. An ergodic heuristic for simulating longitudinal inquiry is also suggested, as well as an alternative to current "stage" theories of moral development.

### Cognitive Algebra of Deservingness

Numerous, sometimes subtle, factors are integrated to determine judgments of deservingness. Such judgments have great social interest because they underlie the rewards and punishments that each person gets from society. Some possibilities for a general cognitive algebra of deservingness will be noted briefly here (see also Anderson, 1974b, 1976d).

An averaging rule for integration of motivation and act seems to have some empirical validity. In general form,

Deservingness = Motive + Act.

Various realizations of this equation would arise according to the kinds of motives and acts. For example, the modal integration rule in Leon's developmental study of deserved punishment was

Punishment = Intention + Damage.

A complementary result was obtained by Lane and Anderson (1976) for adult's judgments of gratitude as a function of intention and actual value of the action:

Gratitude = Intent + Help.

A simple extension of the model incorporates the effect of Ability:

Deservingness = Motive + Act – Ability.

The negative sign on the Ability term reflects the fact that Act is evaluated relative to Ability, the same action being seen as more meritorious in a less able person. Although no experiments have been designed specifically to test this model, three articles that provide some support are discussed in Anderson (1974b, pp. 40-43, 1976d).

A somewhat different determinant of deservingness is the person's need. The developmental study of Fig. 1.9 supported the simple model

Deservingness = Act + Need,

uniformly from age 4 to 8.

Negative forms of deservingness may be considered similarly. The all-pervasive judgment of blaming is postulated to obey the rule

Blame = Motive + Act – Extenuation – Personal Goodness.

The role of the Extenuation term is self-explanatory. The last term reflects the empirical result that even irrelevant personal qualities may act to reduce blame (see Brooks & Doob, 1975). An analogous equation of justice can be written:

Punishment = [(Responsibility – Extenuation) × Crime]
– Prior Punishment – Personal Goodness.

Clearly these verbal formulas can be elaborated indefinitely. The present approach makes it possible to go past the verbalisms to study them as qualitative integrations and as quantitative social rules.

## Equity Theory

A basic idea of equity is that a person's outcome should be proportional to his input. This goes back as far as Aristotle, who actually suggested a mathematical model to define the state of equity. In modern times, alternative models have been suggested by Adams (1965), Walster, Berscheid, and

Walster (1973), and also by workers in information integration theory (Anderson, 1974b, 1976a, 1976d; Anderson & Farkas, 1975; Farkas, 1977; Farkas & Anderson, 1979), who have provided strong experimental tests as well as theoretical criticism of all these models. These tests have shown that the models of Adams and of Walster et al. are incorrect in their representation of the psychological structure of the judgment process. Aristotle's model and the integration theory model both gave correct representations of the psychological structure. In algebraic form, however, Aristotle's model was less appropriate than the integration theory model.

When a fixed sum is to be divided between two persons, A and B, the equity model from integration theory states that A's proportionate share is given by the relative input

Fair Proportion = A's Input/(A's Input + B's Input).

Support for this ratio equity model has been obtained with adults and also with children in the deservingness experiments summarized previously.

This equity model may be extended to include many other determinants of input besides actual work accomplished. Indeed, input may be identified with the concept of deservingness discussed above. Study of main effects of these various determinants would provide a cogent mapping of the child's sense of social fairness.

Moreover, model analysis can help delineate the structure of the underlying processing. Thus, it was possible to determine whether the child first integrates the deservingness information for each person and bases the equity judgment on these two deservingness values (hypothesis of input integration) or alternatively makes a separate equity calculation for each dimension of information and then integrates these separate, partial equity judgments (hypothesis of equity integration). The data show that children, like adults, follow the rule of equity integration (Anderson & Butzin, 1978). Other extensions that consider three or more persons, interpersonal salience, etc. are discussed in Anderson (1976d) and Farkas (1977).

## Perception of Persons

Interactions with other persons, in the family, at play, and in school, form the basis of much of the child's cognitive development. The person being perceived in any such interaction may be conceptualized as a complex informational field in which the informational elements include traits, attitudes, characteristics of face and voice, and various capabilities for reward and punishment. Any response to another person, no matter how intuitive or empathic it may seem, rests on integration of such information.

Person perception in adults has formed one of the empirical pillars of information integration theory (e.g., Anderson, 1974c, 1980). Many theoretical problems were first worked out in this area. An extensive and rather complex pattern of results has been shown to obey an exact averaging model of information integration.

But person perception in children, despite its obvious importance, has been neglected. Many possibilities lie open. One broad line of attack would be to replicate the adult experiments with children. At issue are basic questions dealing with amount, kind, and reliability of information, and the various algebraic integration rules. Developmental aspects of these questions have special interest.

Moreover, there are numerous social dimensions of judgment besides the central area of interpersonal attraction. Some of these concern concepts of equity, deservingness, and attribution, on which some work has been done as noted previously. Various others have yet to be considered.

## Causal Schemes as Integration Models

The core question in attribution theory can be epitomized as "Why did that person act that way?" This question reflects the everyday tendency to attribute causes to explain the actions and behaviors of other people. This section contrasts the integration theory approach (Anderson, 1974b, 1976d, 1978) with that of Kelley (1972). A basic difference between the two theories concerns the nature of causal scheme. Kelley defines causal schemata as specific patterns of three particular kinds of information. The integration–theoretical approach defines causal schemes in terms of cognitive algebra.

This theoretical contrast can be set out with the specific question "Why was the boy afraid of the dog?" In integration theory, this situation may be represented by the general Motive × Incentive model. Here Motive would correspond to the fearfulness of the boy, considered as a personality trait. Incentive would be negative, corresponding to the frightfulness of the dog. Thus, the observed fear would follow the causal scheme

Fear = Fearfulness × Frightfulness.

It is worth remarking that this model points to two distinct loci of causal forces. One is in the person, the other in the person's environment. This pattern of forces is sufficiently common to deserve separate emphasis as the general causal scheme

Action = Person $\circledast$ Environment,

where $\circledast$ is a generalized integration operation. In the given example, the causal forces of Person and Environment, boy and dog, are explicitly acknowledged in the very wording of the question.

The attribution problem is one of causal inference. The Action is given and judgments are to be made about the two terms on the right of the causal equation. With two unknown terms, of course, a unique solution cannot be obtained. Accordingly, it is necessary to impute a value to one or the other of the causal forces, or to obtain auxiliary information about them. If it was known that the dog had previously bitten several people, for example, a natural response would take the dog as the primary causal factor.

Such auxiliary information has a straightforward analysis. Judgments of fearfulness of the boy fall under the general theory of person perception (Anderson, 1974c) and are expected to obey the averaging rule. The same holds for frightfulness of the dog. This is the "first integration problem" of attribution theory (Anderson, 1978).

The "second integration problem" refers to the causal scheme itself. Any answer to the given question reflects this causal scheme, together with auxiliary knowledge about the causal forces.

Kelley's theoretical analysis is quite different. Three kinds of information are taken as basic: Distinctiveness, which refers to past reactions of the person to similar environmental objects; Consensus, which refers to past reactions of other persons to the same environmental object; and Consistency, which refers to reactions of the same person to the same object in the past. Specific patterns of values of these three types of information are taken as "causal schemata": "As such, the three patterns enter into the inferential process itself. Information is compared with them and is interpreted in terms of the pattern(s) with which it is consistent" (Orvis, Cunningham, & Kelley, 1975, p. 606). The HHH pattern, in which all three kinds of information have high value, constitutes a causal scheme that leads to an environment attribution. Any given pattern of stimulus information is compared to this standard causal scheme; to the degree that it is similar, it will lead to the same attribution.

Causal schemes are thus conceptually quite different in the two theories. For Kelley, the causal scheme is a prescribed pattern of values of three specified dimensions of information, and it serves a template function for comparison with given values of these same three dimensions of information. For information integration theory, in contrast, the causal scheme is the integration rule itself.

The basic difference in the qualitative conception of causal schemes ramifies throughout the theoretical analysis. Among the advantages of integration theory is its primary attention to the first and second integration problems, both of which are essentially ignored in Kelley's approach. This permits theoretical analysis of any kind of information, not just the three dimensions allowed by Kelley. Similarly, integration theory explicitly recognizes associated informational factors, such as communicational constraints. It also provides a quantitative framework in which both causal forces are jointly operative in producing the response.

This array of conceptual differences is a controlling factor in experimental work, from choice of task to large and small details of experimental design and data analysis. The long-term value of the experimental work depends heavily on these experimental specifics. The choice between these two theoretical approaches thus deserves careful consideration.

### An Ergodic Heuristic for Developmental Analysis

Longitudinal investigations are time-consuming and so development is usually studied using cross sections at various ages. However, cross-sectional studies have two well-known limitations. First, group averages almost necessarily ignore important individual differences within an age group. Second, age is confounded with other factors, such as secular trends in culture, mass media, education, and general socioeconomic changes.

The ergodic heuristic represents a possible way to avoid some difficulties with cross-sectional analysis. The term ergodic comes from stochastic theory in which longitudinal and cross-sectional properties are equivalent (Halmos, 1956; for a psychological application see Anderson, 1959). An analogous equivalence is expected to hold for cognitive development.

The essential idea of the ergodic heuristic is that behavior on a simple task at one age is expected to foretell behavior on a similar but more difficult task at a later age. The converse should also hold. Some part of a person's longitudinal development will thus be reflected in a cross-sectional picture of processes and abilities. In the subjective probability experiment of Fig. 1.11, for example, increases in task difficulty would presumably cause the 5-year-olds to regress to an adding-type rule. Similarly, in judgments of number, the ergodic heuristic would suggest that older children will treat larger numbers in much the same way that younger children treat small numbers. Thus, the frontier region of understood and partially understood numbers would increase gradually with age, a view that is at least in part similar to that of Gelman (1972, p. 163).

Full utilization of the ergodic heuristic requires batteries of tasks that are related in structure and graded in difficulty. Present performance on the easier tasks is expected to be reflected in future performance on the more difficult tasks. Similarly, present performance on the harder tasks should reflect past performance on the easier tasks. To the degree that this is true, the present cross-section of performance across the battery of tasks reflects the longitudinal development. If such batteries of tasks can be developed, a single time point will provide longitudinal information for individual children.

Judgments of deservingness, discussed previously, provide an attractive domain for developing a battery of tasks. Kind and quality of information can be manipulated in numerous ways. Amount of information, in both homogeneous and heterogeneous combination, is also easily manipulated. The same basic judgmental task can thus be varied from simple to complex along several different dimensions. Such a battery of tasks would serve the double purpose of providing a structural analysis of one major domain of moral judgment and of subserving the ergodic heuristic.

A second domain for development of a task battery would be in judgments of groups. Judgments of group deservingness, in particular, could be studied essentially in parallel with the above judgments of individual deservingness. This has the technical advantage that quite different information can be given about different members of the group that would be inconsistent within a single individual. Among other advantages, the group judgment could serve as a control for the study of how children develop sensitivity to inconsistency and what methods they develop to handle it.

## Stage and Continuity

At an essentially descriptive level, stage concepts are inherent in the very term developmental. Furthermore, there seem to be qualitative temporal changes in behavior patterns and cognitive structure that merit consideration as distinct stages. Beyond that, however, anyone who tries to bring the stage concept down to a working level soon learns that it is indeed "a notion abounding in pitfalls and intricacies" (Pinard & Laurendeau, 1969, p. 124; see also Brainerd, 1973, 1978). This state of affairs is a direct reflection of the lack of methods that can provide a firm empirical basis for stage analysis, a basis that gets beyond phenomenology to construct validity. Integration theory may be useful for this purpose.

Stage and continuity concepts are both clearly necessary. Different stages would usually be expected to manifest themselves as different integration rules or, perhaps, as different valuation rules. Within any stage, continous changes would be expected in the developmental parameters of the rules. In this way, both stage and continuity concepts can be harmoniously accommodated within the theory. This approach does not pretend to solve all or even most problems of stage analysis. When it is applicable, however, it can provide a penetration not available with other methods. Developmental studies of integration rules and their parameters (e.g., Anderson & Butzin, 1978; Anderson & Cuneo, 1978a; Butzin, 1978; Cuneo, 1978; Kun, 1977; Kun, Parsons, & Ruble, 1974; Leon, 1976, Chapter 3, this volume; Wilkening, Chapter 2, this volume) thus constitute an immediate frontier in stage analysis.

## Nonstage Approach to Moral Development

Integration theory provides an alternative to the stage theories that currently dominate studies of moral development (Kohlberg, 1976; Rest, 1976; Turiel, 1976). The simplest criticism of these stage theories is that they are very narrow. Three aspects of this criticism will be noted briefly.

An initial objection to the cited stage theories is that they are not applicable to children under 10. That is a direct consequence of the basic conceptual framework that attempts to base moral judgment on a set of abstract, largely adult moral dilemmas. Whatever the value of such attempts may be, their incapacity to go below age 10 indicates that they are basically inadequate to the study of moral development.

Furthermore, these stage theories are noncognizant of moral actuality. Five decades of research have only amplified the conclusions of Hartshorne and May (1928) that moral behavior depends strongly on situational specifics. The stage theories were not intended to address such questions, it is true, but that is still a proper criticism of the limits of their relevance.

Finally, these stage theories lack analytical power. They assume that each stage represents a complex structure of thought processes, but they provide little beyond introspection to delineate the nature of these structures. As useful as introspection can be, the history of psychology has repeatedly shown that some further validational base is necessary. The stage theories do not provide such a validational base.

The main product of the stage theory studies has been a test that is supposed to locate the person along the sequence of stages. Attempts to validate the test, and the associated sequence of stages, rest on correlations with gross variables such as age, education, profession, etc. Such correlations are too vague to allow meaningful assessment of the test or of the stages.

Integration theory provides methods that can analyze the structure of moral thought. It becomes possible to assess the strengths of various forces, both moral and nonmoral, that control moral judgment. These methods work with younger children as well as adults. They replace the stage–correlational approach with experimental analysis. They allow a delineation of moral algebra, a step forward in analyzing the structure of moral thought, which forms part of the basis needed for an adequate conceptualization of developmental stages.

## ACKNOWLEDGMENTS

This chapter is deeply indebted to Clifford Butzin, Diane Cuneo, and Manuel Leon, who have been my coworkers in applying information integration theory to developmental psychology. Their ingenuity and industry has formed a foundation for the present exposition. Our work was supported by Grants GS-36918, BMS74-19124, and BNS75-21235 from the National Science Foundation, and by grants from the National Institute of Mental Health to the Center for Human Information Processing, University of California, San Diego.

## REFERENCES

Adams, J. S. Inequity in social exchange. In L. Berkowitz (Ed.), *Advances in experimental social psychology* (Vol. 2). New York: Academic Press, 1965.

Anderson, N. H. An analysis of sequential dependencies. In R. R. Bush & W. K. Estes (Eds.), *Studies in mathematical learning theory.* Stanford, Calif.: Stanford University Press, 1959.

Anderson, N. H. Algebraic models in perception. In E. C. Carterette & M. P. Friedman (Eds.), *Handbook of perception* (Vol. 2). New York: Academic Press, 1974. (a)

Anderson, N. H. Cognitive algebra. In L. Berkowitz (Ed.), *Advances in experimental social psychology* (Vol. 7). New York: Academic Press, 1974. (b)

Anderson, N. H. Information integration theory: A brief survey. In D. H. Krantz, R. C. Atkinson, R. D. Luce, & P. Suppes (Eds.), *Contemporary developments in mathematical psychology* (Vol.2). San Francisco: W. H. Freeman, 1974. (c)

Anderson, N. H. On the role of context effects in psychophysical judgment. *Psychological Review,* 1975, *82,* 462–482.

Anderson, N. H. Equity judgments as information integration. *Journal of Personality and Social Psychology,* 1976, *33,* 291–299. (a)

Anderson, N. H. Integration theory, functional measurement, and the psychophysical law. In H.-G. Geissler & Yu. M. Zabrodin (Eds.), *Advances in psychophysics.* Berlin: VEB Deutscher Verlag, 1976. (b)

Anderson, N. H. How functional measurement can yield validated interval scales of mental quantities. *Journal of Applied Psychology,* 1976, *61,* 677–692. (c)

Anderson, N. H. *Social perception and cognition* (Tech. Rep. CHIP 62).La Jolla, Calif.: University of California, San Diego, Center for Human Information Processing, July, 1976. (d)

Anderson, N. H. Note on functional measurement and data analysis. *Perception & Psychophysics,* 1977, *21,* 201–215.

Anderson, N. H. Progress in cognitive algebra. In L. Berkowitz (Ed.), *Cognitive theories in social psychology.* New York: Academic Press, 1978.

Anderson, N. H. Integration theory applied to cognitive responses and attitudes. In R. Petty, T. Ostrom, & T. Brock (Eds.), *Cognitive responses in persuasion.* Hillsdale, N.J.: Lawrence Erlbaum Associates, 1979.

Anderson, N. H. *Information integration theory: A case history in experimental science.* New York: Academic Press, 1980.

Anderson, N. H., & Butzin, C. A. Integration theory applied to children's judgments of equity. *Developmental Psychology,* 1978, *14,* 593–606.

Anderson, N. H., & Cuneo, D. O. *The height + width rule in children's judgments of quantity.* (Tech. Rep. CHIP 69). La Jolla, Calif.: University of California, San Diego, Center for Human Information Processing, June, 1977.

Anderson, N. H., & Cuneo, D. O. The height + width rule in children's judgments of quantity. *Journal of Experimental Psychology: General,* 1978, *107,* 335–378. (a)

Anderson, N. H., & Cuneo, D. O. The height + width rule seems solid: Reply to Bogartz. *Journal of Experimental Psychology: General,* 1978, *107,* 388–392. (b)

Anderson, N. H., & Farkas, A. J. Integration theory applied to models of inequity. *Personality and Social Psychology Bulletin,* 1975, *1,* 588–591.

Anderson, N. H., Lindner, R., & Lopes, L. L. Integration theory applied to judgments of group attractiveness. *Journal of Personality and Social Psychology,* 1973, *26,* 400–408.

Anderson, N. H., & Shanteau, J. C. Information integration in risky decision making. *Journal of Experimental Psychology,* 1970, *84,* 441–451.

Bogartz, R. S. Comments on Anderson and Cuneo's "The height + width rule in children's judgments of quantity." *Journal of Experimental Psychology: General,* 1978, *107,* 379–387.

Brainerd, C. J. Neo-Piagetian training experiments revisited: Is there any support for the cognitive–developmental stage hypothesis? *Cognition, 1973, 2,* 349–370.

Brainerd, C. J. The stage question in cognitive–developmental theory. *The Behavioral and Brain Sciences,* 1978, *2,* 173–213.

Brooks, W. N., & Doob, A. N. Justice and the jury. *Journal of Social Issues,* 1975, *31,* 171–182.

Buchanan, J. P., & Thompson, S. K. A quantitative methodology to examine the development of moral judgment. *Child Development,* 1973, *44,* 186–189.

Butzin, C. A. *Developmental study of effects of extenuation on judgments of naughtiness.* Unpublished experiment, University of California, San Diego, 1977.

Butzin, C. A. *The effect of ulterior motive information on children's moral judgments.* Unpublished doctoral dissertation, University of California, San Diego, 1978.

Butzin, C. A., & Anderson, N. H. Functional measurement of children's judgments. *Child Development,* 1973, *44,* 529–537.

Costanzo, P. R., Coie, J. D., Grumet, J. F., & Farnill, D. A re-examination of the effects of intent and consequences on children's moral judgments. *Child Development,* 1973, *44,* 154–161.

Cuneo, D. O. *Children's judgments of numerical quantity: The role of length, density, and number cues.* Unpublished doctoral dissertation, University of California, San Diego, 1978.

Dion, K. K., & Berscheid, E. Physical attractiveness and peer perception among children. *Sociometry,* 1974, *37,* 1–12.

Farkas, A. J. *A cognitive algebra for bystander judgments of interpersonal unfairness.* Unpublished doctoral dissertation, University of California, San Diego, 1977.

Farkas, A. J., & Anderson, N. H. Multidimensional input in equity judgements. *Journal of Personality and Social Psychology,* 1979, *37,* 879–896.

Flavell, J. H. *The developmental psychology of Jean Piaget.* New York: van Nostrand Reinhold, 1963.

Gelman, R The nature and development of early number concepts. In H. W. Reese (Ed.), *Advances in child development and behavior* (Vol. 7). New York: Academic Press, 1972.

Halmos, P. R. *Lectures on ergodic theory.* New York: Chelsea, 1956.

Hartshorne, H., & May, M. A. *Studies in deceit.* New York: Macmillan 1928.

Hartup, W. H. Peer interaction and social organization. In P. H. Mussen (Ed.), *Carmichael's manual of child psychology* (3rd ed., Vol. 2). New York: Wiley, 1970.

Hebble, P. W. The development of elementary school children's judgment of intent. *Child Development,* 1971, *42,* 1203–1215.

Hendrick, C., Franz, C. M., & Hoving, K. L. How do children form impressions of persons? They average. *Memory & Cognition,* 1975, *3,* 325–328.

Keasey, C. B. Children's developing awareness and usage of intentionality and motives. In C. B. Keasey (Ed.), *Nebraska symposium on motivation* (Vol. 25). Lincoln: University of Nebraska Press, 1978.

Kelley, H. H. *Causal schemata and the attribution process.* New York: General Learning Press, 1972.

Kohlberg, L. Moral stages and moralization: The cognitive–developmental approach. In T. Lickona (Ed.), *Moral development and behavior.* New York: Holt, Rinehart, and Winston, 1976.

Kun, A. Development of the magnitude–covariation and compensation causal schemata in ability and effort attributions of performance. *Child Development, 1977, 48,* 862–873.

Kun, A., Parsons, J. E., & Ruble, D. N. Development of integration processes using ability and effort information to predict outcome. *Developmental Psychology*, 1974, *10*, 721–732.

Leon, M., & Anderson, N. H. A ratio rule from integration theory applied to inference judgments. *Journal of Experimental Psychology*, 1974, *102*, 27–36.

Lane, J., & Anderson, N. H. Integration of intention and outcome in moral judgment. *Memory & Cognition*, 1976, *4*, 1–5.

Leon, M. *Coordination of intent and consequence information in children's moral judgments.* Unpublished doctoral dissertation, University of California, San Diego,1976.

Leon, M. *Coordination of intent and consequence information in children's moral judgments* (Tech. Rep. CHIP 72). La Jolla Calif.: University of California, San Diego, Center for Human Information Processing, August, 1977.

McArthur, L. A. The how and what of why: Some determinants and consequences of causal attribution. *Journal of Personality and Social Psychology*, 1972, *22*, 171–193.

McArthur, L. Z., & Eisen, S. V. Achievements of male and female storybook characters as determinants of achievement behavior by boys and girls. *Journal of Personality and Social Psychology*, 1976, *33*, 467–473.

Mehler, J., & Bever, T. G. Cognitive capacity of very young children. *Science*, 1967, *158*, 141–142.

Oden, G. C. Fuzziness in semantic memory: Choosing exemplars of semantic categories. *Memory & Cognition*, 1977, *5*, 198–204.

Orvis, B. R., Cunningham, J. D., & Kelley, H. H. A closer examination of causal inference: The role of consensus, distinctiveness, and consistency information. *Journal of Personality and Social Psychology*, 1975, *32*, 605–616.

Parducci, A. Contextual effects: A range–frequency analysis. In E. C. Carterette and M. P. Friedman (Eds.), *Handbook of perception* (Vol. 2). New York: Academic Press. 1974.

Piaget, J. *The moral judgment of the child.* [M. Gabain, translator]. New York: The Free Press, 1965. (Originally published, 1932.)

Piaget, J. Quantification, conservation, and nativism. *Science*, 1968, *162*, 976–979.

Piaget, J. [*The child's conception of movement and speed*] (G.E.T. Holloway & M. J. Mackenzie, translators) New York: Ballantine, 1971. (Originally published 1946.)

Piaget, J., Inhelder, B., & Szeminska, A. *The child's conception of geometry* (E. A. Lunzer, Trans.). New York: Basic Books, 1960.

Pinard, A., & Laurendeau, M. "Stage" in Piaget's cognitive–developmental theory: Exegesis of a concept. In D. Elkind & J. H. Flavell (Eds.), *Studies in cognitive development.* New York: Oxford University Press, 1969.

Pringle, R., Andrews, J., & Shanteau, J. A functional measurement analysis of children's judgments of numerosity. *Developmental Psychology*, in press.

Pufall, P. B., & Shaw, R.E. Precocious thoughts on number: The long and short of it. *Developmental Psychology*, 1972, *7*, 62–69.

Rachlin, H. C. Scaling subjective velocity, distance, and duration. *Perception & Psychophysics*, 1966, *1*, 77–82.

Rest, J. R. New approaches in the assessment of moral judgment. In T. Lickona (Ed.), *Moral development and behavior.* New York: Holt, Rinehart, & Winston, 1976.

Ruble, D. N., & Feldman, N. S. Order of consensus, distinctiveness, and consistency information and causal attributions. *Journal of Personality and Social Psychology*, 1976, *34*, 930–937.

Singh, R., Sidana, U. R., & Saluja, S. K. Playgroup attractiveness studied with information integration theory. *Journal of Experimental Child Psychology*, 1978, *25*, 429–436.

Singh, R., Sidana, U. R.., & Srivastava, P. Averaging processes in children's judgments of happiness. *Journal of Social Psychology*, 1978, *104*, 123–132.

Suls, J. M., & Gutkin, D. C. Children's reactions to an actor as a function of expectations and of the consequences received. *Journal of Personality*, 1976, *44*, 149–162.

Surber, C. F. Developmental processes in social inference: Averaging of intentions and consequences in moral judgement. *Developmental Psychology,* 1977, *13,* 654–665.

Svenson, O. A functional measurement approach to intuitive estimation as exemplified by estimated time savings. *Journal of Experimental Psychology,* 1970, *86,* 204–210.

Turiel, E. A comparative analysis of moral knowledge and moral judgment in males and females. *Journal of Personality,* 1976, *44,* 195–208.

Verge, C. G., & Bogartz, R. S. A functional measurement analysis of the development of dimensional coordination in children. *Journal of Experimental Child Psychology,* 1978, *25,* 337–353.

Walster, E., Berscheid, E., & Walster, G. W. New directions in equity research. *Journal of Personality and Social Psychology,* 1973, *25,* 151–176.

Wilkening, F. Combining of stimulus dimensions in children's and adult's judgment of area: An information integration analysis. *Developmental Psychology,* 1979, *15,* 25–33.

Wohlwill, J. F. From perception to inference: A dimension of cognitive development. *Monographs of the Society for Research in Child Development,* 1962, *27,* 87–112.

# 2
# Development of Dimensional Integration in Children's Perceptual Judgment: Experiments with Area, Volume, and Velocity

Friedrich Wilkening
*Technische Universität Braunschweig, West Germany*

In perceiving our world, we usually consider more than one dimension at a time and in nearly all situations. Most situations do not only require that we consider the relevant dimensions, but also that we coordinate them in an adequate manner. It is important, therefore, to study how the coordination of dimensions develops.

Previous studies of dimensional coordination in children have been dominated by Piaget's conception of cognitive development. According to Piaget (1970c), children cannot coordinate stimulus dimensions before the concrete–operational stage, that is at an age of about 7 years. Once they enter this stage, however, they can coordinate the relevant dimensions exactly to that rule that corresponds to the physical properties of the stimulus. In judging the area of rectangles, for example, these children use a multiplicative rule to combine width and height. Children in the preoperational stage, on the other hand, are unable to consider more than one dimension. They either "center" on one aspect of the stimulus or vacillate between single dimensions, so that the question of coordination does not effectively occur.

During the last few years, however, it has become evident that Piaget's view of dimensional coordination in perceptual and cognitive development should be modified. The results of studies using the methods derived from information integration theory and functional measurement have shown very convincingly that young children can and do base their judgments on more than one stimulus dimension. No less interesting is the evidence for "cognitive algebra" in children. Not only do the young children consider more than one dimension, but they also combine information from the different dimensions according to consistent rules.

Of special relevance are the studies of Anderson and Cuneo (1978a) and Wilkening (1978, 1979). In a series of experiments with American children, Anderson and Cuneo found that 5-year-olds' judgments of rectangular area followed an additive rule, Height + Width. This rule proved to be reliable across a variety of experimental conditions. Anderson and Cuneo (1978a) suggested, therefore, that the Height + Width rule represents a general-purpose adding rule that operates in young children across many situations.

Independently from Anderson and Cuneo, this author made similar discoveries with German children, using slightly different experimental techniques (Wilkening, 1978, 1979). As a result, a research program having three aims was begun to: (1) see if the additive rule is task specific or if it has, in fact, the general character hypothesized by Anderson and Cuneo; (2) study the transition from the additive rule to the multiplicative rule that is obtained with older children and adults; (3) investigate the processes underlying the different rules, especially what contributes to the transition from one rule to the other.

The present chapter reports on that part of the research program that has been completed so far. Special emphasis is given to the experimental techniques developed within the framework of the information integration approach and to the results obtained by these methods. The reader interested in more detail about the theoretical foundation of the experiments is referred to the chapter of Anderson (Chapter 1, this volume).

## EXPERIMENT 1: AREA JUDGMENT

As mentioned previously, the starting point of the present work was a study by Wilkening (1979, Experiment 1). Subjects from two age groups, 5-6-year-olds and adults, had to judge the area of nine rectangles in a 3 × 3, Width × Height design, using a numerical, rating-scale type of response. Whereas the judgments of the adults followed the expected multiplicative model, Width × Height, the children seemed to use an additive rule in combining the two dimensions. Doubts in the validity of this finding were still possible, however, because the additive pattern was marred by a one-point discrepancy that appeared to reflect an end effect in the response scale.

A second study was carried out, therefore, in which an attempt was made to avoid the undesirable end effect. This study also included a larger range of stimulus levels, as well as two intermediate age groups. The latter two groups were added in order to investigate a possible developmental transition from an additive to a multiplicative rule. Because this experiment has been described in greater detail elsewhere (Wilkening, 1979, Experiment 2), only a brief summary of the methods and results together with some additional data will be presented here.

## Method

*Subjects.*   Four age groups were tested: 5-year-olds, 8-year-olds, 11-year-olds, and adults, with mean ages of 5.5, 8.5, 11.6, and 26.4 years, respectively. Each age group consisted of 10 subjects, 5 male and 5 female. The children were attending a kindergarten, primary, or secondary school in the Frankfurt area; the adults were students at the University of Frankfurt.

*Materials.*   The experimental stimuli were 16 rectangles cut out of 8-mm-thick plastic and were wrapped in silver paper so as to look like chocolate bars. A 4 × 4 design was used, with widths and heights of 4, 8, 12, and 16 cm on each dimension. A real chocolate bar served as an end anchor. This bar was a 4 × 4 square and consisted of four pieces of 2 × 2 cm each. The response scale was a board, 150 cm long and 6 cm wide, which was laid on the table between experimenter and subject.

*Procedure.*   The experimenter gave the child the real chocolate bar, asked him or her to unwrap it, to break it into pieces, and to form a row out of the four pieces, beginning at the left side of the response scale. After that, the child could keep or consume the end anchor. The same introductory procedure was used for adults.

The experimenter next told the subjects that they would see other chocolate bars. The subjects were asked to imagine that each bar was broken into pieces of the same size as those of the end anchor and that all the pieces were arranged side by side to form a row.

The bars were then shown one after another for about 5 sec each. After each presentation, the subjects pointed to that position on the scale they thought the imaginary row would reach. This judgment could be read in centimeters by the experimenter from a scale concealed at the rear end of the response board. Following four preliminary practice trials, the 16 rectangles were presented in two different random orders for each subject. For the 5-year-olds, the two replications were separated by a 2-day interval. All subjects were tested individually.

## Results

*Group Data Analyses.*   The results for the 5-year-olds and adults are clear from Fig. 2.1. The graphical representation of the *multiplicative* model, Area = Width × Height, is a fan of diverging lines. As can be seen in the right panel of Fig. 2.1, this pattern was obtained for the adults. In contrast, the

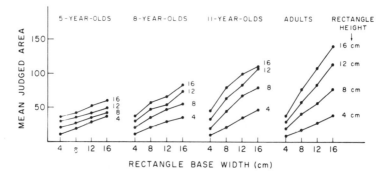

FIG. 2.1.    Mean graphic ratings of rectangle area as a function of rectangle width and height for the four different age groups in Experiment 1.

graphical representation of an *additive* model, Area = Width + Height, is a set of parallel lines. As can be seen from the left panel of Fig.2.1, the data of the 5-year-olds followed this pattern very closely.

The judgment patterns of the two intermediate age groups, however, cannot be unequivocally associated with either integration rule. The two middle panels of Fig 2.1 show departures from the parallelism pattern but do not yet exhibit the clear linear fan pattern of the adult data.

These data for the two intermediate age groups raise an interesting developmental question. Two interpretations are possible. First, each individual might use an ill-formed integration rule, transitional between addition and multiplication. Second, the group data could result from averaging over individuals, some of whom used an additive and others a multiplicative rule.

*Single Subject Data Analyses.*    To investigate the development of the integration rules in more detail, single subject analyses were performed. Inspection of the individual subject graphs revealed that most patterns could easily be classified as either additive or multiplicative. Each graphical classification could be tested by an analysis of variance because each subject served in two replications. The results of these tests on individual subjects are summarized in Table 2.1.

Three aspects of the findings shown in Table 2.1 deserve special mention. First, there is no sign of centration (single dimension solutions) in any individual subject. Except for Subject #5, all 5-year-olds had significant main effects for both width and height. This finding rules out an objection that the additive rule for the 5-year-olds is an artifact of averaging over children, some of whom centered on width and some on height. Second, only 2 out of 40 individual judgment patterns were not classifiable as either additive or multiplicative. For Subject #5, the response variability was so high that it masked even main effects. For Subject #22, the significant residual interaction component seemed to be caused by a one-point discrepancy in an otherwise clear bilinear pattern. Third, the number of subjects with an additive integration pattern decreased with age and the number of subjects with a multiplicative pattern increased.

It should be noted that a significant bilinear component can be obtained both for a pure multiplicative rule and for a combined additive–multiplicative rule (cf. Anderson, 1970, Equation 18). In the present case, inspection of the individual graphs can help in distinguishing between these two models. With width and height, it seems reasonable to assume that subjective and objective length are approximately linearly related. For a multiplicative rule, therefore, the lines of the bilinear fan should have a common intersection at the zero point of the objective scale. In contrast, the intersection for the combined additive–multiplicative rule should clearly be to the left of the zero point (cf. Anderson & Cuneo, 1978a, p. 362). The data patterns classified as multiplicative in Table 2.1 all seemed to be of the former type. This argues against the possibility that an additive and a multiplicative rule operated at the same time in individual children.

## Discussion

In the present study, children at all age levels based their judgments of rectangular area on both relevant stimulus dimensions, that is, width and height. Moreover, children as well as adults combined these dimensions according to simple algebraic rules. What changed over age was not the number of dimensions attended to, but the rule that describes the coordination of the dimensions. Whereas the judgments of the adults followed the expected multiplicative pattern, the 5-year-olds combined width and height additively.

Individual subject analyses showed that the above findings were not artifacts of averaging over children. On the basis of the individual analyses of variance, 38 out of the 40 subjects could be classified as showing either an additive or a multiplicative integration pattern. These results suggest that there is no gradual transition between the two rules. Rather, the developmental change from the additive to the multiplicative rule seems to occur relatively fast for an individual child.

The psychological processes involved in this transition could not be clarified by the present experiment because the design was cross-sectional with respect to age. Also, only speculations can be given as to the processes underlying the additive rule of the younger children. Several mechanisms can be entertained, for example, a Height + Width rule, a perimeter rule, or a general-purpose type additive rule (cf. Anderson & Cuneo, 1978a; Wilkening, 1979). Before such speculations are carried too far, the present findings

TABLE 2.1

Summary of F Ratios in Analyses of Variance for Single Subjects and Individually Assessed Integration Rules, Experiment 1

| Age Group | Subject | Main Effects | | | Interaction | | Integration Rule[a] |
|---|---|---|---|---|---|---|---|
| | | Width | Height | Overall | Bilinear | Residual | |
| 5 years | 1 | 10.31** | 18.16** | .70 | 1.40 | .61 | + |
| | 2 | 8.52** | 7.02** | .49 | .33 | .50 | + |
| | 3 | 8.69** | 6.59** | .51 | 1.05 | .45 | + |
| | 4 | 10.53** | 22.01** | .50 | 1.61 | .36 | + |
| | 5 | 2.53 | 1.79 | .47 | 2.00 | .28 | 0 |
| | 6 | 16.39** | 11.59** | .49 | .48 | .49 | + |
| | 7 | 9.32** | 9.89** | 1.28 | 4.39 | .83 | + |
| | 8 | 23.54** | 21.34** | 1.12 | .04 | 1.25 | + |
| | 9 | 14.01** | 10.94** | .46 | 1.34 | .35 | + |
| | 10 | 30.59** | 36.45** | .94 | 6.56* | .24 | × |
| 8 years | 11 | 17.04** | 15.48** | 2.24 | 15.56** | .58 | × |
| | 12 | 22.14** | 22.82** | 1.87 | 15.25** | .20 | × |
| | 13 | 8.61** | 5.56** | .37 | .30 | .38 | + |
| | 14 | 30.58** | 37.72** | .96 | .01 | 1.07 | + |
| | 15 | 104.98** | 112.03** | 9.23** | 57.60** | 2.19 | × |
| | 16 | 10.28** | 15.00** | 1.30 | 3.61 | 1.01 | + |
| | 17 | 17.44** | 17.47** | 1.12 | .39 | 1.21 | + |
| | 18 | 32.01** | 32.08** | 1.02 | 3.65 | .70 | + |
| | 19 | 35.85** | 33.88** | .27 | .34 | .26 | + |
| | 20 | 32.46** | 31.99** | .82 | .90 | .81 | + |

|     |          |          |        |          |        |     |
| --- | -------- | -------- | ------ | -------- | ------ | --- |
| 21  | 143.04** | 127.91** | 4.44   | 20.92**  | 2.38   | ×   |
| 22  | 79.87**  | 83.76**  | 9.23   | 21.16**  | 7.73** | 0   |
| 23  | 57.95**  | 50.60**  | 1.84   | .00      | 2.07   | +   |
| 24  | 229.44** | 220.76** | 9.52   | 67.69**  | 2.25   | ×   |
| 25  | 70.37**  | 63.54**  | .96    | 4.48     | .52    | +   |
| 26  | 136.86** | 139.03** | 10.92  | 78.02**  | 2.53   | ×   |
| 27  | 27.80**  | 28.20**  | 1.44   | 1.18     | 1.48   | +   |
| 28  | 45.70**  | 37.22**  | 1.14   | .12      | 1.27   | +   |
| 29  | 17.43**  | 8.34**   | .39    | .15      | .42    | +   |
| 30  | 60.25**  | 59.83**  | 2.47   | 14.85**  | .93    | ×   |

11 years

|     |          |          |         |          |        |     |
| --- | -------- | -------- | ------- | -------- | ------ | --- |
| 31  | 123.33** | 116.49** | 8.27**  | 61.68**  | 1.59   | ×   |
| 32  | 275.58** | 251.55** | 15.26** | 119.44** | 2.24   | ×   |
| 33  | 56.58**  | 58.44**  | 3.00*   | 23.33**  | .45    | ×   |
| 34  | 207.97** | 195.15** | 11.91** | 96.65**  | 1.31   | ×   |
| 35  | 53.82**  | 47.61**  | 4.11**  | 32.94**  | .51    | ×   |
| 36  | 121.63** | 119.88** | 8.63**  | 75.26**  | .30    | ×   |
| 37  | 65.36**  | 61.67**  | 3.53*   | 19.94**  | 1.48   | ×   |
| 38  | 781.44** | 758.57** | 39.97** | 356.63** | .39    | ×   |
| 39  | 10.81**  | 11.79**  | .77     | 5.30*    | .20    | ×   |
| 40  | 11.49**  | 11.31**  | 1.77    | 6.52**   | 1.18   | ×   |

Adults

*Note.* $df$ are 3/16, 9/16, 1/16, and 8/16 for main effects, overall interaction, bilinear, and residual, respectively.

[a] + = additive, × = multiplicative, 0 = unclassifiable.

*$p < .05$.

**$p < .01$.

should be verified by other, converging methods to test the robustness of the additive integration rule.

## EXPERIMENT 2: AREA PRODUCTION

To test the generality of the above findings, an area production task was designed. The subject had to adjust the width of a rectangle with a variable height such that its area appeared equal to the area of a standard comparison square.

## Method

*Subjects.* Four age groups participated: 5-6-year-olds, 8-9-year-olds, 11-12-year-olds, and adults. There were 10 subjects in each group. About half of the subjects in each age group were female, and about half were male. The children were irregularly selected from a kindergarten in Frankfurt or from classes in a primary or secondary school in the Frankfurt area. The adults were largely students at the University of Frankfurt.

*Materials.* The following apparatus was used for the production of rectangular area. A board, 75 cm long, 25 cm wide, and 1 cm thick, was laid flat at the edge of the table with its length parallel to the subject. The board was painted chocolate brown. The upper section of the board could be covered by one of five strips of white cardboard, 75 cm long, and 15, 17, 19, 21, or 23 cm wide, thereby posing a brown area with a height of 10, 8, 6, 4, or 2 cm.

Lying on the brown board and the white cardboard strip was a thin white board, also 75 cm long and 25 cm wide. This white board could be moved back and forth over the brown board below, thus producing a brown rectangle of variable width in the lower left corner. The width of this produced rectangle could be read on a millimeter scale along the edge of the brown board, opposite to the subject and in view of the experimenter.

A 10 × 10 cm square, cut out of 1 cm thick brown plastic, served as a standard comparison. A real chocolate bar of the same size as the standard was used in each experiment.

*Procedure.* At the beginning of the experiment, the child was given the real chocolate bar. The experimenter asked the child to lay it on the standard square, in order to find out if the two squares were equal in area. After this introduction, the child was acquainted with the area production apparatus that showed a brown rectangle with a height of 10 cm and a width of 15 cm at the start of the experiment. The child was told to imagine that this rectangle was a chocolate bar and that it should be adjusted to have the same size as the real chocolate bar. After the child had adjusted the width to about 10 cm, the experimenter reduced the height of the rectangle to either 4 cm or to 8 cm (balanced over subjects within each age group) and asked the child how long the adjustable bar would now have to be in order to provide the same amount to eat as the real chocolate bar. This judgment had to be given by moving the white cover board. A further trial with a rectangle height of either 8 or 4 cm (depending on the level presented before) terminated the practice period.

For the main phase of the experiment, the real chocolate bar was removed from the standard square, only the latter serving as a comparison stimulus. The five height levels were presented three times in different random permutations for each child. The response was not reset between trials so that the last adjustment remained in position until the next response was made. No time restrictions were imposed by the experimenter, but the children were encouraged to judge spontaneously. With few exceptions, judgments were made in 5-10 sec.

The procedure for the adults paralleled that for the children. The main difference was that no real chocolate bar was used in this age group.

## Results

*Age Group Analyses.*   Figure 2.2 shows the mean judgments for the four age groups separately. The heavy, solid curve in each panel represents the rectangle width produced by the subjects, plotted as a function of the rectangle height presented by the experimenter. The dotted lines in each panel indicate the values to be expected on the basis of additive or multiplicative combination rules. The straight line labelled + stands for the additive model,

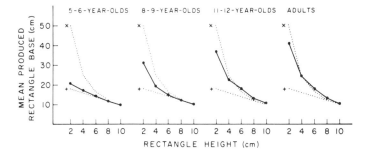

FIG. 2.2.   Area production results: The solid curves show the mean adjusted rectangle width for different levels of height presented. The dotted curves show the theoretical values to be expected on the basis of an additive model, Area = Width + Height (+), or a multiplicative model, Area = Width × Height (×), respectively; Experiment 2.

Area = Width + Height; the hyperbolic curve labelled X stands for the multiplicative model, Area = Width × Height. These are calculated so that the sum of edge lengths (20 cm) or the area (100 cm$^2$) is exactly adjusted to that of the standard.

Figure 2.2 shows that the average judgments of the 5-6-year-olds are very close to the linear function, whereas the average judgments of the adults are very close to the hyperbolic function. Considering the gradual change across the four age levels, it appears as if the additive model, Area = Width + Height, gradually unfolds into the multiplicative one, Area = Width × Height.

In the present experiment, trend analysis can be used as a statistical test for an additive or a multiplicative model. The trend analyses to be reported in the following rest on the assumption that subjective length is proportional to physical length. For width and height, this assumption does not seem unreasonable, as is shown by the linearity of the data obtained in Experiment 1 (cf. Fig. 2.1).

For the 5-6-year-olds, a significant linear component was obtained, $F(1, 9) = 64.32$, $p < .01$, whereas the departure from linearity was not significant, $F(3, 27) = 2.55$, $p > .05$. For the three older age groups, the over-all test for the departure from linearity was always significant, the only significant higher-order component being the quadratic, $F(1, 9) = 11.79$, 37.54, and 43.78, $p < .01$, for the 8-9-year-olds, 11-12-year-olds, and adults, respectively. These results suggest that an additive coordination rule operates in the 5-6-year-olds, whereas a multiplicative rule provides the best description for the older age groups.

*Single Subject Analyses.* To study the unfolding of the judgment patterns to be seen in Fig. 2.2 in more detail, a parametric trend analysis was computed for each subject. An additive model was assigned if the linear component was significant, $p < .05$, and the over-all departure from linearity was not significant, $p > .05$. A multiplicative model was assigned if the quadratic trend component was significant, $p < .05$.

The results in Table 2.2 show that the majority of the 5-6-year-old children

TABLE 2.2
Number of Subjects in Each Age Group Showing Additive or
Multiplicative Rule in Area Production, Experiment 2

| | Integration Rule | | |
|---|---|---|---|
| Age Group | Additive | Multiplicative | Unclassifiable |
| 5–6 years | 6 | 3 | 1 |
| 8–9 years | 3 | 7 | 0 |
| 11–12 years | 1 | 9 | 0 |
| Adults | 2 | 8 | 0 |

are classified as additive, whereas the majority of subjects in the three older age groups are classified as multiplicative. This frequency distribution shows little trend over the three older groups and so cannot account for the gradual age trend that appears in Fig. 2.2. This apparent difference results in part because the judgment patterns classified as multiplicative in the 8-9-year-old age group had a very small slope and in part because the two adults classified as additive had a much steeper slope than the linear patterns in the other age groups.

## Discussion

The main findings of Experiment 1 were replicated in the present study: The majority of 5-year-old children combined width and height according to an additive rule while the majority of the older children used a multiplicative rule.

Some characteristics of the production response are also of interest. The children's behavior suggested that they found this production task easier than the rating-type response of Experiment 1. However, the task appears to have both positive and negative aspects. The positive aspect was that the coordination of dimensions was enforced by the coordination of actions performed by the experimenter and the child on the height and width dimension, respectively. The negative aspect was that the equal-difference variation of height carried out by the experimenter could mislead the subjects to use an equal-difference judgment strategy. In order to produce a data pattern to conform to a multiplicative model, however, subjects had to give nonlinearly increasing judgments on the width dimension. This task characteristic may perhaps explain the additive pattern found with two adults.

The importance of task characteristics can be illustrated further by comparing the present results with those of Verge and Bogartz (1978), who also used an area production technique. In their procedure, children had to match the area of an adjustable square to that of a stimulus rectangle. Verge and Bogartz found that half of the 5-year-olds and about one third of the 7-year-olds equated one side of the square either to the width or to the height of the rectangle. Children showing this behavior were called "centerers." The side matching strategy seems to be caused, however, by some peculiarity of the stimulus display rather than to reflect a general inability to attend to more than one dimension. For the adjustable square, variation in width was always accompanied by the same variation in height, and vice versa. This redundancy may have led some children to think that attention to one dimension of a rectangular area was sufficient. When the adjustable square and the rectangle were displayed side-by-side, moreover, the geometrical configuration may have led some children to match sides on aesthetical grounds. The view that this side matching strategy is not true centration is supported by the finding of

Verge and Bogartz that all of their "centerers" who were questioned could correctly identify the stimulus with the larger area (cf. Anderson & Cuneo, 1978b).

## EXPERIMENT 3: VOLUME JUDGMENT

With the change from an additive to a multiplicative integration rule in area judgment as children become older having been shown to occur across variations in method, the next step of research suggested itself, namely, to investigate if similar rules apply to judgment of volume.

Volumes that can be described by two dimensions have special interest here. These volumes include cylinders and cones, in which the two dimensions are height and diameter. These volume judgments are similar to area in that the two basic dimensions have to be integrated by multiplying to arrive at a physically correct solution. But volume differs from area in that only the height dimension enters linearly into the multiplicative model. The other dimension, that is diameter, has to be integrated nonlinearly, the correct rule being a quadratic function of the radius. The mathematical formulas are $V = \pi r^2 \times h$ and $V = (\pi/3)r^2 \times h$, for cylinder or cone volume, respectively, when $V$, $r$, and $h$ denote volume, radius, and height.

The Quadratic × Linear rule for cylinders and cones would seem to be more difficult than the Linear × Linear rule for rectangles and therefore should appear at a later age. Between an additive coordination, $r + h$, and the correct Quadratic × Linear rule, $r^2 \times h$, an interesting transition stage is conceivable, namely the Linear × Linear model, $r \times h$. It was hypothesized, therefore, that the integration rules would develop in an additive, Linear × Linear, and Quadratic × Linear order.

To test this hypothesis, two experiments were conducted, one on cylinder volume and one on cone volume. Because the methods and results of both studies were very similar, only one will be reported in detail. Because some findings of cylinder volume are presented elsewhere in this book (Anderson, Chapter 1, this volume), the cone experiment was selected for this chapter.

### Method

The method used here was analogous to that of Experiment 1. The subjects had to judge the volume of cones, which were constructed on the basis of a factorial, Height × Radius design. Absolute judgments were obtained on a linear graphic rating scale.

*Subjects.*    Subjects from the following four age groups participated in the experiment: 5-6-year-olds, 8-9-year-olds, 12-13-year-olds, and adults. There were 10 subjects in each age group, 5 male and 5 female. The demographic characteristics and sampling procedures resembled those of the two former experiments. The data of one child from the youngest age group were not considered in the main analyses, because her judgments did not differentiate between eight of the nine cones.

*Materials.*   The stimuli to be judged were nine cones with a radius of 1, 3, or 5 cm and a height of 4, 8, or 12 cm. The mantles of the cones were formed out of thin red plastic; the base of each cone was uncovered. In addition to these nine experimental stimuli, two end-anchor cones were used. The lower had a height and radius of 3 cm and of 1 cm, respectively; the upper had height and radius of 14 cm and 6 cm, respectively.

The judgment scale was a glass tube 100 cm high and with inner and outer diameters of 26 mm and 30 mm. The tube stood vertically on a chair, the lower opening of the tube being fixed on a wooden block. A centimeter scale was placed on the side of the tube that was in view of the experimenter. The tube was encircled by a paper ring 7 cm high, which the subjects could move vertically in order to indicate their judgments.

*Procedure.*   At the beginning of each experiment, the two end anchor stimuli were presented. The experimenter filled the larger with red liquid from a large glass reservoir, holding the cone with its top down and its base horizontal. Then the experimenter said she would pour the liquid from the cone into the tube. The subject was asked to observe this transformation and to move the paper ring upwards during this process such that its lower edge always matched with the liquid level in the tube. When the final level of 99 cm was reached, the subject's attention was again directed to the large end anchor cone, in order to ensure that he or she remembered that the liquid in this cone had filled the tube to the 99-cm height. The liquid from the tube was poured back into the reservoir, and the procedure was repeated for the lower end anchor, which produced a level of less than 1 cm in the tube.

For the experimental stimuli, the subject was asked to imagine that each cone was filled up with liquid and that this liquid was poured from the cone into the tube. The experimenter held each cone with her finger tips at the subject's eye level and turned it around, thus allowing the subject to look at it from all perspectives outside and inside. The subjects judged by shifting the lower edge of the paper ring up or down the tube to that position they thought the imaginary liquid column would rise. For the next judgment, the experimenter moved the paper ring back to the bottom of the tube.

Each subject went through three replications of the 3 × 3 design. Within each replication, the nine trials were presented in different random orders for each subject.

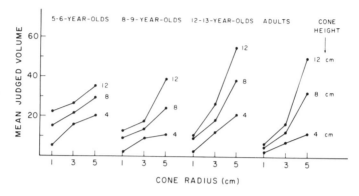

FIG. 2.3. Mean graphic ratings of cone volume as a function of cone radius and height for the four different age groups in Experiment 3.

## Results

*Graphical Analysis.* Figure 2.3 shows the mean judgments of the four age groups. The volume judgments are plotted as a function of cone radius ($r$), with one curve for each value of height ($h$). According to the Quadratic × Linear model, $V = (\pi/3)r^2 \times h$, the curve for each height value should be of parabolic form. The upward curvature should increase with increasing levels on the height dimension.

This Quadratic × Linear pattern is clearly visible for the three older age groups. In contrast to these patterns, the data for the 5-6-year-olds appear parallel. Thus, an additive integration rule seems to operate in this group.

*Statistical Analysis.* For the 5–6-year-olds, main effects for both dimensions were significant, $F(2, 16) = 21.59$ and $21.07$, $p < .01$, for radius and height, respectively. The interaction was not significant, $F(4, 32) = .77$. Thus, the additive integration rule found in above area experiments was also found with the volume judgment in the youngest age group.

For the three older age groups, the main effects and interaction were all significant. The interactions, which are important for determining the nature of the integration rule, were $F(4, 36) = 8.67, 32.10$, and $41.91, p < .01$, for the 8–9-year-olds, 12–13-year-olds, and adults, respectively. Partitioning this interaction into the Linear × Linear, Linear × Quadratic, Quadratic × Linear, and Quadratic × Quadratic components, using the standard orthogonal polynomial coefficients, yielded a significant Quadratic × Linear component in each of the three age groups, $F(1,9) = 24.51, 6.18$, and $27.21$, $p < .05$, for the 8-9-year-olds, 12-13-year-olds, and adults, respectively. The Quadratic × Linear pattern corresponds directly to the physical formula for cone volume, $V = (\pi/3)r^2 \times h$, as already noted.

It would have been desirable to test if the above integration rules are valid for each individual child, as was done for area judgments in Experiments 1 and 2. However, the individual analyses of variance yielded significant main effects and interactions in few instances only. For these volume judgments, the within-subjects variability was too high to provide statistically clear data.

## Discussion

The data of the present study show that the main findings of Experiment 1 and 2 are not limited to judgments of rectangle area. The integration rules found for area seem to apply for volume as well. The rules proved to be valid not only for cylinders, which have rectangular cross-sections, but also for cones that cannot be as easily represented by a rectangular area.

The 5-6-year-olds again exhibited an additive, Diameter + Height integration rule. Various processes might account for this additive rule. For example, the child may estimate diameter and height of the cone separately and add the two estimates. Again, the child may circumscribe the triangular cross-section of the cone by a rectangle and estimate the perimeter of the rectangle, which would be twice (cone diameter + cone height). As still another possibility, the child may transform the isoscelic triangular cross-section into two right triangles, put them together at their diagonal to form a rectangle with cone height and radius as edges, and judge the perimeter of this rectangle. At present, no information is available on this question. It may be of some interest, however, that the data are rather close to the predictions from the third perceptual process when untransformed scale values of height and radius are used.

Children aged 8 years and older combined the relevant stimulus dimensions according to a multiplicative rule. A new and interesting finding was that children as young as 8 years in age not only combined height and radius multiplicatively, but also seemed to realize that the two dimensions enter into the multiplicative integration rule with different functions. Height was processed linearly and radius according to a quadratic function, in agreement with the mathematical formula for cone volume.

It is worth mentioning that the 8-year-olds did not know this mathematical formula from school or from elsewhere. Therefore, the possible interpretation that these children made their judgments by calculating volume can be ruled out. Even for the older children and adults, who might know the formula for cone volume, a mental arithmetic process seems implausible. Judgments were made spontaneously and much faster than such a conscious calculation would have taken. They seem to reflect, therefore, a relatively direct perceptual–cognitive process rather than some abstract logical or mathematical operation.

The speculation that children may pass through the transitional stage of a Linear × Linear integration rule before they arrive at the Quadratic × Linear dimensional combination was not supported in the present experiment. Neither the group data nor the individual graphs showed any clear evidence for a bilinear model.

The hypothesis of a Linear × Linear transition stage had an implicit assumption, namely that two basic operations are involved in cognitive algebra of volume judgment. One operation is the integration of dimensions, the process that has main interest in the studies reported in this chapter. The other operation is the valuation process, by which the physical stimuli on each single dimension receive their subjective values (cf. Anderson, 1974, p. 217). In the present experiment, a correct integration rule was apparently coupled with a correct valuation function, and vice versa.

Two basically different interpretations can be given for this finding. First, integration and valuation may, in fact, be operative as different psychological processes. If this is true, it appears that a correct integration rule and a correct valuation function emerge at about the same time in the course of development. It would be of further interest, then, to study if and how these processes are dependent on each other.

The other interpretation would deny that the older subjects really integrated the dimensions. Instead of producing estimates on each single dimension and integrating them multiplicatively, the subjects may respond to a global percept of volume. They may, for example, subdivide the total volume into small units and count or estimate their total amount. The underlying process, then, would be additive in character rather than multiplicative, and the multiplicative model describing the data would only have an "as if" status. This interpretation, which seems to be favored by Anderson and his coworkers (Anderson, 1974, p. 261; Anderson & Cuneo, 1978a; Anderson & Weiss, 1971), could also apply of course, for the multiplicative area data in Experiment 1 and 2.

## EXPERIMENT 4: TIME AND VELOCITY INTEGRATION

From a developmental point of view, the most important result of the three experiments reported so far was that 5-year-old children attended to both relevant stimulus dimensions and combined them according to an additive rule. All the tasks had in common the facts that geometric dimensions were involved and that a multiplicative combination was required on a priori grounds. A search was made, therefore, for a theoretical model that prescribed the multiplication of dimensions other than geometrical and to see if young children would still apply an additive rule for these non-geometric dimensions. A simple model that seemed to be suited for investigation was given by the formula Distance = Time × Velocity.

Up to now, comparatively little research has been conducted on the development of time and velocity concepts (for a recent review of time development see Friedman, 1978). In this field also, most findings and experimental paradigms originate in the work of Piaget (1969, 1970a, 1970b). Nearly all of his experiments had the same structure: Two objects moved with different velocities for equal or unequal times, and the child had to judge which of the two objects had travelled for the longer time or at a higher velocity. According to Piaget, children in the preoperational stage showed no adequate understanding of time and velocity in these tasks and are also unable to coordinate them. Instead, their judgments are dominated by irrelevant and misleading cues such as stopping position and overtaking. However, Piaget's conclusions from his choice tasks may be doubted for various reasons. One main reason is given by the results of the above studies on area and volume judgment, which clearly showed that young children can coordinate perceptual dimensions.

One purpose of the present study was to investigate the development of time and velocity integration in nonchoice tasks. Beyond that, it was hoped that the use of a kinematic rather than a geometric task would yield further information about processes in dimensional integration at different ages.

## Method

In the experimental situation, subjects judged how far animals of different natural speeds would run during different lengths of time. To make this realistic to the children, the animals were portrayed as fleeing from a barking dog.

*Subjects.*   Three age groups were tested: 5-6-year-olds, 9-10-year-olds, and adults. Each age group consisted of 15 subjects, about half of either sex. The children were attending kindergarten or primary schools in the Frankfurt area. The adults were mostly students at the University of Frankfurt.

*Design and Stimulus Materials.*   A 3 × 3 design, time × velocity, was used. The three levels of time were represented by a barking dog, played over a tape recorder lasting 2, 5, or 8 sec. The three levels of velocity were represented by a turtle, guinea pig, and cat. Pictures of these animals were painted on cardboard pieces that showed one animal measuring about 10 × 6 cm in outline. A small magnet was mounted at the back of each cardboard piece to enable its attachment to the judgment scale (see following).

A screen 3 m long and 1 m high was mounted on the wall at the subject's eye level. On this screen, the following situation was depicted. On the left side, a frightful looking dog was sitting close to the exit of a den. A straight footbridge 250 cm long led away from the exit to the right. This footbridge served as the judgment scale. A metal band was fixed on it, containing a centimeter scale not noticeable to the subject.

*Procedure.*    After the child entered the room, the experimenter showed him or her the scene depicted on the large screen. At that time, the turtle, guinea pig, and cat were sitting together in a random order near the exit of the den. The child was told that all three animals were extremely frightened by the barking of the dog and that each animal started running over the footbridge when the dog began to bark and stopped when he became silent.

The child was asked which animal would be the fastest and which would be the slowest if all three animals ran a race. Having answered this question, the child had to rearrange the animals at the den exit correspondingly, the slowest one sitting on the left and the fastest on the right. All subjects produced the correct velocity order, that is, turtle, guinea pig, and cat. This part of the introduction had two purposes: to ensure that the three levels on the velocity dimension had the same subjective order for each child and to acquaint the children with the fastening function of the magnet.

For the first practice trial, the guinea pig and cat were removed from the screen, leaving only the turtle in the den exit. Then the child was told that the dog was about to bark and that he or she should imagine that the turtle started running as fast as possible immediately after the dog began to bark and stopped when he became silent. The experimenter then started the tape recorder, and the dog barked for 8 sec. Thereafter, the child was asked to put the turtle on that position on the footbridge he or she thought the turtle would have reached. This procedure was repeated for the guinea pig and the cat, with barking times of 5 and 8 sec, respectively.

Following these three practice trials, the nine time-velocity combinations were presented in three different random orders, with the only restriction that the same time or velocity level did not appear in succession.

The children indicated their judgments by putting the animal at that position on the footbridge they thought the animal would have reached in the time presented. This judgment was read in centimeters by the experimenter. The animal was then removed from the footbridge, and the animal for the next trial was placed in the den exit, which was the zero point of the judgment scale.

A similar procedure was used for the adults. The main difference was that the experimenter gave the adults some information to explain the childlike character of the experiment.

## Results

*Graphical Analyses.*    Figure 2.4 shows the mean judgments for the three age groups separately. Judged distance is plotted as function of time, with one curve for each velocity level. According to the multiplicative model,

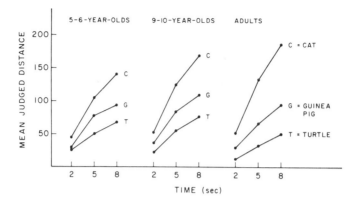

FIG. 2.4.    Mean graphic ratings of distance as a function of time and velocity
for the three different age groups in Experiment 4.

Distance = Time × Velocity, the three curves should form a diverging fan of
straight lines.

The data follow this pattern very closely in each age group. The main
deviation from a perfect bilinear pattern in each age group is the slight
downward bowing of some curves, especially of the mean judgments for the
higher levels of velocity. This finding may be of some interest in itself, because
it shows that the subjective difference between 2 and 5 sec is larger than that
between 5 and 8 sec, in agreement with previous psychophysical time
functions for children (Fraisse, 1948; Goldstone & Goldfarb, 1966). These
deviations from linearity do not cause any serious difficulty for the
multiplicative model because they could be largely eliminated by using
functional measurement methods to transform the objective time scale in Fig.
2.4 to a subjective scale.

Visual inspection of the individual graphs showed that most of them could
be classified as multiplicative in each age group. Although the individual
patterns are not as smooth as the group data, they suggested that the results of
Fig. 2.4 did not represent an artifact of averaging over children.

*Statisical Analysis.*    Analysis of variance yielded significant main effects
both of time and of velocity in each age group. The interaction was also
significant in each age group, $F(4, 56)$ = 8.11, 17.82, and 33.91, $p < .01$, for
the 5-6-year-olds, 9-10-year-olds, and adults, respectively. Decomposition of
these interactions into bilinear and residual seemed unnecessary because it is
evident from Fig. 2.4 that bilinearity is the principal component in each
age group.

Analyses of variance for single subjects did not provide much information
in this experiment. Many $F$ ratios that were expected to be significant from
inspection of the individual graphs failed to reach the critical value, as was the
case in Experiment 3. These somewhat weak results contrast with the high

effectiveness of the respective analyses in Experiment 1, in which a 4 × 4 design was used (cf. Table 2.1). A lesson suggested by comparison of single-subjects results of Experiments 1, 3, and 4 is that a 3 × 3 design with three replications may not provide sufficient power for reliable classifications of the individual integration rules. Larger designs with larger ranges of the stimulus variables may be necessary. This is especially true for research with young children, because the variation of their judgmental data is usually relatively high.

## Discussion

The results of the present study were surprising. Children as young as 5 years not only based their judgments on both dimensions, but also combined them according to the multiplicative rule, Distance = Time × Velocity. No age differences were found in the integration model used by the subjects. The data of the 5-6-year-olds showed the same diverging fan pattern as those of the 9-10-year-olds and adults.

The question is what processes enabled young children to produce such apparently sophisticated judgments. Observations of the children's eye movements provide an answer. Almost every child followed the imaginary movement of the animal on the footbridge with his or her eyes for the time the dog barked. When the dog stopped barking, the child pointed to that position the imaginary movement had reached on the judgment scale. Their eyes moved at a slow constant rate for the turtle, fast for the cat, and in between for the guinea pig. It follows logically from this behavior that the differences between the distance judgments become larger with increasing levels of time, thus corresponding with a multiplicative model. Interestingly enough, the same judgment strategy was apparently used by the older children and adults.

Although the young children's ingenuity in finding the eye-movement strategy is striking, caution seems in order against an overestimation of their cognitive abilities. The multiplicative data pattern does not necessarily mean that the children have an abstract concept of time and velocity and, in addition, have a complete understanding of the correct integration rule. This is hard to believe. It seems to be more likely that the multiplicative data pattern found here reflects only an "as if" model (as may be true for the area and volume judgments). The present task was apparently constructed such that a simple perceptual strategy would produce multiplicative data.

## SUMMARY AND CONCLUSIONS

*Problem.* The four experiments reported in this chapter studied how children integrate information from different perceptual dimensions in three tasks. Two of these tasks were geometric: height and width of rectangles in judgments of area, and height and radius of cones in judgments of volume. The third task was nongeometric: time and velocity of moving objects in judgments of distance. In all three tasks, the physically correct combination rule for the two relevant dimensions was multiplicative.

*General Method.* The methodological approach was that of information integration theory (Anderson, 1974). With the exception of Experiment 2, methods of functional measurement were adopted for the use with children. Perceptual dimensions were experimentally combined by factorial design, and subjects made numerical judgments on a graphic rating-type scale. Different age groups over the range from 5-year-olds to adults participated in each experiment.

*Integration Rules.* Children as well as adults combined the stimulus dimensions according to common algebraic rules. For the two geometric tasks, the youngest children (5 years) used additive rules. These rules shifted developmentally to the physically correct rule of multiplication, which was used by the older children and adults. For time and velocity, however, all ages used a multiplicative rule.

*The Centration Issue.* In all experiments, even the youngest children took account of both relevant stimulus dimensions. This finding contradicts a fundamental postulate of Piaget's (1970c) theory of cognitive development, namely that preoperational 5-year-old children "center" on one aspect or dimension of the stimulus array. Two concepts of centration have appeared in the literature. The stronger one asserts that young children are generally unable to attend to more than one dimension at a time. This presumption is clearly invalidated by the present results. The weaker one states that the children may attend to more than one dimension, but, if they do, they vacillate between the dimensions and are unable to coordinate them. This weaker concept of centration is also invalidated by the present results, for the additive rule found here shows that coordination did occur.

*Note on Choice Tasks.* Piaget's centration assumption is based on the results from choice tasks. The present results suggest that choice responses are inadequate for investigating dimensional coordination because they cannot distinguish between different integration rules, for example, centration and addition (cf. Wilkening, 1978). The same objection applies to recent studies using the rule assessment methodology developed by Siegler (1976, 1978), which also failed to consider the possibility that children's false answers may have been caused by a false combination rule rather than by centration.

*Individual Subject Analyses.* The power of the information integration approach used here is especially notable in the single-subject analyses. They show that the integration rules reported above for age groups as a whole are also valid for single members of each group and are not artifacts of averaging over subjects. In the experiments on area judgments, in particular, the individual analyses of variance yielded remarkably clear-cut results. Nearly every child had a data pattern that was clearly either additive or multiplicative.

*The Transition Period.* The single-subject analyses from Experiment 1 suggest that the transition from the additive to the multiplicative rule is discontinuous rather than gradual. If this were not true, more children should have been detected with graphs showing an additive and multiplicative rule being operative at the same time. This conclusion has to be taken with some caution, however, because the design was cross-sectional with respect to age. However, a discontinuous transition seems plausible, because the two integration rules appear to embody qualitatively different strategies.

*"As If" Integration Models.* The results of the experiment on time and velocity integration show that a multiplicative outcome is even possible in children as young as 5 years, provided they find an adequate judgment strategy. For this particular task, however, it has to be emphasized that the multiplicative model obtained for the 5-year-olds probably has only an "as if" character. Presumably, these children did not really perform a two-dimensional multiplication of time and velocity information, but rather employed the simple, perceptual eye-movement strategy discussed previously.

It would be interesting to test this interpretation by varying the experimental procedure so as to eliminate the eye-movement strategy. For example, the room might be darkened during the presentation of each time level. If the multiplicative model remained unchanged under this manipulation, this would argue against the "as if" interpretation, and it might be concluded that the children have a conceptual understanding of time, distance, and velocity integration.

An alternative prediction would follow from Anderson and Cuneo's (1978a) hypothesis of a general-purpose additive rule that applies to situations in which the children lack a clear, adult conception of the specific quantity to be judged. In such a situation, children may still be sensitive to relevant dimensions, and these dimensions would be integrated by the general-purpose additive rule. In the present task, the relevant dimensions are time and velocity. Hence, this theoretical rationale implies that the judgments should follow the additive rule, Distance = Time + Velocity.

## ACKNOWLEDGMENTS

I wish to thank Hannelore Buchholz, Michael Hartmann, Gudrun Lindner, Marlise Praeg, Michael Russ, and Sigrid Schwalm for their assistance in conducting the experiments. I am also indebted to Norman Anderson, Viktor Sarris, and Tom Trabasso for helpful comments on an earlier draft of this chapter.

## REFERENCES

Anderson, N. H. Functional measurement and psychophysical judgment. *Psychological Review,* 1970, *77,* 153–170.

Anderson, N. H. Algebraic models in perception. In E. C. Carterette & M. P. Friedman (Eds.), *Handbook of perception* (Vol. 2). New York: Academic Press, 1974.

Anderson, N. H., & Cuneo, D. O. The height + width rule in children's judgments of quantity. *Journal of Experimental Psychology: General,* 1978, *107* 335–378. (a)

Anderson, N. H., & Cuneo, D. O. The height + width rule in children's judgments of quantity. *Journal of Experimental Psychology: General,* 1978, *107,* 335–378. (a)

Anderson, N. H., & Weiss, D. J. Test of a multiplying model for estimated area of rectangles. *American Journal of Psychology,* 1971, *84,* 543–548.

Fraisse, P. Etude comparée de la perception et de l'estimation de la durée chez les enfants et chez les adultes. *Enfance,* 1948, *1,* 199–211.

Friedman, W. J. Development of time concepts in children. In H. W. Reese & L. P. Lipsitt (Eds.) *Advances in child development and behavior* (Vol. 12). New York: Academic Press, 1978.

Goldstone, S., & Goldfarb, J. L. The perception of time by children. In A. H. Kidd & J. L. Rivoire (Eds.), *Perceptual development in children.* New York: International University Press, 1966.

Piaget, J. *The child's conception of time.* New York: Ballantine, 1969.

Piaget, J. *The child's conception of movement and speed.* New York: Ballantine, 1970. (a)

Piaget, J. *Genetic epistemology.* New York: Columbia University Press, 1970. (b).

Piaget, J. Piaget's theory. In P. H. Mussen (Ed.), *Carmichael's manual of child psychology* (Vol. 1). New York: Wiley, 1970. (c)

Siegler, R. S. Three aspects of cognitive development. *Cognitive Psychology,* 1976, *4,* 481–520.

Siegler, R. S. The origins of scientific reasoning. In R. S. Siegler (Ed.), *Children's thinking: What develops?* Hillsdale, N.J.: Lawrence Erlbaum Associates, 1978.

Verge, C. G., & Bogartz, R. S. A functional measurement analysis of the development of dimensional coordination in children. *Journal of Experimental Child Psychology,* 1978, *25,* 337–353.

Wilkening, F. Beachtung und Addition zweier Dimensionen: Eine Alternative zu Piagets Zentrierungsannahme. *Zeitschrift für Entwicklungspsychologie und Pädagogische Psychologie,* 1978, *10,* 99–102.

Wilkening, F. Combining of stimulus dimensions in children's and adults' judgments of area: An information integration analysis. *Developmental Psychology,* 1979, *15,* 25–33.

# 3 Integration of Intent and Consequence Information in Children's Moral Judgments

Manuel Leon
*University of California, Los Angeles*

The purpose of this study was to examine the rules children use to coordinate intent and consequence information in their moral judgments. The child is viewed as an information integrator, evaluating each piece of incoming information and combining the various pieces of information into a unitary response. It is a basic assumption that young children have the capacity to comprehend and combine multiple dimensions of stimulus information, including subjective dimensions such as intentionality. The results presented in this chapter not only support this assumption but also reveal the exact nature of children's moral integration rules.

This integration–theoretical approach stands in sharp contrast to the approach of Piaget (1932) that has dominated work on children's moral judgment. This work has been largely directed at questions other than those concerning information integration. Indeed, Piaget denied that even older children integrated intent and consequence information. Instead, he concluded that older children's judgments were based on intentions, and when particularly salient, on consequences. However, Piaget's methodology is subject to serious difficulties that cast doubt on his theoretical interpretation. Because of the major role that Piaget's methodology has played in this research, it requires close examination.

## Critique of Piaget's Moral Choice Task

In his study of children's moral judgment, Piaget (1932) asked children to compare two stories and say which of the two central characters was the naughtier and why. In one story, a child intent on mischief does a little damage. In the other, a child accidently causes considerable damage. The child is classified as moral subjective or moral objective according as he chooses the bad intent or the considerable damage as being naughtier. Piaget concludes that there are "two distinct moral attitudes—one that judges actions according to their material consequences, and one that only takes intentions into account" (p. 133). In Piaget's view, these moral judgments have an all-or-none character. The possibility that both intent and consequence affect the judged naughtiness does not seem to be theoretically admissible. Even the older children are not considered to integrate the two kinds of information.

One obvious shortcoming of this choice task is that it does not discriminate between one-dimensional and multidimensional response strategies. There is no way of showing whether a choice favoring intent is based exclusively on intent or on an integration with intent receiving greater weight than consequence in the overall judgment. Similarly, a choice in favor of consequences does not rule out the possibility of a multidimensional response with consequences receiving greater weight.

Piaget did not base his all-or-none interpretation on the choices alone, of course, but relied on children's justifications of their choices to eliminate the possibility of multidimensional judgments. This procedure is questionable because the children had to rationalize their choices immediately after making them. Presumably, their explanations would emphasize those aspects of the story situations that supported their choices. Moreover, if a child did use both intent and consequences in his explanation, he was classified as being in a transitional stage between the two poles of the intent–consequence dimension. Multidimensional response rules would thus be nondetectable with Piaget's choice task. These limitations of the choice task are now widely recognized (e.g., Buchanan & Thompson, 1973; Chandler, Greenspan, & Barenboim, 1973; Kohlberg, 1969, p. 407).

A second problem is that the choice task may overload the information capabilities of younger children, or that the choice comparison process may cause the subject to ignore the less salient dimension. The choice task requires the child to deal with four discrete pieces of information on two different stimulus dimensions. Hence, unidimensional response strategies may represent cognitive simplification of the task. Such strategies may seriously misrepresent the child's evaluative capabilities for moral judgments.

A related difficulty with the choice task has recently been brought to light by Ruble, Trabasso and their associates (Austin, Ruble, & Trabasso, 1977; Feldman, Klosson, Parsons, Rholes, & Ruble, 1976). These investigators showed that the lesser effect of intent in the choice task was, in large part, a memory effect. As the task is ordinarily given, the intent information is given first, followed by the consequence information. The studies cited indicate that the greater effect of consequence information in young children is largely a recency effect related to memory factors.

Finally, there is the problem that the "intent" manipulation in the choice stories is typically so ill-defined that results are difficult to interpret. This methodological shortcoming is clear in the three stories used by Piaget. For example, the scissors theme was used to generate the following two stories (Piaget, 1965):

> There was once a little girl who was called Marie. She wanted to give her mother a nice surprise and cut out a piece of sewing for her. But she didn't know how to use the scissors properly and cut a big hole in her dress.
>
> A little girl called Margaret went and took her mother's scissors one day that her mother was out. She played with them for a bit. Then as she didn't know how to use them properly, she made a little hole in her dress [p. 122].

Two aspects of the construction of these stories deserve notice. First, the children's motives for initiating the behavior are not causally linked with the damage done. The damage in both stories is accidental, resulting from clumsiness and having nothing to do with the children's motives. The older children especially might be expected to recognize this lack of causal relation. Hence, a shift to an intent-only response strategy may be built in by the stimulus stories themselves.

Second, of more immediate relevance, motives are manipulated by attributing good intentions to one character and none to the other. Thus, in the second story above, the child is only playing with the scissors. The same analysis applies to the two stories based on the ink pen theme. In Piaget's stories about the broken cups, the only deviation from this pattern is that in one story it is explicitly stated that the damage was accidental.

It is clear from Piaget's description of the stories that he meant the absence of an explicit motive to be regarded as signifying an ill-intentioned act:

> We therefore tried to make the children compare the stories of two kinds of clumsiness, one, entirely fortuitous or even the result of a well-intentioned act, but involving considerable material damage, the other negligible as regards the damage done but happening as the result of an ill-intentioned act [p. 121].

It is possible, of course, that children infer that Margaret had bad intentions in taking her mother's scissors, but this is unknown. Certainly, the results of the present study differ considerably depending on whether intent is specified explicitly or implicitly. Alternatively, there may be no inference about an "ill-intentioned act." Instead, the good intentions of Marie may be taken by older children as mitigating the damage. These shortcomings of

Piaget's stories are important because they have been used extensively in subsequent research and have served as the model for stimulus construction (e.g., Chandler et al., 1973; Crowley, 1968; Gutkin, 1972; Surber, 1977).

This arbitrariness in stimulus construction continues to be a problem. Crowley (1967) has attempted to remedy this problem by standardizing the stories. However, his work seems rather to further emphasize the problems of Piaget's approach. Crowley's standardization criterion was that story pairs should discriminate between " objective" and "subjective" children. However, this criterion is poorly related to the causal coupling of intent and consequence. For example, the following story (Crowley's pretraining item #6) is judged to have poor intent–consequence coupling:

> Ann doesn't care very much for finger painting. When the class was finger painting that afternoon, Ann didn't do much finger painting. She just played with the paint, and a little paint dribbled on her desk [p. 75].

There are two things wrong with this story. First, Ann's bad intentions consisted of nothing more than lack of enthusiasm for finger painting. Second, it is not clear whether or not Ann purposely spilled paint on her desk. Presumably, children were expected to infer that Ann was naughty for not wanting to paint and that she spilled paint on her desk either out of anger for being made to paint or out of carelessness. What children actually did infer is unknown.

Crowley used this story because it and its companion item discriminated well between moral objectives and moral subjectives. However, the lack of specificity in such stimulus stories makes the results of the choice task difficult to interpret. Much of this work has been criticized on the grounds that the moral relevance of such stories is dubious (Chandler et al., 1973; Turiel, 1966).

The items rejected by Crowley because of poor discriminative properties seem to be better constructed than some of those found acceptable. Here is a representative example of an item rejected because too many "objective" children made intent-based choices:

> *Bad intent-little damage.* One day Irving found a piece of wood. He wants to saw the wood in pieces to make a box. But his father won't let him. Irving doesn't like that, so he pushes the board. It falls on the ground and a little piece breaks off the end of the board.
> *Accident-high damage.* One day Fred notices that a large board on the fence was loose. He figured he'd better hammer the board to the fence so his dog wouldn't get out. So he got some nails. But they were too big, and as he hammered them in, they split the board to pieces. So next day, Fred's father had to buy another large board and had to spend Saturday morning fixing the fence [p. 109].

Elimination of items on which "objective" children make "subjective" choices may have been acceptable for Crowley's specific goal of testing effects of training. However, it clearly does violence to the children's actual moral sense. Certainly, Crowley's results vitiate any conclusion that children below a certain age do not take account of intent.

## Averaging Model for the Integration Process

The central problem in an information integration study is to determine the rule by which the given information is integrated. The present study was designed to test the hypothesis that intent and consequence information are integrated by an averaging rule. According to the theory, each piece of information is specified by two parameters: a scale value that represents the evaluation of the information with respect to the response dimension; a weight that represents the relative importance of that information in the overall judgment. For an averaging rule, the response is the weighted average of the scale values of the various pieces of information included in the integration process. The algebraic rule is

$$R_{ij} = w_I I_i + w_C C_j$$

where $I_i$ and $C_j$ are the scale values of the $i$ and $j$ levels of the intent and consequence factors, respectively, and $w_I$ and $w_C$ are the importance of intent and consequence information in the overall judgment. $R_{ij}$ is the response on a continuous, numerical scale for the single story defined by the $i$ level of intent and the $j$ level of consequence. In the present application, the weight parameters $w_I$ and $w_C$ are assumed to remain constant over various levels of intent and consequences.

The statistical test of the model requires that the stories be defined by a factorial design so that every level of the intent factor is paired with every level of the consequence factor. Given this design constraint, the averaging rule predicts that the row × column plot of the data, that is, the intent × consequence graph, should be a series of parallel curves. Statistically, this parallelism prediction is equivalent to a zero row × column interaction term in a two-way analysis of variance (see Anderson, Chapter 1, this volume). The factorial graph thus becomes a key tool in the theoretical analysis.

## Review of Previous Work

Three previous reports (Buchanan & Thompson, 1973; Costanzo, Coie, Grumet, & Farnill, 1973; Hebble, 1971) aimed to show that younger children make multidimensional moral judgments. For this purpose, Piaget's choice task was modified in two important ways. First, the story characters were

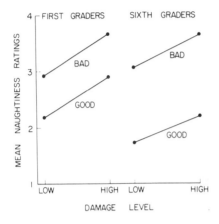

FIG. 3.1. Parallelism test for averaging rule of intent and consequence information. Data estimated from Hebble (1971, Fig. 1). Curves correspond to positive and negative intent.

rated one at a time on degree of badness. Second, Piaget's bad intent–low damage and good intent–high damage stories were supplemented by two more stories, bad intent–high damage, and good intent–low damage. These four stories form a 2 × 2, intent × consequence design. The main effects of this design provide evidence on the joint use of the intent and damage cues. The main finding of all three studies was that intent and damage cues both had substantial main effects. Contrary to Piaget, children as young as kindergarten age readily made multidimensional moral judgments. Intent and consequence are both integrated into the overall judgment.

The authors in these studies were not especially concerned with the nature of the intent–consequence integration rule. Indeed, their 2 × 2 designs are too small and other aspects of procedure not adequate enough to shed much light on this issue. Nevertheless, their results are suggestive and are reanalyzed here for their bearing on the integration rule.

Hebble (1971) used seven different story themes, each varied in a 2 × 2, intent × consequence design. Each child rated all 28 stories on a 4-point naughtiness scale. Figure 3.1 shows the data averaged over story themes and over 86 subjects in each of the first and sixth grades. The essential feature of Fig. 3.1 is the parallelism supporting the averaging rule for the integration process. However, this support must be interpreted with caution because there was considerable variation in response pattern over story themes.

Constanzo et al. (1973) used procedures similar to those of Hebble, the main difference being that consequences could be positive as well as negative. The data for the three grade levels are shown in Fig. 3.2. The curves for the second and fourth grades are essentially parallel, in support of the averaging integration rule. However, the kindergarten group shows an interesting configural effect: Intent is ignored for the negative outcome but not for the positive outcome.

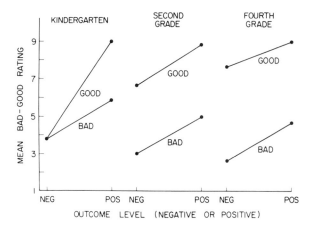

FIG. 3.2. Parallelism test for averaging rule of intent and consequence information. Data reanalyzed from Costanzo, et al. (1973, Table 2). Curves correspond to positive and negative intent.

Buchanan and Thompson (1973) adopted a suggestion by Norman Anderson to employ the methodology of information integration theory to study moral judgment in children. This entailed a shift from the Piagetian choice task to numerical judgments of single story characters obtained from factorial designs. Subjects were 48 children in first, second, and third grades. They were first classified as "moral subjective" and "moral objective" using Piaget's choice task and then given the integration task.

The results for the two moral groups are shown in Fig. 3.3. As would be expected, the difference between the two intent curves, malice and accident, is greater for the subjective than for the objective group. But even the objective children show a substantial effect of intent, contrary to Piaget's claim that

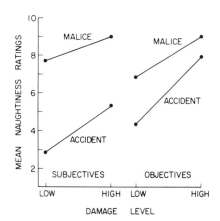

FIG. 3.3. Parallelism test for averaging rule of intent and consequence information. Data reanalyzed from Buchanan and Thompson (1973).

these children tend to ignore intent. These data bring out the crudeness of the subjective–objective dichotomy. Reanalysis of these data showed no significant deviations from parallelism, in support of the averaging rule. It may be noted, however, that Fig. 3.3 shows some apparent nonparallelism that would be consistent with the averaging rule if the more extreme level of intent or of damage received greater weight than the less extreme level (Leon, Oden, & Anderson, 1973).

Since the completion of this thesis, Surber (1977) independently tested the averaging rule for the intent–consequence judgments. The data fit the parallelism prediction of the averaging rule for kindergarten through fifth grade children. Separate tests also supported averaging over adding for the children. Adults, however, ignored the damage cue and based their judgments solely on intent. In contrast, the present results indicate that adults also average damage and intent. Present results also suggest that Surber's age trend largely reflects failure to causally link the consequences to the intent of the story characters by the younger children.

## METHOD

Subjects listened to tape recorded stories that gave intent and/or consequence information about an action of a boy. They judged how much punishment the boy should receive. Two types of stories were used. In the simple stories, intent was explicitly stated. In the standard stories, similar to those used in previous studies, intent was implicit and had to be inferred. A standard Piagetian choice task was also used. Subjects were first, second, third, fifth, and seventh graders and a group of college students.

### Stimulus Stories

*Simple Stories.*   In these stories, intent was manipulated with two short sentences that simply and directly specified the motives underlying the behavior. The consequences were damage that resulted when the actor interfered with workmen painting a house. Three levels of intent and four levels of consequences were combined to make 12 stories according to a 3 × 4, intent × consequence design. The single intent and consequence items were also used for a total of 19 stories. The stimulus levels were as follows:

#### Intent Statements

1. Perry got in the way on purpose. He wanted to mess things up.
2. John had a tough day at school. He took it out on the workmen.
3. Jim did not mean to get in the way. It was an accident.

*Consequence Statements*

1. He knocked the ladder over. The ladder broke the front window.
2. He knocked a paint can off the ladder. The can broke a flower pot.
3. He knocked a paint brush off the ladder. The brush got very dirty.
4. He bumped the ladder. Nothing fell off.

*Story Example.* Jim did not mean to get in the way. It was an accident. He bumped the ladder. Nothing fell off.

*Standard Stories.* The design for the standard stories was identical to that for the simple stories. Intent was manipulated by varying the manner of aggression. Consequences were degrees of personal injury caused by the story character throwing an object at another child. The consequence-alone stories were introduced by the statement, "Harry threw a rock at a friend." Stimulus levels were as follows:

*Intent Statements*

1. *Malicious aggression.* John was very mad at one of his friends. He saw his friend coming. He picked up a rock and threw it at his friend.
2. *Displacement.* Harry was very angry at his parents for not letting him do what he wanted. A friend came by to play catch. Harry threw the ball before his friend was ready to catch it.
3. *Accident.* Mike and a friend were throwing rocks against a wall. Mike threw a rock against the wall. The rock bounced back toward Mike's friend.

*Consequence Statements*

1. The rock hit Mike's friend on the head and made a very bloody cut.
2. The rock knocked John's friend down. He cut his knees pretty bad when he fell.
3. The rock hit Harry's friend on the leg and made a bruise.
4. The rock missed John's friend. John's friend was not hurt.

*Story Example.* John was very mad at one of his friends. He saw his friend coming. He picked up a rock and threw it at his friend. The rock hit John's friend on the leg and made a bruise.

## Procedure

All subjects went through one complete replication of the simple stories and, beginning with the third grade, one replication of the standard stories. The standard stories were not used with first- and second-graders because they showed no effect of intent in pilot work. The standard stories followed the simple stories after a three- to five-minute rest period.

The simple stories were presented in four phases as follows.

*Phase 1.*   In this phase, subjects were introduced to the stimulus stories with the following remarks:

> I want you to listen to some stories about boys who are in trouble with their parents for something they did. All the stories are about boys who got in the way of workmen painting houses. The stories tell why the boys got in the way of the workmen; and how much damage the boys did.

Three examples were then given. In the first example, the actor got in the way on purpose and broke a flower pot. In the second, the dirty brush outcome was presented alone. In the third, the displacement motive was presented alone. With each example, the subject was asked to explain why the boy in the story had gotten in the way and/or how much damage the boys had done. In the first example, if the subject omitted mention of either intent or consequences, the procedure was repeated. This happened infrequently.

*Phase 2.*   The second phase introduced the stimulus stories in a choice situation. Subjects listened to three pairs of stories and then told the experimenter which of two actors in each pair should be punished more and why. In the first pair, consequences were the same for both stories (the dirty brush outcome), while intent was varied (accidental vs. purposive interference). In the second pair, intent (displacement) was the same for both stories and the consequences were varied (no damage vs. a broken flower pot). In the third pair, intent and consequences were pitted against each other in the Piagetian manner, that is, accident + broken window vs. purposive interference + no damage. The purpose of the first two pairs and the verbal justification of the choices was to sensitize children to the multidimensional aspect of the stimulus stories. With few exceptions, the children based their choices on the variable factor. On the third pair, subjects' choices were recorded without comment.

*Phase 3.*   The third phase introduced the integration task with the following instructions:

> I am going to show you stories like these, one at a time. Listen carefully and pay attention to everything in the stories. Then tell me how much the boy should be punished. To make it easier for you, we'll use these sticks. The more you feel the boy should be punished, the longer should be the stick to which you point. Remember, all the stories are about boys who got in the way of workmen painting houses. The stories tell why each boy got in the way and how much damage each did.

These introductory remarks were followed by two stories used to define the end points of the response scale. These end-anchors serve to establish subject's frame of reference on the response scale. For the simple stories, the shortest stick of the response scale was defined as "no punishment" and anchored with the following story: "Harry was trying to help the workmen. He wanted to help. He just touched the ladder. Nothing happened." The longest stick of the response scale was defined as the punishment suitable to the following story: "Art set out to really mess things up. He did it on purpose. He pushed the ladder over. The ladder broke the front window. The glass and paint ruined the rug." Each time they were presented, the anchor stories were paired with the end points of the response scale. This phase ended with a short practice set consisting of the two anchor stories plus six practice stories taken from the intent × consequence design.

*Phase 4.* The fourth phase began with the two anchor stories and continued with the 19 test stories. This phase followed the practice set after a summary of the nature of the stories and response scale.

*Standard Stories.* The standard stories were presented in the same manner as the simple stories. The one main difference was that only one choice pair was used in Phase 2 because of the previous practice. The choice pair pitted intent against consequence in the Piagetian manner, that is, accident motive + most severe consequence vs. malice motive + no damage consequence.

*Response Scale.* The response scale consisted of 12 sticks of increasing length mounted on a box. Subjects responded by pressing switches mounted directly beneath the sticks. The sticks were numbered 1 to 12 from shortest to longest. Pressing a switch lit up the corresponding number at the rear of the box where it was visible only to the experimenter.

*Stimulus Presentation.* All stimulus stories were recorded on a portable cassette by the author. Except for the stimulus end-anchors, each stimulus story was repeated immediately after the initial presentation. Thus, a trial consisted of two renderings of the same story. In the three instructional phases, the stories were given in the same order for all subjects. In Phase 4, the 19 test stories were presented in one of 10 randomized orders, under mild balancing requirements (e.g., successive stories could not share common levels of intent or consequence). Playing times were approximately 6.5 minutes for the 19 simple stories, and 7.5 minutes for the 19 standard stories. Intertrial interval was seven seconds, though occasionally the tape had to be stopped to await a subject's response. The simple stories took about 20 minutes, and the standard stories an additional 20 minutes including the rest period.

## Subjects

One complication arose in the selection of subjects. The main pilot work had been done with the standard stories, and the simple stories were added later in order to extend the experiment to cover the first and second grades. In the course of the experiment, it became apparent that the simple stories were evoking a configural response in some subjects: Consequences were ignored when they were accidental, but not with other motivations. In their spontaneous verbalizations, these subjects indicated that the actor was not responsible for adverse consequences resulting from accidents. This occurred only for the simple stories in which intent was explicit, not for the standard stories in which intent was implicit.

To handle this complication, subjects were classified into an auxiliary group if the difference in response to the two extreme consequence levels (no damage and broken window) for the accident motive was one response category or less. This classification criterion selects out not only the indicated configural subjects, but also those subjects who used an intent only rule. Enough subjects were run to obtain eight males and eight females at each age level. These subjects make up the main group of subjects.

The subjects were 115 children and 24 college students. The data for seven additional children were rejected: one because of experimenter error, three because they used only the extreme ends of the response scale, and three others because of an inability to concentrate on the task. In the auxiliary group there were a total of 43 subjects with 29 females and 14 males. The mean age and age range (in parentheses) for each grade in the main group were: first-graders, 6 years, 10 months (6-3 to 7-2); second-graders, 8-0 (7-5 to 8-4); third-graders, 9-0 (8-0 to 9-5); fifth-graders, 10-10 (10-4 to 11-3);seventh-graders, 12-11 (12-3 to 13-8); college students, 19-7 (17-10 to 21-4). The children were all from white middle-class homes. The fathers were businessman or professional people. The experimental sessions with the children were run in the parents' home. The college students were introductory psychology students and participated to fulfill a course requirement.

## RESULTS

The results for the standard stories require only brief consideration and will be discussed first. The simple stories yielded a more complicated pattern of data and will be discussed second. Then the results for the auxiliary group of subjects will be taken up, followed by a comparison between the choice and the judgment data. Further details on these and related analyses can be found in Leon (1976, 1977).

## Standard Stories

The purpose of these stories, which are similar to those used by previous investigators, was to test the integration rule for intent and consequence information when the subjects had to infer the underlying motive from the story. It was thought that the difficulty of abstracting intent information from verbal descriptions would produce a steady developmental trend in the effect of the intent information. Indeed, these standard stories were not given to the younger children because a pilot study showed that 9 out of the 10 first-graders ignored the intent information.

*Parallelism Test.*  Mean judgments of naughtiness to the standard stories are shown in Fig. 3.4. Because the third-, fifth- and seventh-graders showed the same pattern, these data were pooled and are shown in the left panel. The upward sweep of the curves reflects the effect of severity of consequences listed on the horizontal axis, while the vertical spread of the curves reflects the effect of intent listed as curve parameter. Both intent and consequences appear to be integrated together to produce the judgment of naughtiness. The adult data in the right panel show the same picture.

The theoretical interest in these data concerns the rule that governs the integration of the intent and consequence information. An averaging or adding integration rule will produce a pattern of parallelism in the factorial plot. Because both panels of Fig. 3.4 exhibit parallelism, these data support a linear integration rule. The question of whether this linear rule is adding or averaging is discussed later.

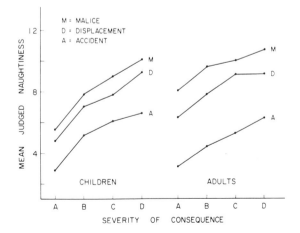

FIG. 3.4.  Parallelism test, standard stories. Punishment responses plotted as a function of intent and consequences.

The parallelism of Fig. 3.4 was supported by the statistical analysis. Parallelism is equivalent to absense of interaction in the analysis of variance. The intent × consequence interaction did not approach significance, $F(9, 504) = .69$. Deviations from parallelism in Fig. 3.4 can thus be attributed to chance.

*Developmental Trends.*   No developmental trend appeared in the integration rule. All age groups exhibited the same pattern of parallelism as indicated by the nonsignificant intent × consequence × age interaction, $F(27, 504) = 1.26$. There was a developmental trend in the effect of the intent information, as shown by the significant intent × age interaction, $F(9, 168) = 2.40$. This effect reflects a moderate increase in effect of intent information with age.

*Single-Cue Data: Attribution Problem.*   The attribution problem concerns the inferences that people may make about missing information. Harmful intent creates a likelihood of harmful consequences, while harmful consequences create suspicion of harmful intent. Accordingly, a subject who receives only one piece of information might make an inference about the value of the other.

Attribution based on intent information has primary interest. These data are presented for each age group in Fig. 3.5. The dashed curve represents the judgment of naughtiness based on the intent information alone, that is, accident, displacement, or malice, as listed on the horizontal axis. The two solid curves represent the same intent information but paired with two levels of consequence, "no harm" and "cut knees."

Two aspects of these data are important. First, the intent-only curve lies above the intent + no-harm curve. Second, the three curves for each age

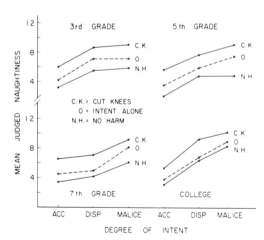

FIG. 3.5. Test for implicit inferences of missing information. Punishment responses plotted as a function of intent alone, and intent plus consequences, standard stories.

group are parallel. These data support an attributional hypothesis as follows. When only intent is given, subjects first infer a mildly negative consequence. This inferred consequence is then integrated with the given information. This attribution hypothesis requires justification in terms of the integration rule. The parallelism test is consistent with both an adding or an averaging model. Accordingly, these two models will be considered in turn.

The adding rule is simple. If no harm was inferred from the intent, then the intent-only information would be equivalent to intent + no-harm information, and the two curves would be the same in Fig. 3.5. Instead, the intent-only curve (labelled 0) lies uniformly above the no-harm curve (labelled N.H.). This means that subjects infer an implicit negative consequence when only intent is specified. It can be seen that the implicit consequence is only mildly negative, less than "cut knees" as shown by the relative elevations of these curves.

The averaging rule reaches the same conclusion, but the theoretical rationale is more complex. With no implicit inference, the averaging rule does not imply that the intent-only and no-harm curves in Fig. 3.5 would be the same: instead, the intent-only curve would have a steeper slope than the no-harm curve. That is, because the relative weights of intent and consequence information must sum to unity, the intent-only curve would have steeper slope than the intent + no-harm curve. Thus, under the averaging rule, the observed parallelism requires implicit inference about consequences.

A similar analysis applies to the consequence-only stories. These data are not presented here, but the consequence-only curves were parallel to the other curves for consequence + intent in Fig. 3.4. The consequence-only curve was higher than the consequence + displacement curve. Hence the reasoning above applies without change to show that subjects made implicit inferences about intent when given only consequence information.

## Simple Stories

The simple stories produced a fairly complicated array of results. Whereas a single integration rule appeared adequate for the standard stories, the simple stories led to a number of alternative integration rules. This was especially true for the first graders, but alternative rules were found at all age levels. The presentation of these data is somewhat involved and will continue through the next subsection on alternative integration rules. This section considers the results from the main group, first for the older children, then for the first graders.

*Parallelism Test.* The primary concern in the analysis of the simple stories is to study the integration rule for intent and consequence information. The mean naughtiness judgments for the five older age groups are shown in Fig.

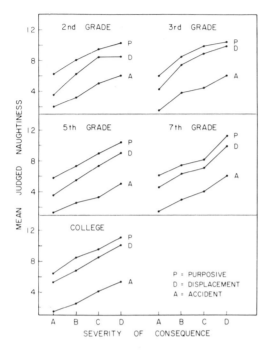

FIG. 3.6.   Parallelism test, simple stories. Punishment responses plotted as a function of intent and consequence information for the five age levels.

3.6. The plots for all five age groups look parallel. The interaction term did not approach significance for any of these groups separately or combined. For the older subjects then, these results support a linear-type rule, the same as for the standard stories above.

No developmental trends appeared beyond the second grade. The analysis, including all five age groups of Fig. 3.6, showed no significant interactions of age with either intent or consequence information. In contrast, the standard stories did show an age trend for intent information. This difference presumably reflects the fact that intent had to be inferred in the standard stories.

*First-Graders.*   The first-graders are a singular exception to the general result. The intent × consequence interaction was significant, $F(6, 64) = 2.51$, indicating a reliable deviation from the parallelism prediction of the simple linear model. The data, given in the upper left panel of Fig. 3.7, show that the effect of intent becomes larger as damage increases.

Inspection of the individual data revealed three strikingly different patterns of response among the first graders. One group ignored the intent information. The significant interaction was due to a second group. The third group roughly followed the parallelism prediction.

Subjects were separated into these groups on the basis of their use of the intent cue at the no damage and highest damage conditions. If the accident

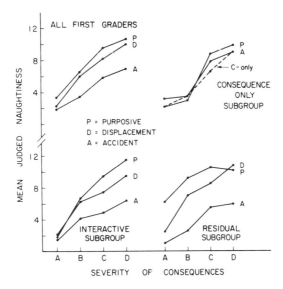

FIG. 3.7.   Three integration rules for first-graders. Punishment responses plotted as a function of intent and consequence information, simple stories.

and on-purpose levels of intent had effects within one step on the response scale, then the subject was considered to be ignoring the intent cue. Under these criteria, four subjects ignored intent for both no damage and high damage. The data for this consequence-only subgroup are plotted in the upper right panel of Fig. 3.7. The curves for the different levels of intent are very close together. The displacement curve was not plotted because it overlapped the others. The dashed curve gives the corresponding data for the stories that specified only the consequences, with no information about intent. Because this curve is the same as the others, it is clear that this subgroup judged on the basis of consequences only. They represent the prototype of Piaget's moral objective child.

A second subgroup of subjects ignored intent only when there was no damage. The data of these seven subjects are plotted in the lower left panel of Fig. 3.7. The interaction was significant for this group, $F(6, 36) = 4.20$, and they seem to be the source of the interaction for the first graders. Graphically, these data form a diverging fan that suggests a multiplying rule of integration.

The third subgroup of subjects made use of intent information for both no damage and high damage. The data of these five subjects are shown in the lower right panel of Fig. 3.7. These data are roughly parallel, and the deviations from parallelism were not significant, $F(6, 24) = 1.47$. These subjects appear to follow a simple linear rule for integration.

It should be emphasized that the criterion for classifying subjects into these three subgroups contains a built-in validational check. The consequence-only subjects were classified according to their response to intent under the two extreme damage conditions. If this classification is valid, then it should also hold for the two intermediate damage conditions. That is clearly the case for the consequence-only subgroup in the upper right panel of Fig. 3.7. The differences between the intent curves is no larger for the two intermediate levels of damage than for the two extreme levels. For the other two subgroups, the responses at the two intermediate damage levels fit in with the responses to the two extreme damage levels. This issue deserves emphasis because any such classification procedure introduces possible selection-regression effects. The present validational check allows this possibility to be ruled out.

*Single-Cue Data: Attribution and Averaging.*    Judgments of naughtiness were also obtained when the intent and consequence information were presented separately rather than in combination. The responses based on intent information alone are shown as the dashed curves in Fig. 3.8. The solid curve represents the response to the given intent cue combined with "dirty brush" damage. (For completeness, the residual subgroup of first-graders is included in the graph, although it is not considered in the analysis.)

The critical aspect of these data for the integration model is the crossover of the two curves in each panel except for the adult group. This crossover supports the averaging rule and infirms the adding rule. The rationale is as follows. According to the averaging rule, pairing intent with a moderately

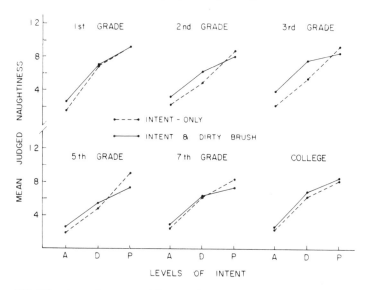

FIG. 3.8.   Averaging versus adding test, simple stories. The levels of intent are A = accident, D = displacement, and P = purposive.

negative outcome, such as "dirty brush" will increase naughtiness judgments for mildly negative intent, but will decrease naughtiness judgments for extremely negative intent. This follows because the average value of "accident" and "dirty brush" is greater than the value of "accident" alone, whereas the average value of "purposeful interference" and "dirty brush" is less than the value of "purposeful interference" alone. Hence, the intent + dirty brush curve should have lower slope than the intent-only curve and also should cross over it.

Statistically, the crossover in Fig. 3.8 implies an intent × consequence interaction. This was significant for the four grade levels from second to seventh, $F(2, 28) = 4.08$, 7.95, 14.03, and 6.30, respectively. These data, therefore, rule out an adding model and support the averaging model for the children.

The adults, in contrast to the children, do not exhibit the crossover, as can be seen in the lower right panel of Fig. 3.8. This pattern requires the assumption that the adults inferred an implicit level of consequence that was integrated in with the intent, according to the above reasoning for the corresponding data for the standard stories.

Judgments of consequence-only stories were analyzed in a similar manner. Crossover-type interactions were obtained for second and third graders, but the three older age groups exhibited parallelism. The present interpretation is that all groups employ an averaging rule but there is a developmental trend toward implicit inferences about missing information.

It should be emphasized that the data provide direct support for the conclusion that the older subjects infer implicit values for missing information. If no implicit inference was made, then intent-only would produce the same response as intent and no damage. In fact, intent-only produces.a more severe response, as can be seen by comparing Fig. 3.8 with Fig. 3.6 in which "dirty brush" is Consequence B. Similarly, consequence-only would produce the same or even less severe response than consequence + accident, whereas the opposite is true. This shows that the older subjects implicitly attributed a mildly negative motive when given only the consequence information.

## Alternative Integration Rules for Simple Stories

For the simple stories, a number of subjects at all ages adopted a configural integration rule in which the consequence information was discounted when it was accidental. Although these subjects were like the others in their use of the non-accident levels of intent, this configural aspect made it desirable to treat them separately. Accordingly, a criterion was applied to screen these subjects into an auxiliary group. This criterion was that the difference between the response to the most and least severe consequences, when paired with the accident motive, be at most one step on the response scale. This criterion screened out not only the accident–configual subjects but also those subjects who used a one-dimensional, intent-only rule. That is desirable, of course, because the data for the intent-only subjects would plot as a set of flat parallel lines and so would not be detected if averaged in with the data of the main group.

*Accident-Configural Rule.* Twenty-nine subjects in the auxiliary group obeyed an accident–configural rule: Consequences were discounted when they were accidental. This is clear in the graph shown in the left panel of Fig. 3.9 in which the accident curve (A) is essentially horizontal. Except for the accident curve, however, the data seem to follow an averaging rule. The two curves for the purposive and displacement motives are nearly parallel. The consequence-only curve, not included in the graph, was also approximately parallel to these two motive curves.

The flatness of the curve for accident in the left panel of Fig. 3.9 validates the screening criterion for this subgroup. The criterion requires the leftmost and rightmost points on the accident curve to lie at the same level, but it imposes no constraint on the two interior points of this curve. The fact that the interior points also lie at the same level means that the screening did not suffer from selection–regresssion effects and thereby validates the interpretation in terms of the accident–configural rule.

There were 8, 5, 5, 5, 3, and 3 accident–configural subjects in the first, second, third, fifth, seventh, and college age groups, respectively. The

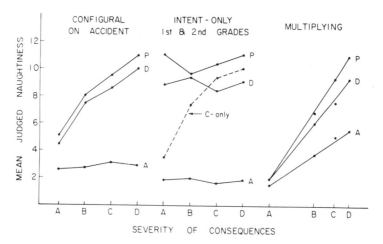

FIG. 3.9. Alternative integration rules for the simple stories. The curves represent the levels of intent (A = accident, D = displacement, P = purposive). The levels of consequence on the horizontal axis go from A = no damage to D = broken window.

frequency is largest for first graders, but an analysis of variance indicated no significant age effects on the pattern of data. Thus, the only age trend seems to be the decrease in frequency of the configural rule. The group included 21 females and 8 males, significantly different from chance by a post hoc binomial test. This was one of the few signs of sex effects in this study.

*Intent-Only Rule.* The remaining 14 subjects in the auxiliary group based their judgments largely or solely on intent. The data for the six first and second graders are shown in the center panel of Fig. 3.9. The curve for accident is flat, of course, but so are the solid curves for the other two levels of intent. Because consequences had no effect, this pattern reflects an intent-only rule. This intent-only rule is the prototype for Piaget's moral subjective child. The present results indicate that this response mode is confined to a small percentage of first and second graders (6 out of 51 or less than 12%). The eight older children in this subgroup exhibited a small but significant effect of consequence, $F(3, 21) = 4.14$, and so do not obey a strict intent-only rule. It should be added that even the first and second graders pay attention to consequences when presented alone. This is shown by the sharp upward trend of the dashed, consequence-only curve in the center panel of Fig. 3.9.

*Consequence-Only Rule.* Four first-graders from the main group based their judgments solely on the consequence information, as noted previously in the discussion of Fig. 3.7. Similar screening of all other individuals in the main group revealed 4 similar second-graders, as well as two older subjects who will not be further considered. The data for the second-graders were similar to that for the first-graders, shown previously in the top right panel of Fig. 3.7. These eight subjects showed no effect of intent. The mean difference between accident and on-purpose was only .2 and this was nonsignificant, $F(2, 14) = .45$. Even these subjects, moreover, made good discriminations on the basis of intent in the intent-only stories. The mean judgments were 8.0, 4.2, and 2.6 for purposive, displacement, and accident, respectively. These subjects thus comprehend and can react to the intent information, even though this did not appear in the two-cue task.

The most interesting aspect of these data is that these subjects are, in terms of the two-cue judgments, the prototype of Piaget's moral objective child. Yet these eight subjects constitute only a small minority of the 51 first and second graders. If this response mode represents a developmental phase, it is largely over by the first grade.

*Multiplying Rule.* As noted, above, seven first-graders in the main group appeared to discount intent when there was no damage. Inspection of all other subjects in the main group revealed 12 more with a similar pattern, scattered about equally over the different age levels. Analysis of variance showed no difference between the first graders and the older children in the pattern of judgment. Accordingly, the following analyses consider this group of 19 subjects as a whole.

The data of this group are plotted in the right panel of Fig. 3.9. This graph forms a linear fan, and so suggests that these subjects obeyed a multiplying rule, that is, naughtiness = intent × consequence. In this graph, the consequences are spaced on the horizontal axis in accord with their functional scale values from the factorial design as is required by the analysis (Anderson, 1974). The multiplying rule requires that the interaction be concentrated in the linear × linear component, and that the residual component be nonsignificant. The linear × linear component was significant, $F(1, 18) = 14.32$, and accounts for 97% of the interaction variance. Graphically and statistically, therefore, these data appear to obey the multiplying rule.

The appearance of a multiplying rule was unexpected and should be taken provisionally. Lane and Anderson (1976) proposed a multiplying rule for integration of positive intent and consequence information. However, their adult subjects used an averaging rule, much like the present adult group. The present results suggest, however, that a few adults use a multiplying rule, a possibility that would not be detected in Lane and Anderson's group analysis.

## Choice Data

The choice task in this experiment used pairs of stories contrasting intent and consequence information in the Piagetian manner, for example, accidentally interfering + severe damage versus purposely interfering + no damage. Subjects were asked which boy was naughtier and why. On the basis of these choice responses, subjects were classified as moral objectives (damage choice), or moral subjectives (intent choice). For the simple stories, eight subjects scattered across all age levels could not be classified, either because they said both were equally bad or because they could not reach a decision. The choice data for the simple stories for the remaining 131 subjects are shown in Table 3.1.

*Age Trends.*   These choice data show the age trends expected from Piaget's work. The moral objectives constitute 69% of the first graders, but only 24% of the seventh graders, a complete reversal of choice proportion. The main reduction in damage based choice occurs between first and second grade. Beyond the second grade there is a gradual decrease in choices based on damage, right up to the adult group. A similar trend was observed for the standard stories. In further analyses, only the data from the simple stories for first, second, and third graders were used. In this age range, damage and intent based choices occurred nearly equally often, 33 versus 35, respectively. A chi-square test on the 2 × 3, moral orientation × age frequency table was

TABLE 3.1
Responses in Choice Task as a Function of Age

| Grade[a] | Number of Choices Based on | | |
|---|---|---|---|
| | Damage | Intent | % Damage |
| First | 18 | 8 | 69 |
| Second | 8 | 14 | 36 |
| Third | 7 | 13 | 35 |
| Fifth | 5 | 19 | 21 |
| Seventh | 4 | 13 | 24 |
| College | 2 | 20 | 9 |

[a]Eight subjects could not be classified.

significant, $\chi^2 (2)$ = 7.18, indicating a reliable age trend over the three grades. Further analysis revealed a strong sex bias. Of the 35 moral subjectives, 24 were females; of the 33 moral objectives, 12 were females. This sex effect was reliable as indicated by a significant chi-square, $\chi^2 (1)$ = 5.84.

A second analysis was performed on the judgment data by adjoining the objective–subjective factor to the intent × consequence design. The range between the means for low and high levels of intent was 6.1 for the moral subjective, 3.2 for the moral objectives. This difference was significant, as shown by the interaction between moral type and intent, $F(2, 128)$ = 17.43. Similarly, the range between the means for the low and high levels of consequence was 3.2 for the moral subjectives, 5.5 for the moral objectives. This difference was also significant, $F(3, 192)$ = 6.51.

Both of these differences in means show agreement between the behavior in the choice task and that in the judgment task. To this extent, the present results agree with those of Buchanan and Thompson (1973) shown in Fig. 3.3. However, there are important qualifications on attempts to relate the choice data with the judgment data. The present results on integration rules show that the Piagetian dichotomy into moral "objectives" and moral "subjectives" is simplistic, even with allowance for a so-called transitional stage. Contrary to Piaget, even the first-graders use multicue strategies and generally take account of both intent and consequence information.

An important illustration of the use of multiple cues comes from the accident–configural subgroup. These subjects ignored consequences when they were accidental, but otherwise integrated consequence and intent by a simple linear rule. This accident–configural rule reflects a striking sensitivity to the configuration of given information. It is notable that it was proportionately most frequent among the first-graders. The standard Piagetian choice task is incapable of delineating this configural strategy. Thus, choice data misrepresent the child's capacity for moral judgment, a fact that becomes clear when the judgmental data are considered.

# DISCUSSION

The picture that emerged from the information integration analysis was that of a highly adaptive information processor. For the simple stories, three multidimensional integration rules were observed. The dominant rule was an averaging rule in which both intent and consequences made additive contributions to the judgments. In addition, about one of every five subjects exhibited an accident–configural rule and discounted consequences in the simple stories when they were accidental. This configural rule was not applied to the standard stories and may be restricted to situations where consequences are obviously accidental. Finally, there was some evidence to support a multiplying rule in which the response was the product of the values assigned the intent and consequence information.

Only a small number of subjects used one-dimensional response rules. These were virtually all first- and second- graders, about equally divided between consequence- and intent-only rules. Although these rules correspond to Piaget's moral objective and moral subjective types, respectively, they provide no support for Piaget's formulation. Not only are they a small minority even in these two youngest age groups, but the subjective types are about as frequent as the objective types.

For the standard stories, which were similar to those used in previous work, the results generally supported an averaging rule. In one respect, this simple picture may be misleading because these stories elicited consequence-only responses in the first- and second-graders. This consequence-only rule might seem to provide support for the concept of a moral objective stage. However, such a conclusion is unjustified because the first- and second-graders generally took account of intent when it was explicitly specified in the simple stories. In other words, their seeming inability to integrate the intent information in the standard stories has nothing to do with their moral type or their integrational capacity. Instead, it reflects a failure to make an inference about intent. Because of this confounding in the standard stories, their usefulness for the study of moral judgment seems rather limited.

Finally, the results on implicit inference about missing information are also important for the study of integration rules. When subjects received only intent or only consequence information, they sometimes inferred a value for the missing information and integrated the inferred value with the given information. Such implicit inferences seem reasonable on commonsense grounds. Given negative intent, some negative consequence is to be expected. Given negative consequence, some negative motivation is not unlikely. Thus, some subjects commented on the consequence-only simple stories that the boy in the story "shouldn't have been messing around" where the men were working. Implicit inferences represent a high level of cognitive activity and deserve careful study. The present method provides a penetrating tool for diagnosing the operation of such covert information processing strategies.

Recent reviews (Karniol, 1978; Keasey, 1978) indicate that research using the intent–consequence choice paradigm has been largely directed at determining the age at which children first use intent, and at assessing the relative influence of intent and consequences in children's judgments. The present results indicate that neither effort is likely to be successful because the meaning of the response in the choice task depends jointly on the choice rule adopted and on stimulus story characteristics.

Suppose, for example, that the choice is based on the output of an averaging integration rule applied to each story. In this case the relation of the choice to the intent and consequence values is extremely complex. For example, the relative naughtiness of the boy who accidently broke the window and the boy who tried but failed to mess things up depends both on the extremity and on the importance of the stimulus information. In principle at least, the magnitude of the damage associated with the accident can be varied so that the average of "accident plus damage" becomes more or less extreme than the average of "malice plus no-damage." Similarly, the importance of information can be enhanced by increasing its salience. Moreover, both value and weight depend on the ability of the child to extract information from the stimulus materials. Thus, the lack of an intent effect in the standard stories for first- and second-graders resulted from their failure to infer the implied intent, not from any inability to integrate intent and damage information.

The indeterminacy in the relation between the choice response and functional stimulus values makes choice behavior inadequate as a developmental index. The choice task does dichotomize subjects according to the relative magnitude of intent and consequence effects. However, subjects classified in this manner do not appear to differ in their integrative or evaluative strategies.

Although judgmental tasks can provide a picture of the child's integrative capacity for moral judgment, they have their own limitations and need to be treated with some caution. Two points deserve comment. The first is that different subjects may employ different integration rules. In itself, this is not surprising, for integration rules will reflect stage of development as well as other individual differences. However, this variety of integration rules does limit any interpretation based on group mean data. The second is that the same subject may employ different response strategies for different combinations of information. The accident–configural rule represents a case in which consequences are discounted for accident, but averaged in for other values of intent.

This picture of inter- and intra-individual differences suggests that moral judgment is fairly situation-specific. Fifty years of work have largely reaffirmed the conclusion of Hartshorne and May (1928) in this respect.

Daily observation makes clear the complexity of moral judgment, so it is no surprise to find such complexity in the present results. It is important, therefore, to develop methods that have sufficient sensitivity to elucidate these subtleties of moral judgment. The potential of the present approach is illustrated by the examination of individual integration rules.

## ACKNOWLEDGMENTS

This chapter is based on the writer's Ph.D. dissertation at the University of California, San Diego. My thanks to Norman Anderson for his generous assistance in the preparation of this chapter. This work was supported by Grants GS-36918 and BNS 75-21235 from the Social Psychology and Development program of the National Science Foundation and by grants from the National Institute of Mental Health to the Center for Human Information Processing, University of California, San Diego.

## REFERENCES

Anderson, N. H. Information integration theory: A brief survey. In D. H. Krantz, R. C. Atkinson, R. D. Luce & P. Suppes (Eds.), *Contemporary developments in mathematical psychology*. San Franscisco: Freeman, 1974.

Austin, V. D., Ruble, D. N., & Trabasso, T. Recall and order effects as factors in children's moral judgments. *Child Development*, 1977, *48*, 470–474.

Buchanan, J. P., & Thompson, S. K. A quantitative methodology to examine the development of moral judgment. *Child Development*, 1973, *44*, 186–189.

Chandler, M. J., Greenspan, S., & Barenboim, C. Judgments of intentionality in response to videotaped and verbally presented moral dilemmas: The medium is the message. *Child Development*, 1973, *44*, 315–320.

Costanzo, P. R., Coie, J. D., Grumet, J. F., & Farnill, D. A reexamination of the effects of intent and consequence on children's moral judgment. *Child Development*, 1973, *44*, 154–161.

Crowley, P. M. *Effect of training upon objectivity of moral judgment in grade-school children.* Unpublished doctoral dissertation, The Catholic University of America, 1967.

Crowley, P. M. Effect of training upon objectivity of moral judgment in grade-school children. *Journal of Personality and Social Psychology*, 1968, *8*, 228–232.

Feldman, N. S., Klosson, E. C., Parsons, J. E., Rholes, W. S., & Ruble, D. N. Order of information presentation and children's moral judgments. *Child Development*, 1976, *47*, 556–559.

Gutkin, D. C. The effect of systematic story changes on intentionality in children's moral judgments. *Child Development*, 1972, *43*, 187–195.

Hartshorne, H., & May, M. A. *Studies in deceit.* New York: Macmillan, 1928.

Hebble, P. W. The development of elementary school children's judgment of intent. *Child Development*, 1971, *42*, 1203–1215.

Karniol, R. Children's use of intention cues in evaluating behavior. *Psychological Bulletin*, 1978, *85*, 76–85.

Keasey, C. B. Children's developing awareness and usage of intentionality and motives. In C. B Keasey (Ed.), *Nebraska Symposium on Motivation* (Vol. 25). Lincoln: University of Nebraska Press, 1978.

Kohlberg, L. Stage and sequence: The cognitive–developmental approach to socialization. In D. Goslin (Ed.), *Handbook of socialization theory and research.* Chicago: Rand McNally, 1969.

Lane, J., & Anderson, N. H. Integration of intention and outcome in moral judgment. *Memory & Cognition,* 1976, *4,* 1–5.

Leon, M. Coordination of intent and consequence information in children's moral judgments. Unpublished doctoral dissertation, University of California, San Diego, 1976.

Leon, M. *Coordination of intent and consequence information in children's moral judgments* (Tech. Rep. CHIP 72). La Jolla, Calif.: University of California, San Diego, Center for Human Information Processing, August, 1977.

Leon, M., Oden, G. C., & Anderson, N. H. Functional measurement of social values. *Journal of Personality and Social Psychology,* 1973, *27,* 301–310.

Piaget, J. *The moral judgment of the child.* (M. Gabain, translator). New York: The Free Press, 1965. (Originally published, 1932.)

Surber, C. F. Developmental processes in social inference: Averaging of intentions and consequences in moral judgment. *Developmental Psychology,* 1977, *13,* 654–665.

Turiel, E. An experimental test of the sequentiality of developmental stages in the child's moral judgments. *Journal of Personality and Social Psychology,* 1966, *3,* 611–618.

# 4

# Information Processing in Children's Choices Among Bets

Wilfried Hommers
*University of Kiel, West Germany*

## ABSTRACT

Children's information processing of risky choice alternatives was investigated in two studies without using verbal reports. In Study 1, the ability to integrate the probabilities and the payoffs of simple bets was examined using the rating scale methodology. Children's choices among three of those simple bets were recorded also. By cross-classifying the children's choice and rating behavior it was shown that a three-stage developmental hypothesis of decision making is not sufficient. A four-stage hypothesis is proposed.

In Study 2, the influence of enlarging the presented number of alternatives from two to three and the influence of the similarity of the alternatives on children's choice probabilities was examined with those bets. Children's choice behavior was probabilistic and was influenced only by enlarging the presented number of alternatives. These results suggest that a Bayesian approach, based on two probabilistic choice models, should not be applied in order to analyze children's choice behavior. The functional measurement approach is, as was demonstrated in Study 1, a powerful implement to further the understanding of the development of decision making.

# INTRODUCTION

This paper is concerned with children's information processing when they make decisions among conflicting alternatives. Developmental studies may contribute generally to the understanding of decision making in human beings. This developmental approach to decision making is a research strategy that avoids various difficulties with the common strategy of comparing human behavior with normative or statistically optimal decision theories.

Schmidt (1966) adopted this point of view in a study of children's information processing when they made risky decisions among five alternatives. Each alternative consisted of a box into which 10 marbles of two colors (blue and yellow) were placed. The subjects were told that they would receive a specified amount of money or candy if they got a blue marble in a blind draw. The number of the blue marbles and the magnitude of the prize inversely varied across the alternatives. Thus, no alternative "dominated" another (see, e.g., Table 4.3 later).

Schmidt found three stages of choice behavior with this task. The youngest children, 4 and 6 years in age, chose most often the alternative with the highest payoff; 8-year-old children chose the alternative with the highest probability of winning, while the 11-year-olds chose the alternatives with medium payoffs and probabilities. To investigate the information processing of these three stages of choice behavior more closely, Schmidt asked the children for retrospective explanations of their choices. He concluded that the youngest children paid attention only to the payoff, that children at the second level considered only the probability, and that children at the third level took both attributes into account.

The main argument against these conclusions is that Schmidt relied too much on the validity of the children's explanations of their choices. These explanations have questionable value because they depend on verbal skills that may portray only part of the process. Also, only the older children may have the conceptional and verbal abilities for more detailed answers. In addition, some authors (Kleber, 1970; Hommers & Gloth, 1978) have found a high percentage of verbal explanations that cannot be attributed to any of the three levels. In order to analyze children's information processing of risky choices, other approaches using nonverbal techniques may be necessary.

Nonverbal techniques were used by the present author (Hommers, 1975, 1976) to analyze the information processing of the third level children more carefully. Among other results, it was found that third level children chose the largest expected value of the alternatives more likely than could be expected. Because the expected value of these alternatives is defined as the product of probability and payoff, this result supports the hypothesis of a multiplying rule applied by the third level children. However, similar studies have not been done for the first two stages.

STUDY 1

Problem

The hypothesis of Schmidt (1966), that subjects in the first or second stage base their decisions on either the payoff or on the probability and do not combine these two attributes, is questioned here. The functional measurement approach of information integration theory may be able to determine whether younger children can integrate these two attributes. Anderson and Shanteau (1970) found additive and multiplicative combination rules for single and duplex bets with adult subjects. However, a similar study with children has not been made. One advantage of the functional measurement approach is that it allows statistical analysis for the individual child. Such individual analysis is a necessity to avoid artifacts that can arise from pooling data over children who have different strategies.

Method

A 3 × 3, probability × payoff stimuli design was employed. The probability levels .10, .50, and .90 and the payoff levels 5, 25, and 45 Deutsche Pfennigs were used. Two replications of the nine stimuli from the design were given. In each replication the nine stimuli followed in a different order. Forty-two children (24 male; age 5-10 to 13-10) were tested in single sessions at their homes.

On each trial, a colored picture of a bag was shown that contained 10 marbles, some red, some green. The number of red marbles (1, 5, 9) indicated the probability of winning. Below the bag, yellow coins were seen that represented the prize (5, 25, or 45 Pfennigs). The children were told that picking a red marble in a blind draw would win the prize. Before drawing, however, the experimenter wanted to learn how much they liked each bet.

To indicate their liking of each bet, the children used a graphic rating scale of 20 small circles, each 1 cm in diameter. At the left end of the scale a frowning face was shown. At the right end a smiling face was shown. Anchors were placed at each end of the scale. The upper anchor consisted of a bag with 10 red marbles and a prize of 50 Deutsche Pfennigs. The lower anchor showed a bag with 10 green marbles and no coins.

After the instructions, six practice stimuli were presented to train the children in the use of the scale. Following this, the two replications of the main design were given.

Finally, the children chose one alternative from each of 10 three-alternative decision tasks. Before they chose, they had been introduced to all 10 tasks in order to avoid artificial risk tendencies. All 10 tasks had the inverse arrangement of probabilities and amounts of win, but varied in the specific values of these attributes. The first of the decision tasks had the alternatives with the highest, lowest, and medium payoff of Schmidt's (1966) study and will be considered later. Payoffs were given immediately so that choices in later tasks that might be influenced by the gains or no-gains were not considered.

## Results

The main purpose of the data analysis was to relate the rating data to the choice data in order to obtain behavioral evidence on the three stages considered previously. The first step was to calculate an analysis of variance separately for each individual subject. The main effects in this analysis provide a sensitive index of the child's utilization of the two stimulus cues in the factorial design.

Raw data for three illustrative children are shown in Table 4.1, and the corresponding analyses of variance are summarized in Table 4.2.

The child in the first row of Table 4.1 employed a payoff-only response strategy. His responses vary markedly as a fuction of the amount to be won, but are independent of the probabilities. This one-dimensional, payoff-only strategy reappears in the analysis of variance of Table 4.2: The mean square for payoff is very large compared to the error mean square, showing a highly significant payoff effect, while the probability effect does not approach significance.

The second row of Table 4.1 shows a probability-only response strategy. The responses of this child vary markedly as a function of the probabilities, but are independent of the amounts of win. This one-dimensional, probability-only strategy reappears in the analysis of variance of Table 4.2: The mean square for probability is very large compared to the error mean square, showing a highly significant probability effect, while the payoff effect does not approach significance.

TABLE 4.1
Rating Data for Three Subjects Selected to Illustrate Three Response Strategies, Study 1

| | *Probability × Payoff Levels* | | | | | | | | |
| | .1 | | | .5 | | | .9 | | |
| *Strategy* | 5 | 25 | 45 | 5 | 25 | 45 | 5 | 25 | 45 |
|---|---|---|---|---|---|---|---|---|---|
| Payoff only | 3,1 | 11,11 | 20,20 | 2,1 | 11,11 | 20,20 | 3,1 | 11,11 | 20,20 |
| Probability only | 1,5 | 2,4 | 5,4 | 15,17 | 15,17 | 17,17 | 17,20 | 20,20 | 20,20 |
| Payoff + Probability | 3,5 | 7,6 | 8,9 | 10,9 | 12,16 | 17,16 | 13,11 | 18,19 | 20,20 |

TABLE 4.2
Summary of Analysis of Variance for Three Selected Subjects, Study 1

| | | Mean Square | | |
|---|---|---|---|---|
| Source | df | Payoff Only | Probability Only | Payoff + Probability |
| Replications | 1 | 1.4 | 8.0 | .5 |
| Probability | 2 | .1 | 430.7 | 171.5 |
| Payoff | 2 | 495.1 | 2.7 | 66.5 |
| Interaction | 4 | .1 | .5 | 2.5 |
| Error | 8 | .4 | 1.4 | 1.8 |

The child in the last row of Table 4.1 utilized both stimulus factors in a probability + payoff strategy. This two-dimensional, probability + payoff strategy reappears in the analysis of variance of Table 4.2: The mean squares for both factorial effects are considerably large compared to the error mean square. This means that this child took account of both factors in making his judgment. By virtue of the logic of functional measurement, the nonsignificant interaction implies that these two stimulus dimensions were integrated by an adding-type rule.

The next step in the analysis is to relate the response strategies in the rating task to the behavior in the choice task. Table 4.3 correlates these rating strategies with the choice behavior of the children in the first three-alternative decision task. Table 4.3 shows that nearly one-half of those children who chose the alternative with the highest or the lowest payoff used a one-

TABLE 4.3
Attributes of Alternatives in Choice Task and Subjects Cross-
Classified by Behavior in Rating Task and Choice Task

| | Alternative | | |
|---|---|---|---|
| Dimension | A | B | C |
| Probability | .1 | .5 | .9 |
| Payoff value | 25 | 15 | 5 |
| Expected value | 2.5 | 7.5 | 4.5 |

| Rating Task Classification | Number of Subjects[a] | | |
|---|---|---|---|
| Two-dimensional subjects | 5 | 14 | 7 |
| One-dimensional subjects | 7 | 0 | 9 |

[a]Entries indicate number of subjects who chose the given alternative in the first choice trial.

dimensional response strategy. Contrarily, all subjects who chose the alternative with the medium payoff in that choice task employed a probability + payoff response strategy in the rating tasks, $\chi^2(2) = 12.92$, $p < .001$.

All the one-dimensional subjects who chose the alternative with the highest payoff had just the factor "payoff" significant. Similarly, all the one-dimensional subjects who chose the alternative with the highest probability had just the factor "probability" significant.

In summary, Study 1 showed that the children who chose the alternative with the intermediate attribute levels differ in their rating behavior from the children who chose other alternatives. In accord with Schmidt's conclusions, they were able to combine the two attributes of single, simple bets in their judgments. Also, if a child significantly responded in the rating task to only the probability (payoff) factor, then he or she chose the alternative with the highest probability (payoff). However, some children who chose the alternative with the highest payoff or with the highest probability were actually able to combine probabilities and payoffs. This result does not fit into the framework of three developmental stages of decision making as given by Schmidt (1966).

## STUDY 2

### Problem

One might regard the integration of information present in a single alternative as a complete elucidation of children's information processing in decision making. This view is adequate only if choices among two or more alternatives depend on the rank order of subjective values obtained from the rating of single bets alone. But as Tversky (1972) showed with adolescents, the number and the similarity of the presented alternatives can have important influences on choices. Thus, the set of alternatives presented to the children may affect their decision making in two ways. First, there may be an influence of the presented number of alternatives on their choices. Second, there may be an effect of the similarity[1] of the alternatives on their choices. Study 2 examines whether these aspects of a specified set of alternatives have an effect on children's choice probabilities of the alternatives.

---

[1]Let $(p/v)$ denote the attributes of an alternative, then a similarity pattern of three alternatives may consist within the set $(.1/45)$, $(.2/40)$, $(.9/5)$, where the first two alternatives are apparently similar. But that apparent similarity would vanish in the set $(.1/45)$, $(.2/10)$, and $(.9/5)$. So, a similarity pattern exists in a set of three alternatives when a difference in the distances of one attribute across adjacent alternatives is not compensated by a contrary pattern in the distances of the other attribute.

## Method

A 2 × 2 design was used with two sets of alternatives and two response modes
as factors. By employing two sets of alternatives, the effects of the presented
number of alternatives and of the similarity within each set on the choice
probabilities were studied. The two response modes were used to assess the
choice probabilities because each of them seemed desirable to answer certain
questions.

The influence of the presented number of alternatives was examined by
comparing the choice behavior in two-alternative decision tasks with that in a
three-alternative decision task, all of them derived from the same total set of
three alternatives. The elements of each set were combined to obtain three
two-alternative and one three-alternative task. Thus, eight decision tasks
were derived from the two sets of alternatives that are listed in Table 4.4. Each
task was presented as a colored picture of two or three bags in the same
manner as in Study 1. Each bag represented an alternative option for the
child.

The influence of the similarity of the alternatives was investigated by
comparing behavior of two sets of choice tasks that differ in their apparent
similarity of the three alternatives. Probabilities and payoffs for Set I define
the similarity pattern so that the pair of alternatives B and C (see Table 4.4) is
more similar than the pair A and B or the pair A and C. Set II was constructed
so that no apparent similarity of alternatives appears.

Assessment of the choice probabilities was done in two ways, both of which
have possible objections. One could obtain repeated choices, either within
one session or distributed over several sessions. Repetition over several
sessions would allow possible developmental changes during and between
sessions. Therefore, repeated choices during one session were obtained to
assess the choice probabilities. But repeated choices during one session could
produce boredom, especially with children. As boredom could presumably be
prevented thereby, payoffs were given after each decision depending on the
outcome.

But, giving payoffs could change prior probabilities of choice. Thus, a
second mode, "distributing choices in advance," was applied. With this

TABLE 4.4
Sets of Alternatives from Which Eight Decision Tasks Were Derived

| | Set I Alternatives | | | Set II Alternatives | | |
|---|---|---|---|---|---|---|
| Win | A | B | C | A | B | C |
| Probability | .1 | .4 | .6 | .1 | .5 | .9 |
| Payoff (Pfennigs) | 35 | 12 | 8 | 45 | 25 | 5 |

procedure, one had to assume that, if several choices were to be made in advance for each task, they would picture actual choice probabilities of children's single decisions. Unfortunately, no empirical support for this assumption was available. Thus, both response modes were used as no one other approach was found to be more suitable.

Thirty-seven children (18 male) aged 8 to 15 years (mean age 11-8) were tested in a summer camp. As a pretest, the children were presented with a three-alternative task that had equal expected-value alternatives. The probabilities of this task were .10, .50, and .90. The payoffs were in the same order as the probabilities, 45, 9, and 5 Deutsche Pfennigs.

After the pretest, subjects made hypothetical advance choices for each of the eight tasks. They were asked to indicate in advance how often they would choose each alternative when they had 10 choices in each task during the session. Following this, they were given a sequence of 10 choices on each of the eight tasks. Each such choice was implemented by the child's placing a hand into a bag filled with marbles in the same proportion as the chosen alternative and making a blind draw of one marble. Win received immediate payoff. The same order of tasks was used for all the children and all 10 replications per subject.

## Results

*Level of Decision Making.* In the pretest, 24 subjects chose the alternative with medium payoff. Also, in the 10 single choices, 29 subjects chose this alternative most frequently. Therefore, a majority of the children are considered to be decision makers who were able to consider the expected value of an alternative or at least both pieces of information presented in each alternative.

*Probabilistic Decision Making.* For each child, two sets of choice probability estimates were available from advance hypothetical and actual single choices. If the decision making of the children was not probabilistic, one would expect choice frequencies of 0 or 10 within each set of estimates. Table 4.5 shows the frequencies of modal choice probabilities in the three-alternatives tasks for each set and each response mode. Probabilistic decision making implies high frequencies in the upper rows of Table 4.5 corresponding to near-chance probabilities. Table 4.5 indicates that the majority of subjects made decisions probabilistically with both response modes in both sets. This might suggest that one of the response modes assessed the actual choice probabilities of single decisions. This conclusion can be justified as follows. In Set II, the optimal strategy with 10 choices would be to choose always the medium alternative that has the largest expected value. This can be true only of subjects who consider the expected value in their choices. But although the

TABLE 4.5
Frequencies of Modal Choice Probabilities, Three-Alternative Task,
Study 2

| Choice Probabilities | Hypothetical Choices in Advance | | Single Choices with Immediate Payoff | |
|---|---|---|---|---|
| | Set I | Set II | Set I | Set II |
| .4 | 16 | 12 | 3 | 1 |
| .5 | 15 | 11 | 4 | 2 |
| .6 | 4 | 6 | 10 | 6 |
| .7 | 0 | 4 | 9 | 8 |
| .8 | 0 | 0 | 5 | 3 |
| .9 | 0 | 0 | 5 | 10 |
| 1.0 | 2 | 4 | 1 | 7 |

pretest results indicate that most of the subjects seem to be able to do that, the majority of them behaved probabilistically when several choices among the same alternatives were available.

*Influence of Number of Alternatives.*    Two mathematical conditions were examined to test the influence of the presented number of alternatives. Let $T$ denote a set of three alternatives. Let $P(x;y)$ be the binary choice probability of $x$ when presented together with $y$, and $P(x, T)$ be the trinary choice probability when $x$ is presented together with $y$ and a third alternative. If the addition of a third alternative does not change the order of choice probabilities (order independence), condition (1) holds (see Tversky, 1972, p. 282).

For each pair $x, y, \epsilon T$, $P(x;y) \geq .5$ if and only $P(x,T) \geq P(y,T)$ $[P(y,T) \neq 0]$.(1)

If the addition of a third alternative did not change the ratio of choice probabilities (ratio independence), condition (2) holds (see Tversky, 1972, p. 292).

For each pair $x, y, \epsilon T$, $P(x;y)/P(y;x) = P(x,T)/P(y,T)$ $[P(y;x) \neq 0 \neq P(y,T)]$.(2)

Table 4.6 shows how many subjects matched the ratio or order independence conditions. Order independence was found in a majority of subjects, especially in the real single choices. However, ratio independence was almost completely absent. Furthermore, the hypothetical advance choices showed less order independence than the real choices.

Overall, therefore, these data indicate, on an individual level of analysis, that the response modes of hypothetical choices in advance and of repeated real single choices with immediate payoffs did not yield choice probability

TABLE 4.6
Frequencies of Children ($n$ = 37) Who Fit Order or Ratio
Independence

| Mode | Set I | | Set II | |
|---|---|---|---|---|
| | Order | Ratio | Order | Ratio |
| Hypothetical choices | 21 | 1 | 19 | 2 |
| Single choices | 31 | 0 | 29 | 5 |

estimates that are independent of adding a third alternative. Although the majority of children showed order independence, some subjects showed order dependence. This suggests that children's choice behavior in two-alternative tasks might differ from that in three-alternative tasks, as the enlargement of the presented number of alternatives can change even the order of choice probabilities.

*Group Analysis of Ratio Independence.* The individual analyses of ratio independence in Table 4.6 might not have adequate sensitivity. Accordingly, it seems justified to examine ratio independence on a group level. For each subject, therefore, the individual deviation $d = P(x;y) - P(x,T)/[P(x,T) + P(y,T)]$ was calculated for each pair $x,y$. The observed mean $\bar{d}$ was tested against the expectation $E(d_i) = 0$, which should hold if ratio independence holds because condition (3) then becomes an equality.

The analysis of variance showed no significant effects. The overall mean was $\bar{d}$ = .015. The estimated standard deviation was .011, yielding $z$ = 1.38. Although $\bar{d}$ is not significantly different from 0, this $z$-value indicates that even the group data reflect the influence of the third alternative on the choice probabilities. To understand that conclusion, one should imagine first that, although the $d$ of two pairs of one individual subject were positive, the third $d$ need not be, and second, that the individual analysis showed that individuals might differ in which of their $d$ pairs are positive. Both circumstances reduce the $z$-value of $\bar{d}$. Thus, the influence of adding a third alternative was almost strong enough to be revealed as a trend in the group data analysis.

*Influence of Similarity Perception.* Similarity of alternatives with medium and highest probability (see Table 4.4) was systematically high in Set I. If children take into consideration this similarity, then condition (3) should hold (see Tversky, 1972, p. 292).

$$P(B;A) > P(B,T)/[P(B,T) + P(A,T)] \text{ and}$$
$$P(C;A) > P(C,T)/[P(C,T) + P(A,T)]. \tag{3}$$

This condition can be justified intuitively by the argument that, if an alternative is added that is similar to only one of two already existing alternatives, then it will subtract more from the choice probability for the similar alternative than for the dissimilar alternative.

Perceived similarity need not be bound to the objective similarity that has been arranged in Set I. Children may perceive alternatives A and B or alternatives A and C to be equally similar. These three similarity pairs must be considered separately. This argument can be applied to Set II as well.

The children's choice probabilities were analyzed with regard to how often condition (3) was supported in each possible similarity pair. Table 4.7 shows the frequencies of children to whom one of the three similarity perceptions could be attributed. If the similarity manipulation influenced the individual children, one would expect that the entry in row BC of Set I would be higher than the other entries of the same set and higher than the entry BC in Set II. As can be seen, this expectation was not supported. The real single choices show a strong disagreement with expectation.

It is difficult to estimate the chance probability of an entry in Table 4.7. However, it seems reasonable to assume that a verification of one part of condition (3) is as probable as a falsification, if similarity plays no role in the decision process. This assumption implies a probability of .25 in each of the four rows. Testing the observed frequencies against this expectation yielded only one significant chi-square (see Table 4.7). Because this one significant chi-square partly results from an overly high frequency of "no similarity" judgments, it clearly does not support the similarity hypothesis.

Two further tests for similarity effects were also performed. The first sought for a more sensitive index by comparing attributed similarities across Sets I and II. The second extended the first by allowing for some within-subject variability within each of Sets I and II. Neither test provided any sign

TABLE 4.7
Frequencies of Children Satisfying the Perceived Similarity
Assumptions, Study 2

| Similarity Assumed Between | Hypothetical Choices | | Single Choices | |
|---|---|---|---|---|
| | Set I | Set II | Set I | Set II |
| A    B | 5 | 8 | 8 | 3 |
| B    C | 12 | 8 | 9 | 15 |
| A    C | 10 | 5 | 9 | 4 |
| No similarity | 10 | 16 | 11 | 15 |
| $\chi^2$ ($df = 3$) | 2.89 | 7.22 | .51 | 14.35[a] |

[a] $p < .05$.

of similarity effect. Overall, therefore, these data provide no support for the hypothesis that similarity affected the children's choices.

## DISCUSSION

### Developmental Stages

The results of Study 1, obtained by the combined use of choice and rating responses, helped illustrate the information processing hypotheses of the three developmental stages found by Schmidt (1966). The children who chose the alternative with the highest payoff and also employed a payoff-only strategy in their rating responses represent information processing of the first developmental stage. These children seem to be unaware or to lack understanding of the "probability" attribute of the alternatives.

The second developmental stage was described by Schmidt (1966) as transitional, in which subjects consider only the probability of the alternatives. In the present study, those subjects who chose the alternative with the largest probability and also employed a probability-only rating strategy would seem to correspond to Schmidt's transition stage subjects.

In Schmidt's third developmental stage, subjects are considered to combine the payoff and probability attributes when choosing the medium alternative. Subjects at this stage were found in the present study too. Indeed, all those subjects who chose the alternative with medium attribute values appeared to use a probability + payoff strategy in their ratings. These three groups, defined in terms of choice and rating behavior, seem to accord with Schmidt's three-stage hypothesis.

However, there were two other groups of children who did not fit into Schmidt's three stages. This can be seen in the cross-classification of choice and rating strategies given in the lower part of Table 4.3. The 14 children who chose the medium alternative were not the only ones who employed the two-dimensional probability + payoff rating strategy. Five children who chose on the basis of payoff and seven who chose on the basis of probability also used the two-dimensional probability + payoff strategy in their ratings. The information processing of these children differs from that in Schmidt's stage descriptions. The present results suggest, therefore, that Schmidt's three-stage classification is not sufficient and that other stages exist.

In addition, it is necessary to consider a fourth, more advanced stage not considered by Schmidt. This stage could be characterized by the ability to combine attributes according to a multiplying rule when making decisions and judgments. This fourth stage would be consistent with previous studies of the present author (Hommers 1975, 1976), in which children who chose the medium alternative appeared to be sensitive to the expected value of an alternative, that is, to the product of payoff and probability.

In this hypothesis of four developmental stages, the first two would appear as described by Schmidt. These are one-dimensional subjects; they take account of just one attribute of the bets. The other two stages are two-dimensional, but differ in their integration rule. The third stage might be characterized mainly by its probability + payoff rating strategy, in which the choice behavior depends on the weights of the attributes. At the fourth stage the subjects might employ a multiplying rule in their ratings. This would reveal itself in the choice task as following a maximization of expected value rule.

## Individual Bayesian Analysis of Choices

Wendt (1973, 1975) suggested a Bayesian technique to compare competing probabilistic models of the information processing of nondominated alternative bets. Two formal models were proposed: The constant-ratio model, and the sum-difference model.

The constant-ratio model assumes that the alternatives can be scaled so that choice probability ratios are independent of the number of presented alternatives. However, the results of the present Study II showed that ratio independence did not hold. This result indicates that the constant-ratio model is not valid for children's choices.

The sum-difference model requires that the highest choice probability among three alternatives is not greater than one-half. Table 4.5 shows that this condition failed for nearly all subjects with real choices and for at least some subjects with hypothetical choices. Additionally, the sum-difference model requires order independence. But, in both response modes, some subjects failed this condition. Thus, the validity of the sum-difference model for children's choices is also doubtful.

## Power of the Functional Measurement Approach

The power of the functional measurement approach for the understanding of the development of decision making is demonstrated by the results of Study 1 in several respects. These data confirmed earlier results, but allowed a more penetrating analysis. Subjects who chose the medium alternative, in fact, combine the probability and payoff cues. Also, children who did not integrate probability and payoff in the rating task did not chose the alternative with medium attributes in the choice task. But most importantly, the power of the combined use of factorial design and rating response was shown by the result that the choice behavior of some children was observed together with a two-dimensional rating strategy. Previously, children who chose the alternative with either the highest payoff or the highest probability were not regarded as capable to consider both attributes of the bets simultaneously. This view was based on the choices. But, by the use of the functional measurement approach, it could be shown that they are, in fact, capable of integrating these attributes.

## ACKNOWLEDGMENTS

The author thanks Johannes Becker, Tom Trabasso, John Verdi, and Friedrich Wilkening, who commented on earlier drafts. The author is very indebted to Norman H. Anderson, who made remarks on Study 2 that led to Study 1 and who helped with the writing of the final version of this report during a visit of the author at the University of California, San Diego, which was sponsored by the Stiftung Volkswagenwerk.

## REFERENCES

Anderson, N. H., & Shanteau, J. C. Information integration in risky decision making. *Journal of Experimental Psychology, 1970, 84,* 441–451.

Hommers, W. Zur Gültigkeit des objektiven Erwartungsmaximierungsmodells beim Entscheidungsverhalten von Schulkindern. *Zeitschrift für Psychologie, 1975, 183,* 69–81.

Hommers, W. Zur Validität der Portfolio-Theorie im Entscheidungsverhalten von Schulkindern. *Zeitschrift für Psychologie, 1976, 184,* 604–618.

Hommers, W., & Gloth, J. Alternativenart, persönliche Glückszahl und magisch-animistische Begründungen von Entscheidungen bei Risiko. *Zeitschrift für experimentelle und angewandte Psychologie, 1978, 25,* 407–415.

Kleber, E. W. Uber die Abhängigkeit des Entscheidungsverhaltens von der Begabung. *Psychologische Beiträge, 1970, 12,* 558–579.

Schmidt, H. D. *Leistungschance, Erfolgserwartung and Entscheidung.* Berlin: VEB Verlag Deutscher Wissenschaften, 1966.

Tversky, A. Elimination by aspects: A theory of choice. *Psychological Review, 1972, 79,* 281–299.

Wendt, D. *Bayesian data analysis of gambling preferences.* Technical Report 011013-3-T, Engineering Psychology Laboratory, University of Michigan, 1973.

Wendt, D. Some criticisms of the general models used in decision making experiments. *Theory and Decision, 1975, 6,* 197–212.

# II
## STIMULUS ANALYSIS AND INTEGRATION

# The Relation of Stimulus Structure to Perceptual and Cognitive Development: Further Tests of a Separability Hypothesis

5

Bryan E. Shepp
Barbara Burns
Dorothy McDonough
*Brown University, Providence, Rhode Island*

## INTRODUCTION

### Development Differences in Attention

The concept of attention plays a central role in many contemporary theories of conceptual and cognitive development (e.g., Fisher & Zeaman, 1973; Gibson, 1969; Klahr & Wallace, 1976; Piaget, 1970) and there is a substantial literature that implicates developmental differences in attention in a variety of tasks where multiple sources of information are presented. Unfortunately, however, this literature has not yielded a clear picture of attentional development. Instead, the developmental trends in attention that appear in some tasks do not appear in others.

Consider first tasks in which one aspect or dimension of a stimulus is designated as relevant to successful execution of the task and other aspects or dimensions are designated as irrelevant. Such tasks include selective listening (e.g., Doyle, 1973; Maccoby, 1969), speeded classification (e.g., Pick & Frankel, 1973; Smith, Kemler & Aronfreed, 1975; Strutt, Anderson & Well, 1975), incidental learning and memory (e.g., Kemler, Shepp & Foote, 1976; Hagen & Hale, 1973), and some forms of classification (e.g., Bruner, Olver & Greenfield, 1966; Wohlwill, 1962). The results of experiments using these tasks are highly consistent in showing that older children are more successful than younger children in ignoring irrelevant dimensions. Such results have led to the interpretation that older children focus attention or allocate attention better than do younger children (e.g., Pick & Frankel, 1973; Hagen & Hale, 1973).

Consider next tasks in which two or more aspects or dimensions of the stimulus are relevant to successful task performance. These tasks include learning with redundant relevant cues (e.g., Eimas, 1969; Hale & Morgan, 1973; Hale & Taweel, 1974), perceptual judgment (e.g., Anderson & Cuneo, 1978), conservation (e.g., Piaget, 1970), and some forms of classification (e.g., Wohlwill, 1962). The results of experiments using these tasks are inconsistent. Although older children typically attend to more than one dimension, younger children attend to just one dimension in some tasks (e.g., Hale & Morgan, 1973; Piaget, 1970) but attend to more than one dimension in other tasks (e.g., Anderson & Cuneo, 1978; Wohlwill, 1962).

Taken together, the results of these two classes of experiments indicate that the older child can focus and may allocate or divide attention in relation to the demands of a task, whereas the younger child often fails to focus attention, but in other instances may focus or divide attention. The failure to find consistent trends in attentional development is undoubtedly related to differences in task demands (e.g., Shepp & Adams, 1973; Adams & Shepp, 1975), and it is likely that additional research can clarify, to some extent, the principles of attentional development. We will argue, however, that the nature of the stimulus input can constrain the processing options of the subject and that an understanding of developmental differences in perceived stimulus structure is fundamental to an understanding of developmental differences in attention.

## Stimulus Structure and Attention

Garner (1974, 1976) has recently argued that the structure of the stimulus affects the processing options of the subject. In support of his argument, Garner has identified several different forms of dimensional interactions and has shown how each can affect performances in a variety of tasks. For purposes of the present discussion, only two of these interactions, integral and separable, are considered.

Phenomenologically, integral dimensions (e.g., hue and brightness) are perceived as unitary wholes, whereas separable dimensions (e.g., size of circle and angle of a radial line) are perceived as distinct components. Operationally, integral dimensions produce a Euclidean metric in direct distance scaling, lead to a redundancy gain in speed or accuracy of identification or discrimination when values are correlated, and produce interference in a filtering task. In contrast, separable dimensions produce a city-block metric and yield no redundancy gain when correlated and no interference in a filtering task (Garner, 1974, 1976).

The properties of these dimensional combinations are shown clearly in two tasks used by Garner to converge on these concepts. First, there is the speeded sorting task introduced by Garner and Felfoldy (1970). In this task, subjects are instructed to sort a deck of cards into two piles as quickly as possible. On each card one value on each of two dimensions is displayed, and the subject is instructed to sort on the basis of one of the dimensions. During the course of the experiment, subjects sort decks composed of different subsets of stimuli. To illustrate the composition of the different decks, consider the four stimuli shown in Fig. 5.1. In a one-dimension task, the deck includes stimuli that vary on only one dimension. A one-dimension task for Dimension 1 would include A and D (or B and C). In a correlated-dimensions task, the values of the dimensions are redundant; the deck includes A and C (or B and D). In the orthogonal-dimensions task, all four stimuli are included in a deck (e.g., A,B vs. C,D).

Differences in the perceived structure of integral and separable dimensions are shown by comparing performances on the one-dimension and the correlated-dimensions task. The perceived differences between stimuli composed from integral dimensions are described by a Euclidean metric (Hyman & Well, 1967, 1968; Handel & Imai, 1972), which implies a direct distance relation between stimuli. Thus, the stimuli, A vs. C, are more dissimilar to each other than are stimuli on the one-dimension task (e.g., A vs. D) and should be sorted faster than stimuli in the one-dimension task.

In contrast, the perceived differences between stimuli composed of separable dimensions are best described by a city-block metric (e.g., Shepard, 1964; Handel & Imai, 1972), which implies a perceived dimensional structure. If the subject is instructed to sort on Dimension 1, for example, the basis for the classification in both the one-dimension and correlated-dimensions task are the values on that dimension. Consequently, the two tasks should be

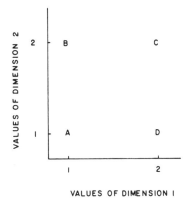

FIG. 5.1.  A schematic representation of four stimuli generated from two orthogonal dimensions.

performed at the same speed. Garner and Felfoldy (1970) observed the expected results for both integral and separable dimensions.

That stimulus structure affects the processing options of the subject is shown by performances on the orthogonal-dimensions task relative to the one-dimension task. Because the stimuli produced by integral dimensions are unitary, selective attention to dimensions is not possible, and the orthogonal-dimensions task should be performed more slowly than the one-dimension task. The levels of separable dimensions, however, are seen as perceptually distinct components and do allow selective attention. Thus, the time to sort with orthogonal dimensions should be no longer than the time to sort with a variation on a single dimension. As predicted, Garner and Felfoldy report interference on an orthogonal-dimensions task with integral dimensions but none with separable dimensions.

A second task that shows the dominant perceived structure of integral and separable dimensions is the restricted classification task. In this task, the subject is presented with subsets of a set of stimuli and instructed to divide them into classes. To illustrate, consider the triad of stimuli shown in Fig. 5.2. Stimuli A and B share the same value on Dimension 1, but differ considerably on Dimension 2. Stimulus C does not share a value with either A or B, but in overall similarity C is closer to B than to A.

The classifications that subjects form from such an arrangement depends on the structure of the stimuli. If stimuli are generated by separable dimensions (e.g., size and brightness), subjects classify A and B together, indicating that dimensional structure is perceived. If stimuli are generated by integral dimensions (e.g., value and chroma), however, B and C are classified together, indicating that the stimuli are perceived by overall similarity (Garner, 1974; Handel & Imai, 1972).

The results of these experiments and others (see Garner, 1974, 1976, 1978) have succeeded in identifying different properties of the stimulus and

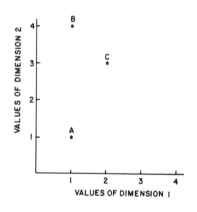

FIG. 5.2. An illustration of an informative triad for classification.

different perceived structures that result from such properties. Further, by showing that stimulus structure can limit the processing options of the subject, Garner has shown that the specification of stimulus concepts takes logical priority over the specification of processing concepts. A priori assumptions about the nature of the stimulus may lead to erroneous or misleading conclusions about processing mechanisms (Garner, 1970; Nickerson, 1972).

## Development of Perceived Structure

Previous research on the development of attention has for the most part ignored the nature of the stimulus, and, as Garner's work (1974; 1976) has shown, questions about the subject's capacity to focus, allocate, or divide attention can be meaningfully asked only with dimensions that are represented as separable. There is no direct evidence that dimensional combinations are separable for younger children, and there is considerable evidence that the perception of dimensional structure is a product of perceptual learning (Gibson, 1969).

Gibson and others (Bruner et al., 1966; Gibson & Olum, 1960; Werner, 1948) have suggested that although older children perceive multidimensional stimuli in terms of their constituent dimensions, younger children perceive stimuli as undifferentiated or wholistic. According to Gibson (1969), the developmental progression from undifferentiated to differentiated properties is accomplished through perceptual learning, which includes the basic processes of abstraction and selective filtering. Through abstraction the child learns to extract invariants, including dimensions, from the stimulus, and by selective filtering the child learns to ignore properties that are irrelevant to specific abstractions.

The evidence to support the claim that children learn to extract dimensional representation during the course of perceptual learning is often indirect (Gibson, 1969; King & Holt, 1970; Miller, 1971; Rogers & Johnson, 1973): The conclusion that the perception of younger children is wholistic is based on their failures to respond dimensionally.

Stronger evidence to document the wholistic to dimensional trend in perceptual development has been provided by Tighe and his colleagues (e.g., Tighe, Glick, & Cole, 1971; Tighe & Tighe, 1972; Tighe, 1973). These investigators have proposed that subjects may solve standard discrimination tasks by either of two alternative modes. Consider Table 5.1 which shows a simultaneous discrimination task. From the experimenter's point of view, color is the relevant dimension and form and position are irrelevant. One mode of solution in this task is consistent with the experimenter's point of view—subjects learn that color is the relevant dimension and consistently

TABLE 5.1
Reversal–Nonreversal Shift Paradigm

| | Array | Original | Learning |
|---|---|---|---|
| | 1 | Red $^+$ Square | Green $^-$ Circle |
| | 2 | Red $^+$ Circle | Green $^-$ Square |

| Array | Reversal Shift | Array | Nonreversal Shift |
|---|---|---|---|
| 1 | Red $^-$ Square  Green $^+$ Circle | 1 | Red $^+$ Square  Green $^-$ Circle |
| 2 | Red $^-$ Circle  Green $^+$ Square | 2 | Red $^-$ Circle  Green $^+$ Square |

*Note.* Only two of the possible four arrays are shown. In practice, two additional arrays, in which the positions of the stimuli are interchanged, would also be presented. The symbols "+" and "−" indicate that a choice of a particular stimulus is rewarded or nonrewarded respectively.

choose red. In this case, the different arrays are treated as instances of the same problem, and the solution is governed by some form of dimension learning.

Tighe et al. (1971) point out that there is another equally plausible description of the task and suggest an alternative type of solution. Notice in Table 5.1 that two stimuli, red square and red circle, lead to a correct response. The subject could, in principle, treat each stimulus as a separate object, in which case each array of the task constitutes an independent subproblem and the solution is based on the choice of specific objects.

The type of solution adopted by the subjects can be revealed by an examination of performance on reversal and nonreversal shift tasks. If subjects have learned the initial task on the basis of object-reward relations, both subproblems must be relearned in the reversal shift, and the errors committed on each subproblem should be equivalent. In the nonreversal shift, however, the object-reward relation remains unchanged in one subproblem (Array 1) and is reversed in the second (Array 2). Only the reversed subproblem must be relearned, and the errors committed on the reversed subproblem should exceed those committed on the unchanged subproblem, which ideally would be zero. "Dimension-reward" learning (Tighe & Tighe, 1972) would, however, lead to a very different outcome in the shift tasks. Because each array is perceived as an instance of the same problem in both types of shift task, error rates should be equivalent for the arrays within each shift task. In particular, the changed and unchanged subproblems of the nonreversal shift should be learned at the same rate.

The work of Tighe and his colleagues is germane to the present discussion because of the assumptions made about the type of solution adopted by children of different ages. They have assumed that children perceive both modes of representation but that younger children are more likely to learn object-reward relations than dimension-reward relations, whereas the reverse is assumed for older children. Tighe & Tighe (1972) and Tighe (1973) report results that support these assumptions. Younger children typically show the distributions of errors on the subproblems of the nonreversal shift that would be expected for an object-reward learner. Older children, however, show equivalent error rates on the two subproblems of the nonreversal task. Thus, the results of Tighe and his associates do suggest that the younger child perceives a multidimensional stimulus as wholistic or unitary, whereas older children perceive the same stimulus in terms of specific dimensions.

In reviewing these trends in perceptual development, Shepp (1978) has observed that the description of the younger child as perceiving stimuli as unitary or wholistic and as failing to attend selectively is very similar to that of an adult faced with the task of processing integral dimensions. On the basis of such trends, Shepp (1978) has proposed a separability hypothesis of perceptual development. The hypothesis assumes that dimensional combinations that are perceived by older children and adults as separable are perceived by the younger child as integral, and it is through perceptual learning that dimensional structure is abstracted from the stimulus (Gibson, 1969).

This view differs somewhat from that of Garner (1974). Garner has argued that integral and separable dimensions are stimulus concepts: The distance or similarity structure of integral combinations or dimensions and the dimensional structure of separable dimensions are properties of physical stimuli, and any set of stimuli is characterized by both a similarity and a dimensional structure. For Garner, the psychological question is which structure is perceived by the subject for a particular set of stimuli. With integral combinations, a similarity structure is primary in perception, whereas a dimensional structure is extracted only at a more derived or cognitive level. For separable dimensions, dimensional structure is the primary process, and similarity is derived.

We accept Garner's argument that similarity and dimensional structures are properties of the stimulus. We are suggesting, however, that, of the two structures, the similarity structure is the more fundamental, and it is during the course of perceptual learning and development that dimensional structure becomes extracted. We are stressing, then, a process whereby a multidimensional stimulus that is perceived initially as unitary becomes divided into its constituent dimensions. The plausibility of such a process has been shown by Lockhead (1972), who points out that both integral and separable dimensions are analyzable. Multidimensional stimuli are analyzable if the subject can respond accurately to the values of one dimension while values on the others vary orthogonally.

According to a separability hypothesis, young children perceive the similarity structure of multidimensional stimuli, and during the course of perceptual experience learn to analyze multidimensional stimuli. The result of perceptual analysis over a number of varying objects or events is abstraction of the dimensional structure (Gibson, 1969). Some dimensional combinations, separable dimensions, are more easily analyzed than others, integral dimensions, and dimensional structure would be more easily extracted from the former than from the latter. It is also likely that some tasks either require or encourage more perceptual analysis than others (see Lockhead, 1972).

The separability hypothesis also speaks to the question of attentional development. As Garner (1974, 1976) has shown, integral dimensions do not allow selective attention. Thus, if young children do perceive dimensional combinations as integral, an observed failure to attend selectively is the result of perceived stimulus structure and not a failure in the ability of these children to either focus or allocate attention. A similar conclusion holds for results that suggest efficient integration of information through divided attention (e.g., Wohlwill, 1962). If redundancy gains are observed in the presence of integral dimensions, they are made possible by distance relations between the stimuli. It is not necessary to assume that the child has divided or broadened attention in order to improve performance (Shepp, 1978).

The argument that there is a developmental progression from perceived similarity to dimensional structure does deny the importance of attentional development. Clearly, attention is a cognitive resource over which children gain increasing control during the course of development, and there are some studies (e.g., Smith, Kemler, & Aronfreed, 1975) that document this progression. We do argue, however, that the results of many studies that appear to show developmental differences in attention may also be reflecting developmental differences in perceived structure. The development of control over attentional resources cannot be demonstrated unless it can be shown that the sources of information are independent.

To summarize, a separability hypothesis is a view of perceptual development that can be incorporated within Gibson's (1969) general theory of perceptual development. Like Gibson, we assume that invariants in the structure of the stimulus are detected during the course of perceptual learning and that children extract these invariants through the processes of abstraction and selective filtering. A separability hypothesis speaks to a specific aspect of perceptual development, namely, the progression of representation from a perceived similarity to a dimensional structure.

Although there is considerable experimental evidence that can be reasonably claimed by a separability hypothesis (Shepp, 1978), there have been only two studies that provide direct support. The first such experiment was by Shepp and Swartz (1976), who used a version of the speeded sorting task (Garner & Felfoldy, 1970). First- and fourth-grade children were instructed to sort decks of cards that displayed either the dimensional combinations of hue and brightness or color and form. The composition of the decks was varied so that three tasks, one-dimension, correlated-dimensions, and orthogonal-dimensions, were presented to each subject. The measure of performance was the time to sort on each task.

Hue and brightness are integral dimensions for the adult (Garner, 1974) and should also be integral for children. Although Shepp and Swartz did find differences in the absolute sorting times for first and fourth graders, the pattern of sorting times within an age group was consistent with the performance of adults with integral dimensions (Garner & Felfoldy, 1970). Relative to the performance on the one-dimension task, both first and fourth graders showed facilitation on the correlated-dimensions task and interference on the orthogonal-dimensions task.

The theoretically important results were obtained with the dimensional combination of color and form. Color and form are perceived by the adult as separable dimensions (Garner, 1974; Handel & Imai, 1972), but according to a separability hypothesis, color and form should be integral for young children and separable for older ones. Shepp and Swartz (1976) confirmed this prediction. First graders showed facilitation on the correlated-dimensions task and interference on the orthogonal-dimensions task. Fourth graders, on the other hand, performed equally well on all three tasks.

The second study that provides support for a separability hypothesis is due to Smith and Kemler (1977). They used a restricted classification task in which the subject is instructed to partition subsets of stimuli according to which go together. Their subjects were groups of kindergarten, second-grade, and fifth-grade children, who were instructed to classify stimuli that varied in size and brightness. In one experiment the children classified triads, and in another they classified tetrads.

Size and brightness are separable dimensions (Garner, 1974; Handel & Imai, 1972) and should be classified according to dimensional structure. Consider again the subset of stimuli shown in Fig. 5.2. The stimuli A and B share a value on Dimension 1. Stimulus C does not share a value with either A or B, but in overall similarity, C is more similar to B than to A. With separable dimensions, such as size and brightness, A and B should be classified together, whereas with integral dimensions, such as hue and brightness, B and C should be classified together.

According to a separability hypothesis, size and brightness should be integral for young children and separable for older children. Smith and Kemler (1977) confirmed this prediction in both experiments. Kindergarten children consistently classified the triads according to overall similarity, whereas fifth graders classified by dimensional structure. Second graders divided their responses evenly between similarity and dimensional classifications. Thus, Smith and Kemler have shown a clear developmental trend from a perceived similarity structure to a dimensional structure.

Taken together, the results of Shepp and Swartz (1976) and Smith and

Kemler (1977) provide convincing evidence for a separability hypothesis. Both studies show that younger children perceive the similarity structure of multidimensional stimuli whereas older children extract dimensional structure. Shepp and Swartz also show that the observed failure of younger children to attend selectively must be attributed in some instances to the perceived stimulus structure rather than the inability of these children to focus or allocate their attentional resources.

Despite the initial success of a separability hypothesis, there are many theoretical issues to be resolved in order to determine its relation to more general theories of perceptual development (e.g., Gibson, 1969), and to determine the role of perceived structure in other aspects of cognitive development (Shepp, 1978). It is to some of these issues that the remainder of the present paper is directed.

## SOME NEW TESTS OF A SEPARABILITY
## HYPOTHESIS: EXPERIMENT 1

In our previous discussion, the distinction between integral and separable dimensions has been treated as a simple dichotomy, and the results of experiments using certain dimensional combinations support the idea of a dichotomy. Research with the combination of circle size and angle of a radial line, for example, yields consistent evidence that these dimensions are separable. Similarly, dimensions such as value and chroma are clearly integral. There are other dimensional combinations, however, such as size and brightness, color and form, and vertical and horizontal position of a single dot, for which the picture is much less clear.

According to Garner (1970, 1974), dimensions are integral if in order to specify a level on one dimension, a level on another must also be specified. By this definition, dimensions such as size vs. brightness, color vs. form, and vertical vs. horizontal position of a dot are integral and in some tasks yield results that are typical of integral dimensions. Thus, when the values of such dimensional combinations are correlated, there is a redundancy gain in speeded classification (Biederman & Checkosky, 1970; Gottwald & Garner, 1972; Garner & Felfoldy, 1970). Morever, such dimensional combinations appear to be integral in absolute judgment tasks (e.g., Levy & Haggbloom, 1971).

Given that these dimensions produce a redundancy gain when correlated, we would also expect interference when selective attention is required to orthogonal dimensions in speeded classification. This result has been obtained by Garner and Felfoldy (1970), and Gottwald and Garner (1972). The amount of interference, however, is much smaller than for value and chroma, and, in some instances, no interference is observed (e.g., Gottwald & Garner, 1975).

In speeded tasks, then, these dimensions give somewhat mixed results. When correlated, the dimensions behave as integral dimensions, but when orthogonal, some selective attention is possible, indicating that dimensional structure is perceived by the subject. That dimensional structure is extracted by subjects for such dimensions is shown by Handel and Imai (1972), who report that color and form and size and brightness are classified by dimensional relations in a restricted classification task.

In addressing these types of results, Garner (1974) suggests that instead of a dichotomy between separable and integral dimensions, there exists a continuum with degrees of integrality. We further suggest that the continuum exists because of differences in the analyzability of stimulus combinations. Specifically, we would argue that the perceptual analyzers that operate on stimuli composed of physically separable dimensions extract dimensional structure automatically; no analysis is required. For stimuli generated by physically integral dimensions, however, the situation is more complicated. Such stimuli are initially represented as wholistic and only by subsequent analysis can dimensional structure be extracted. For some combinations (e.g., color vs. form) dimensional structure is easily accessed, whereas for others (e.g., chroma and value) the accessing of dimensional structure may not be possible (Burns, Shepp, McDonough, & Wiener-Ehrlich, 1978; Smith, 1977).

Thus far, the argument for a continuum of integrality has dealt only with adult perceptions, but the argument has a clear bearing on the development of perceived structure. The previous tests of a separability hypothesis have used the dimensions of color and form (Shepp & Swartz, 1976) and size and brightness (Smith & Kemler, 1977). These dimensional combinations are physically integral (Garner, 1970) but can be analyzed into dimensional structure. A fundamental assumption of a separability hypothesis is that children, through experience with different correlational structures and tasks, learn to analyze the stimulus according to a dimensional structure, and, as the results of Shepp and Swartz (1976) and Smith and Kemler (1977) indicate, there is a developmental trend from perceived similarity to dimensional structure with these particular dimensions. In principle, however, a developmental trend in perceived structure should also exist for physically separable dimensions (e.g., size of circle vs. angle of a radial line). One could also expect a somewhat different trend in the development of perceived structure for physically separable dimensions from that observed with physically integral dimensions (e.g., size vs. brightness). Because levels of physically separable dimensions can be varied independently, it is plausible that the dimensions would also be perceived as independent earlier in development than would be the case for dimensions that are physically integral.

The purpose of the present experiment was to compare developmental trends in perceived structure for dimensional combinations that are either physically separable or physically integral. Four-, six-, and 11-year-old children were administered a restricted classification task similar to that of Smith and Kemler (1977). One group of children at each age classified triads of stimuli generated by combinations of circle size and angle of a radial line and another group classified triads that varied in size and brightness.

As shown in Fig. 5.3, three different types of triads were presented. Type I and type II triads pit dimensional similarity against overall similarity. In both triads, stimulus A and B share a value on one dimension and differ considerably on the other. Stimulus C shares no dimensional value with either A or B, but in overall similarity C is nearer to B than to A. Note, however, that the distance relations between A and C differ considerably between the two triads. In type II triads, the distance between A and C is much less than in type I triads. The difference between type I and type II triads was introduced to determine if some distance relations would enhance the perception of dimensional relations more than others would. By making the distance relations (B and C vs. A and C) more similar in type II triads, we assumed that the classification would be more difficult and, by closer inspection of the array, the dimensional relation (A and B) might be discovered.

Type III triads are included as a measure of dimensional preference. Garner (1974) has shown that separable dimensions are characterized by dimensional preferences, whereas integral dimensions show no such preferences. Garner has also shown that dimensional preferences dominate classification despite variations in the nonpreferred dimension. Type III triads provide two dimensional classifications; in one of the classifications (i.e. B and C),

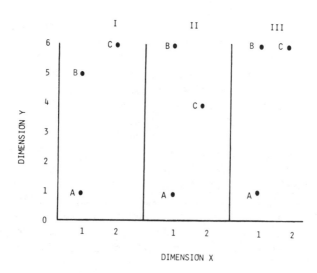

FIG. 5.3.    A schematic of three types of triads used in Experiments 1 and 2.

similarity is also maximized. If subjects classify type I and II triads by overall similarity, then similarity relations should also govern the classifications of type III triads. If, on the other hand, subjects classify by dimensional relations on type I and type II triads, some subjects should show dimensional preferences. That is, the subject should classify by the preferred dimension when it provides either the AB or BC relation.

By hypothesis, we expected 4-year-olds to classify both stimulus sets by overall similarity. Moreover, because there is no evidence of dimensional perception by children of this age, we expected no difference between classifications of type I and type II triads nor the appearance of dimensional preferences on type III triads.

In accord with previous evidence, we expected 6-year-olds to be more sensitive to dimensional structure than 4-year-olds. Smith and Kemler (1977) have reported that although kindergarten subjects classify primarily on the basis of an overall similarity structure, these children can access dimensional relations. Similarly, Shepp and Swartz (1976) and others (e.g., Miller, 1971) report results that imply the perception of dimensional relations by at least some 6-year-olds. It is by no means clear, however, that children of this age have a generalized concept of dimensions, and it is likely that several factors might influence the perception of dimensional relations. First, different types of dimensional combinations may promote differences in the perception of dimensional relations. Thus, physically separable dimensions may produce more dimensional classifications than physically integral dimensions. Second, subjects of this age may be especially influenced by task variables such that the distance relations of type II triads are more favorable for the perception of dimensional relations than are the distance relations of type I triads. Finally, previous perceptual learning will undoubtedly affect the perception of dimensional relations. If a subject has acquired information about variations on one dimension of a set, such a subject might classify by dimensional relations on that dimension but might not be sensitive to dimensional relations on the other dimension of a set. In this event, the classifications would be asymmetric and are analogous to a form of response that Piaget (1970) has called centration.

Classifications by 11-year-olds typically resemble those of adults (Smith & Kemler, 1977). Thus, we expected that the subjects would classify both dimensional sets according to dimensional relations. Moreover, subjects of this age should show consistent dimensional preferences on type III triads.

## Method

*Subjects.*   The subjects for the first experiment were 60 children, with 20 subjects selected randomly from each of the following age groups: 4 years (9 males), 6–7 years (12 males) and 11–12 years (9 males). Ten subjects in each age group were assigned to the Size × Brightness set, and 10 were assigned to the Circle × Angle of Line set. Children in the youngest age group attended a day care center, while those in the older groups attended a summer day camp, both in the Providence, R.I. area.

*Stimuli: Size and Brightness.* The stimuli were Munsell chips varying in brightness and cut into squares of different sizes. Brightness levels corresponded to Munsell values of 3 (very dark), 4, 5, 6, 7, and 8 (very light). The sides of the squares measured 1.9, 2.4, 3.1, 3.9, 4.9, and 6.2 cm. Differences between levels of both dimensions were shown to be equal from previously obtained adult similarity judgments. Thirty-six stimuli were prepared by combining the six levels of the two dimensions in a 6 × 6 matrix. Stimuli were mounted on cardboard covered with gray paper and viewed under illumination approximating Illuminant C, as specified by the Munsell system.

*Stimuli: Size of Circle and Angle of Line.* The stimuli were circles cut from heavy white paper and increasing in area on a logarithmic scale. Lines cut from black tape 0.08 mm wide and 8mm long extended from the center of the circles and varied in angle of inclination from the vertical. The areas of the circles were 4.5, 6.4, 9.0, 12.8, 18.1 and 25.8 cm$^2$. The angles of the lines were 5, 35, 65, 95, 125 and 155 degrees. These levels were also obtained from adult similarity judgments. Stimuli were mounted as above.

*Design and Procedure.* From each matrix of 36 stimuli, 16 triads were selected in the following manner: Type I and type II triads put classification by similarity structure and by dimensional structure into conflict; that is, two of the three stimuli (A and B) share a level of dimension $X$ and greatly differ on dimension $Y$, while another pair of stimuli (B and C) are closer in overall similarity, but do not share a level of either dimension. Type I and type II triads differ in the nature of the stimulus relations within the two-dimensional ($X$ vs. $Y$) matrix. In type I triads, A and B share a level of dimension $X$ and are four levels apart on the other, B and C are one level apart on both dimensions, and A and C are one level apart on dimension $X$ and five levels apart on dimension $Y$. In type II triads, A and B share a level of dimension $X$ and are five levels apart on dimension $Y$, B and C are one level apart on dimension $X$ and two levels apart on dimension $Y$, and A and C are one level apart on dimension $X$ and three levels apart on dimension $Y$. Therefore, in type II triads, the distances between the pairs A and B, and B and C are greater than comparable distances in type I triads, and the distance between A and C is less in type II than in type I triads. For both type I and type II triads, three classifications are possible: classification by dimensional structure (A and B); classification by similarity structure (B and C); or classification by neither structure (haphazard; A and C).

Type III triads do not put classification by dimensional structure or by similarity structure directly into conflict. A level on each dimension is shared by two pairs of stimuli; however, only one of the pairs also maximizes similarity along the other dimension. Again, three classifications are possible: Classification by the dimensional structure with no regard for similarity (dimension only), classification by the dimensional structure that also maximizes similarity (similarity plus dimension), or classification by neither (haphazard).

From each matrix of 36 stimuli, six type I and four type II triads were selected such that half of the triads shared a level of dimension $X$, and half shared a level of dimension $Y$. Six type III triads were selected such that half of the triads maximized similarity on the shared dimension $X$, and half maximized similarity on the shared dimension $Y$. The 16 triads were presented four times each in random order for a total of 64 trials. On two trials for each triad, stimuli were placed in a row: on the other two trials, stimuli were placed as if at the vertices of a triangle. In addition, on two trials, the most similar stimuli were placed adjacently in the rows or at the base of the triangle; on the other two trials, stimuli that shared a dimension level were so placed.

The subject was seated at a table facing the experimenter, and the three stimuli were placed in front of him. The subject was asked to indicate, for each trial, which two of the three stimuli went together the most. The experimental session averaged about 30 minutes.

## Results

For each stimulus set, proportions of the three possible classifications in the three triad types (Dimensional, Similarity, and Haphazard for types I and II; Dimension Only, Similarity plus Dimension, and Haphazard for Type III) were calculated for each subject. The data of interest in the present study are the relative proportions of systematic classifications. Because the proportion of haphazard responses did not exceed 7% for any age group in either stimulus set, the proportion of systematic classifications that was based on dimensional structure (type I and II) or dimensional structure only (type III) was calculated for each subject.

Because type I and type II triads could result in classifications based on one of two competing stimulus structures (dimensional or similarity), these triads were analyzed together. For each stimulus set (Size × Brightness and Circle × Angle of Line), the mean proportions of systematic classifications that were based on dimensional structure were submitted to analysis of variance for Age (4, 6, or 11 yrs.) × Triad type (I or II) × Shared dimension (Size or Brightness; Circle or Angle) × Subjects. Both analyses revealed a main effect of age; for the Size × Brightness set, $F(2,27) = 53.26, p < .01$; for the Circle × Angle set, $F(2,27) = 50.08, p < .01$. Neither analysis revealed

TABLE 5.2
Proportions of Dimensional (Type I and Type II) and Dimension-Only (Type III) Classifications for Triads Generated by (a) Size and Brightness and (b) Size of Circle and Angle of Line

| Triad Type | Age | Size and Brightness Classification[a] | Size of Circle and Angle of Line Classification[a] |
|---|---|---|---|
| | | Dim | Dim |
| I | 4 | .13 (.133) | .15 (.119) |
| | 6–7 | .48 (.122) | .50 (.079) |
| | 11–12 | .79 (.170) | .67 (.126) |
| | | Dim | Dim |
| II | 4 | .22 (.141) | .22 (.193) |
| | 6–7 | .58 (.239) | .61 (.110) |
| | 11–12 | .83 (.190) | .72 (.149) |
| | | Dim Only | Dim Only |
| III | 4 | .26 (.122) | .22 (.128) |
| | 6–7 | .43 (.073) | .39 (.082) |
| | 11–12 | .39 (.110) | .33 (.153) |

[a]Standard deviations are given in parentheses.

effects due to triad type or the shared dimension involved in a dimension classification. The age related trend in classification is shown in Table 5.2 for size and brightness and for size and angle. As these figures show, 4-year-old children classify both size and brightness and size and angle by overall similarity, whereas 11-year-old children classify by dimension. Six-year-old children fall in between the younger and older children.

These age-related trends were further substantiated by comparing the proportions of classifications based on dimensional structure in each triad type to a chance level of response (.50 for dimensional vs. similarity structure). For the Size × Brightness set, 4-year-old subjects classified by dimensional structure at a level significantly less than chance in both triad types, $t(9) = 5.62$, $p < .01$ and $t(9) = 3.92$, $p < .01$ for types I and II respectively. Six-year-old subjects responded at a chance level in both triad types, $t(9) = .49$ and $t(9) = 1.0$ for types I and II, respectively. Eleven-year-old subjects responded with dimensional classifications at a level significantly greater than that expected by chance, $t(9) = 5.98$, $p < .01$ and $t(9) = 5.24$, $p < .01$ for types I and II, respectively.

The proportion of dimensional classification in the Circle × Angle of Line set showed a similar age-related trend. In both triad types, 4-year-old subjects classified by dimensional structure at a level significantly less than chance, $t(9) = 8.82, p < .01$ and $t(9) = 4.38, p < .01$ for types I and II, respectively. Six-year-old subjects classified by dimensional structure at chance level for type I triads, $t(9) = .12$ but in type II triads they showed a level of dimensional classifications that was reliably greater than that expected by chance, $t(9) = 2.97, p < .05$. Eleven-year-old subjects classified both type I and type II triads by dimensional structure at a level significantly greater than chance, $t(9) = 4.04, p < .01$ and $t(9) = 4.4, p < .01$ for types I and II, respectively.

Type III triads could result in classification based on dimensional structure alone or in a classification by dimensional structure that also maximized similarity along the second dimension. For each stimulus set, the mean proportions of systematic classifications that were based on a dimensional structure only were submitted to an analysis of variance for Age (4, 6, 11) × Dimension Shared by the most similar pair (Size or Brightness) (Circle or Angle) × Subjects. Both analyses revealed main effects of age (for Size and Brightness, $F(2,27) = 11.4, p < .01$; for Circle and Angle, $F(2,27) = 4.66, p < .05$) but no effects of dimensions shared and no significant interaction.

The classifications shown in Table 5.2 for type III triads are somewhat misleading because dimensional preferences are obscured by averaging responses to each dimension. Four-year-old subjects are, as predicted, highly consistent in making classifications based on overall similarity relations. For the size and brightness set, these subjects classified by dimension-only at a level reliably less than chance when the shared dimension was size, $t(9) = 3.54, p < .01$, or when the shared dimension was brightness, $t(9) = 4.37, p < .01$. Similar results were observed for size of circle and angle of line. The proportion of dimension-only responses was reliably less than chance for both size of circle, $t(9) = 4.80, p < .01$, and angle of line, $t(9) = 4.37, p < .01$. Thus, it is clear that 4-year-olds show no dimensional preferences.

Unlike the 4-year-olds, many of the older children did show dimensional preferences. Consider first the classifications of 6-year-olds. Eight subjects showed dimensional preferences in the size and brightness set (six preferred size, two preferred brightness). These subjects classified by their preferred dimension in both in AB relations (92%) and the BC relation (99%). Eight subjects also showed dimensional preferences in the size of circle and angle of line set (three preferred size, five preferred angle). These subjects also consistently classified by their preferred dimension in the AB (77%) as well as the BC relation (92%).

Many of our 11-year-olds also showed dimensional preferences. With size and brightness, seven subjects showed preferences (four preferred size, three preferred brightness). These subjects classified by their preferred dimension in both the AB (81%) and the BC (91%) relations. Simlarly, the four subjects who preferred angle and the two subjects who preferred circle size classified consistently by their preferred dimension in both AB (79%) and BC (94%)

TABLE 5.3
Percentages of Dimensional Classifications by 6-year-olds for Preferred and Nonpreferred
Dimensions in Type I and Type II Triads

| | Dimensional Set | | | |
| | Circle Size vs. Angle of Line Dimension | | Size vs. Brightness Dimension | |
| Triad Type | Preferred | Nonpreferred | Preferred | Nonpreferred |
|---|---|---|---|---|
| I | 87.6 | 0.01 | 88.5 | 13.9 |
| II | 70.3 | 69.1 | 89.5 | 26.4 |

relations. Thus, the 11-year-olds do exhibit dimensional preferences and show consistent classifications by dimension in type I and type II triads.

In contrast to the 11-year-old performances, the classifications by 6-year-olds on type I and type II triads yield a different picture when their performances are considered in relation to their dimensional preferences. The percentages of dimensional classifications for preferred and nonpreferred dimensions are given in Table 5.3. With circle size and angle of line, these subjects show reliable classification ($p < .01$) by dimensional relations when a value is shared on the preferred dimensions in both type I and type II triads. When the nonpreferred dimension shares a value, however, these subjects classify by similarity in type I triads ($p < .01$) and by dimension in type II triads ($p < .01$). Subjects who classified size and brightness also classify by dimension when the preferred dimension shares a value in both type I and type II triads ($p < .01$) but classify by overall similarity in both type I and type II triads when a value is shared on the nonpreferred dimension ($p < .01$).

## Discussion

The results of the present experiment show a clear trend in the development of perceived dimensional relations for physically separable as well as physically integral dimensions. Four-year-olds classify both size of circle vs. angle of line and size vs. brightness by overall similarity relations, regardless of which dimension shares a value. Moreover, these subjects show no dimensional preferences. In contrast, 11-year-olds classify the same stimulus sets by dimensional relations and many of these subjects show dimensional preferences. Thus, our results support the separability hypothesis (Shepp, 1978) and extend the domain of stimulus structure to which the hypothesis applies. As we indicated earlier in the paper, previous tests of the hypothesis used dimensions that were physically integral, but which, to varying degrees, allow the extraction of dimensional structure. Our present results indicate that the separability hypothesis applies to dimensions that are physically separable as well.

The classifications produced by our 6-year-olds, combined with the results of Smith and Kemler (1977) for second-grade children suggest that there is a transitional age range, 6 to 8 years, in which the child has some knowledge about dimensions, but consistent classification by dimensional relations may be affected by a variety of variables. First, there is some evidence to indicate that type of dimensional structure combines with distance relations between stimuli to improve the detection of dimensional relations. With size of circle and angle of line, the 6-year-olds made dimensional classifications in type I triads when their preferred dimension shared a value but classified by overall similarity relations when the nonpreferred dimension shared a value. In type II triads, on the other hand, these subjects classified consistently by dimensional relations when either dimension shared a value. With size and brightness, however, these subjects classified by dimensional relations in both type I and type II triads when the preferred dimension shared a value, but classified by overall similarity relations when the nonpreferred dimension shared a value.

It seems clear, then, that the classifications of these subjects are guided by their preferred dimensions in both stimulus sets but that dimensional relations on the nonpreferred dimension are easier to detect with circle size and angle of line than with size and brightness. These consistently asymmetric classifications with size and brightness could be interpreted in several ways. First, it could reflect the specific effects of perceptual learning. The subjects know something about size but little about brightness as dimensions. Second, the size dimension may be more salient than brightness and serve to control the classification. In either of these cases, the subject is, in effect, performing the task with one dimension. Finally there is the possibility that the performances of 6-year-olds with size and brightness are revealing a characteristic in the trend of perceptual development for this type of dimensional combination. These children have some knowledge of dimensions that they apply when possible; otherwise, they classify on the basis of overall similarity. Thus, when their "preferred" dimension shares a value, they classify by dimensional relations, but when their "nonpreferred" dimension shares a value, they classify by overall similarity. This third alternative is the most appealing of the three because it is consistent with results reported by Smith and Kemler (1977) that still older children, that is second graders, do not consistently classify size and brightness by either dimensional or similarity relations. By this view, the emergence of perceived dimensional structure occurs slowly, and the perceptual organization of dimensional sets depends upon the relative dominance of dimensional and overall similarity relation. The dominance of dimensional relations would appear to depend upon the analyzability of dimensional combinations, knowledge about specific dimensions, the symmetry of dimensional knowledge, and the distance relations between stimuli.

## EXPERIMENT 2: PERCEPTION OF RECTANGLES

The fact that younger children perceive the overall similarity relations between multidimensional stimuli clearly sets some limit on the achievement of these children in any task in which success depends upon the extraction and coordination of dimensional information. There is little doubt, of course, that even young children can learn to extract dimensional structure because such learning has been repeatedly demonstrated in studies of discrimination shifts (e. g., Shepp & Turrisi, 1966; Wolff, 1967). However, the stimulus and task variables that are most favorable for such extraction are not well understood. Thus, a priori assumptions about the existence of dimensional structure may be erroneous.

Although we have previously raised this issue in connection with work on selective attention, the issue is a general one in studies of cognitive development and is fundamental to such questions as the development of logical operations (e.g., Elkind, 1975; Ginsburg & Opper, 1969; Piaget, 1970). To illustrate, consider a conservation of quantity task. Two identical glasses of liquid are shown to a child and the child, beyond the age of 4, says the glasses have the same amount of liquid. The contents of one of the glasses are then poured into another, taller and narrower glass. Faced with this situation, the preoperational child is likely to choose the latter glass as having more liquid, and, according to Piaget, such performance is governed by centration or the tendency to focus on just one dimension. The concrete operational child, however, will conserve on this task. These children are capable of decentering, meaning that the relevant dimensions are apprehended simultaneously. This broadened attention makes the child aware of transformations in the task and makes possible such operations as reversibility. For Piaget, the stimulus dimensions in such tasks are independent, meaning that selective attention can occur to either or to both and that each dimension contributes independently when the dimensions are coordinated or combined. Thus, the theoretical burdens of this view are placed entirely on the development of logical operations and no attempt is made to relate perceptual and cognitive development.

A similar problem exists in the work of Anderson and his colleagues (e.g., Anderson & Butzin, 1978; Anderson & Cuneo, 1978; Anderson, Chapter 1, this volume) who have attempted to relate perceptual judgment to the development of conservation and logical operations. In an extensive series of studies using the techniques of information integration theory, these investigators have shown a developmental difference in the rule by which children combine dimensions in perceptual judgment tasks. Like Piaget, Anderson assumes that the stimulus dimensions are independent. Unlike Piaget, however, Anderson and his colleagues are attempting to identify the perceptual mechanisms that underlie specific combinational rules.

Although there is no doubt that the development of logical operations plays a central role in cognitive development, and that Anderson's information integration theory offers important insights into the relation between perceptual judgment and logical operations, we believe that the specification of stimulus structure and the development of perceived stimulus relations are misrepresented in these views. Furthermore, we would argue that the nature of stimulus structure and the development of perceived structure must be understood if the development of judgmental processes and logical operations are to be accurately characterized.

To illustrate these issues, consider the properties of rectangles. These stimuli are typical of those used in the conservation of quantity task and have been used by Anderson and Cuneo (1978) to demonstrate developmental differences in the combination of height and width to produce judgments of area. For both Piaget and Anderson, height and width are independent dimensions at all developmental levels. Developmental differences in performance are due to developmental differences in thought (Piaget, 1970) or combinatorial rules (Anderson & Cuneo, 1978).

The assumptions that height and width are independent and combine in some simple fashion to produce judgments of area or quantity are seriously challenged by several studies in the adult literature that deal with the perception and processing of rectangles. First, Felfoldy (1974) has shown that height and width of rectangles are integral dimensions. Subjects were required to classify rectangles by height or width in a speeded sorting task. In comparison with the control task, a redundancy gain was observed when height and width were correlated and interference was observed when the dimensions were combined orthogonally. Second, there is evidence from the absolute identification task that height and width are integral and that these dimensions combine to produce shape as well as area. Monahan and Lockhead (1977) required subjects to identify rectangles chosen from either a linear or a scattered pattern. The rectangles of the scattered pattern were identified more accurately and faster than rectangles arranged linearly along the primary diagonal. This result shows that the stimuli are integral. Weintraub (1971), also using absolute identification, has shown that height and width combine to produce shape as well as area. Subjects performed the task with different subsets of stimuli in which the rectangles varied (1) in width, (2) in height, (3) in area, or (4) in shape. The last condition produced the most accurate identification.

Finally, there are results by Wender (1971) and Krantz and Tversky (1975), who used a dissimilarity judgment task to determine if height and width and area and shape would exhibit dimensional structure according to the assumptions of an additive difference model. In both studies these dimensions were shown to interact strongly, a finding that is consistent with the argument that they are integral (cf., Burns, Shepp, McDonough, & Wiener-Ehrlich, 1978).

The results obtained with adult subjects in several tasks show that height and width are integral dimensions that combine to produce both area and shape. Although the evidence is less conclusive, area and shape may also be integral. Such evidence in adult perception raises a number of interesting questions in the development of perceived structure.

The first is whether there is any developmental difference in perceived structure. If height and width are integral for the adult, it seems most unlikely that these dimensions are anything but integral for children. But what of area and shape? These are derived dimensions and, although the evidence is suggestive, it is not entirely clear that these dimensions are integral in adult perception. If they are integral for the adult, however, it is still possible that the young child does not perceive variations in rectangles as involving both area and shape. The child may first perceive area and only later perceive shape. Unfortunately, there are no data that speak to these questions, and the purpose of Experiment II is to determine if there are developmental differences in the perception of rectangles.

Our subjects were administered a restricted classification task in which triads that varied in height and width or area and shape were presented. A hypothetical set of such stimuli is shown in Fig. 5.4. Triads varying in height and width were chosen from the 6 × 6 matrix defined by height and width, whereas triads varying in area and shape were chosen from the matrix produced by the 45° rotation of the height and width matrix. As in Experiment 1, three types of triads were presented and the distance relations between the stimuli in these triads were the same as in Experiment 1 (see Fig. 5.3).

## Method

*Subjects.*   The subjects were 30 children and 10 adults. The children were selected randomly from the same facilities as in Experiment 1. Ten children were 4–5 years (5 males), 10 were 6–7 years (5 males), and 10 were 11–12 years (5 males). Adult subjects were paid volunteers from Brown University.

*Stimuli.*   The stimuli were rectangles drawn in black ink on white cardboard squares. Two sets of rectangles were prepared from levels of dimensions, the differences between which were shown to be psychologically equal from previously obtained adult similarity judgments. In the first set, the dimensions of height and width increased on logarithmic scale, with values of

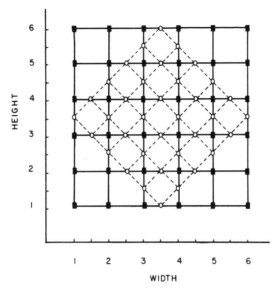

FIG. 5.4.  A schematic representation of height × width and area × shape
dimensions (units on the coordinates are arbitrary).

.48, .62, .81, 1.05, 1.37, and 1.77 cm for height and 2.31, 3.0, 3.9, 5.1, 6.59, and
8.56 cm for width. In the second set of stimuli, the dimensions of area and
shape were formed by a 45° rotation of the height and width matrix. Area was
defined as the product of height and width and increased on a logarithmic
scale, with values of 2.15, 2.79, 3.63, 4.73, 6.13, and 7.97 cm$^2$. Shape was
defined as the ratio between width and height, with values of 2.5, 3.2, 4.2, 5.5,
7.2 and 9.4.

*Experimental Design and Procedure.*    Six type I, four type II, and six type
III triads were selected from each matrix of 36 rectangles in a manner similar
to that used in Experiment 1. For type I and type II triads selected from the
height × width matrix, half of the triads shared a level of the height dimension
and half shared a level of the width dimension. For type III triads, half
maximized similarity on the shared dimension of height and the other half
maximized similarity on the shared dimension of width. Similar constraints
occurred in the selection of 16 triads from the area × shape matrix.

Type I and type II triads put classification by dimensional or similarity
structures into conflict with respect to the particular matrix from which the
triads were selected (height × width or area × shape). In type I triads, the
possibility of a classification based on a dimension from the other matrix was
not excluded. A pair of stimuli in each type I triad necessarily shared a level of
a dimension from the other matrix; this pair formed the similarity
classification. An experimenter-defined similarity classification from one

matrix could thus be conceived of as a dimensional classification from the other matrix, reflected in a predominance of similarity classifications for triads selected from one matrix and a predominance of dimensional classifications for triads selected from the other matrix. For example, if similarity classifications for triads from the height × width matrix were actually based on the dimension of area (or of shape), then triads from the area × shape matrix should result in dimensional classifications based on area (or on shape). In type II triads, however, experimenter-defined similarity classifications could not be based on a dimension defined by the other matrix; triads were selected so that no pair of stimuli from a particular matrix also shared a level of a dimension from the other matrix. Type III triads could result in a classification based on dimensional structure alone or a classification by dimensional structure that also maximized similarity on the second dimension of the matrix.

The task was administered in a single session. For the three oldest groups of subjects, triads from both the height × width matrix and the area × shape matrix were presented in a random order. Each subject classified on 128 trials and the session lasted for approximately 50 minutes. Because the session was lengthy, a modification was made for the four-year-olds. Five subjects classified rectangles from the height × width matrix and five classified rectangles from the area × shape matrix. Thus, each subject received 64 trials and the sessions averaged 30 minutes. Otherwise, the procedures used in Experiment 1 were repeated in Experiment 2.

## Results

The experimental manipulation of the rectangle dimensions allowed an analysis of the classification data in terms of two possible dimensional combinations: triads from the height × width and triads from the area × shape matrix. For each set of dimensions, proportions of the three possible classifications in the three triad types were calculated for each subject. Because the proportion of haphazard responses did not exceed 6% for any age group, the proportions of systematic classifications that were based on dimension structure (type I and II) or dimensional structure alone (type III) were computed for each subject. These proportions are presented for each age group in Table 5.4.

An inspection of Table 5.4 suggests that subjects of all ages made classifications consistently on the basis of overall similarity relations in all three triads. Analyses similar to those conducted in Experiment 1 confirmed this impression. Consider first type I and II triads. The results of an analysis of variance for proportions of dimensional responses indicated that there were no main effects of age, triad type, or shared dimensions, or interactions between these factors that even approached significance. The results of $t$ test comparisons in which the proportions of dimensional classifications were

TABLE 5.4
Proportions of Dimensional (Type I and Type II) and Dimension-Only
(Type III) Classifications for Triads Generated by Height × Width and
Area × Shape of Rectangles

| Triad Type | Age | Height × Width Classification[a] | Area × Shape Classification[a] |
|---|---|---|---|
| | | Dim | Dim |
| I | 4 | .06 (.053) | .15 (.178) |
| | 6-7 | .04 (.047) | .05 (.055) |
| | 9-10 | .02 (.041) | .02 (.030) |
| | Adult | .10 (.120) | .12 (.145) |
| | | Dim | Dim |
| II | 4 | .10 (.120) | .10 (.142) |
| | 6-7 | .06 (.133) | .04 (.049) |
| | 9-10 | .02 (.042) | .02 (.042) |
| | Adult | .10 (.120) | .12 (.152) |
| | | Dim Only | Dim Only |
| III | 4 | .06 (.080) | .07 (.062) |
| | 6-7 | .05 (.088) | .02 (.032) |
| | 9-10 | .01 (.018) | .01 (.018) |
| | Adult | .05 (.068) | .04 (.071) |

[a]Standard deviations are given in parentheses.

compared with a chance level of responding (.50) were also highly consistent. For both type I and type II triads, the proportions of dimensional classifications were reliably less than chance (all $t > 4.00, p < .01$) at each age level, meaning that all subjects classified by similarity rather than by dimensional relations. Similar conclusions were confirmed by an analysis of Type III triads. No effects due to age or dimension shared were observed, nor was the interaction significant. Comparisons of the proportion of dimensional only classifications with chance (.50) at each age level revealed that these classifications were reliably below chance (all $t's > 10.0, p < .01$), meaning that subjects consistently classified by the dimensional classification that also honored similarity.

## Discussion

The results of Experiment 2 are very clear. Height and width are integral dimensions that combine to produce area and shape, which are also integral. Moreover, there is not a hint of a developmental difference in the perceived structure of these stimuli. In type I triads there is of course the possibility that classification by similarity in one matrix (e.g., height and width) is based on the dimensional relations (e.g., area or shape) of the other. This type of arrangement was presented to determine the strength of dimensional classifications between the two matrices. If, for example, younger subjects were to centrate on width, dimensional classifications would have appeared with height and width, and some of the area and shape triads (those with the same width) would have been classified by similarity. This pattern of response did not appear; in both height × width and area × shape triads subjects classified by similarity. Thus, to argue that subjects used dimensional classifications, it is necessary to assume that the similarity classifications of height and width were made by dimensional relations of area or shape and vice versa. Given the results of Experiment 1, it seems unlikely that younger children are capable of such mental gymnastics and it seems unparsimonious to assume that older children and adults would make such dimensional classifications.

The implausibility of such an argument is also shown by performances of the subject on type II triads. As on type I triads, subjects made classifications of both height × width and area × shape on the basis of similarity relations. Unlike type I triads, however, type II triads were arranged such that classification by similarity in one matrix (e.g., height × width) could not be achieved by a shared dimensional value in the second (e.g., area × shape). Nevertheless, type II triads were classified in a manner identical to classifications of type I triads. Thus, it is reasonable to conclude that both types of triads were classified by overall similarity relations.

Classification of type III triads were in general agreement with those of Experiment 1, with two notable exceptions. First, the proportions of similarity plus dimensional classifications were higher for rectangles than for the dimensional combinations of Experiment 1. This difference would seem to reflect the difficulty of extracting dimensional structure from stimuli like rectangles that are composed of several integral dimensions. Second, there was no tendency for subjects of any age to show dimensional preference. This result differs from that of Experiment I, which showed that many of the 11-year-olds who classify consistently by dimensional relations also show dimensional preferences.

The fact that the dimensions composing rectangles are integral and that the perceived structure of these stimuli is invariant during the course of perceptual development raises some significant issues for theories of perceptual and cognitive development. First, our results illustrate the general importance of identifying the properties of the stimulus prior to making assumptions about the nature of processing or cognitive operations. Garner (1974, 1976) has clearly documented the consequences of failing to take stimulus structure into account in studies of adult information processing. We have shown that such issues are even more pronounced in the context of developmental studies. During the course of development, not only does the nature of processing change, but perceived stimulus structure may change, as in Experiment 1, or remain invariant, as in Experiment 2.

Second, our results speak to previous interpretations on the conservation of quantity and judgment of area. As noted previously, the young child is characterized as centering on just one dimension and as being unable to decenter to take into account other relevant information. These concepts are attentional, and with stimuli like rectangles they cannot apply. With integral dimensions, selective attention is not possible (Garner, 1974); instead, attention is mandatorily distributed.

Observed centration with integral dimensions can, of course, occur. As Lockhead (1972) has observed, integral dimensions can be analyzed into dimensional structure, which means that the subject can respond accurately to one dimension even though the other varies. Thus, in principle, subjects could analyze integral dimensions and respond on the basis of one of them. In situations in which speed of response was not measured, there would be no basis for inferring any effect due to the second dimension and the experimenter could erroneously conclude that such selective responding was the result of selective attention.

It is also possible that observed centration can occur with integral dimensions even though subjects do not extract dimensional structure. Centration is typically inferred when judgments of the subject vary with variations of one physical dimension but not the other. Variations of the physical dimensions change the perceived similarity or distance relations between stimuli when the dimensions are integral, and the similarity relations that are correlated with one of the physical dimensions may provide a more optimal basis for judgment than similarity relations of the other. Under these conditions, judgments will seem to be based on just one dimension, but, in this case, centration is based upon distance relations between the stimuli and not upon dimensional structure.

Generally, then, centration does not appear to be a useful concept. With integral dimensions, such as the rectangles of Experiment 2, selective attention is not a logical possibility and observed centration must be explained in terms other than the young child's inability to decenter. Moreover, the strong centration effects observed for 6-year-olds in Experiment 1 appear to be the result of previous perceptual learning and stimulus factors rather than a general inability to decenter. The latter observation is also supported by the results of Anderson and Cuneo (1978).

The results of Experiment 2 also speak to the question of the coordination or combination of dimensions in producing judgments of area. Anderson and Cuneo (1978) report a developmental difference in the rule by which children combine height and width in making judgments of area. Younger children use an addition, Height + Width rule, whereas older children use a multiplication, Height × Width rule. These rules have been shown to hold for a variety of stimulus sets, and this consistency provides considerable support for information integration theory. Our results with the classification of rectangles, however, indicate that their formulation does not adequately characterize the stimulus structure of rectangles and raises the possibility, at least, that the structure of other stimulus combinations are more complex than they have assumed.

Anderson and Cuneo assume that height and width are psychologically independent, and that the source of development differences in the judgment of area stems from the rule by which the dimensions are combined. Our results that height and width are integral indicate that these dimensions interact. Furthermore, height and width combine to produce rectangles that vary in both area and shape. Thus, our data are in clear conflict with the view of Anderson and Cuneo (1978), and their data, on the other hand, provide a puzzle for our view. Although we cannot reconcile these differences at this point in time, we can raise issues that are critical to a resolution.

From the point of view of Anderson and Cuneo, it is necessary to demonstrate that height and width are independent at some level of cognitive analysis. It is also necessary to show either that differences in shape do not contribute to judgments in their task or that subjects in making judgments of area compensate for differences in shape. In their task, subjects are given an "amount" instruction and it is possible that such an instruction separated area and shape at least at a conceptual level of processing.

From our point of view, the issue is somewhat different. Given our results that the perceived structure of rectangles is invariant with development, we are faced with the question as to why Anderson and Cuneo obtained a developmental difference in the judgment of rectangles. We do not rule out the possibility that both area and shape contributed to the results of Anderson and Cuneo. If both area and shape contributed to their results, then the distance relations between stimuli could be perceived differently at different developmental levels and could result in developmental differences in judgment. Short of performing a classification experiment using rectangles like those of Anderson and Cuneo, there is no way to evaluate this possibility.

There is also another stimulus property that may be present in the rectangles employed by Anderson and Cuneo and that may produce developmental differences in perceived structure. Unlike the rectangles of the present study, they varied height and width symmetrically in 2-cm steps, that is, 7, 9, 11 cm. Thus, the primary diagonal was a series of squares, whereas the secondary diagonal was a series of shapes varying from tall and narrow to short and wide. This arrangement introduces the possibility that judgments could have been affected by the configural properties of stimuli. A 7 × 11 and 11 × 7 rectangles are members of the same rotation and reflection subset. They are identical with a 90° rotation. Such stimulus properties are important in adult perceptual judgments. The data of Anderson and Cuneo are highly suggestive. Their older children judged configurally identical rectangles as equal, and the data of older children conformed to the Height × Width rule. In contrast, younger children judged such rectangles as equal in some experiments but not in others. When configurally identical rectangles were not assigned the same rating, height and width did not interact, but in experiments when such rectangles were judged as equal, the interaction between height and width was reliable. Thus, while the perception of configural properties by young children may vary in the judgment task, such properties cannot be ruled out as contributing to the results in such tasks.

From our point of view, then, the perceived structure of rectangles has not been completely specified, nor have developmental differences in perceived structure been ruled out. We contend, however, that in order to understand the development of logical operations or rules of combination, it is necessary to specify the perceived structure of the stimulus and the developmental differences in perceived structure.

## SUMMARY

The experiments in the present paper have attempted to outline some fundamental principles of perceptual development. In the first experiment we attempted to further elaborate the scope of the separability hypothesis proposed by Shepp and Swartz (1976) and Shepp (1978). According to this view, the wholistic, unitary perception of young children is characterized by the overall similarity structure that is typical of integral dimensions, and that, with increasing perceptual learning, the dimensional relations that characterize separable dimensions may emerge. Experiment 1 showed such a developmental trend for dimensional combinations that are physically separable as well as those that are physically integral. Moreover, Experiment 1 showed that the developmental trend from perceived overall similarity to dimensional relations differs for the two types of dimensional structure.

Although our view has borrowed heavily from Garner's work (1970, 1974), it differs from his conception. Garner has argued that similarity and dimension relations are the properties of physical stimuli; we, on the other hand, are stressing the nature of perceptual representation and the course of its change during development. We argue that all dimensional combinations are initially perceived by overall similarity and that dimensional structure is extracted through perceptual learning. For physically separable dimensions, the process of dimensional extraction becomes increasingly automatic. We assume that a dimensional representation can also occur for physically integral dimensions. These dimensional combinations are initially perceived by overall similarity and only subsequently analyzed by dimensional structure. For some of these dimensions (e.g., color vs. form) the extraction of dimensional relations may become relatively automatic, whereas others (e.g., hue vs. saturation) may be analyzed only at a conceptual level.

In Experiment 2, we examined the proposition that some dimensional combinations are represented by overall similarity relations throughout the course of development. The results of Experiment 2 show that the properties of rectangles lead to classification by overall similarities throughout the course of development. We would argue on the basis of these results that conservation of quantity (Piaget, 1970) or judgment of area (Anderson & Cuneo, 1978, Wilkening, Chapter 2, this volume) is the result of operations initiated at a conceptual level of representation. This view is consistent with contemporary theories that assume that different information is represented at different levels of processing and that attention may be directed at any of these levels (e.g., LaBerge, 1975).

## ACKNOWLEDGMENTS

This research and preparation of this paper were supported by Research Grant HD 04320 from U.S.P.H.S. We are deeply indebted to June L. Shepp for her very able assistance in the conduct of the experiments and preparation of figures for the paper, and to Margaret Furey for her painstaking efforts in typing the manuscript.

We are also greatly indebted to Omer Leclerc, Ron Mayer, and Beverly Tellier of the MacColl Field YMCA Camp Ugoto, and to Richard Garceau and Lizbeth Simpson of the Pawtucket Day Nursery for making their facilities available to us and for their cooperation in facilitating this research.

## REFERENCES

Adams, M. J., & Shepp, B. E. Selective attention and the breadth of learning: A developmental study. *Journal of Experimental Child Psychology,* 1975, *20,* 168–180.

Anderson, N. H., & Butzin, C. A. Integration theory applied to children's judgments of equity. *Developmental Psychology,* 1978, *14,* 593–606.

Anderson, N. H., & Cuneo, D. O. The height + width rule in children's judgments of quantity. *Journal of Experimental Psychology: General,* 1978, *107,* 335–378.

Biederman, I., & Checkosky, S. F. Processing redundant information. *Journal of Experimental Psychology,* 1970, *83,* 486–490.

Bruner, J. S., Olver, R. R., & Greenfield, P. M. *Studies in cognitive growth.* New York: Wiley, 1966.

Burns, B., Shepp, B. E., McDonough, D. & Wiener-Ehrlich, W. K. The relation between stimulus analyzability and perceived dimensional structure. In G. H. Bower (Ed.), *The psychology of learning and motivation* (Vol. 12). New York: Academic Press, 1978.

Doyle, A. Listening to distraction: A developmental study of selection attention. *Journal of Experimental Child Psychology,* 1973, *15,* 100–115.

Eimas, P. D. Multiple-cue discrimination learning in children. *Psychological Record,* 1969, *19,* 417–424.

Elkind, D. Perceptual development in children. *American Scientist,* 1975, *63,* 533–541.

Felfoldy, G. L. Repetition effects in choice reaction time to multidimensional stimuli. *Perception & Psychophysics,* 1974, *15,* 453–459.

Fisher, M. A., & Zeaman, D. An attention-retention theory of retardate discrimination learning. In N. R. Ellis (Ed.),*International review of research in mental retardation* (Vol. 6). New York: Academic Press, 1973.

Garner, W. R. The stimulus in information processing. *American Psychologist,* 1970, *25,* 350–358.

Garner, W. R. *The processing of information and structure.* Potomac, Md.: Lawrence Erlbaum Associates, 1974.

Garner, W. R. Interaction of stimulus dimensions in concept and choice processes. *Cognitive Psychology,* 1976, *8,* 98–123.

Garner, W. R. Aspects of a stimulus: Features, dimensions, and configurations. In E. Rosch & B. Lloyd (Eds.), *The nature and principles of categories.* Hillsdale, N.J.: Lawrence Erlbaum Associates, 1978.

Garner, W. R., & Felfoldy, G. L. Integrality of stimulus dimensions in various types of information processing. *Cognitive Psychology,* 1970, *1,* 225–241.

Gibson, E. J. *Principles of perceptual learning and development.* New York: Appleton-Century-Crofts, 1969.

Gibson, E. J., & Olum, V. Experimental methods for studying perception in children. In P. H. Mussen (Ed.), *Handbook of research methods in child development.* New York: Wiley, 1960.

Ginsburg, H., & Opper, S. *Piaget's theory of intellectual development.* Englewood Cliffs, N.J.: Prentice-Hall, 1969.

Gottwald, R. L., & Garner, W. R. Effects of focusing strategy on speeded classification with grouping, filtering, and condensation tasks. *Perception & Psychophysics,* 1972, *11,* 179–182.

Gottwald, R. L., & Garner, W. R. Filtering and condensation tasks with integral and separable dimensions. *Perception & Psychophysics,* 1975, *18,* 26–28.

Hagen, J. W., & Hale, G. A. The development of attention in children. In A. Pick (Ed.), *Minnesota symposia on child psychology* (Vol. 7). Minneapolis, Minn.: University of Minnesota Press, 1973.

Hale, G. A., and Morgan, J. S. Developmental trends in children's component selection. *Journal of Experimental Child Psychology,* 1973, *15,* 302–314.

Hale, G. A., & Taweel, S. S. Children's component selection with varying degrees of training. *Journal of Experimental Child Psychology,* 1974, *17,* 229–241.

Handel, S., & Imai, S. The free classification of analyzable and unanalyzable stimuli. *Perception & Psychophysics,* 1972, *12,* 108–116.

Hyman, R., & Well, A. Judgments of similarity and spatial models. *Perception & Psychophysics,* 1967, *2,* 233–248.

Hyman, R., & Well, A. Perceptual separability and spatial models. *Perception & Psychophysics,* 1968, *3,* 161–165.

Kemler, D. G., Shepp, B. E., & Foote, K. E. The sources of developmental differences in children's incidental processing during discrimination trials. *Journal of Experimental Child Psychology,* 1976, *21,* 226–240.

King, W. L., & Holt, J. R. Conjunctive and disjunctive rule learning as a function of age and forced verbalization. *Journal of Experimental Child Psychology,* 1970, *10,* 100–111.

Klahr, D., & Wallace, J. G. *Cognitive development: An information-processing view.* Hillsdale, N. J.: Lawrence Erlbaum Associates, 1976.

Krantz, D. H., & Tversky, A. Similarity of rectangles: An analysis of subjective dimensions. *Journal of Mathematical Psychology,* 1975, *12,* 4–34.

LaBerge, D. Perceptual learning and attention. In W. K. Estes (Ed.), *Handbook of Learning and Cognitive Processes* (Vol. 4). Hillsdale, N. J.: Lawrence Erlbaum Associates, 1975.

Levy, R. M., & Haggbloom, S. J.  Test of a multidimensional discrimination model of stimulus identification. *Psychonomic Science,* 1971, *25,* 203–204.

Lockhead, G. R.  Processing dimensional stimuli: A note. *Psychological Review,* 1972, *79,* 410–419.

Maccoby, E. E.  The development of stimulus selection. In J. P. Hill (Ed.), *Minnesota symposia on child psychology* (Vol. 3). Minneapolis, Minn.: University of Minnesota Press, 1969, 68–96.

Miller, S. A.  Developmental investigation of hypotheses in attribute identification. Unpublished doctoral dissertation, University of Colorado, 1971.

Monahan, J. S., & Lockhead, G. R.  Identification of integral stimuli. *Journal of Experimental Psychology: General,* 1977, *106,* 94–110.

Nickerson, R. S.  Binary-classification reaction time: A review of some studies of human information-processing capabilities. *Psychonomic Monograph Supplements,* 1972, *4,* 275–317.

Piaget, J.  Piaget's theory. In P. H. Mussen (Ed.), *Carmichael's manual of child psychology* (Vol. 1). New York: Wiley, 1970, 703–732.

Pick, A. D., & Frankel, G. W.  A study of strategies of visual attention in children. *Developmental Psychology,* 1973, *9,* 348–357.

Rogers, J. C., & Johnson, P. J.  Attribute identification in children as a function of stimulus dimensionality. *Journal of Experimental Child Psychology,* 1973, *15,* 216–221.

Shepard, R. N.  Attention and the metric structure of the stimulus space. *Journal of Mathematical Psychology,* 1964, *1,* 54–87.

Shepp, B. E.  From perceived similarity to dimensional structure: A new hypothesis about perceptual development. In E. Rosch & B. Lloyd (Eds.), *The nature and principles of categories.* Hillsdale, N. J.: Lawrence Erlbaum Associates, 1978.

Shepp, B. E., & Adams, M. J.  Effects of amount of training on type of solution and breadth of learning in optional shifts. *Journal of Experimental Psychology,* 1973, *101,* 63–69.

Shepp, B. E., & Swartz, K. B.  Selective attention and the processing of integral and nonintegral dimensions: A developmental study. *Journal of Experimental Child Psychology,* 1976, *22,* 73–85.

Shepp, B. E., & Turrisi, F. D.  Learning and transfer of mediating responses in discriminative learning. In N. R. Ellis (Ed.), *International review of research in mental retardation* (Vol. 2). New York: Academic Press, 1966.

Smith, L. B.  Levels of experienced dimensionality in children and adults. Unpublished doctoral dissertation, University of Pennsylvania, 1977.

Smith, L. B., Kemler, D. G., & Aronfreed, J.  Developmental trends in voluntary selective attention: Differential effects of source distinctness. *Journal of Experimental Psychology,* 1975, *20,* 352–362.

Smith, L. B., & Kemler, D. G., & Aronfreed, J.  Developmental trends in voluntary selective attention: Differential effects of source distinctness. *Journal of Experimental Psychology,* 1975, *20,* 352–362.

Strutt, G. F., Anderson, D. R., & Well, A. D.  A developmental study of the effects of irrelevant information on speeded classification. *Journal of Experimental Child Psychology,* 1975, *20,* 127–135.

Tighe, T.  Subproblem analysis of discrimination learning. In G. H. Bower (Ed.), *The psychology of learning and motivation* (Vol. 7). New York: Academic Press, 1973.

Tighe, T. J., Glick, J., & Cole, M.  Subproblem analysis of discrimination-shift learning. *Psychonomic Science,* 1971, *24,* 159–160.

Tighe, T. J., & Tighe, L. S.  Stimulus control in children's learning. In A. Pick (Ed.), *Minnesota symposia on child psychology* (Vol. 6). Minneapolis, Minn.: University of Minnesota Press, 1972.

Weintraub, D. J. Rectangle discriminability: Perceptual relativity and the law Pragnanz. *Journal of Experimental Psychology*, 1971, *88*, 1–11.

Wender, K. A test of independence of dimension in multidimensional scaling. *Perception & Psychophysics*, 1971, *10*, 30–32.

Werner, H. *Comparative psychology of mental development* (Revised edition). Chicago: Follett, 1948.

Wilkening, F. Combining of stimulus dimensions in children's and adults' judgments of area: An information integration analysis. *Developmental Psychology*, 1979, *15*, 25–33.

Wohlwill, J. From perception to inference: A dimension of cognitive development. *Monographs of the Society for Research in Child Development*, 1962, *72*, 87–107.

Wolff, J. L. Concept-shift and discrimination-reversal learning in humans. *Psychological Bulletin*, 1967, *68*, 369–408.

# 6 Where Does One Part End and Another Begin? A Developmental Study

Stephen M. Kosslyn
*Harvard University*

Karen H. Heldmeyer
*Vanderbilt University*

Arnold L. Glass
*Rutgers University*

One way to approach questions of cognitive development is to examine a model of adult processing and consider how such a system could have developed. Kosslyn (1978) does just this with the Kosslyn & Shwartz (1977, 1978) model of visual memory. This model posits that one's memory for an object's appearance is usually encoded in multiple representations. One representation is of the global shape or central element, and the rest are details that may be integrated into the global shape, producing a more elaborated representation of the object. The present paper extends the "teleological approach" of Kosslyn (1978) by exploring the principles that dictate how children and adults perceptually "parse" objects into separate units. In these experiments we shall attempt to determine what sorts of stimulus properties serve to delineate part boundaries at different ages. This is an important topic not only from the point of view of the Kosslyn & Shwartz model, but for any theory of how people abstract and integrate visual information.

## The Problem of Centration

In constructing our model, we hypothesized that people first encode a global representation of an object and then encode details about parts of the object. Thus, we postulate that people encode both information about the whole configuration and about particular components of it. This seems to be a reasonable supposition for adults, but can we assume the same for children? Apparently not: Elkind, Koegler, & Go (1964) presented children with a task they call the "Picture Integration Test." This task required children to describe complex pictures, each of which was composed of several small pictures of individual objects that together formed the outline picture of another object. For example, one of the pictures was a face with cherries for eyes, a banana for a mouth, and a pear for a nose. In this study, children rarely named the larger composite figure, but usually named all the component parts. Interestingly, when a child did name a global figure, he or she tended not to name the parts. The child could seemingly see only one thing, one level or the other—but could not see both at the same time. This finding was interpreted in terms of Piaget's ideas about "centration," the tendency for children to attend to only one dimension or stimulus attribute at a time. If this is so, it questions a basic assumption of our model, namely, that a global encoding serves as the "peg" upon which to hang encodings of parts.

Before accepting the notion that children's visual memory may be structured in a qualitatively different way from that of adults, we decided to examine the Elkind et al. (1964) claim. It seemed possible that their results tell us more about the child's understanding of the task than about what the child actually saw. That is, perhaps the child simply interprets the instructions as a request to describe parts; if asked whether anything else is seen, the child may think that the experimenter is asking whether the picture contains any other parts (e.g., fruit). We therefore designed an experiment that would replicate the Elkind et al. (1964) procedure but that would also tap the children's memory of parts and wholes nonverbally. In this experiment, children (mean age 5 years, 9 months; range 4-10 to 6-2) saw composite drawings very much like those used by Elkind et al. (1964). Following this, we showed the child pairs of pictures and asked him or her to pick out which member of the pair he or she had seen in the original set. Half of these pairs included parts of the composites and half had line drawings of the emergent configuration. Finally, after going through all of the pairs, we again repeated the first part, asking the child to describe the contents of the pictures. An example of the sort of stimuli we used is illustrated in Fig. 6.1. At the top is an example of the kind of composite drawing shown initially and underneath it are the memory test pairs, one showing wholes and the other one parts.

The main results of this experiment are illustrated in Fig. 6.2. In the leftmost panel, we see that we replicated the findings of Elkind et al. (1964). As they had reported, we found that children tended to name parts, and even when they did name wholes, they rarely named both. In contrast, adults tended to name both parts and wholes. In the middle panel are the results of the memory trials. Interestingly, children and adults alike remembered both types of information. Although the adults were better overall, they did not have a relative advantage in memory of one type of information over the other. Clearly, children remembered the configural information, thus

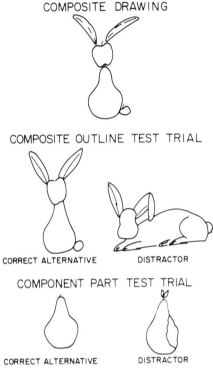

COMPOSITE DRAWING

COMPOSITE OUTLINE TEST TRIAL

CORRECT ALTERNATIVE      DISTRACTOR

COMPONENT PART TEST TRIAL

CORRECT ALTERNATIVE      DISTRACTOR

FIG. 6.1. Examples of stimuli used to examine whether children encode both parts and wholes. At the top is an example of a figure made of nameable parts and beneath that are examples of the forced-choice alternatives used to assess the child's memory for configurations and parts.

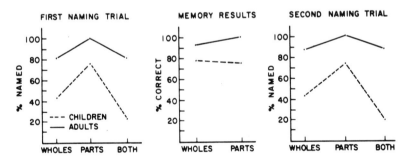

FIG. 6.2. Results of the experiment on perception of parts and wholes. The leftmost and rightmost panels depict the percentage of times a subject mentioned a part, a whole, or both a part and whole (if a subject named both, he was given a point in all three categories; "both" was not an exclusive class). The middle panel depicts the results of the forced-choice memory test.

providing strong evidence that they initially saw it. Further, as can be seen in the rightmost panel, we find that even after seeing the memory trials and correctly choosing the wholes, the children *still* did not name them when presented with the composite pictures again! These results seem to indicate that the results of Elkind et al. (1964) are due to the child's interpretation of the naming task and not due to his or her failure to see both kinds of information.

The results of our study persuaded us that it made sense to suppose that children encoded both configural/global information and information about component parts. Thus, it seemed sensible to go on to study how wholes were parsed at different ages.

## How Are Parts Defined

In the course of perceptual development, children become increasingly sensitive to the various stimulus properties of objects. One way in which they may learn to distinguish between objects is by comparing their relevant parts. That is, parts of objects may come to serve as "distinctive features," as does the oblique line in a "Q," which allows us to distinguish it from an "O". It is not immediately apparent, however, how particular regions come to be perceived as "parts," whereas others do not. After all, the world is not divided up by dotted lines, like a cow diagrammed on a butcher's wall. Psychologists have not yet fully explained how stimulus properties serve to delineate the parts of an object for adults, let alone approached this problem developmentally. If children do not parse objects into parts as do adults, it may be dangerous to formulate theories of concept attainment, semantic development, and perceptual learning based on adults' perceptions and intuitions.

It seems clear that two sorts of processes work to define an object's parts: On the one hand, "bottom-up" processes operate such that certain stimulus properties impose part boundaries. On the other, "top-down" processes should result in one's expectations and preconceptions also imposing an organization of an object into component parts. The present studies represent an attempt to begin to investigate "bottom-up" processes, to begin to explore how various stimulus properties delineate part boundaries at different ages. These experiments are concerned with the effects of changes in the contour, color, and texture of objects in defining parts.

## EXPERIMENT 1

In this experiment we are interested simply in whether children and adults consistently use the same stimulus properties in perceiving the boundaries of parts and in whether these boundaries are ever assigned on bases other than changes in stimulus properties of an object.

## Method

Children and adults viewed a simple L-shaped line drawing that had one segment colored red, one segment striped, and one segment placed at a right angle to the main section. Subjects simply marked with a pencil the perceived boundaries of the component parts of the form.

*Materials.*   A simple outline drawing was constructed in the shape of an "L." The vertical segment was 2 cm wide and 7 cm high. The horizontal segment was 2 cm wide and 22 cm long. Two 5-cm-long patches were placed along the horizontal leg, such that their centers were one-third and two-thirds of the distance from the left end. The left-most patch was colored red, and the right patch was filled with blue diagonal stripes spaced 4 mm apart. The boundaries of these areas were not demarcated by vertical lines, nor did any lines cut across the interior of the figure at any point. The figure itself was outlined in blue, and, except for the red patch, was left blank (white) internally.

*Procedure.*   Subjects were given a copy of the stimulus drawing and told that it was a picture of a roadway built for a model car. This roadway was described as having been built out of scraps of paper. The subject was told that we were interested in where he or she thought the pieces of the roadway joined together. Specifically, we asked the subjects "If a breeze came up and blew apart the road, where do you think it would come apart?" A subject was to indicate his or her assessment simply by drawing a line where he or she thought the parts joined. Following this, the experimenter presented an example. First, two small rectangles were shown, then one rectangle was presented that was as long as the two initial ones placed end to end. If the larger one had been constructed by placing the two smaller ones next to each other, the subject was asked, "Where would they meet?" The experimenter then drew a line vertically down the middle of the larger rectangle and explained that this was how we wanted them to indicate where they thought the pieces of the roadway met. At this point questions were solicited and answered, and subjects were asked to draw where they thought the part boundaries lay in the roadway drawing.

*Subjects.*   Twenty-eight first graders (mean age 6-6; range, 6-2 to 7-1) and 28 Johns Hopkins and Goucher undergraduates were subjects. None of the people in this or any of the other experiments reported herein had gross color vision impairment.

## Results

Because we were interested in discovering which of the possible perceptual cues the subjects used to define the boundaries of parts, we first simply tabulated how many times each subject used the contour change (where the vertical end joined the horizontal segment) and the edges of the color and texture variation as indications of such boundaries. Adults in general used these cues more than did children, $F(1,54) = 4.78, p < .05$. Further, people of both ages tended to use the contour change more than the edges of color and texture change. Children chose available contour, color and texture variations .71, .50, and .55 of the time, respectively; adults selected these cues .86, .73, and .77 of the time. The tendency to select the contour change more often than the others was significant ($p < .01$).

We further analyzed the data by tabulating how many subjects of each age group ever used each of the possible strategies (contour, color or texture change, equal intervals, or idiosyncratic) to delineate parts. Additionally, in this second analysis we also examined how many subjects placed demarcations at equal intervals along the figure and how many used idiosyncratic strategies. In general, more subjects relied on apparent physical properties instead of a non-perceptual strategy to infer where part boundaries would occur, $F(4,216) = 18.47, p < .001$. Interestingly, this was much more the case for adults than for children, as indicated by a significant age by choice-type interaction, $F(4,216) = 6.24, p < .01$. The proportions of people using contour, color, texture, equal spacing, and "other" strategies were .61, .57, .64, .18, and .61 for children, and .79, .79, .79, .18, and .14 for adults. Clearly, children used many more idiosyncratic notions of parsing the "roadway" than did the adults.

## Discussion

Adults, in general, were more constrained in how they parsed the stimulus drawing. They tended to assume continuity unless some physical change in the stimulus indicated otherwise. The children also made wide use of changes in physical dimensions but apparently also more readily assumed that boundaries existed even when no physical evidence was available. However, before we can speculate about how the developing individual becomes more constrained in his or her perception of part boundaries, we first need to get a better notion of what aspects of physical variation are used at different ages. In the present experiment, the perceptual "salience" of the dimensions was not controlled. Perhaps children at first simply pay attention only to striking changes in physical properties of an object. If the contour change were most striking, then, a propensity to rely on it tells us nothing about the importance of that class of stimulus changes per se. Further, the sort of texture variation used in the present experiment is peculiar because one could argue that stripes constitute both a change in texture and a change in color. Finally, the results of the present experiment may, in part, simply reflect children's confusion about the task, as simple as it was. The following experiment was an attempt to examine how different sorts of physical variation index part boundaries and how this function changes over age. This experiment corrected the major deficiencies of Experiment 1 and provided an opportunity to obtain convergent evidence corroborating our earlier findings.

## EXPERIMENT 2

In this experiment we explicitly varied the relative perceptual saliency of the different dimensions. We assessed the relative effectiveness of changes along various dimensions by pitting a change in one dimension against a conflicting change in another. In addition, we now examined five different age groups in order to chart this sort of perceptual growth in more detail.

### Method

People of different ages viewed forms and indicated where they thought the form would best be divided into two pieces. Each form displayed two of the following: A change in color; a change in texture; and/or a perturbation in outer contour. In addition, one dimension was made more perceptually salient than the other. The change in each dimension occurred at a different location on the figure. All possible pairs of dimensions and relative saliency were combined on various forms equally often.

*Materials.* The stimuli were constructed of stiff poster paper and were rectangular with rounded edges; each stimulus was 17.5 cm long and 7 cm wide. Seven different stimuli were constructed. One stimulus was blank whereas the others were constructed so as to include a manipulation of the color, texture, or contour dimensions. If color was included, the figure was colored blue 5.25 cm from one end, and the remainder was colored red. If texture was included, the figure was filled in with "x" patterns in the area up to 5.25 cm from one end, and the remaining area was filled with "o" patterns. If a contour manipulation was included, an indentation in the outer contour occurred 5.25 cm from one end. The change in value of the two dimensions included in a single form occurred at opposite ends of the figure. Further, each dimension was constructed to be the perceptually "dominant" member of the pair in one figure, with dominance being defined by potency of the stimulus property. That is, the color change was defined as nondominant if the blue and red were only lightly colored in or dominant if heavily saturated colors were used. The texture was defined as nondominant if the patterns were drawn lightly or dominant if heavy ink was used. The contour change was defined as nondominant if there was only a 1 cm indentation on each side or dominant if there was a 2 cm indentation. Ratings from an independent group of 10 adults confirmed the experimenters' intuitions as to which dimension was dominant on each form.

*Procedure.* The subjects were first shown a blank form and asked, "If we were going to divide this thing into two pieces, where do you think we should divide it?" The child or adult was handed a small stick and asked to lay it on the place on the shape where we should divide it. The subject was told to divide it any way that she or he thought was best, and that the pieces need not be even. If the child did not understand the instructions, the experimenter elaborated them by asking the child to suppose the form came apart like a puzzle and to indicate where the parts joined, by asking the child where would be a good place to cut it into parts with a pair of scissors and by asking the child to anticipate where it would come apart if the experimenter dropped it. This amplification continued through the use of paraphrasing, etc. until the child indicated unambiguously that he or she clearly understood the instructions.

Following this, the same instructions were repeated prior to presenting the child with the actual test stimuli. The subject was shown the six test stimuli in a random order and the forms were presented in a horizontal orientation. The subject placed a small stick on each form indicating where he or she thought was the most likely boundary between two parts. After all stimuli were presented, they were rotated 180° (out of sight of the subject) and presented a second time in a new random order. Thus, each stimulus was judged twice by each subject.

The subjects were encouraged to divide the forms by placing the stick vertically (perpendicular to the longest axis of the forms) and to divide the forms into only two pieces. If the subject wanted to divide the figure into three parts, he or she first was asked to divide it into only two pieces and then was allowed to divide it further. The trials in which this occurred were recorded and submitted to a further analysis. If a child chose a point that did not mark a locus of dimensional change, he or she was asked for a second choice and then asked to indicate which of the two boundaries were preferred.

*Subjects.* The 64 children (16 each from nursery school and grades 1, 3, and 6) were all students at the same racially-mixed, predominantly middle-class private school. There were 6 male and 10 female nursery school children (mean age 4–4; range 4–1 to 4–9), 10 male and 6 female first-graders (mean age 6–7; range 6–0 to 7–6), 7 male and 9 female third-graders (mean age 8–8; range 8–0 to 9–8), and 9 male and 7 female sixth-graders (mean age 11–8; range 11–0 to 12–4).

In addition, 16 Johns Hopkins University students (8 male, 8 female) volunteered to participate as subjects.

## Results

We first tabulated the number of times each subject chose the dominant dimension when it was paired with each of the other dimensions and then considered these data in an analysis of variance. In general, subjects chose the change in the dominant dimension as the most likely place at which two parts of the object may have joined. This was much more the case for older subjects, however, $F(4,75) = 5.42$, $p < .01$. In general, more choices were made for contour when it was dominant than was the case for color or texture, $F(2,150) = 12.96$, $p < .01$. In fact, when contour was included as the non-dominant alternative, there was a tendency for the dominant dimension to be chosen less often than when color or texture was the nondominant dimension $F(3,225) = 2.49$, $.05 < p < .1$. The number of choices for contour when it was dominant changed little over age, whereas color became more important, and the effectiveness of texture improved even more markedly. These results were evident in a significant interaction between age and choice type, $F(8,225) = 2.49$, $p < .01$. These results are evident in Table 6.1.

We also examined the total number of times each dimension was chosen, independent of its dominance, and also included in this analysis the choices that were not based on changes in any dimension. Again, each subject's choices were tabulated and an analysis of variance performed on the data. In general, contour was preferred over other dimensions, $F(3,225) = 25.46$, $p < .001$. As before, preference for texture notably improved over age whereas—again, as in Experiment 1—preference for marking boundaries at which no stimulus properties change decreased over age, $F(2,225) = 3.27$, $p < .01$. These data are presented in Table 6.2.

Finally, we performed an analysis to determine whether or not our subjects were consistent in their choices. Because each object occurred twice, we simply assessed how often each subject made the same choice on both trials using the same stimulus object. If the subject was consistent, we scored the pair a "1," if not, we assigned it "0." These data then were considered in an analysis of variance. The nursery school children were consistent 45% of the time, whereas the first-, third-, sixth-graders and adults were consistent 80, 77, 77, and 77% of the time, respectively. Although this difference was significant, $F(4,75) = 6.57$, $p < .01$, it should be noted that even the subjects in the youngest age group clearly were not simply responding at random, which would have been indicated by 0% consistency. One of the reasons the youngest children appear relatively inconsistent may be that they often use strategies not tied to changes in the physical dimensions we examined. For example, choosing the left side on both trials would have resulted in two

TABLE 6.1

Mean Number of Choices for Each Type of Dominant Dimension over Each Type of Nondominant Dimension (out of two possible)

| Dominant Dimension | Nondominant Dimension | | |
|---|---|---|---|
| | Contour | Color | Texture |
| Contour | | | |
| Grade: Nursery Children[a] | — | 1.250 | 1.500 |
| 1st Graders | — | 1.750 | 1.750 |
| 3rd Graders | — | 1.312 | 1.375 |
| 6th Graders | — | 1.250 | 1.000 |
| College | — | 1.312 | 1.438 |
| Color | | | |
| Grade: Nursery Children | .562 | — | .937 |
| 1st Graders | .375 | — | 1.250 |
| 3rd Graders | .875 | — | 1.500 |
| 6th Graders | 1.250 | — | .937 |
| College | 1.125 | — | 1.438 |
| Texture | | | |
| Grade: Nursery Children | .312 | .625 | — |
| 1st Graders | .500 | .875 | — |
| 3rd Graders | .562 | .562 | — |
| 6th Graders | 1.125 | 1.000 | — |
| College | 1.250 | 1.500 | — |

[a]See text for the ages of children in each grade.

TABLE 6.2

Mean Number of Choices for Each Age for Each Dimension Irrespective of Dominance (out of 12 possible)

| Grade | Choice Determinant | | | |
|---|---|---|---|---|
| | Contour | Color | Texture | Other |
| Nursery[a] | 4.75 | 2.69 | 1.50 | 3.06 |
| 1st | 6.62 | 2.12 | 1.69 | 1.56 |
| 3rd | 4.81 | 3.94 | 2.00 | 1.25 |
| 6th | 4.06 | 3.25 | 4.19 | .50 |
| College | 4.31 | 3.50 | 3.69 | .50 |

[a]See text for ages of subjects in each grade.

different choices according to our scoring method, even though the same strategy—"smaller parts occur on the left"—was used consistently. Interestingly, the nature of the dominant dimension and of the nondominant alternatives had no effects on consistency (all effects and interactions $p > .1$).

## Discussion

As in the first experiment, we found age changes in how parts seem to be defined. While contour dictated part boundaries for all ages, color and texture changes become potent indicators only with increasing age. Furthermore, although the more dominant dimension generally tended to override the less dominant one, this was not true for the younger ages if contour was the less dominant dimension. This result probably says something about age changes in what is "salient" (see Odom & Cunningham, this volume).

One could argue that the methods used in the two previous experiments have problems of interpretation. This sort of conscious assessment may bring into play strategies and processes that do not operate when we view an object without trying to ascertain its component parts. The next experiment used a different method in order to circumvent these possible problems.

## EXPERIMENT 3

In this experiment, we attempted to show that the stimulus properties that seemed to dictate the perception of part boundaries in the earlier experiments also dictate what portions of a figure are encoded into memory as a unit. In addition, we also varied relative dominance of color and texture without pitting the dimensions against each other. Thus, in this experiment we asked our subjects to try to remember a series of figures, each of which was divided into parts, as dictated by changes in color, texture, or contour. After each figure was presented, we then showed the subject a pair of parts, one of which was in fact a component of the figure just seen. The subject was asked to indicate which of the two was taken from the previous figure.

## Method

The eight test stimuli, illustrated in the top line of Fig. 6.3, were simple, enclosed shapes; a contour change divided the figures into two lobes, or parts. Within each half of each figure, another part was demarcated by a color change or a texture (i.e., a region of "x's" or "o's") change. For half of the subjects, the leftmost or top part was defined by coloring it in red, and the right or bottom part was filled in with a pattern of "o's." For the other subjects, the parts were defined by the other stimulus property. Thus, the

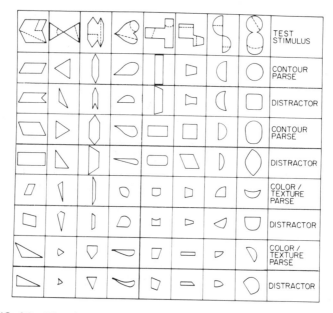

FIG. 6.3. The stimuli used in Experiment 3. The top row depicts the test
stimuli. The dotted lines demarcate the regions that were different colors or
textures. Beneath each test stimulus are the various parses and distractors
(directly beneath the correct part) used in the forced choice recognition test.

same part could be defined either by color or texture patterning. Within each
of these groups, the relative perceptual saliency of both color and texture was
completely counterbalanced for each stimulus over subjects. The relative
saliency was varied by the saturation of the color and the thickness of the
pattern. In addition, all possible combinations of stimulus, part type, and
saliency were counterbalanced completely within each age group.

The test stimuli were drawn on sheets of paper 21.6 × 27.9 cm, which were
protected by plastic covers and mounted into booklets. Each booklet
contained all eight stimuli, with the order of presentation, part type, and
salience of parts counterbalanced between booklets. Within a booklet, each
test stimulus was preceded by a blank dividing page and followed by another
divider sheet. Following this, four pages containing pairs of parts were
presented. Each of these pairs contained one of the parts of the test stimulus,
in its original color and orientation. Next to each bona fide part was a similar
distractor (also illustrated in Fig. 6.3). The correct parts and their distractors
were rated as equally complex by 12 Johns Hopkins University
undergraduates. The order of the part types and the position of the correct
alternative were counterbalanced both within each individual booklet and
over subjects.

*Procedure.* Subjects were presented first with a practice stimulus booklet. They were told that each picture contained several different parts and were asked to point these parts out. If they were not able to do so, the experimenter asked them, "If this were a puzzle, where would the parts be?" If the subject did not identify all the parts, he or she was asked to show the experimenter another kind of part, and—if necessary—the experimenter helped in locating the other parts.

After it was clear that the subject understood what constituted a part, the subject was told to remember all of the parts of an object. The children were then given 8 sec to study each picture. The adults were only given 3 sec, however, as they tended to make no errors at all with the longer exposure. The page of the booklet was then turned to the first pair of parts and the subject was told to mark under the part that was taken from the figure just seen. After all four of the practice pairs had been marked, and any questions answered, the test booklet was introduced. The same procedure was repeated with the booklet until all 8 figures had been seen and all 32 pairs had been marked.

*Subjects.* The children were 16 kindergarten students (11 male and 5 female) from a multiracial private school. They ranged from 4-4 to 6-0 years, with a mean age of 5-5 years. The 16 adults (6 male and 10 female) were Johns Hopkins undergraduate volunteers.

## Results

We calculated the percentage of errors in each of the conditions two ways: for each condition for each subject and for each condition for each item. Thus, we performed two analyses of variance, one testing for significance over subject error and one testing over item error. The type of boundary change affected part encoding over subjects, $F(2,56) = 10.0$, $p < .01$, and over items, $F(2,14) = 4.84$, $p < .05$. Parts defined by contour changes were most effectively encoded, with an error rate of 21%, followed by parts defined by color changes and then those defined by texture changes, which had error rates of 30% and 34%, respectively. The patterns of the children's errors mirrored that of the overall means, 27% for contour-defined parts, 34% for color-defined parts, and 45% for texture-defined parts. The adults' errors, in contrast, followed a slightly different pattern: 15% for contour-defined parts, 25% for color-defined, and 22% for texture-defined parts. This interaction of age by part definition type was significant, $F(2,56) = 3.19$, $p < .05$, for subjects, but due to the small number of items, it was only marginally significant over items ($p < .10$). In addition, even though they studied the parts for a shorter period of time, adults still performed better than did children, 21% errors vs. 35%, $F(1,28) = 15.92$, $p < .01$, for subjects, $F(1,7) = 9.51$, $p < .05$, for items. The relative saliency of the color and texture did not significantly affect either the adults or the children ($p > .10$), although there was a trend in the expected direction.

## Discussion

Once again, contour was the overriding factor in determining which parts were encoded. Increasing the saliency of the part-defining stimulus dimension did not significantly affect the performance of either children or adults. This may be because the dominant and the nondominant dimensions did not differ sufficiently from one another. Also, in this experiment we did not vary the saliency of contour, the most effective determinant of how parts were defined.

An interesting finding in this study is that whereas children again performed better with colored parts than with those defined by texture, the adults showed the opposite trend (although the absolute difference between error rates for adults was small). In discussing the experiment with the adults afterwards, several of them mentioned that they knew that the texture-defined parts would be more difficult to remember, and hence allotted more time and effort towards encoding them. This suggested that age-related changes in parsing could be due in part to the effects of how one chooses to organize a stimulus.

## EXPERIMENT 4

The previous experiments converged in demonstrating that contour changes serve to delineate parts at a very early age, but that color and texture variations begin to play this role only later, with increased age. The contour changes we studied, however, have been those in the outer shape of a figure. Our treatment of contour up until now may have been too gross to expose any differences in the way in which the contour itself may serve to delineate or organize parts over age. This experiment investigated another way in which contour may define parts, in terms of the organization of segments of a contour. The Gestalt Laws of perception describe how line segments and the like are organized into units. We wished to study whether such Gestalt principles dictated organization of line drawings into parts in the same way for children and adults.

The materials used here were adapted from a recent study by Bower and Glass (1976). Bower and Glass formalized the Gestalt principles of "good continuity" and "proximity" (see Wertheimer, 1938) and used their set of rules to parse a set of patterns into good structural units. In their first experiment, they found that such a structural unit was about five times as effective as a recall cue for the entire original pattern than a part of the pattern that, although equal in area to the "structually good" unit, was not organized according to the Gestalt principles mentioned. In their second experiment, they found that two patterns containing the same structural units were more confusable in a recognition task than two patterns containing different structural units.

In the following experiment we modified the materials of Bower and Glass for use in a recognition task. First, adults and children were shown a set of study patterns. They were then shown a pair of test patterns, and were asked to choose which of the two had been a part of a study pattern. All the study patterns and test parts were taken from the first experiment of Bower and Glass. There were two kinds of parts used. The "good parts" corresponded to the good recall cues of Bower and Glass; that is, they corresponded to the a priori defined structural units of the study patterns. The "bad parts" corresponded to the bad cues of Bower and Glass; that is, they did not correspond to any structural units of the study patterns. If the Gestalt laws really do reflect innate tendencies, then both adults and children should recognize significantly more of the parts organized according to the principles of good continuity and proximity than patterns not so organized. Furthermore, if the Gestalt rules operate to the same extent in children and adults, then the relative advantage in recognizing good parts over bad ought to be about the same over age.

Two study patterns, along with their good and bad parts and distractors, are shown in Fig. 6.4. The study pattern in the top row of Fig. 6.4 contains the structural units (ABCD), (EFGH), (JK), and (MN) while the good part for it contains the units (ABCD) and (JK). Similarly, the study pattern in the bottom row of Fig. 6.4 is parsed into four vertical lines cut by a diagonal and its good part is parsed into two vertical lines cut by a diagonal. Bad parts, on the other hand, are misleading because the parsing rules assign to them structural units that do not correspond in any way to the units of the original pattern. For example, the two jagged lines in the bad part in the top row of Fig. 6.4 each comprise a structural unit that does not exist in the study pattern. Similarly, in the bottom row of Fig. 6.4, the diagonal segment and the vertical segments that are members of a single structural unit in the bad part belong to different structural units in the study pattern. A detailed description of how the patterns are parsed into structural descriptions is given in Bower and Glass (1976).

Also shown in Fig. 6.4 are the distractors presented with each part. Initially, three distractors were constructed for each part. Thirty-six Johns Hopkins students rated the distractors (on a standard 7-point scale) in terms of how similar they were to the corresponding "good" or "bad" part. Every good part and the distractor paired with it in the experiment were rated on the average to be slightly more similar to each other than was the case for the bad parts and their distractors. This procedure ensured that any advantage in recognizing good parts could not be attributed to how easily the distractor was rejected.

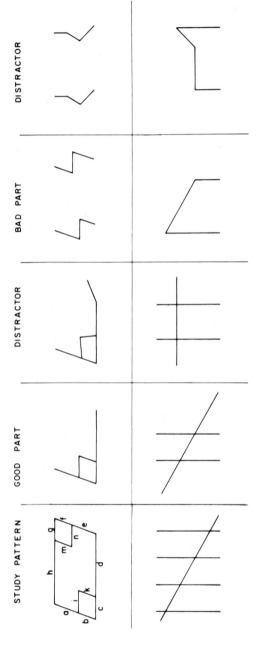

FIG. 6.4. Examples of the stimuli used in Experiments 4 and 5. The figures on the left are examples of the patterns the subjects originally saw (without the letters, in the top row), and the figures to the right of this are the corresponding "good" and "bad" pairs used in the forced-choice recognition task.

162

## Method

*Materials.*   The 12 original study patterns, the good and bad parts and the distractors, were originally drawn with a black felt tip pen on white cardboard 23 × 30 cm. A tracing procedure was used so that each part appeared exactly the same as in the original pattern. Then, all drawings were transferred to dittos and reproduced as blue lines on white paper. The twelve study patterns were randomly ordered and bound together in a booklet. Immediately in front of each pattern was a blank page, which prevented a subject from seeing through one drawing to the one following it. The parts and distractors were mounted in a second booklet such that a part and its distractor were on opposite pages, facing each other. Half of the good and bad parts appeared on the left, and half appeared on the right. Half of the good parts appeared before the bad part for the same study pattern and half the good parts appeared after the corresponding bad part. The parts were collated in approximately the same order as the study patterns, except for the fact that parts of adjacent study patterns were interleafed so that both parts of the same pattern never appeared successively in the test booklet.

*Procedure.*   Subjects were tested in small groups. They were told that they soon would see some drawings and should try to remember what they looked like. The experimenter would tell them when to look at a new drawing, and they would wait until told before turning the page. Following this, subjects viewed each drawing for about 5 sec. Prompts to turn the page were given every 7 sec for the children and every 6 sec for adults. The additional time given children was deemed necessary, as they tended to turn the pages more slowly. Even this time is only a rough indicator of viewing time, however, as the children frequently fell out of synch and had to be corrected by the experimenters.

After all study patterns had been viewed, subjects returned the study booklets. The test booklets were then distributed. The subjects were asked not to open these booklets until told to do so. Subjects were then informed that the booklets contained parts of pictures, and that two parts could be seen at the same time on pages that faced each other. For every pair, only one of the two parts actually was taken from a picture that they had just seen. They were told to indicate which one was from a picture by making an "x" under that part. If a subject was not sure, he or she was to guess. Following this, an example was given. First, a pattern not included in the twelve seen previously was shown. Then, a pair of test patterns consisting of a good part of the pattern just shown and a distractor were presented. The subjects were asked which of the two parts was taken from the picture just shown. The study pattern was exposed again and the location of the good part was marked. Next, a second pair of test patterns consisting of a bad part and distractor for the study pattern was shown, and the procedure was repeated. Questions were solicited and misconceptions were corrected. At the conclusion of the instructions and example, everyone seemed to understand the task. Subjects then were told to examine the pairs in the booklet before them, marking which page contained the correct test pattern. This task was self-paced, but subjects were not allowed to view a pair a second time.

*Subjects.*   Eleven children (ages 6-0 to 7-4, mean 6-4), 5 boys and 6 girls, were tested. These children attended a racially mixed, predominantly middle/upper-middle class elementary school. The adult subjects, 2 males and 9 females, attended Johns Hopkins University or Goucher College.

## Results

As before, correct choices were scored as 1 and incorrect choices as 0. These data were then considered in two analyses of variance, one considering generality over subjects and one considering generality over items.

Adults recognized 85% of the good parts and 67% of the bad parts, while children recognized 67% of the good parts and 48% of the bad parts. Hence, both adults and children recognized good parts more often than bad parts for subjects, $F(1,20) = 27.17$, $p < .001$ and for items, $F(1,11) = 14.27$, $p < .01$. In addition, the adults' performance was generally superior to the children's for subjects, $F(1,20) = 18.88$, $p < .001$ and for items, $F(1,11) = 27$, $p < .01$. The advantage of good parts over bad was about the same over age, as indicated by the fact that there was not a significant interaction between age and part-type, $F < 1$, for both analyses.

## Discussion

Although adults recognized more parts than did the children, the effects of part type were the same for both ages. This result seems to indicate that line segments are organized into units in about the same way in 6-year-olds as in adults. These results suggest that much of the development in perceptual parsing between these ages involves the effects of color, texture and other variables.

In the next experiment, we wished to study the development of a nonstructural variable in dictating the organization of segments into parts. On the basis of our previous results, we expected that an organization dictated by contour would override one dictated by color—even if color were perceptually dominant—for children, but not for adults.

## EXPERIMENT 5

In this study, new groups of adults and children were presented with the same study patterns used in the previous experiment. But at this time, the segments of the patterns corresponding to bad parts were colored dark blue, while the remainder of the pattern was colored a very light red. All of the pairs of test patterns used in later testing were also colored blue. We expected the Gestalt principle of similarity to induce adults to encode the parts of the study pattern that were the same color as members of the same structural units. If a bad part (as defined by continuity of form and proximity) is encoded separately as a unit when the study pattern is initially presented, recognition of parts ought to improve greatly relative to performance in Experiment 4. For example, if in the top row of Fig. 6.4 the fact that (AJK) and (MNE) are colored differently induces an adult to encode them as structural units, then recognition of the bad part of the study pattern should improve. Conversely, the new organization induced by the color similarity should debilitate recognition of the good parts, because their structural units will no longer correspond to those of the study pattern. For example, if (AJK) is a structural unit, then (ABCD) cannot be a structural unit, and thus, the structural units of the "good" part no longer correspond to those of the study pattern itself.

In contrast to the expected performance of the adults, we did not expect the color variation to affect the children's performance. The results of our first three experiments were that color is less effective than form in defining parts for young children. If an organization dictated by the form of the drawing conflicts with one dictated by common coloring, we expected children to attend to form over color. Thus, it seemed unlikely that the principle of similarity would operate to induce children to organize the patterns in terms of the homogeneously colored areas. Therefore, we did not expect the children to recognize the bad parts more often than in the previous experiment, in which color variations were not presented. Similarly, we expected children, again in contrast to adults, to recognize the good parts in the test phase as frequently as in Experiment 4, even though a good part now contained segments that were initially colored differently.

### Method

*Materials.* Study booklets were used that were identical to those in Experiment 4 in all respects other than the fact that the portions corresponding to bad parts were dark blue and the remainder was light red in color. The same test booklets used in Experiment 4, containing pairs that included a correct part and a distractor, both in blue ink, were also used here.

*Procedure.* The procedure was identical to that of Experiment 4.

*Subjects.*   Eleven children were drawn from the same population as those of Experiment 4. The adult subjects, 4 males and 7 females, also were from the same population as those of Experiment 4. None of the subjects who participated in the experiment, however, took part in Experiment 5.

## Results

Data were analyzed as in Experiment 4. Adults now recognized 70% of the good parts and 74% of the bad parts; children, in contrast, recognized 64% of the good parts but only 55% of the bad parts. These effects of part type were reliably different for the different ages when tested over subject error variance, as documented by a significant interaction between part type and age, $F(1,20) = 4.56$, $p < .05$. When item variance was included in error term, however, this interaction was not significant, $F < 1$. In addition, adults generally recognized more parts correctly than did the children, $F(1,20) = 5.08$, $p < .05$ over subjects and $F(1,11) = 7.12$, $p < .05$ over items.

In order to examine more fully the interaction between part type and age, data from Experiments 4 and 5 were combined and analyzed separately for each age. For the adults, the effects of part type were reliably different in the two experiments. Relative to Experiment 4, recognition of bad parts improved here, but recognition of good parts suffered, $F(1,20) = 12.36$, $p < .01$ over subjects and $F(1,11) = 6.11$, $p < .05$ over items. For the children, in contrast, the effects of part type were the same in the two experiments: for the interaction of part type and experiments, $F(1,20) = 1.99$, $p > .1$ over subjects and $F(1,11) = 2.96$, $p > .1$ over items. No other differences between the two experiments were evident in these analyses. Finally, an analysis of all the data together was performed. This analysis lacked the power to detect the age differences noted above; however, the interaction between part-type, age, and experiment failed to reach an acceptable level of significance, $F(1,40) = 1.52$, $p > .1$ over subjects and $F(1,11) = 1.17$, $p > .1$ over items.

The children's apparent failure to make use of color information could have been a consequence of their not encoding it initially. Alternatively, they may have encoded the color variation but simply not made use of it in organizing the drawings. After they had performed the task, the children in this experiment were asked which colors had been used in the drawings; all of these subjects noticed that both red and blue had been used. Thus, the children would appear to have encoded the color information, but not made use of it in organizing the stimulus patterns.

## Discussion

As expected, then, for adults the principle of (color) similarity played a significant role and they often encoded together the configurations of lines that were the same color. This occurred even though the commonly colored portions of patterns were defined as bad parts by other Gestalt principles of structural organization, by the structural variables that had proved so potent in Experiment 4, but only when we examined the data from the adults. When we considered the data from the children, in contrast, there were no differences between the results of Experiments 4 and 5. Although both subject and item analyses were consistent in these comparisons, they were not consistent when we considered the interaction of part type and age. Although the standard $F$ test (including subject error variance) indicated that part type had reliably different effects for the two ages, the analysis including item error variance did not. Apparently, color interacted with the structural variables differently for different stimuli.

## GENERAL DISCUSSION

At all ages, parts were delineated by changes in the stimulus properties of objects, although the types of such changes that were used to define boundaries increased with age. We consistently found that contour changes in the outer fringe of a figure, or the structural organization of line segments composing it, dictated which portions constituted parts for very young children. In contrast to older children and adults, young children were less likely to organize figures in accordance with constancy of texture or color in some region. Furthermore, while older people's units were defined by variations in the most perceptually salient dimension, young children persisted in parsing according to structural changes.

One reason children may not use color information in tasks like ours is because the color of an object is not consistently correlated with other features of an object. That is, as Rosch, Mervis, Gray, Johnson, and Boyes-Braem (1976) suggest, most features may group into highly correlated clusters (e.g., the shapes defining wings, feathers, and beaks often occur together). Color, in contrast, may not often cluster with other features, and thus would be a poor index of the likelihood of other given features being present. This same low correlation may also be true of texture changes, although to a lesser degree. Furthermore, colors and textures often change arbitrarily (e.g., as with clothing) and in many instances may be irrelevant for pattern identification. Hence, it often may not behoove the learning child to pay too much attention to these dimensions.

In closing, it may be worthwhile to return to the distinction between "bottom-up" and "top-down" parsing. We have shown that although there are differences over age in the effectiveness of different stimulus dimensions in delineating part boundaries, the changes appear to be gradual and not qualitative. Thus, a model of perceptual development could posit that the same sorts of rules are used in performing bottom-up processing at different ages, with development proceeding largely by changing weighting functions for different rules at different ages. But what about "top-down" parsing? In Experiment 3 we seemed to find age differences that were easily explained by reference to increased top-down, intentional-strategic processing by older subjects. These types of strategies, however, are not unique to adults. In Experiments 1 and 2 we also found children using strategies that did not utilize the physical properties of the stimulus object. The general process—perception being influenced by more "conceptual" factors—seems similar at all ages. The major changes over age in such "top-down" perceptual processing may be in the types of strategies that are used and not in the fact of strategy use per se.

In conclusion, our findings suggest that a model like that of Kosslyn and Shwartz (1977, 1978) may not require qualitatively different procedures to model perceptual parsing at different ages. This sort of model seems consistent with our findings thus far, but is obviously in need of further development before any real tests of specific assumptions can be made.

## ACKNOWLEDGMENTS

We would like to thank Jan Berie, Eileen Locklear, Janet Michaliszyn, and Gusty Taler for their assistance in collecting the data reported herein. This research was supported by NSF grants BNS 76-16987 and BNS 77-21782, awarded to the first author.

## REFERENCES

Bower, G. H., & Glass, A. L. Structural units and the redintegrative power of picture fragments. *Journal of Experimental Psychology: Human Learning and Memory,* 1976, *2,* 456–466.

Elkind, D., Koegler, R. R., & Go, G. Studies in perceptual development II: part-whole perception. *Child Development,* 1964, *35,* 81–90.

Kosslyn, S. M. Imagery and cognitive development: a teleological approach. In R. Siegler (Ed.), *Children's thinking: What develops?* Hillsdale, N.J.: Lawrence Erlbaum Associates, 1978.

Kosslyn, S. M., & Shwartz, S. P. A simulation of visual imagery. *Cognitive Science,* 1977, *1,* 265–295.

Kosslyn, S. M., & Shwartz, S. P. Visual images as spatial representations in active memory. In A. R. Hanson & E. M. Riseman (Eds.), *Computer vision systems.* New York: Academic Press, 1978.

Rosch, E., Mervis, C. B., Gray, W. D., Johnson, D. M., & Boyes-Braem, P. Basic objects in natural categories. *Cognitive Psychology,* 1976, *8,* 382–439.

Wertheimer, M. Laws of organization in perceptual forms. In W. D. Ellis (Ed.), *A source book of gestalt psychology.* New York: The Humanities Press, 1938.

# 7
# Integrating and Disintegrating Information: The Role of Perception and Conception in the Development of Problem Solving

Richard D. Odom
Joseph G. Cunningham
*Vanderbilt University*

A large body of research in developmental psychology is devoted to the topic of problem solving. The general purpose of this research has been to identify the kinds of psychological processes reflected by goal-directed performance in different types of problems and to determine whether these processes change or remain similar with development. Problem-solving tasks in both familiar and unfamiliar contexts typically contain information that may be described as multirelational. To solve any particular problem, the use of either one or several of these relational sources of information may be necessary. For some problems, it may be necessary to integrate, combine, or coordinate several sources of information. Others may require the disintegration, decomposition, or analysis of information so that a single relational source may be used for solution. Therefore, depending on which of the available relations are (is) relevant for problem solution, it may be necessary to integrate several relations or to analyze for one among many.

Research designed to investigate the development of the integration process has, in one way or another, been linked to Piagetian theory. From their work with matrix problems, Inhelder and Piaget (1964) viewed the young child's evaluation of multirelational information as limited by preoperational thought, which is characterized by centration on single relations and an inability to integrate or coordinate information. These investigators proposed that only with the emergence of concrete operational thought around 7 or 8 years of age was integration likely to manifest itself in the accurate choice of the missing cell that completed a matrix problem. From this perspective, the development of evaluative or conceptual processes would proceed from an initial analysis of only single relations to the later integration and combination of several. Therefore, subjects at both younger and older developmental levels might be expected to solve unirelational problems in which there is only one relevant relation, but only older subjects would be expected to solve multirelational problems, such as the matrix task.

Much of the developmental research devoted to the study of the analysis of information is represented by work in the field of selective attention. One view of the development of this process is summarized in Hagen and Hale's (1973) review of some of the research using incidental learning tasks. From this work, these authors concluded that young children are less capable than older children of analyzing or selectively attending to only the relevant information in a problem. Hagen and Hale proposed that the conceptual ability to attend selectively and analyze sources of information becomes more proficient with development. From this account, the development of evaluative and conceptual processes would proceed from an initial integration of relations to a later analysis of each. Therefore, subjects at all developmental levels might be expected to evaluate multirelational sources of information in problems requiring the integration and combination of those sources, but only older subjects would be expected to solve unirelational problems.

Because separate research paradigms have been used to study the development of integration and analysis processes, the development of each in relation to the other has not been considered. As a result, seemingly incompatible accounts of change in conceptual development have been proposed. This may be, in part, the result of each account's common ties to a general conceptual-change perspective. From such a perspective, age-related improvement in problem solving is considered to be a function of qualitative or quantitative changes in conceptual processes that function in a general sense to evaluate information. Thus, when the performance of older children was found to be more accurate than that of younger children in an analysis or selective attention problem (Hagen & Hale, 1973), the younger children were said to be conceptually less able to analyze and attend to only the relevant information than the older children. However, when similar age related improvement in performance was associated with the matrix problem (Inhelder & Piaget, 1964), the younger children were said to be analyzing and centering on only one relation, and therefore they were unable to integrate as the older children could. The incompatibility of these accounts lies in the fact that the deficiency attributed to the younger child in each account is viewed as the achievement of the older child in the other account.

Within a conceptual-change position, little or no consideration is given to the development of perceptual processes nor to how the perceptual characteristics of the information in a problem may change with development. An inherent assumption of conceptual-change accounts seems to be that children at different developmental levels perceive, and subsequently evaluate through conceptual processes, the same relations from a given set of information. But are all sources of information equally likely to be conceptually evaluated at all developmental levels? There is now substantial evidence indicating that they are not.

In an alternative view of the development of problem solving, Odom and Guzman (1972) have emphasized the role of the perceptual system. In part, this view derives from certain of the ideas about perception and perceptual development that have been advanced by the Gibsons (1966, 1969). These ideas are (1) that information is represented in the structure of the stimulus as relations, (2) that such relations are directly perceived with no dependence on their enhancement or elaboration through conceptual processes, and (3) that with development, the perceptual system discovers an increasing number of relations that are available in the environment.

In addition to these ideas, Odom and Guzman proposed that the increasing perceptual experience that comes with development serves to increase the sensitivity of the perceptual system to relations that have already been discovered. Furthermore, it has been shown that perceptual sensitivity, as measured by traditional salience tasks, determines the likelihood that relations will be conceptually evaluated. In a number of different problem-solving situations, information that is highly salient has been shown to have a greater likelihood of being conceptually evaluated than information that is less salient, regardless of its relevance for problem solution.

From this position it is assumed that more relations are discovered perceptually and become more salient as the child has increasing experience with them. Because this is likely to occur during the course of development, the greater accuracy typically shown by older subjects in solving problems may be due to an increasing number of relations becoming more perceptually salient and consequently increasing the probability of their conceptual evaluation. It would be expected, therefore, that subjects at any developmental level would be more likely to demonstrate the conceptual ability to solve problems requiring the integration or analysis of information when the relevant information is sufficiently salient.

The role of perceptual salience in the development of integration and disintegration processes has been investigated within the separate research paradigms noted earlier, that is, matrix and incidental learning tasks. In studies that utilized incidental learning tasks to investigate the disintegration or analysis of information, the salience of the relevant and incidental relations was found to be positively related to recall of values of both relations for younger and older children alike (Odom, 1972; Odom, Cunningham, & Astor-Stetson, 1977; Odom & Lemond, 1975). Younger children clearly demonstrated evidence of analysis and disintegration processes when the relation relevant for solution was high in salience. Furthermore, there was no evidence in these studies to suggest that older children are more proficient at analyzing or selectively attending to only relevant information. In each of these three studies, older children recalled more irrelevant information than younger children.

There is also evidence from salience research of the ability of young children to solve problems requiring the integration of relations. Odom, Astor, and Cunningham (1975) demonstrated that children as young as 4 and 6 years of age could successfully coordinate and integrate values representing two highly salient relations to solve matrix problems. In another type of integration task, Odom and Corbin (1973) found that 6-year-old children were able to solve problems requiring the recall of the array location of compounds that were comprised of values from two highly salient relations. The evidence from salience research, therefore, seems contrary to what one would predict from the conceptual-change accounts.

Because previous studies have been limited to the investigation of either integration or analysis in any given task, comparisons of the relative rate of development for each process have been impossible to make. This is the case, because performance differences that may have occurred as a function of differences in the quantity, type, or structure of the information comprising each task cannot be differentiated from those that may have occurred as a function of the types of conceptual process required for the solution of each task. For example, if the abilities of children to analyze and integrate were to be compared using incidental learning and matrix tasks, any obtained performance differences could not be clearly attributed to differences in conceptual processes, because the tasks also differ in the type and structure of the information they contain. Therefore, in order to get a better understanding of the development of each process in relation to that of the other, it would be advantageous to have tasks in which both the conceptual process required for solution and the characteristics of the information are systematically varied.

The following two studies were designed to accomplish this and to provide data about the relative rates of development of conceptual processes that integrate and disintegrate information in problem-solving tasks. They also provide an assessment of how the perceptual salience of solution-relevant and -irrelevant information influences the manifestation of these processes.

In both studies, the subjects were given a salience task to assess their perceptual sensitivity to the dimensions (categories or relations) of form, color, and position (location). This was done several weeks prior to the time that the problem-solving tasks were presented. During salience assessment, subjects were asked to match items that were most alike in values representing particular dimensions or categories. In these tasks, there was no problem to solve, and therefore no solution-relevant choices. Several choice alternatives were provided, and no feedback regarding the appropriateness of choices was given by the experimenter. (For details on the construction of salience tasks see Odom and Guzman, 1972.) Based on the salience scores associated with the assessed dimension, a rank-ordered ABC hierarchy, with A designating the most salient and C the least salient dimension, was obtained for each child. Within this approach, the salience hierarchy is seen as a product of the perceptual system's detection of, experience with, and organization of information.

## STUDY 1

In the first study to be reported, Astor-Stetson (1977) investigated the ability of 4-, 5-, and 6-year-old children to solve matrix problems that required either the selective evaluation of one dimension or the integrated evaluation of two dimensions. Within each grade level, half of the children were assigned to Condition AB and received nine 3 × 3 matrices comprised of three different values from each of their A and B dimensions. The other half of the children were assigned to Condition AC and received nine structurally identical matrices comprised of three values from each of their A and C dimensions. Within each salience condition, half of the children received unidimensional matrices in which the selective evaluation of values from either their A dimension (Condition AB) or their C dimension (Condition AC) was required. The other half of the children received bidimensional matrices in which the coordinated evaluation of values from two dimensions (A and B or A and C) was required. (For a fuller description of each matrix type see Odom, Astor, and Cunningham, 1975, and Astor-Stetson, 1977).

In unidimensional problems, only the values of the relevant dimension were systematically ordered across either the rows or the columns of the matrix. Figure 7.1 is an example of a unidimensional matrix in which form is the relevant dimension and position is the irrelevant dimension. The three cells of the left column of this matrix contain only crosses, the middle column only squares, and the right column only triangles. None of the values representing position is ordered in any row or column. Rather, they are located randomly with respect to rows and columns. In bidimensional problems, the values of one relevant dimension were ordered across the rows of the matrix while the values of the other relevant dimension were ordered across the columns. An example of a bidimensional matrix with form and position relevant is shown in Figure 7.2.

In both types of problem, the children were required to select that response compound from a set of four alternatives that correctly filled the empty cell of the matrix. (In Figs. 7.1 and 7.2, the response choices are presented just below each matrix.) In the unidimensional matrices, the correct compound was the only alternative that contained the value from the relevant dimension that was appropriate to the row or column occupied by the empty cell. One of the

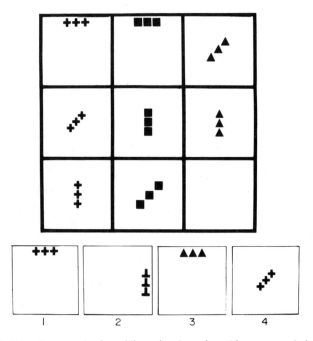

FIG. 7.1.   An example of a unidimensional matrix and its response choices.

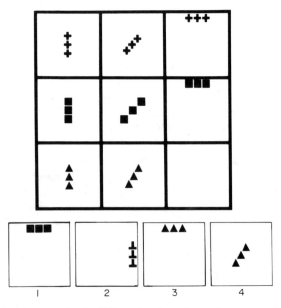

FIG. 7.2.   An example of a bidimensional matrix and its response choices.

174

incorrect compounds contained an inappropriate value from the relevant dimension paired with the same value of the irrelevant dimension as the correct response compound. Another contained that same inappropriate value of the relevant dimension paired with the value from the irrelevant dimension that only occurred twice in the matrix. The values that comprised the remaining compound were both inappropriate and did not appear in the matrix. In the bidimensional matrices, the correct compound was the only alternative that contained the values appropriate to the row and column occupied by the empty cell. Two of the other compounds each contained an appropriate value from one of the dimensions and an inappropriate value from the other dimension. The appropriate value in one of these compounds was from the more salient dimension, and that in the other compound was from the less salient dimension. The inappropriate value in each of these compounds appeared in one of the filled matrix cells. Both values of the remaining compound were inappropriate and did not appear in the matrix.

Table 7.1 contains the mean number of errors made by each age group in the two salience conditions of each matrix problem. The results revealed that children performed more accurately on both unidimensional and bidimensional problems in which the relevant information was high in salience ($M$ errors = 3.4) than on problems in which the relevant information was low in salience ($M$ errors = 4.8). For all conditions combined, errors decreased with increasing age; however, age-related similarities in performance also occurred as a function of salience. For example, 4-year-old children who received their more salient information as relevant in the unidimensional problem performed ($M$ errors = 4.5) as well as 5-year-old children who received their less salient information as relevant ($M$ errors = 5.0). Similarly, 5-year-old children who received their more salient information as relevant in the bidimensional problem ($M$ errors = 2.4) performed as well as 6-year-old children who received their less salient information as relevant ($M$ errors = 2.9).

In order to determine whether the children evidenced the ability to solve the problem, $t$-tests were conducted to compare observed performance with

TABLE 7.1
Mean Errors Made by the Age Groups in the Salience Conditions of Each Matrix Problem

| Age Group | Unidimensional | | Bidimensional | | Combined |
|---|---|---|---|---|---|
| | AB | AC | AB | AC | |
| 4 years | 4.5 | 6.6 | 6.5 | 6.7 | 6.08 |
| 5 years | 3.4 | 5.0 | 2.4 | 5.2 | 4.0 |
| 6 years | 2.1 | 2.4 | 1.5 | 2.9 | 2.22 |
| Combined | 3.33 | 4.67 | 3.47 | 4.93 | |

that expected on the basis of chance ($M$ errors = 6.75). In the bidimensional problem the youngest children failed to perform better than chance (AB, $M$ errors = 6.5; AC, $M$ errors = 6.7), while both 5-year-old (AB, $M$ errors = 2.4; AC, $M$ errors = 5.2) and 6-year-old children (AB, $M$ errors = 1.5; AC, $M$ errors = 2.9) demonstrated the ability to solve the problem. In the unidimensional problem, only the 4-year-old children in Condition AC ($M$ errors = 6.6) failed to perform better than chance.

## STUDY 2

In the second study, Cunningham and Odom (1978) investigated the ability of 6- and 11-year-old children to solve problems requiring the analysis or the integration of salience-assessed relations. Within each age group, half of the children were assigned to Condition BA and received problems comprised of values from their B and A dimensions, while the remaining children were assigned to Condition BC and received problems comprised of values from the B and C dimensions. Within each salience condition, half of the children received analysis problems that required the selective evaluation of values from their B dimension, while the remaining children received integration problems that required the combined evaluation of values from both dimensions.

The analysis and integration problems were both location-recall tasks in which the same horizontal stimulus array was used. The array consisted of six compounds, each of which was comprised of a different value from two dimensions (B and A or B and C). In both problems, each of 24 5-sec array exposures was followed by the covering of the stimulus array and the presentation of a four-compound response array from which the child was asked to select that compound which accurately matched the covered compound occupying the stimulus-array location being indicated by the experimenter. For a given problem there were six different response arrays, each corresponding to one of the stimulus-array compounds. A sample trial with three types of array used in problems involving form and position relations is shown in Fig. 7.3. The arrow indicates the probed location in the stimulus array for that trial.

In both analysis and integration problems, each response array included one correct and three incorrect compounds. In the analysis problem, the correct compound contained a value from the relevant B dimension that was identical to the one on the probed compound in the stimulus array. It also contained a value from the irrelevant dimension (A or C) that was unlike the one on the probed compound. One of the incorrect compounds was comprised of a value from the irrelevant dimension that was identical to that on the probed compound and a value from the relevant B dimension that was

STIMULUS ARRAY

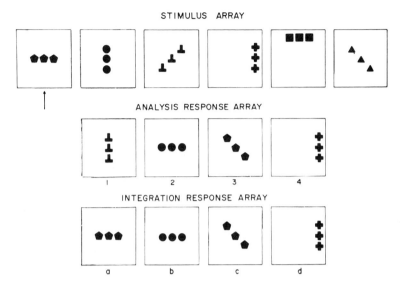

FIG. 7.3.   Examples of stimulus and response arrays containing values from the form and position relations.

different from the one on the probed compound. Each of the remaining two compounds was comprised of values from both dimensions that were unlike those on the probed compound. One of those compounds was identical to a stimulus compound in another location, while the other was a novel compound. This novel compound was replaced in the integration response array by the correct compound that contained values from both dimensions that were identical to those on the compound in the probed location. Therefore, the incorrect compounds of the integration response array included one that contained a correct value from one of the dimensions, another that contained a correct value from the other dimension, and a third that contained two incorrect values that were paired as a compound in another location of the array.

The mean recall errors made by the age groups during the four trial blocks of each problem are presented in Table 7.2. Although fewer errors were made by older ($M$ = 8.61) than by younger subjects ($M$ = 10.52), performance of both younger and older children in analysis and integration problems clearly varied as a function of the salience of the relevant information. In integration problems, children made fewer errors when they evaluated their more salient dimensions (BA, $M$ errors = 7.56) than when they evaluated their less salient dimensions (BC, $M$ errors = 11.30). Similarly, children who received analysis problems and were required to evaluate selectively a more salient dimension in the presence of a less salient dimension made fewer errors (BC, $M$

TABLE 7.2
Mean Recall Errors Made by the Two Age Groups in the Different Salience Conditions of
the Two Problems

| Problem | Age Group | Salience Condition | Trial Blocks | | | | Combined |
|---------|-----------|--------------------|---|---|---|---|----------|
| | | | 1 | 2 | 3 | 4 | |
| Analysis | 6 yrs. | BA | 4.12 | 3.50 | 3.37 | 2.62 | 13.61 |
| | | BC | 3.00 | 2.37 | 1.50 | 1.12 | 7.99 |
| | 11 yrs. | BA | 3.25 | 3.12 | 2.75 | 2.87 | 11.99 |
| | | BC | 2.62 | 1.37 | 1.12 | .12 | 5.23 |
| Integration | 6 yrs. | BA | 3.12 | 2.25 | 1.75 | 1.25 | 8.37 |
| | | BC | 3.37 | 2.87 | 3.00 | 2.87 | 12.11 |
| | 11 yrs. | BA | 2.37 | 2.37 | 1.00 | 1.00 | 6.74 |
| | | BC | 3.12 | 3.00 | 2.50 | 1.87 | 10.49 |
| Combined | | | 3.12 | 2.61 | 2.12 | 1.72 | |

errors = 6.61) than children who evaluated a less salient dimension in the presence of a more salient dimension (BA, $M$ errors = 12.80). The effects of salience were also manifested in the rate of solution. The decrease in errors across trial blocks was greater in Condition BA than in Condition BC of the integration problem. In the analysis problem the decrease was greater in Condition BC than in Condition BA of the analysis problem.

Further evidence of the effects of salience was revealed in the age related similarities in performance. In the analysis problem, younger children in Condition BC ($M$ errors = 7.99) made no more errors than older children in Condition BA ($M$ errors = 11.99). In the integration problem, the performance of younger children in Condition BA ($M$ errors = 8.37) was similar to that of older children in Condition BC ($M$ errors = 10.49)

To ascertain whether the subjects' performance in each problem reflected those processes required for solution, $t$-tests were performed to determine whether fewer errors were made than would be expected if subjects had been performing at chance level ($M$ errors = 18.00). The performance of both younger and older children in both salience conditions of analysis and integration problems alike exceeded that expected by chance alone ($t$'s (56) $\geq$ 10.37, $p < .001$).

In none of the analyses of the data were performance differences seen to occur as a function of type of problem. Both younger and older subjects demonstrated the ability to solve analysis and integration problems.

## DISCUSSION

In the two studies just described there is no clear evidence that either integration or analysis precedes the other in the course of development. Given that the results revealed no main effect associated with problem type, one might nevertheless see the matrix performance of the 4-year-olds in the first study as supportive of the claim that an analysis or disintegration process precedes that of integration in development. However, this result is just as reasonably, and perhaps more parsimoniously, explained by perceptual salience. That 4-year-olds can solve analysis problems is demonstrated by their performance in the AB unidimensional task in which the more salient dimension (A) was relevant, and their failure to solve the AC unidimensional problem can be attributed to the infrequency with which they evaluated the relevant C dimension, which was low in salience. Likewise, their failure to solve the bidimensional tasks may also have been due to the salience of the relevant B and C dimensions being too low to cause their frequent evaluation. In other words, there is no evidence that the youngest subjects could solve any problem except the one requiring the conceptual evaluation of only the most salient relation (A) in their hierarchy.

Little support from the results of these two studies is realized for conceptual-change positions. As younger and younger children demonstrate the ability to solve problems requiring theoretically important conceptual processes, then the thesis, crucial to most conceptual-change positions, that such processes are absent in the younger child and emerge in the older, more developmentally mature child becomes less and less tenable. All age groups in both studies clearly demonstrated an ability to disintegrate and analyze information. With the exception of the 4-year-olds in the first study, evidence for an ability to integrate was also found. These findings were reflected by the level of performance accuracy being above that expected by chance or guessing.

The pattern of data associated with the salience conditions and age groups in the two studies represents yet another instance of a finding that continues to create a problem for conceptual-change theories. The problem is the décalage, which is primarily associated with Piagetian research but which also exists in other developmental research. As noted elsewhere (Odom, 1978), the décalage is not a theoretical construct, but is rather a description of the unreliable manifestation of a particular conceptual process. Instances of the décalage in the developmental literature involve performance differences in tasks that require the same conceptual processing for solution but differ in the characteristics of the information to be conceptually evaluated. Such findings are difficult to explain within conceptual-change positions that attribute age-related performance differences to the availability of some particular conceptual process in the problem solver. This is because there is no clear rationale to account for the presence of the process, or more accurate performance, when a problem solver is given a problem involving one type of information and the absence of the process, or less accurate performance, when the same problem solver is given a problem with identical solution requirements but different information.

In contrast, the perceptual-change position that we have advanced provides a rationale that may best be presented in terms of two components of the décalage. The first component involves within-age comparisons of performance in problems that contain different information but have the same solution requirements. In the studies described herein, the performance differences that occurred as a function of salience in both the analysis (unidimensional) and integration (bidimensional) problems provide two examples of this décalage component within each of the age groups. That is, the rate of accuracy shown by each age group was affected by the salience of the information in each type of problem.

The second component of the décalage involves between-age comparisons of performance on problems that again have the same solution requirements but different types of information. This component is reflected in the age related similarities in both analysis and integration performance that occurred as a function of the salience of the information. The 4-year-olds given an AB unidimensional matrix performed as accurately as 5-year-olds given an AC unidimensional matrix, and 5-year-olds given an AB bidimensional matrix performed as well as 6-year-olds given an AC bidimensional matrix. In the second study, the younger children who evaluated their more salient relation (BC analysis task) or relations (BA integration task) made no more errors than the older children who evaluated respectively their less salient relation (BA analysis task) or relations (BC integration task). These results indicate that, contrary to conceptual-change views, younger children can analyze and integrate relations in a way similar to that of older children. Further, the occurrence of both components of the décalage in each type of problem provides additional support for a perceptual-based, rather than a conceptual-based, model of developmental change in problem solving.

As is the case in most developmental studies, the older subjects made fewer errors than the younger subjects. That is, the results of both studies yielded a significant main effect of age group. For reasons just given, it would be unreasonable to conclude from this that only older subjects are capable of integrating and disintegrating information. Instead, we may assume that if more information becomes more salient in the course of development, then older subjects would be more likely than younger subjects to evaluate more of the available information in any given problem. Furthermore, because of their greater perceptual sensitivity to information, older subjects might be expected to accept or reject relevant or irrelevant information more rapidly than younger subjects. If speed of conceptual processing is to be considered a part of conceptual development, then it would be important to determine its relation to the perceptual system and to perceptual development. It is obvious to most developmental psychologists that understanding conceptual-evaluative processes such as integration and disintegration is an important goal. It should also be obvious from studies like those described above that understanding perceptual processes and the perceptual characteristics of information is equally important and perhaps necessary if the development of conceptual processes is to be understood

# REFERENCES

Astor-Stetson, E. *The effects of salience on children's multidimensional and unidimensional problem solving.* Unpublished doctoral dissertation, Vanderbilt University, 1977.

Cunningham, J. G., & Odom, R. D. The role of perceptual salience in the development of analysis and synthesis processes. *Child Development,* 1978, *49,* 815-823.

Gibson, E. J. *Principles of perceptual development.* New York: Appleton-Century-Crofts, 1969.

Gibson, J. J. *The senses considered as perceptual systems.* Boston: Houghton Mifflin, 1966.

Hagen, J. W., & Hale, G. A. The development of attention in children. In A. D. Pick (Ed.), *Minnesota symposia on child psychology* (Vol. 7). Minneapolis: University of Minnesota Press, 1973.

Inhelder, B., & Piaget, J. *The early growth of logic in the child.* New York: Norton, 1964.

Odom, R. D. Effects of perceptual salience on the recall of relevant and incidental dimensional values: A developmental study. *Journal of Experimental Psychology,* 1972, *92,* 285-291.

Odom, R. D. A perceptual salience account of décalage relations and developmental change. In L. S. Siegel & C. J. Brainerd (Eds.), *Alternatives to Piaget: Critical essays on the theory.* New York: Academic Press, 1978.

Odom, R. D., Astor, E. C., & Cunningham, J. G. The effects of perceptual salience on the matrix task performance of four- and six-year-old children. *Child Development,* 1975, *46,* 758-762.

Odom, R. D., & Corbin, D. W. Perceptual salience and children's multidimensional problem solving. *Child Development,* 1973, *44,* 425-432.

Odom, R. D., Cunningham, J. G., & Astor-Stetson, E. The role of perceptual salience and type of instruction in children's recall of relevant and incidental dimensional values. *Bulletin of the Psychonomic Society,* 1977, *9,* 77-80.

Odom, R. D., & Guzman, R. D. Development of hierarchies of dimensional salience. *Developmental Psychology,* 1972, *6,* 271-287.

Odom, R. D., & Lemond, C. M. The recall of relevant and incidental dimensional values as a function of perceptual salience, cognitive set, and age. *Journal of Experimental Child Psychology,* 1975, *19,* 524-535.

# 8

# Information Integration Through Structural Abstraction in Discrimination Learning

Richard S. Bogartz
*University of Massachusetts, Amherst*

## The Conditional Discrimination and Transverse Patterning Problems

The *conditional discrimination* problem and the *transverse patterning* problem are of special interest in the study of discrimination learning because they involve different, higher levels of information organization than that found in simple discrimination. In a simple discrimination, the solution consists of identifying the correct stimulus attribute, so that, for example, always choosing the red stimulus or always choosing the square one is a solution. The conditional discrimination cannot be solved by learning to choose a specific stimulus attribute. Instead, its solution requires selection of combinations of attributes. At a higher level of complexity, the transverse patterning problem (Berch & Israel, 1971, 1974; Spence, 1952) cannot be solved even on the basis of combinations of stimulus attributes but requires solution on the basis of combinations of stimuli.

An example of the conditional discrimination would be the problem in which, when a red square and a red triangle are presented, the square is correct, but when a blue square and a blue triangle are presented, the triangle is correct. Four- and 5-year-old children who solve simple discriminations easily, find the conditional discrimination difficult or impossible, but 9-year-olds have no difficulty with it.

The transverse patterning problem is exemplified by presenting the three different pairs from the forms triangle, circle, and square. When triangle and circle are presented, triangle is correct; when circle and square, circle is correct; and when square and triangle are presented, square is correct. Thus, there is no correct stimulus attribute, as in the conditional discrimination, and also there is no absolutely correct stimulus, in that whether or not a stimulus is correct depends upon which other stimulus is paired with it. Nine-year-old children ordinarily find the transverse patterning problem impossible to solve (Berch & Israel, 1974; Experiment 3, later), and even adults solve it with great difficulty, if they solve it at all (Berch & Israel, 1971).

The occurrence of this developmental sequence from the simple to the conditional to the transverse patterning problem jibes with our intuitive appreciation of the increasing complexity of these problems. The hypothesis naturally arises that increasingly complex cognitive structures are required for solution of this sequence of increasingly complex problems. But this hypothesis requires considerable elaboration in that it in turn raises questions of how to represent such cognitive structures and how the information from the stimulus presentations and the experimenter-provided feedback is integrated into these structures to provide solutions. The purpose of the present paper is to begin to answer, theoretically and experimentally, some of the questions relating to the nature of these cognitive structures and information integration processes.

## Form and Content

Haygood and Bourne (1965) found it useful to distinguish between two aspects of conceptual behavior:

> (a) rule learning, in which the subject attains or discovers the principle for partitioning the stimuli in a particular problem and *acquires the rule in general form so that he can use it in any problem;* and (b) attribute identification, in which the subject attains or discovers the relevant attributes (p. 180, italics added).

The transferable rule provides a form or generalized structure to which the attributes are assimilated as content, completing the formation of the specific concept. Haygood and Bourne also noted that the process that they called rule learning is not unlike what Piaget refers to as concept formation, as, for example, in the formation of the concept of conservation of quantity. They agree with Piaget in emphasizing the importance of rules or cognitive structures separate from attributes or content. The relevance of Piagetian theory to the present work is further considered later.

Bourne (1970) later showed that college students given experience with successive concept identification problems, each based on the same bidimensional rule (conjunctive, disjunctive, conditional, or biconditional), attained perfect errorless performance by at most six problems (the relevant attributes were indicated to the subject in advance on each problem). This demonstrated both the acquisition of the general form of the conceptual rule and its availability for assimilation of new attributes.

The present chapter: (1) provides a similar analysis of the conditional and transverse patterning and discrimination learning problems in terms of separating form and content; (2) shows experimentally that abstract forms or structures analogous to conceptual rules can be brought into operation to facilitate acquisition of these two types of problems; and (3) adduces evidence concerning the specific nature of those structures.

## The Structure and Content of Solutions in Discrimination Learning

In this section we introduce a set–theoretical representation of solutions to discrimination learning problems. This in turn permits representation of the notions of structure and content. There are major similarities and only minor differences between the conceptual rules studied by Haygood and Bourne and the solution structures for discrimination learning problems studied here. In each, the same type of logical transformation can represent the psychological differences between knowledge of a specific problem solution and knowledge of a general, transferrable structure. Therefore, in passing, the form of conceptual rules will be developed parallel to the development of central interest, representation of the structures of discrimination learning solutions. This latter representation will then provide a precise means for expressing the theoretical predictions and discussion for the experiments to be presented.

According to Haygood and Bourne, a conceptual rule partitions a stimulus set into two classes, + and –. This partition maps the stimulus set into the response set $R = \{+, -\}$. It will be convenient to represent such functional graphs as subsets of the Cartesian product of the stimulus set $S$ with the response set $R$. Consider the set of stimuli differing in Color (Rd or Bl, for red or blue) and Form (Sq or Tr, for square or triangle). Letting Rd and Sq be the focal attributes, we can express the conceptual rule Rd ∩ Sq as

$$\text{Rd} \cap \text{SQ} = \{(x,y) \mid x \in S \wedge y \in R \wedge (x = \text{RdSq} \leftrightarrow y = +)\}$$

which reads, the conjunctive conceptual rule "Red and Square" is a relation in $S \times R$ such that for any ordered pair $(x,y)$ in $S \times R$, the stimulus $x$ is a red square if and only if the response is +. As a second example, the conditional conceptual rule Rd → Sq may be written

$$\text{RD} \rightarrow \text{SQ} = \{(x,y) \mid x \in S \wedge y \in R \wedge (x \neq \text{RdTr} \leftrightarrow y = +)\}$$

and read in similar fashion. Clearly, each of Haygood and Bourne's 10 conceptual rules for partitions of stimulus populations with two focal attributes can be described similarly.

In discrimination learning problems, instead of identifying a stimulus as being or not being an instance of a concept, the person chooses one of two stimuli presented together (we exclude problems with more than two stimuli per presentation to preserve simplicity of exposition). Let (+) and (–) mark the stimuli that are respectively called correct and incorrect by the experimenter. The problem in which choosing the red stimulus is the correct response may be characterized by a set of stimulus *presentations*. Each presentation is itself a set consisting of the two stimuli presented on some trial. For red correct, an example of the set of stimulus presentations, with the correct and incorrect stimuli marked, would be {{RdSq(+), BlSq(–)}, {BlTr(–), RdTr(+)}}, and their spatial reversals, in which the left–right positions of the stimuli are changed, but position is an irrelevant dimension. (The irrelevance of order in the specifications of the elements of a set will be used here to correspond to the experimental condition of irrelevance of the left–right dimension, so a single set will be used for a stimulus presentation and also its spatial reversal.) Again, as with concept identification, we see a partitioning of the stimulus set into those that are positive choices or instances of the correct stimlulus and those that are not. However, although a mapping of the stimulus set into the response set $R = \{+, -\}$ is sufficient for concept identification, a different treatment is required in general for discrimination learning. The transverse patterning problem is an instance in which no such mapping from $S$ into $R$ exists as a solution. Instead, the correct mapping for discrimination learning problems is from the set of stimulus presentations to the set of stimuli (more precisely, to a set of responses that are in one-to-one correspondence with the stimuli.) Thus, for the discrimination learning problem in which choosing the red stimulus is correct, the solution is a subset of the Cartesian product $P_1 \times S$, in which $P_1 = \{\{RdSq, BlSq\}, \{RdTr, BlTr\}\}$ is the set of stimulus presentations and $S = \{RdSq, BlSq, RdTr, BlTr\}$ is the set of stimuli. The solution is

$$Rd(+) = \{(x,y) \mid x \in P_1 \land y \in S \land y = \{RdSq, RdTr\} \cap x\}$$

which reads that the solution "Red is correct" is a relation in $P_1 \times S$ such that for any ordered pair $(x,y)$ in $P_1 \times S$, the chosen stimulus $y$ is that stimulus in the intersection of the set of red stimuli and the presentation set $x$.

As a second example, we consider the conditional discrimination problem, using the same stimuli. Here the set of stimulus sets that are presented is $P_2 = \{\{RdSq, RdTr\}, \{BlSq, BlTr\}\}$. The correct solution is to choose the square when the presented stimuli are both red and the triangle when they are both blue. The solution is

$$\{(x,y) \mid x \in P_2 \wedge y \in S \wedge y = \{\text{RdSq, BlTr}\} \cap x\} \tag{1}$$

which says that the chosen stimulus $y$ should be in the intersection of the presented set $x$ with the set of correct stimuli that contains RdSq and BlTr. The representation in (1) is intended to denote a list solution of the problem. The subject learns a list of correct stimuli and selects that presented stimulus that is on the list. It will be of theoretical interest in considering Experiments 1 and 2 that an alternative solution can be formulated for the same problem. Let RED = {RdSq, RdTr}, BLUE = {BlSq, BlTr}, SQUARE = {RdSq, BlSq}, and TRIANGLE = {RdTr, BlTr}. Then the solution can be written

$$\{(x,y) \mid x \in P_2 \wedge y \in S \wedge (x = \text{RED} \rightarrow y = \text{RED} \cap \text{SQUARE}) \wedge$$
$$(x = \text{BLUE} \rightarrow y = \text{BLUE} \cap \text{TRIANGLE})\} \tag{2}$$

which reads that if the red stimuli are presented, the choice is the red square and if the blue stimuli are presented the choice is the blue triangle. We will propose that these two solutions, (1) and (2), which are identical mappings from $P_2$ to $S$, are in fact psychologically and experimentally distinguishable.

With this set–theoretical notation in hand we now can represent, for both the concept identification and the discrimination learning problems, the notion of *a rule or structure that is acquired in general form and can transfer from problem to problem.* Expressions such as (1) and (2) are logical sentences (Tarski, 1965) in which $x$ and $y$ are *bound variables,* bound by the operator $(x,y)$, and the other terms, such as $P_1$, $S$, BLUE, and RdSq are constants. When the constants in such a sentence are replaced by *free variables,* the sentence becomes a sentential function (see Tarski, 1965 or Quine, 1965 for discussion of bound and free variables, and Tarski for discussion of sentential functions). The sentential function

$$\{(x,y) \mid x \in \Pi \wedge y \in \Sigma \wedge y = \{\kappa_1, \kappa_2\} \cap x\} \tag{3}$$

is the abstract form of the solution (1) to the conditional discrimination problem, in which $P_2$, $S$, RdSq and BlTr have been replaced respectively by the free variables $\Pi$, $\Sigma$, $\kappa_1$, and $\kappa_2$, in which $\{\kappa_1, \kappa_2\}$ is a list of the correct stimuli. We say that this sentential function expresses the form or structure of the solution, freed of its content, the constants. To express the form of solution (2), let $\Sigma = \{\sigma_1 \sigma_2, \sigma_1 \bar{\sigma}_2, \bar{\sigma}_1 \sigma_2, \bar{\sigma}_1 \bar{\sigma}_2\}$.

$$\Sigma_1 = \{\sigma_1 \sigma_2, \sigma_1 \bar{\sigma}_2\} \quad \bar{\mathrm{E}}_1 = \{\bar{\sigma}_1 \sigma_2, \bar{\sigma}_1 \bar{\sigma}_2\}$$
$$\Sigma_2 = \{\sigma_1 \sigma_2, \bar{\sigma}_1 \sigma_2\} \quad \bar{\mathrm{E}}_2 = \{\sigma_1 \bar{\sigma}_2, \bar{\sigma}_1 \bar{\sigma}_2\}$$

and $\Pi = \{\Sigma_1, \bar{\Sigma}_1\}$. Then the form of solution (2) is represented by

$$\{(x,y) \mid x \in \Pi \wedge y \in \Sigma \wedge (x = \Sigma_1 \rightarrow y = \sigma_1\sigma_2) \wedge (x = \bar{E}_1 \rightarrow y = \bar{\sigma}_1\bar{\sigma}_2)\} \qquad (4)$$

Similarly, in concept identification, the form of the conditional rule is just

$$\sigma_1 \rightarrow \sigma_2 = \{(x,y) \mid x \in \Sigma \wedge y \in R \wedge (x \neq \sigma_1\bar{\sigma}_2 \leftrightarrow y = +)\}$$

in which $\sigma_1$ and $\sigma_2$ are the focal attributes and $\bar{\sigma}_2$ is the alternative value on the same dimension as $\sigma_2$.

To summarize, we have seen that both Haygood and Bourne's conceptual rules and the solutions of discrimination learning problems can be represented set–theoretically as relations that are expressible by logical sentences, and that the notion of a general rule or solution structure can be represented as a sentential function in which some or all of the constants of a particular solution have been replaced by free variables.

## Overview of the Experiments

The four experiments described below are all concerned with the use of structure in the solution of discrimination learning problems. Experiment 1 is an attempt to identify the structure used by children in solving the conditional discrimination problem. The procedures employed toward that end are obtaining postexperimental verbal descriptions of the solution from the children and analyzing the distribution of post-solution probe trial responses. The results indicate that all children who solve the conditional discrimination use a structure such as that in (4) rather than that in (3).

Experiment 2 shows that the same solution structure found in children in Experiment 1 is used by adults in solving the conditional discrimination. Further, it demonstrates the validity of a very interesting prediction that distinguishes clearly between the two structures (3) and (4). This is done using a transfer design in which the adults repeatedly solve conditional discriminations with content changing from problem to problem. In each problem, the presentation set is of the form $\Pi = \{\{\sigma_1\sigma_2, \sigma_1\bar{\sigma}_2\}, \{\bar{\sigma}_1\sigma_2, \bar{\sigma}_1\bar{\sigma}_2\}\}$. Because the stimulus presentations, that is, the sets that are members of $\Pi$, are presented in random order at the start of each new problem one of them, say FIRST $= \{\sigma_1\sigma_2 \ \sigma_1\bar{\sigma}_2\}$, will be presented at least once and sometimes two or three times before the first presentation of SECOND $= \{\bar{\sigma}_1\sigma_2 \ \bar{\sigma}_1\bar{\sigma}_2\}$, the other stimulus presentation. One solution structure, (3), suggests that performance on this *very first occurrence* of SECOND will be at a chance level; the other solution structure, (4), suggests that such performance will exceed the chance level. The results clearly indicate greater than chance performance on this class of presentations. This is a very interesting effect because the greater-than-chance performance is with stimulus presentations *never* seen before and cannot be explained by generalization from stimulus sets in previous problems. The result is analogous to the errorless performance in concept identification found by Bourne (1970) in the later rule learning problems.

Experiment 3 presents a very exciting result. It shows that the ordinarily impossible transverse patterning problem becomes soluble by nine-year-olds if they are first told and use the solution to another transverse patterning problem in which the content is that of a familiar childhood game. The solution to this game is structurally identical to the solution to a transverse patterning problem and it was expected that the solution structure might be easily abstracted from it. A striking feature of the results is that this procedure using the content from the childhood game is as effective in promoting solution of a subsequent transverse patterning problem as is telling the children the exact solution of the subsequent problem in its entirety.

Finally, selected results from a fourth experiment are presented that provide convincing evidence for distinguishing between two possible solution structures for the transverse patterning problem.

## EXPERIMENT 1: THE FORM OF THE SOLUTION IN THE CONDITIONAL DISCRIMINATION

The purpose of this experiment was to determine if children solving the conditional discrimination tended to use solution structure (3) or solution structure (4). Two approaches to this problem were taken. The first was to obtain the children's descriptions of their solutions in a postexperimental interview. It was assumed that children using (3) would tend to list the correct stimuli as the solution, but children using (4) would tend to make conditional statements such as "If the stimuli were red, I chose the square, but if they were blue, I chose the triangle." The second approach rests on the following logic.

Suppose that children learn the conditional discrimination with the presentation set being $P_2 = \{\{RdSq, RdTr\}, \{BlSq, BlTr\}\}$. After the problem is solved, probe trials consisting of presentations from the set $P_3 = \{\{RdSq, BlSq\}, \{RdTr, BlTr\}\}$ are presented. If, because the child does not know that the probe trial presentations are not members of $P_2$, the expression $y = \{RdSq, BlTr\} \cap x$ from solution (1) is applied, the response will be choosing $y = \{RdSq, BlTr\} \cap \{RdSq, BlSq\} = RdSq$ when $\{RdSq, BlSq\}$ is presented and $y = \{RdSq, BlTr\} \cap \{RdTr, BlTr\} = BlTr$ when $\{RdTr, BlTr\}$ is presented. On the other hand, application of $(x = RED \rightarrow y = RED \cap SQUARE) \wedge (x = BLUE \rightarrow y = BLUE \cap TRIANGLE)$ from solution (2) can not occur with presentation sets from $P_3$ because for any $x \in P_3$, $x \neq RED$ and $x \neq BLUE$. In the absence of an applicable solution, the child would be expected to behave in accordance with other factors such as chance or pre-experimental preferences that should not lead to systematic choices on probe trials.

In summary, use of solution structure (3) implies greater-than-chance selection of the stimuli in the role of RdSq and BlTr on probe trials, but use of solution structure (4) implies a chance distribution.

## Method

*Subjects.* Ninety-six children, 32 children per grade, from the first-, third-, and fifth-grades of two Amherst, Massachusetts public schools, participated in the experiment. The mean age, standard deviation, and range for the first graders were 6 years-4 months, 4.28 months, and 5 years-10 months to 7 years-8 months. The values for the third- and fifth-grade children were: 8-5, 3.86, and 7-2 to 8-10; and 10-6, 4.28, and 10-0 to 11-10.

*Design.* For each of four sets of stimuli, the stimuli varied on two dimensions. Let $A_1$ and $A_2$ be the values on dimension A, and let $B_1$ and $B_2$ be the values on dimension B. In training, when dimension B varied within presentations and A varied between presentations, the four possible presentations were $\{A_1B_1, A_1B_2\}$ and $\{A_2B_1, A_2B_2\}$, the first set standing for $A_1B_1$ on the left, $A_1B_2$ on the right, and also for its spatial reversal, and similarly for the second set. The four probe trials after training were a random ordering of the four possible presentations with A now varying *within* presentations and B varying *between*: $\{A_1B_1, A_2B_1\}$ and $\{A_1B_2, A_2B_2\}$.

For each of the four stimulus sets, which dimension varied between presentations and which varied within was counterbalanced over sex and age group. For each child, a different random sequence of stimulus presentations was generated. The four different training presentations occurred randomly three times in every 12-trial block and the position of the correct stimulus was balanced in accordance with Fellows' sequences (Fellows, 1967, Table 4).

*Stimuli.* The stimuli were four sets of Chartpak Transfer pictures (Chartpak Co., Leeds, Mass.). Each set varied on two dimensions. For Set I, the dimensions were form (snowflake or flower) and number (one or two). Set II combined form (arrow or diamond) with color (black or white). In Set III, form (three bicycle-crossing signs or three cow-crossing signs) and linear array orientation (horizontal or vertical) were the dimensions. Set IV varied in form (man walking or man riding a bicycle) and size (small or large).

*Procedure.* The children were tested individually. Each child was escorted from the classroom by one of two female experimenters who, on the way to the testing area, informed the child that he or she could return to the classroom at any time he or she wanted to. In the test room, the child was seated at a table opposite the experimenter. A card with two pictures of a car on it was then shown. The cars were similar, except that one was totally black and one was white with a black outline and details. The experimenter said:

> We are going to play a game today. I will show you some cards like this one. Each of the cards has two pictures on it. One of the two pictures is right and the other is not right. You have to try to pick the right picture as many times as you can. I already know which one is right; and after you have picked one, I will tell you whether or not you picked the right one. If you pick the right one, I will say "That is right." If you pick the one which is not right, I will say, "That is not right." Let's practice one time. Look at this card again and tell me what you see.

If the child did not indicate a knowledge of the difference between the two stimuli, the experimenter asked, "How are these two pictures different?" The experimenter then continued, "O.K. Now tell me which one you think is right." Regardless of the child's response, the experimenter said, "That is right. Very good."

The experimenter then displayed a card with all of the forms used in the experiment and said, "This card shows all of the different pictures in the game. Can you tell me what all of these things are?" The experimenter accepted whatever names the child gave to the pictures. If the child could not name something, the experimenter told the child the appropriate name. The experimenter then said, "O.K. Now we can begin the game. Be sure to look carefully at the pictures on each card. Let's see how many times you can pick the right one."

The testing continued until the child had made nine correct choices in 10 consecutive trials, or until 80 trials had been completed, whichever occurred first. If the child had not learned the problem, he or she was taken back to the classroom. Those children who learned the problem were then presented with the four probe trials. The experimenter said, "Very good. Now I'm going to show you some more cards. This time I won't tell you whether or not you made the right choice, but I still want you to point to the one you think is right." After the probe trials, the child was asked, "In the first part of the game, how did you know which pictures were right?" The experimenter recorded the child's answer and escorted the child back to the classroom.

## Results and Discussion

*Training.*   Sixty-eight of the 96 children reached criterion. Thirty-three were boys; 35 were girls. The number of solvers in grades one, three, and five were 18, 24, and 26. A chi-square test of the hypothesis of equal frequency of solvers in the three grades gave a nonsignificant chi-square statistic of 5.25 on 2 df, the .05 level critical value being 5.99.

A three by two by eight (grades by sex by stimulus sets) analysis of variance of training trials to criterion, scoring nonsolvers as 80 trials to criterion, yielded no significant main effects or interactions. Excluding nonsolvers, a two by three (sex by grades) analysis of variance of trials to criterion yielded no significant effects, with $F$-statistics less than one for Sex, Grades and Sex by Grades effects. This indicates that there were no systematic selection effects due to excluding nonsolvers.

The mean number of trials to criterion (including the criterion run of trials) for solvers were 34.0, 34.1, and 32.2 for the first-, third-, and fifth-grade girls. Apparently, within the age range of about 6 to 10 years, about two thirds of the children solve the conditional discrimination, and age and sex appear to be slightly or not at all related to frequency or rate of solution. The question of central interest is how this solution occurs.

*Verbal Description Results.* Only eight of the 68 solvers gave verbal descriptions that could unambiguously be classified concerning their method of solution. All of these were judged to indicate the use of solution structure (4) rather than (3). Two examples were "When it was snowflakes, two was right; and when it was flowers, one was right." and "I found out that when it's double, one is right; and when there's only one, another is right."

*Probe Trial Response Distribution Analysis.* A positive probe trial response is the choice of the stimulus that was "right" during the training phase. As noted above use of (4) should produce a chance distribution of probe trial responses. The number of positive probe trial responses would therefore be binomially distributed with $p = .5$. For the 60 solvers whose verbal descriptions could not be categorized, there were 121 positive probe trial responses in 240 probe trials, for an overall proportion of .504, which is obviously not significantly different from the predicted value of .5. The observed frequencies for 0, 1, 2, 3, and 4 positive responses were 5, 13, 24, 12 and 6. Assuming $p = .5$, the expected frequencies are 3.75, 15, 22.5, 15, and 3.75, giving a chi-square statistic of 2.73 on 4 df, which is not significant. Thus the distribution of probe trial responses for those subjects who could not be identified by their verbal descriptions as using solution structure (4) agreed almost perfectly with the behavior predicted under the hypothesis that they were using solution structure (4) and would produce chance responding on the probe trials.

The evidence supporting solution structure (4) is of two kinds. A small group of children gave descriptions clearly suggesting its use. From the large remainder of solvers the evidence is statistical. Although the logic is no less rigorous, it may still be less persuasive. Because the logic rests on the prediction of chance responding, it can be impugned by offering alternative reasons for such responding. It might be argued, for instance, that the shift from the training sequence to the probe trials may have suggested that a new problem was beginning. Actually, the instructions did not suggest such a change. The child was told "Very good. Now I'm going to show you some more cards. This time I won't tell you whether or not you made the right choice, but I still want you to point to the one you think is right." The phrase "more cards" suggests continuity with the previous task, as does the phrase "still want". The instruction itself suggests a change of some sort, but the indication that feedback will now be omitted is the operative statement characterizing the change. Instructions that much more strongly suggest a change in the problem have been used in numerous discrimination transfer tasks in which explanations of transfer task responding have assumed tendencies learned in the first task transfer to the second.

A related but weaker argument would be that the children thought that a new problem began when they were shown the new presentations. But if they had been using a solution like (3), in which the problem is solved by learning a list of correct stimuli, there is nothing "new" for them about the probe trials, because the same stimuli are being presented and the solution learned during training would still apply. For the sake of argument it can be granted that perhaps some small number of subjects did decide that a new problem was beginning. It seems very improbable, however, that the number was so large that the almost perfect fit to a binomial distribution with $p = .5$ would be found. If such a massive effect did occur in response to so weak a suggestion, it would call for an extensive reevaluation of the discrimination transfer literature. Fortunately, the simpler explanation that (4) was in effect for the larger, less articulate group as well as for the smaller group that verbalized such a solution avoids these ramifications and explains the present data.

One final matter requires consideration. In any experiment employing a learning criterion, the question of chance attainment of the criterion and its implications for interpretation of the results must be considered (Bogartz, 1965). If subjects reached criterion in training by guessing and then were found to be guessing on the probe trials, this would say nothing about how the training task is solved. In the present study, the criterion that was used was not very stringent. It can be shown (Bogartz, 1965, Appendix B) that if all of the subjects were simply guessing during the training trials, approximately 30% of them would have reached criterion by the 80th trial. Even after eliminating the eight clear cases, it was found that 60 out of the remaining 88 subjects, or 68%, reached criterion, unequivocally indicating that the hypothesis of chance responding for all subjects during training is untenable. It may therefore be concluded that nonchance solution of the training task occurred for an unknown proportion of the subjects, but that performance by all subjects on the probe trials is compatible with the hypothesis of chance performance, and therefore with the hypothesis of solution structure (4) during training.

The results of this study, then, suggest that with a large class of stimuli, learning of the conditional discrimination occurs on the basis of solution structure (4) or it does not occur. Eight children made statements that clearly indicated that solution. The remaining 60 children did not clearly indicate either solution in their explanations but collectively indicated (4) by their chance distribution of positive probe responses. These results raise some puzzling questions. Why were there no solutions based on a list structure? The list is short. It contains only two items. The items in the list are not similar, so no confusion should occur. And what were the nonsolvers doing? We have no definite answers to these questions. I conjecture that the nonsolvers were still trying for a solution based on a single attribute combination, or were being confused by the spatial reversals. When solution by list did occur, the simple list was unsatisfying. The question perhaps arose for the subject as to why sometimes one member of the list was correct and sometimes the other. This question found its answer in the integration of all of the information that (4) provides. Having integrated all of this information into (4), the simple elements of the list that might have used to choose the "right" stimuli during the probe trials were now embedded within (4) and tended not to be retrieved out of that context. Obviously these conjectures go far beyond the data and further research is needed to test them.

## EXPERIMENT 2: STRUCTURAL TRANSFER IN THE CONDITIONAL DISCRIMINATION

Although Experiment 2 was originally designed to answer a variety of preliminary questions, its central relevance in the present context lies in the demonstration that it provides of structural transfer across repeated conditional problems. Assume that, in the course of solving repeated conditional discriminations, the structure of the problem is abstracted from the particular problems that have been solved. Formally, the constants in the solution structure have been transformed into free variables. Assume further that the subject's approach to a new problem is to process the available information on each trial in order to determine the values to be assigned to as many as possible of the free variables in this abstracted structure. If the subject is using (3), then the information on each trial is processed to determine a correct stimulus, and its value is substituted for a free $\kappa_i$ in the set $\{\kappa_1, \kappa_2\}$ from (3). If the subject is using (4), then the available information on a trial is processed to substitute as many constants as possible into the phrase

$$(x = \Sigma_1 \rightarrow y = \sigma_1\sigma_2) \wedge (x = \bar{\Sigma}_1 \rightarrow y = \bar{\sigma}_1\bar{\sigma}_2) \tag{5}$$

in (4). Let $\Sigma_1 = \{\sigma_1\sigma_2, \sigma_1\bar{\sigma}_2\} = $ FIRST be the stimulus presentation that the subject is shown on the first one or more trials before being shown the other presentation, SECOND = $\bar{\Sigma}_1 = \{\bar{\sigma}_1\sigma_2, \bar{\sigma}_1\bar{\sigma}_2\}$, on a later trial. Assume further that $\sigma_1\sigma_2$ = RdSq and $\bar{\sigma}_1\bar{\sigma}_2$ = BlTr, so that the solution to the problem is that given in (2). On the first trial, including the feedback that RdSq is correct, the subject is given the information that $\Sigma_1$ = RED, $\sigma_1$ = Rd, $\sigma_2$ = Sq, and $\bar{\sigma}_2$ = Tr. Substituting these values for the appropriate free variables in phrase (5) gives the phrase

$$(x = \text{RED} \rightarrow y = \text{RdSq}) \, \Delta \, (x = \overline{\text{RED}} \rightarrow y = \bar{\sigma}_1\text{Tr}). \qquad (6)$$

With phrase (6) available, the subject can evaluate the stimulus presentation SECOND before making a choice and determine that $\overline{\text{RED}}$ = BLUE and $\bar{\sigma}_1$ = Bl, completing the substitution of constants for free variables and making the selection of the correct stimulus BlTr possible without the subject ever having received feedback information for responding to the presentation BLUE.

By contrast, if the subject is filling in constants for variables in (3), at least one feedback to a presentation of SECOND will be required before solution can be completed. The strong prediction can therefore be made that if (3) is in use, responding to the first presentation of SECOND will be at the chance level, but if (4) is in use, perfect memory and information processing would give perfect responding on the first presentation of SECOND, and less than perfect functioning of these processes should still produce better than chance responding. Portions of the results of Experiment 2 provide a test of this contrast between two possible modes of integrating the information from FIRST and SECOND trials. Adult subjects were used rather than children, because they maximize the chances of discriminating between these two modes.

## Method

*Subjects.* The subjects were 75 University of Massachusetts undergraduate psychology students, 18 to 25 years in age, who volunteered in order to earn extra credits or to meet a course requirement.

*Procedure.* Each student was introduced to the discrimination learning task as follows. The experimenter said:

A discrimination is a choice based upon distinguishing differences between two or more alternatives. In this study, I will give you pairs of things to look at. Your job is to choose one. I will tell you "Yes" if your choice was right, and "No" if not. Try to get as many right as you can. On your first trial in any new problem, you will have no new information yet, so just guess.

All students were given 15 problems consisting of two 12-trial problems and 13 eight-trial problems. The order of problems was random, as was the order of presentations within problems. The position of the correct stimulus was varied according to truncated Fellows' sequences (Fellows, 1967). The problems were either conditional discriminations as described previously, or two-dimensional simple discriminations. In the two-dimensional simple discrimination, the presentation set is the same as in the conditional discrimination, but solution is on the basis of a single value that is on the dimension varying within presentations but not between. For example, with the presentation set {{RdSq, RdTr}, {BlSq, BlTr}}, the solution could be the choice of the square stimulus in each presentation.

Group I received 15 simple discrimination problems. Group II received 15 conditional discriminations. Group III was given 10 simple discrimination problems followed by five conditional discriminations. Group IV had 10 conditional discriminations followed by five simple discrimination problems. Group V received 15 problems with 7 or 8 of each type of problem intermixed randomly. Groups I and II were run to contrast performance on these two types of problems. Group V was run to assess performance involving shifting at random between problem types.

*Stimuli.*   The stimuli were black Chartpak (Chartpak Co., Leeds, Mass.) symbols depicting human figures, letters, numbers, and road signs. One image was centered on each half of a white, 5- × 7-inch card, which in turn was mounted on a black 8.5- × 11-inch sheet of paper and inserted in a cellophane protector.

*Design.*   The design consisted of one between-subject factor, Groups, and three within-subjects factors, type of presentation (FIRST or SECOND), Block of five problems, and Trials within problems pooled over problems within blocks. Except for Group V, all problems in a block were of the same type of discrimination, simple or conditional. Trials refers to presentation of a given presentation set, FIRST or SECOND. Thus, for each presentation set in each problem, performance on Trial 1 refers to performance on the first presentation of that set in that problem; performance on Trial 2 refers to performance on the second appearance of that type of presentation in the same problem, etc. Therefore, Trial 1 for FIRST occurs on the first trial of a problem, but Trial 1 for SECOND occurs no earlier than the second trial of that problem.

The performance of Group V was examined separately, using a within-subjects design. The factors were Problem Type, Blocks, and Trials. Each subject attempted eight problems of one type (simple or conditional) and seven of the other, decided randomly. The problem type with eight problems was blocked into three blocks with three, three, and two problems in blocks one, two and three. The problem type with seven problems was blocked with three, two, and two problems.

## Results

Table 8.1 shows the mean proportion correct responses for each Group on each Trial, for each Presentation Type, in each of the three Blocks. Although the data were extensively analyzed, most of the results are not of interest to the question of transfer of structure and will not be presented here. (The reader wishing to pursue additional analyses may use .035 as a conservative estimate of within-subjects mean square for error and .11 for between-subjects mean square for error for all comparisons involving the first four groups, and .05 for within-subjects mean square for error for Group V.) The central interest for the present purposes lies in performance on the conditional discriminations, that is, all problems for Group II, the first 10 for Group IV, and the last five for Group III. The focus is on a small number of entries in Table 8.1. The entries of greatest interest are the proportion correct in Group II on Trial 1 trials in the second and third blocks for SECOND trials, which are .73 and .72, and the mean proportion correct in Group IV on Trial 1 trials in the second block for SECOND trials, which is .79. These three values, which average .75, are the proportion of correct responses in Conditional discriminations to the *first* presentation of SECOND trials. Thus, the subjects have never seen this presentation, but they have seen FIRST, the other presentations of the same problem, at least once. Each of these proportions is significantly above the chance value of .5.

   This result supports the hypothesis that structure (4) was abstracted from the previous problems, carried into subsequent problems, and integrated with dimensional information from the FIRST presentations and its feedback, and the SECOND presentation before choice and feedback, to enable solution of the problem before choice on the first occurrence of SECOND trials. The fact that the corresponding values of .39, .59, and .51 for performance on Trial 1 of FIRST trials averaged .50 indicates that dimensional transfer from previous problems could not have been responsible for this effect. This is not surprising because great care was taken to produce problems that were dissimilar, and each subject received a different random sequence of problems.

   There is also some supporting evidence from the data for Group V on Trials 1 of SECOND presentations. The proportions of correct responses for these trials averaged close to .5, indicating that it is only when the Conditional problem occurs repeatedly, rather than randomly as in Group V, that the greater-than-chance performance is observed for presentations that have never been seen before. Thus, prior experience with the Conditional problems per se does not produce the effect. Only when the Conditional problem is

## TABLE 8.1
Proportion of Correct Responses for Each Block-Presentation Type-Trial Combination: Experiment 2

| | | | | | | | | | | | | | | | | | |
|---|---|---|---|---|---|---|---|---|---|---|---|---|---|---|---|---|---|
| | | | | | | | | | | Group | | | | | | | |
| | | I | | | II | | | III | | | IV | | | V | | |
| | | Trial | | | Trial | | | Trial | | | Trial | | | Trial | | |
| Presentation Type | Block | 1 | 2 | 3 | 1 | 2 | 3 | 1 | 2 | 3 | 1 | 2 | 3 | 1 | 2 | 3 |
| First | 1 | .51 | .91 | .91 | .44 | .72 | .84 | .52 | .92 | .91 | .52 | .84 | .85 | .45 | .80 | .85 |
| | 2 | .49 | .99 | .99 | .39 | .91 | .87 | .52 | .99 | 1.00 | .51 | .91 | .99 | .52 | .91 | .97 |
| | 3 | .49 | .99 | .99 | .59 | .93 | .91 | .53 | .85 | .87 | .32 | .92 | .91 | .43 | .92 | .99 |
| Second | 1 | .91 | .91 | .95 | .47 | .76 | .83 | .93 | .96 | .97 | .56 | .77 | .81 | .59 | .92 | .78 |
| | 2 | .96 | 1.00 | .97 | .73 | .89 | .88 | .97 | 1.00 | 1.00 | .79 | .97 | .96 | .45 | .92 | .96 |
| | 3 | .99 | 1.00 | 1.00 | .72 | .89 | .95 | .29 | .83 | .95 | .49 | .91 | .94 | .36 | .91 | .97 |

predictable from problem to problem do we observe the better-than-chance responding on previously unseen presentations.

These results support the hypothesis that repeated experience with the Conditional discrimination can result in the abstraction of a solution structure, and that this solution structure transfers to new problems. The structure allows integration of partial information from the new problem to provide a complete solution. A replication of this finding with children would be desirable. It would extend the scope of the finding and suggest at what age children begin to use the logic of the solution structure to assimilate information.

Experiments 3 and 4 do provide further evidence that children can abstract the form of a problem from its content and transfer it to a new problem, the content of which can be assimilated to this abstract structure.

## EXPERIMENT 3: STRUCTURAL TRANSFER IN THE TRANSVERSE PATTERNING PROBLEM

In the simplest form of transverse patterning problem (Berch & Israel, 1971, 1974; Spence, 1952), each of the three combinations of three stimuli, taken two at a time, constitute the stimulus presentations. In each combination (and its spatial reversal) one stimulus is correct but no stimulus is correct in more than one combination. For example, if the stimuli are triangle, circle, and square, the three combinations would be triangle–circle in which, say, the triangle is correct; circle–square, in which the circle would be correct; and square–triangle, in which the square would be correct. Berch and Israel (1974) showed that nine-year-old children were unable to solve the transverse patterning problem. In Experiment III, an attempt was made to see if solution of this problem could be obtained by children of this age if the solution structure were made available. To achieve this, the structural similarity of the transverse patterning problem to a well known children's game, Paper–Rock–Scissors, was employed. In the Paper–Rock–Scissors game, each of two children brings one hand from behind his back and extends it in front of him, at the same time extending all the fingers, only the first two fingers, or none of them. With all fingers extended, the hand represents a flat sheet of paper; with the first two, a scissors, with none, a rock. A child wins if he presents paper and his opponent presents rock because paper covers rock, or if he presents rock and his opponent presents scissors because rock crushes scissors, or if he presents scissors and his opponent presents paper because scissors cut paper. The structure of this game is very similar to the transverse patterning problem. The outcome of a finger configuration depends on the opponent's configuration that accompanies it, just as the correctness of a given stimulus in the transverse patterning problem depends on which stimulus accompanies it. Children in one experimental group learned the Paper–Rock–Scissors game before being given the transverse patterning problem. Two other important groups were a replication group that received the same treatment as subjects in the Berch and Israel (1974) study, and a group that was simply told the solution to the transverse patterning problem before having to solve it. The results for subjects given two other treatments are provided, but consideration of these results is not germane to the present discussion of structural transfer.

## Method

*Subjects.* Eighty fourth-grade children, 30 from Amherst and 50 from Springfield, Mass., participated in the experiment. The children from Amherst were tested in a research trailer in Amherst. The Springfield children were tested at the University of Massachusetts Child Study Center in Springfield. Children from each town were represented proportionately in each of the five conditions of the experiment. Boys and girls were represented proportionately in each cell of the design. There were 16 children in each experimental condition.

*Materials.* Materials consisted of five black posterboard shapes, three pictures encased in laminating plastic, and three white posterboards. The five shapes were a square, 9 mm long on each side, a triangle with a 9 mm base and 9 mm height, a circle 9 mm in diameter, and a crescent moon and a heart of approximately the same dimensions. The pictures were of a rock, scissors, and paper, each on a white background. On one large white posterboard three stick figures were depicted standing in a circle and throwing a ball to one another. On a second white posterboard, two stick-figure bodies were drawn such that the black shapes, when put in place, completed the figures. The third white posterboard was blank.

*Procedure.* Each child was taken individually to an experimental room, seated across the table from the experimenter, and given instructions appropriate to the condition. Performance on the basic transverse patterning problem was tested in all conditions. Three differently shaped stimuli were presented in pairs on white posterboard backgrounds. The problem was defined by the six left–right permutations of the three shapes taken two at a time. The correct response for any given trial depended on the particular combination of shapes. If the triangle and circle were shown, the triangle was correct; if the circle and square, circle was correct; if the square and triangle, square was correct. The instructions and procedure for each of the five experimental conditions follow.

*Replication Condition.* Children in this condition were given the following instructions:

> We're going to play a game with some cutouts. I am going to show you the cutouts two at a time. Each time you point to the one you think is right, and I will say either "right" or "wrong." It is possible to get me to say "right" every time. See if you can get me to say "right" every time.

*Solution Condition.* Here the children were given the same instructions as in the Replication condition and, in addition, were provided the solution to the problem in this way: "The rules are that triangle beats circle, circle beats square, and square beats triangle." As these instructions were presented, the experimenter demonstrated with the cutouts. The children were then required to state the rule for each pair, with the experimenter repeating each correct relation.

*Paper-Rock-Scissors Condition.* Children in this condition were first taught a variation of the children's game according to the following instructions:

> We're going to play some games. In the first game, I am going to show you some pictures two at a time. See these "scissors," "rock," and "paper" (while showing the pictures). Each time you point to the one that you think is right, and I will say either "right" or "wrong." It is possible to get me to say right every time. I'll tell you how you can pick the winner. When scissors and paper are together, scissors cut paper, so scissors win. When paper and rock are together, paper covers rock, so paper wins. When rock and scissors are together, rock smashes scissors, so rock wins.

The experimenter then asked the child to state the appropriate choice for each pair and repeated each correct response. Pairs of the stimuli were presented, and the children were tested to a criterion of two successive errorless six-trial blocks. The children were then told they would now play a similar game with some other cutouts and were instructed as in the Replication condition.

*Hypothesis Verbalization Condition.* In this condition, the children were told to pretend that the two shapes were having a contest. They were instructed to say which shape "beat" the other. This procedure was illustrated using the moon and heart shapes. Testing differed from the Replication condition in that the children verbalized each response (e.g., "Triangle beats circle.") instead of pointing to the choice.

*Circle Condition.* In this condition, the children were first shown how each stimulus could form the head of a stick figure child. They were shown a display of three stick figures with stars as "heads," and instructed as follows:

> Let's pretend that the children are standing in a circle playing ball like this. Imagine that the children keep throwing the ball around the circle. Each child always gets the ball from the same person and throws the ball to the next person. Every once in a while we'll pretend that we stop the game when one of the children is holding the ball. I'll show you two of the children from the circle, and you point to the child that you think will throw the ball. I will say either "right" or "wrong." Remember, each child always throws the ball to the same person. You point to the child who will throw the ball. See if you can pick the right child every time.

The display of stick figures was removed during the test trials. Testing differed from the preceding conditions in that the triangle, circle, and square figures were not presented on plain posterboard, but as the "heads" of stick figures drawn on posterboard.

For all groups, the administration of test trials conformed closely to the procedure used by Berch and Israel (1974). A trial consisted of the presentation of one spatial permutation of two stimuli. The six possible permutations were presented within each block of six trials in prearranged random order, with the restriction that neither position would be correct more than three times in succession. A different random order of the permutations was used in each of 15 blocks. The order of presentation of the 15 blocks was also randomized, with each subject receiving a unique random order. All children were tested until they attained a criterion of two successive errorless six-trial blocks or received a maximum of 90 trials, permitting a better than 99% level of confidence per child that criterion was not reached by chance (Bogartz, 1965). A noncorrection procedure was used throughout testing.

## Results

Table 8.2 summarizes the results. None of the children in the Replication condition reached criterion, replicating the Berch and Israel (1974) result, and therefore validating the condition as a transfer task in tests of training effects. Chi-square tests at the .05 significance level indicated that the number of children reaching criterion in the Solution and the Paper–Rock–Scissors groups did not differ, 13 out of 16 = 81% in the Solution condition and 11 out of 16 = 69% in the Paper–Rock–Scissors condition. The Hypothesis Verbalization and the Circle groups also did not differ, but each of the first pair of groups differed from each of the second pair. As Table 8.2 shows, trials to criterion, errors to criterion, and errors-per-trial to criterion ordered the

TABLE 8.2
Summary Table of Means: Experiment 3

| | Criterion Subjects | | | | | Noncriterion Subjects | | |
| Condition | Percent of Group | Trials to Criterion | Errors to Criterion | Errors/Trial to Criterion | | Percent of Group | Errors | Errors/Trial |
|---|---|---|---|---|---|---|---|---|
| Solution | 81 | 41.54 | 7.07 | .17 | | 19 | 33.00 | .37 |
| Paper–Rock–Scissors | 69 | 40.36 | 7.63 | .19 | | 31 | 39.60 | .44 |
| Hypoth. Verbaliza. | 38 | 57.00 | 14.83 | .26 | | 62 | 42.80 | .48 |
| Circle | 25 | 70.50 | 20.75 | .29 | | 75 | 34.75 | .39 |
| Replication | 0 | — | — | — | | 100 | 42.75 | .48 |

groups in the same way except for one slight inversion for the Solution and Paper–Rock–Scissors groups in number of trials to criterion.

It was impossible for the children in the Paper–Rock–Scissors group to reach criterion in less than 18 trials because they required at least one block of six trials to learn the content of the transverse patterning problem, even assuming they were perfectly primed with the structure. Two subjects did only require one block of six trials to acquire the content, reaching criterion in 18 trials, and another three children took only two six-trial blocks to acquire the content, reaching criterion in 24 trials. On the other hand, the Solution condition permitted children to reach criterion in 12 trials, and three of the Solution condition children did do this, making no errors to criterion. When the Solution condition children did not solve the problem with no errors, however, it took them at least 30 trials to reach criterion. These observations account in part for the slightly smaller average number of trials to criterion for the Paper–Rock–Scissors group than for the Solution group.

To compare the performance of children not reaching criterion, an analysis of variance was performed on the total number of errors, with Condition as the single factor. Table 8.2 shows the mean errors and mean errors-per-trial for noncriterion children in each Condition. The Condition effect was significant at the .05 level, $F(4,41) = 5.72$. Most errors were made in the Hypothesis Verbalization and Replication conditions, and least errors were made in the Solution and Circle conditions. Individual $t$-tests indicated that the mean number of errors made by noncriterion children in the Hypothesis Verbalization and Replication conditions did not differ significantly but did differ from that made by noncriterion children in the Solution and Circle conditions, although the mean number of errors made by children not reaching criterion in these latter two groups did not differ. The noncriterion children in the Paper–Rock–Scissors condition produced a mean total number of errors that fell between these two sets of two groups and did not differ significantly from any of them.

## Discussion

Nine-year-old children in the Paper–Rock–Scissors group reach criterion as often as do those who are given the solution, take the same number of trials to reach criterion, and make the same number of errors to criterion. But the Paper–Rock–Scissors children were only given the structure of the transverse patterning task and were given no prior information about the stimuli. This result, the most striking in the entire study, shows that priming the relevant structure but giving none of the content to be used with that structure is just about as facilitative of solution as telling the children the entire solution, structure and content together.

As in the case of the conditional discrimination, two alternative structures will be considered for the transverse patterning problem. The first is a list structure, listing the correct choice for each presentation. The child is assumed to learn the preferences or choices, one for each pair of stimuli that is presented. For the triangle–circle–square problem, we represent this solution by

$$\{(x,y) \mid (x \in P_4) \wedge (y \in S') \wedge (x' = \{(u,v) \mid (u \in x) \wedge (v \in x) \wedge (u \neq v)\})$$
$$\wedge [(w,z) \in \{(\mathrm{Tr,Ci}), (\mathrm{Ci,Sq}), (\mathrm{Sq,Tr})\} \cap x'] \rightarrow (y = w)\} \tag{7}$$

in which $P_4$ is the set of stimulus presentations $\{\{\mathrm{Tr,Ci}\}, \{\mathrm{Ci,Sq}\}, \{\mathrm{Sq, Tr}\}\}$, $S'$ is the set of stimuli $\{\mathrm{Tr, Ci, Sq}\}$, and (7) says that the subject remembers three ordered pairs, (Tr,Ci), (Ci,Sq), and (Sq,Tr) in which the first element is the correct choice for a presentation containing the two members of the ordered pair. It is further assumed that these ordered pairs are learned separately. This limited form of integration requires at least one feedback trial for each different presentation.

In the case of the second solution structure, the child is assumed to use a more complex representation of the problem in conjunction with a single ordered triple of the stimuli. This solution structure is represented by

$$\{(x,y) \mid x \in P_4 \wedge y \in S' \wedge T = (\mathrm{Tr,Ci,Sq}) \rightarrow$$
$$\mathrm{Ch(Tr,Ci)} \wedge \mathrm{Ch(Ci,Sq)} \wedge \mathrm{Ch(Sq,Tr)}\} \tag{8}$$

in which the phrase $\mathrm{Ch}(u,v)$ is defined to mean $[x = \{u,v\} \rightarrow y = u]$. It is assumed that when a structure such as (8) is used, the feedback information is stored in the triple, $T$, by appropriate positioning of the stimulus values. For example, if the subject starts with the abstract solution structure

$$\{(x,y) \mid x \in \Pi \wedge y \in \Sigma \wedge T = (\sigma_1,\sigma_2,\sigma_3) \rightarrow \mathrm{Ch}(\sigma_1,\sigma_2) \wedge$$
$$\mathrm{Ch}(\sigma_2,\sigma_3) \wedge \mathrm{Ch}(\sigma_3,\sigma_1)\} \tag{9}$$

and the presentation $\{\mathrm{Tr}(+), \mathrm{Ci}(-)\}$ with the indicated feedback occurs, the subject sets $T$ to the value $(\mathrm{Tr,Ci},\sigma_3)$ and at this point can be said to know $\mathrm{Ch(Tr,Ci)} \wedge \mathrm{Ch(Ci},\sigma_3) \wedge \mathrm{Ch}(\sigma_3,\mathrm{Tr})$, although $\sigma_3$ will remain unknown until a presentation containing Sq occurs.

We can now represent knowing *a* transverse patterning problem, e.g., the Paper–Rock–Scissors problem, by

$$\{(x,y) \mid x \in P_4 \wedge y \in S'' \wedge T = (\mathrm{Pa,Ro,Sc}) \rightarrow \mathrm{Ch(Pa,Ro)} \wedge$$
$$\mathrm{Ch(Ro,Sc)} \wedge \mathrm{Ch(Sc,Pa)}\} \tag{10}$$

knowing *some* transverse patterning problems by

$$\{(x,y) \mid x \in P_4 \cup P_5 \wedge y \in S' \cup S'' \wedge (\sigma_1,\sigma_2,\sigma_3) \in \{(\mathrm{Tr,Ci,Sq}),$$
$$(\mathrm{Pa,Ro,Sc})\} \rightarrow \mathrm{Ch}(\sigma_1,\sigma_2) \wedge \mathrm{Ch}(\sigma_2,\sigma_3) \wedge \mathrm{Ch}(\sigma_3,\sigma_1)\} \tag{11}$$

and knowing *the* transverse patterning problem, represented by (9). (A similar generalization from structure (7) can also be stated.)

It is interesting to contrast solutions (7) and (8). Solution (7) has a simple, familar form but uses a three-item list of ordered pairs of stimuli. Solution (8) uses a more complex form but obtains compensation by reducing the data to be stored to a single ordered triple of stimuli. Solution (8) seems to characterize the way adults informed of the problem know the solution. Knowing the structure of the Paper–Rock–Scissors game, it is enough to remember the ordered triple (paper, rock, scissors), although the ideas of covering, smashing, and cutting may help. Moving to the transverse patterning problem, if we recall the sequence triangle–circle–square, we know that triangle beats circle, circle beats square, and square beats triangle by moving through the list and around from the end to the beginning.

The knowledge in (10) might be what the child has when he comes to the experiment or after being taught the Paper–Rock–Scissors game, the knowledge in (11) might be what is known after two or more transverse patterning problems have been solved, and the knowledge in (9) specifies what transfers from one transverse patterning problem to another when the solution structure can be dissociated from the problem content.

I hypothesize that performance by the Paper–Rock–Scissors group can be summarized as follows: learning (or relearning) structure (10) enabled the children to abstract structure (9) and transfer it to the transverse patterning problem, facilitating the complete solution (8). The present study does not, however, conclusively demonstrate that the solution form (9) was transferring rather than an abstract form like (7). Some results from a fourth experiment will be presented to demonstrate a context in which it can be concluded that (9) was used.

## EXPERIMENT 4: THE FORM OF STRUCTURAL TRANSFER IN THE TRANSVERSE PATTERNING PROBLEM

The logic here is analogous to that used in Experiment 2. If, with repeated transverse patterning problems, a list structure such as (7) is used, the correct choice for each presentation will not be known until feedback for each presentation has been provided at least once. But if a structure such as (9) is transferring from problem to problem, and if as many free variables as possible are being transformed into constants as soon as the information is available, then as we saw previously, after only one trial of the new problem the child can know essentially the entire solution. When the values in $T$ are $(c_1, c_2, \sigma_3)$, $c_1$ and $c_2$ being constants, then the child knows $Ch(c_1, c_2)$, $Ch(c_2, \sigma_3)$, and $Ch(\sigma_3, c_1)$. As soon as a presentation containing stimulus $c_3$ occurs, the solution is complete prior to choice or feedback because now it is known that $T = (c_1, c_2, c_3)$. This analysis predicts that transfer of the structure in (9) should enable children to perform better than chance on the second trial of the new problem and thereafter.

To test this hypothesis, Experiment 4 employed multiple transverse patterning problems. Two departures from previous procedure were employed. The first was that word names rather than pictures were used as the stimuli. This enabled computer generation of the numerous stimulus sequences and feedback outcomes. It was assumed that, in the previous studies, verbal encoding of pictures was the predominant approach, so that use of stimulus words, instead of pictures, would be a comparable procedure. The second departure followed a suggestion by Harlow (1959) that maximization of interproblem learning efficiency is achieved by using for each problem the trials on which the learning is greatest, rather than bringing the subject to a learning criterion on each problem. It was assumed that the maximum learning per problem would probably take place in the first 12 trials or so, so each problem used only 12 trials. Also, in order to facilitate early abstraction of the intransitive, cyclic structure, a system of cyclic clues was used for the first one, two, or three problems.

## Method

*Subjects.*    The subjects were 108 nine-, ten-, and eleven-year-old children, 36 from each of grades four, five, and six of the Wildwood Elementary School in Amherst, Mass.

*Materials.*    The materials consisted of a game board with one, two, or three clues in envelopes glued to the front of the board, and 13, 14, or 15 problem sheets in the game board. The top of the board had three rows of four pairs of circular holes. In each hole was a rubber stopper. The stopper in the left hand hole of each pair had a red paper dot on it, and the stopper in the right hand hole had a green paper dot. A strip of paper was pasted under each row of holes, with the numbers 1 through 12 written sequentially on the strips, each number centered beneath a pair of holes. Also on the strip of paper at each pair of holes under the left hand hole was the word "choose" and under the right hand hole was the word "correct". Finally, in the upper left hand corner of the board were one, two, or three clue envelopes, each containing one clue sheet. These envelopes were labeled "First Clue," "Second Clue," and "Third Clue" when all three were present, and obvious deletions were made when less were there.

Inside the board were computer-printed problem sheets on which words were printed such that when the sheets were inserted in the board, a pair of words would appear under each left hand hole of each pair of holes, and a single word that was a member of the pair would appear under the right hand hole. Thus, the left hand pair of words offered a choice for the subject and the right hand word indicated which choice was correct. The first one, two, or three problem sheets were problems to which the clues applied, depending on the number of clues provided, and the remaining 12 sheets were transverse patterning discrimination problems for which no clues were provided. Thus, each pair of holes provided one trial of a twelve trial problem.

*Procedure.*    The children were run in groups of 12 to 18 children. The essentials of the procedure are explained in the following instructions that were read to the children at the beginning of the session.

We have developed a new word game which we are going to give to the school if it turns out to be a good game. To find out if it is a good game we are asking you to help us test it in this experiment. We play this game with words on sheets of paper in a game board. In this game we learn to choose one word each time we see two words. Then we find out if we were correct.

You each have a game board. In this board there are sheets of paper with words on them. Don't look at the sheets of paper in the board now. On the top of the board there are holes to look through and rubber stoppers covering the holes. In a minute I will tell you which stopper to pick up.

Look at the numbers on the board. The numbers go from 1 to 12. Each row has four numbers: 1,2,3, and 4 in the top row; 5,6,7, and 8 in the middle row; and 9,10,11 and 12 in the bottom row. Just above each number there are two rubber stoppers. One rubber stopper has a red dot and the other rubber stopper has a green dot. Under the red dot stopper the board says "Choose" and under the green dot stopper the board says "Correct." The red dot means "*Stop* here and choose a word" and the green dot means "Now *go* and look here to see if you were correct."

We will work across the top row, then across the middle row, and then across the bottom row. So, we will just follow the numbers 1 to 12.

Now here is what to do. Does everyone see the envelope marked FIRST CLUE? Take out your first clue and read it. Now, lift up the red dot stopper at number one and look at the two words underneath it. Now, choose which you think is correct and circle it with a crayon. At first you won't be sure which is the right word, so you may have to guess. You can learn the right word by using the clues and seeing what is under the green dot stopper each time. Did everyone mark a word?

Now look under the next stopper, the green dot stopper over the number one, where it tells which word is the correct one to choose from the two words you just looked at. After we have seen the correct word, we put both stoppers back in their holes. Always put the red dot back where it says choose and the green dot back where it says correct.

We will follow the numbers from 1 to 12, moving across each row and then moving back to the beginning of the next row. When we finish with number 12 at the end of the bottom row, we will take the top sheet of paper out from inside the board and put it in our folder. *This is very important.* Be very sure to take out *only* the top sheet of paper in the board each time you finish with number 12. Then we start over again at the top of the board at number 1 with a new set of words.

Before we go on, I want to tell you a little more about the clues because they make the game easier. On the top of your board there is one, two or three envelopes. How many of you have one envelope? How many have two envelopes? How many have three envelopes? Each sheet of paper in your board has a different set of words. The first envelope gives a clue for the words on the top sheet of paper in your board. It will help you work on the first sheet. If you have three clues, when you finish with number 12 on the first sheet and have taken the first sheet out of the board and put it in your folder, then take the second clue to help you work on the second sheet of words in your board. The third envelope gives a clue for the words on the third sheet of paper in your board. Don't look at it until you have finished with the second sheet and put it in your folder.

If you only have one envelope, you use the clue for the first sheet of paper in the board, and then do the rest of the sheets of paper on your own. If you have two clues, use the first clue for your first sheet of paper, the second clue for your second sheet of paper, and then do all the rest on your own. If you have three clues, use the first clue for the first sheet of paper, the second clue for the second sheet of paper, the third clue for the third sheet of paper, and then do the rest of the sheets in the board without a clue.

Are there any questions?

O.K. Now we will start for real. Read your first clue again. Look again at the word you chose under the red dot at number one, look again at the correct word under the green dot at number 1. Put the stoppers back and now move on to number 2. Don't forget to use your other clues later if you have them.

O.K. Let's begin. If you have any questions, raise your hand and I'll come to your desk to help you.

When you finish raise your hand.

*Design.*    At each grade level, the children were randomly assigned to one, two, or three clues, and to the Class condition or to the Nonclass condition. A clue consisted of three lines of computer print. One clue read: PAPER COVERS ROCK/ROCK SMASHES SCISSORS/SCISSORS CUTS PAPER. Another read: EVENING BEFORE MORNING/MORNING BEFORE NOON/NOON BEFORE EVENING. The third was: TREE GIVES FRUIT/FRUIT GIVES SEED/SEED GIVES TREE. To each clue corresponded a transverse patterning problem. For paper, rock, scissors, the problem solution is obvious. For morning, noon, evening, correct solution required choosing morning when with noon, noon when with evening, and evening when with morning. For tree, fruit, seed, tree was correct with fruit, fruit was correct with seed, and seed was correct with tree. Which clues were assigned and in what order was completely balanced and randomized.

Following the one, two, or three problems for which clues were given, 12 additional transverse patterning problems were given in a different random order of problems for each child. The words were unrelated from problem to problem. The children in the Class condition received triples of words that were related within each problem. Thus they might receive one problem involving turkey, duck and goose; the next problem involving star, sun, and moon; pencil, chalk, and crayon; etc. Children in the Nonclass condition received the same words, but not in classes for each problem. Thus they received problems such as spoon, duck, highway, and couch, ocean, sheep. Which words were correct with which other words were determined randomly and were different for each subject.

## Results

The complete analysis of the data from this experiment is not yet available. A subset of 17 children were selected on the basis of their high performance on the final trials of the final problems. None of the grades or experimental conditions seemed to be overly represented in this group of children. This group provides important evidence concerning the question of central interest here, the form of the structural transfer in the transverse patterning problem. Figure 8.1 shows the proportion of correct responses on each of the 12 trials of the post-clue problems, averaged over the 17 children and over blocks of three problems. The important part of the figure is the performance on Trial 2. It can be seen that for these subjects, the average proportion correct on Trial 2 in the second and third blocks of three problems was about .8, and by the fourth block of three problems it was over .9. The fact that on Trial 1 the performance was at the chance level argues against any specific dimensional transfer between problems. Occasionally the content of Trial 2 was the same

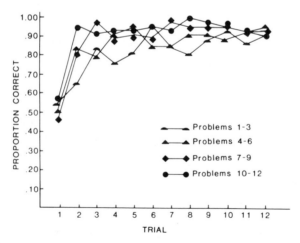

FIG. 8.1.   Proportion of correct responses on each trial, averaged over blocks of three problems, 17 selected subjects.

as Trial 1, due to randomization of presentations, but even with perfect memory for the answer from Trial 1, performance at Trial 2 would only be expected to be at less than .6 if this was the only basis of facilitation. That these children were performing almost perfectly on the second trial of the last three problems strongly suggests, then, that some abstraction of the form of the transverse patterning problem had occurred and that this abstract structure was being integrated with the information from Trial 1 to arrive at the problem solution. But a solution of form (7), a list solution, would not produce such facilitation on the second trial. Having learned one stimulus pair would still leave the other two pairs to be learned. These data suggest that a form such as (9) was being used, where data from Trial 1 would be sufficient to fill in two thirds of the stimulus triple $T$, and presentation of a new set of stimuli on Trial 2, even without choice or feedback yet, would enable completion of the triple and therefore completion of the solution.

## GENERAL DISCUSSION

The results of the four discrimination learning experiments indicate that in addition to the well-known learning of information concerning relevance or irrelevance of dimensions, and correctness or incorrectness of values on those dimensions, new, structural forms of learning can also be demonstrated. The results for Experiment 1 indicate that children who solve the conditional discrimination use structure (4), a compound structure involving the conjunction of two conditional phrases or frames that obscures the correctness or incorrectness of individual stimuli. Experiment 2 suggests the use of that same structure by adults and also demonstrates that, in adults, the structure of the conditional discrimination can be abstracted from its content and transfer across problems. This structure is used to assimilate new content, forming the basis of the integration of information from subsequent conditional discrimination problems.

The results of Experiment 3 are particularly exciting. The difficulty inherent in the transverse patterning problem, so effectively demonstrated by Berch and Israel (1974), and replicated here, is dramatically removed by providing the child with a structural analogue of the problem, the Paper–Rock–Scissors game. Perhaps the most interesting aspect of this finding is that supplying the structural analogue is as effective a facilitation as is telling the children the complete solution to the problem. It appears that the intransitive, cyclic character of the solution is extremely counterintuitive for children, rather than difficult to use. Given the form of the problems, assimilation of content and use of the solution structure does not appear to be inordinately difficult. This conclusion is further supported by the finding in Experiment IV that some children could master the abstract structure of the transverse patterning problem after being exposed to the cyclic clues, even though they were getting only 12 trials per problem.

The theoretical and experimental results presented here indicate that information integration in discrimination learning can occur by assimilation of specific content to abstract structures. Because the theoretical discussion and the representations of solution structures presented here are not a complete theory, a variety of processes remain unaccounted for. Among the most interesting are those involved in forming a specific solution structure by use of the trial-to-trial information in a problem before an abstract structure is available. Answering this question requires a theory of initial discrimination learning. A second process of interest is that of structural abstraction. How does the abstract form become established, free of previous content? Finally, what are the processes involved in the assimilation of new content to an established abstract structure?

With respect to structural abstraction, Piaget's concept of reflective abstraction (Piaget, 1970) appears to be of value in placing the phenomenon within a general context:

> In the case of logico-mathematical abstraction, on the other hand, what is given is an agglomeration of actions or operations previously made by the subject himself, with their results. In this case, abstraction consists first of taking cognizance of the existence of one of these actions or operations.... Second, the action noted has to be "reflected" (in the physical sense of the term) by being projected onto another plane—for example, the plane of thought as opposed to that of practical action, or the plane of abstract systematization as opposed to that of concrete thought (say, algebra versus arithmetic). Third, it has to be integrated into a new structure, which means that a new structure has to be set up, but this is only possible if two conditions are fulfilled: (a) the new structure must first of all be a reconstruction of the preceding one if it is not to lack coherence and congruity; it will thus be the product of the preceding one on a plane chosen by it; (b) it must also, however, widen the scope of the preceding one, making it general by combining it with the elements proper to the new place of thought; otherwise there will be nothing new about it. These, then, are the characteristics of a "reflection," but now we are taking the term in the psychological sense, to mean a rearrangement, by means of thought, of some matter previously presented to the subject in a rough or immediate form. The name I propose to give this process of reconstruction with new combinations, which allows for any operational structure at any previous stage or level to be integrated into a richer structure at a higher level is "reflective abstraction." (pp. 320-21)

The details of the process remain to be spelled out for the specific instances that arise in discrimination learning. Piaget's general approach also suggests that the answer to structural abstraction in terms of reflective abstraction will entail an answer to the question of what processes are involved in the assimilation of new content to an established structure. It is in the nature of reflective abstraction that the scope of the structure constructed on the plane of reflection is wider than the original structure. This widening of scope entails the assimilation of new content. Again, the details will require theoretical elaboration.

A brief example of such elaboration will show how Piaget's conception of reflective abstraction guides a theoretical analysis of what happens when the transverse patterning problem is facilitated. One thing that telling the child the solution to the problem (Solution condition, Exp. 3) shares with both telling the child the solution to the Paper–Rock–Scissors problem (Exp. 3) and giving the child the cyclic clue system (Exp. 4) is that, in each case, an entire problem solution is presented, rather than just the piecemeal trial-to-trial information. Symbolically, the child is not just given Ch(Pa,Ro), Ch(Ro,Sc), and Ch(Sc,Pa). Instead, the child is given Ch(Pa,Ro) $\wedge$ Ch(Ro,Sc) $\wedge$ Ch(Sc,Pa). The activities required of the child in order to cognitively organize this entire solution require that the choice function Ch be intransitive. The child can only notice the counterintuitive intransitivity within the context of an entire solution, because single choices will not reveal this. Noticing this cognitive action provides the opportunity to reflect this action to a different plane at which cyclic structure can be established that will not only completely organize the given solution but will be available to organize new information from other problems. This cyclic structure is itself open to further reflection. Attention to rehearsal of the cycle (Paper–Rock) $\rightarrow$ (Rock–Scissors) $\rightarrow$ (Scissors–Paper) $\rightarrow$ (Paper–Rock) $\rightarrow$ ... may reveal to the subject that repetition of ( –Rock) and (Rock– ) is unnecessary. The cycle may be reduced to Paper $\rightarrow$ Rock $\rightarrow$ Scissors $\rightarrow$ ... with the appropriate inferential rules attached. Reflection of this abbreviated organization leads to the triple of organization, $T$, hypothesized in (9).

In any case, it is clear that structural abstraction occurs as an information integration process in discrimination learning in adults and children and that theoretical conceptions of discrimination learning broad enough to encompass such phenomena will be required. A Piagetian approach, sufficiently elaborated, seems likely to be one of the candidates.

## ACKNOWLEDGMENTS

Experiments 1 and 4 were conducted in collaboration with Betsy Moore. Jeffrey Lowell assisted with conducting Experiment 2. Experiment 3 was conducted in collaboration with Nancy Myers, Marion Perlmutter, Hilary Horn, Betty Lorch, and Robert Lorch. I am indebted to H. Berch for making his transverse patterning data available to me at an early point in the work on Experiment 3 to M. Greenebaum, the principal at Mark's Meadow Elementary School, and to Nancy Morrison and Tom Fowler–Finn, the principal and acting principal at Wildwood Elementary School, for their generous cooperation, and to Tom Trabasso for numerous suggestions in response to an earlier draft.

# REFERENCES

Berch, D. B., & Israel, M.  Solution of the transverse patterning problem: Response to cue–cue relations. *Psychonomic Science,* 1971, *23,* 383–384.

Berch, D. B. & Israel, M.  The effects of setting similarity on children's learning of the transverse patterning problem. *Journal of Experimental Child Psychology,* 1974, *18,* 252–258.

Bogartz, R. S.  The criterion method: Some analyses and remarks. *Psychological Bulletin,* 1965, *64,* 1–14.

Bourne, L. E., Jr.  Knowing and using concepts. *Psychological Review,* 1970, *77,* 546–556.

Fellows, B. J.  Chance stimulus sequences for discrimination learning. *Psychological Bulletin,* 1967, *2,* 87–92.

Harlow, H.  Learning set and error factor theory. In S. Koch (Ed.), *Psychology: A study of a science* (Vol. 2). New York: McGraw-Hill, 1959.

Haygood, R. C., & Bourne, L. E., Jr.  Attribute and rule-learning aspects of conceptual behavior. *Psychological Review,* 1965, *72,* 175–195.

Piaget, J.  *Biology and knowledge.* Chicago: University of Chicago Press, 1970.

Quine, W. V. O.  *Mathematical logic.* Cambridge, Mass.: Harvard University Press, 1965.

Spence, K. W.  The nature of the response in discrimination learning. *Psychological Review,* 1952, *59,* 89–93

Tarski, A.  *Introduction to logic and to the methodology of deductive sciences.* New York: Oxford University Press, 1965.

# III INTEGRATION OF EVENTS IN DISCOURSE PROCESSING

# 9 Memory and Inferences in the Comprehension of Narratives

Tom Trabasso
*University of Chicago*

David W. Nicholas
*Carnegie-Mellon University*

How do things become meaningful? This is a central question in the study of language comprehension. To set the stage for our discussion, we found the following definition of meaning by the American educational philosopher John Dewey most helpful.

> To grasp the meaning of a thing, an event or a situation is to see it in its relations to other things; to note how it operates or functions, what consequences follow from it; what causes it, what uses it can be put to. (1963, p. 135)

Finding relations between things or events in a context is synonymous with making them become meaningful. In comprehending a story, the person must "go beyond the text" and make the necessary connections between statements or fill in the existing gaps (Bartlett, 1932). The process of inferencing is the construction of relations between events and is a central component in language comprehension. Moreover, this process is assumed to be essential to representing information in memory, leading to better recall and the probability of making more inferences.

## NARRATIVES AND MEMORY BY CHILDREN

In a recent review on the development of memory, Brown (1975) discussed evidence showing that children remember best material that is most meaningful. If the material is conveyed in stories or narratives, it is better retained than if it is conveyed via lists of isolated items. Brown interpreted the

215

meaningfulness of stories in a manner different from the definition given above. She indicated that stories convey material in a form that is already known or familiar to the child. In a manner of speaking, narratives are better made to "fit the head of the child." Brown's argument was that the child is forced to use strategies or control processes such as elaboration for the memorization of isolated items or events. Such strategies develop or are accelerated through formal education, which requires the frequent commitment to memory and retrieval of isolated facts. The implication of her discussion is that active strategies are not required in the comprehension and retention of stories, narratives, or connected discourse.

We find this implication hard to accept. Children do develop specific strategies for dealing with laboratory memory tasks such as learning to recall lists of words, but they probably also develop a different set of strategies or processes for dealing with stories, narratives, or connected discourse. One difference between isolated lists and narratives is that the material in a story is already elaborated, at least to some extent. Interrelationships between protagonists, actions, consequences, conflicts, goals, etc., are specified. In this sense, the child does not have to provide meaning or relations; rather, he has to find them. The information in the narrative is structured and organized and can even be described by "grammars" (Rumelhart, 1975; Mandler & Johnson, 1977; Stein & Glenn, 1979; Thorndyke, 1977). When a child is trying to master a list of words, these relations are absent. The child must generate meaningful relations in order to connect the words on the list to each other or to other known concepts (in memory). Elaboration is a strategic behavior that may be a manifestation of a procedure by which the child tries to find meaning in the absence of its surface representation in the stimulus input or text.

Although narratives promote meaning by making explicit at least some of the relations, they are never fully explicit and the child must make *inferences* in order to connect, understand, and retain material. In many instances, making inferences requires considerable knowledge of the world. To illustrate how a child's understanding of a narrative must depend upon knowledge of the world, consider the following three pairs of sentences:

(1) Mary had a little lamb. Its fleece was white as snow.
(2) Mary had a little lamb. She spilled gravy and mint jelly on her dress.
(3) Mary had a little lamb. The delivery was a difficult one and afterwards the vet needed a drink.

In the first pair of sentences, "Mary" refers to a character from a well-known nursery rhyme—a little girl who is followed about by her pet lamb. The verb "had" alludes to ownership, and the animal is alive and well in this context. The sheep does not fare so well in the second example. Here, "Mary" is probably human and female (the pronoun "she" and the noun "dress" allow this inference). "Mary" may also be a child, because children are more likely than adults to spill food on themselves. The references to gravy and mint jelly, however, indicate that the lamb is a meal, not a pet, of which Mary ate only a small portion. Finally, in the third pair of sentences, the references to the veterinarian and a difficult delivery suggest that Mary has given birth to a small lamb and is, herself, a mature female sheep. The vet is probably an adult, male human being whose profession is to tend to sick animals. The drink is presumably an alcoholic beverage intended to enable the vet to relax after the difficult delivery of the newborn lamb.

This brief analysis reveals that a considerable amount of knowledge—about nursery rhymes, ownership, pets, little girls, sheep, food, animal births, veterinarians, and alcohol—must be brought to bear in order to understand these sentences. Information that is implicit in the message has to be *inferred* if the gap between the intended meaning and understanding is to be closed.

## RESEARCH ON INFERENCES BY CHILDREN

In this section, we shall present a selective review of studies that have focused on inferential abilities of children. In particular, we shall consider those studies that involve narratives, the making of inferences, and memory.

### Inferring Internal States

One of the first studies on the retention of information and the child's ability to infer internal states of protagonists in narratives is that of Flapan (1968). Flapan showed *filmed* episodes to children 6 through 12 years in age and asked them to tell what happened as well as what they thought the feeling states were of various characters in the filmed events. Flapan used a direct probe questioning procedure, asking, for example, "How did Mary *feel* when John refused to let her use the skates?" The feelings reported by the children were more likely to occur and to agree with the adult interpretations when the child was older. Because the feelings were not explicitly stated in the dialogue, the assumption was that the child would have to infer them from facial expressions or from reactions to actions and consequences by others. The conclusion reached was that younger children cannot make such inferences or at least have difficulty in doing so.

This conclusion is consistent with Piaget's (1932) pioneering work on inferential ability and moral judgment. Piaget believed that "preoperational" children (children who are less than 7 years old) are "morally objective" and focus only on the consequences of actions. Older and "concrete operational" children are thought to be "morally subjective" and able to take into account intentions or goals of others and to coordinate this information with the consequences of actions. Such judgments on either an intention or an action or a consequence constitute an *evaluative* inference.

When children are asked to recall stories, they tend to recall categories of information in an ordering that is independent of age and story. The order, from the best recalled to the least well recalled, is: major settings, direct consequences, initiating events, attempts, reactions, minor settings, and internal responses (Stein & Glenn, 1979; see also Mandler & Johnson, 1977). Note that, in free recall, internal responses are recalled least well, while consequences and attempts (actions) are recalled better. These data are consistent with the belief that younger children do not focus on internal states. However, Stein and Glenn (1979) carried out a second experiment in which they asked children to tell them what was most important about the story. They also asked the children a series of "Why" questions on each major category of information. When asked for what was the most important aspect of the story, the children stressed motives, feelings, and thoughts of characters to a greater degree than the recall data would suggest. More than one fourth of the children made inferences of a moral nature as answers, and there were no differences related to age for this kind of inference. The developmental differences, contrasting 10- with 6-year-olds, seem to be that the older children drew more general inferences or lessons while the younger children were more specific in their examples. When the probe questions were used, internal responses were given far more often than in recall and were perceived as the immediate cause for other internal responses, attempts, and consequences more than any other category. In short, internal responses were seen as the locus of causality. Stein and Glenn's (1979) procedure of asking *causal* questions may be a more sensitive method than Flapan's direct "feeling" questions to assess what a child knows about internal responses and their relations to other behaviors.

There are several reasons why internal states may not be inferred or recalled. One is that the relation between the internal state and its cause may be uncertain. People react in a variety of ways to a given event, or they may carry out several possible actions for a given motive or feeling. Young children, when uncertain, may not link the actions to the internal states. Another possibility is that internal states are directly implied and are redundant with actions. For example, if a character cries in response to learning of someone's death, then the act of crying entails a state of grief. The child may report the action and convey implicity the state without feeling an obligation to report the state. Information that is redundant in messages is often deleted, and children may be selective forgetters. Finally, in stories, the internal states are not made as explicit as actions. If they were made more explicit, elaborated, or emphasized, then recall for this information might increase. Berndt and Berndt (1975) and Bearison and Isaacs (1975) have shown that when motives and intentions are made explicit in stories, 6- and 7-year-olds will use intentions over consequences in moral judgment.

The conclusion that young children cannot take into account intentions is suspect on other grounds. In Piaget's (1932) experiments (and consequently nearly all of those that use his paradigm), the order or presentation of the intentions and the consequences is confounded. In stories, the intention nearly always precedes the act and its consequences. This confounding of temporal order of events is natural in the sense that episodes have standard structures that correspond to real-life, temporally ordered event sequences. For example, in their story grammar, Stein and Glenn 1979 identify five main sequential events in an episode: (1) an initiating event; (2) an internal state; (3) an action; (4) a consequence; and (5) a reaction. Piaget's (1932) stories are not so well structured but they usually contain events (2), (3), and (4). In his paradigm, two stories are read to the child. In each story, a protagonist's intent, acts, and/or consequences are given. Then the child is asked to make a moral judgment on the protagonists. Typically, the judgment is on a good/bad dimension.

Three studies have shown that there are recency effects for intentions and consequences on evaluative inferences in this context (Feldman, Klosson, Parsons, Rholes, & Ruble, 1976; Nummedal & Bass, 1976; Austin, Ruble, & Trabasso, 1977). the evaluative judgments were strongly affected by the position of the intentional information in the story. When the intentions were described first, the consequences had more influence on the judgment. When the intentions occurred second and were more recent, they had more influence. In the study by Feldman et al. (1976), the data for the 4- and 5-year-old children were virtually mirror images for the two orders of presentation, indicating that intentions and consequences had equal weight in determining the moral judgment.

Austin et al. (1977) controlled memory for the stories and studied the recency effect in Piaget's two-story paradigm. The child had to first recall both stories equally well before making an evaluation comparison between the protagonists on a scale of "naughtiness." The children were 5 to 8 years in age. The consequences in the stories were always negative so that the question was whether or not a positive intention could offset a negative one. The position, either first or last, of the intentions was varied in the experiment. The child's evaluation of the protagonists was measured in three ways: (1) a decision as to which one was naughtier; (2) a justification of this decision; and (3) an award of cookies among the protagonists. All three measures favored the idea that the intentions were more likely to be processed when they were recent. When the children were asked to judge the naughtier protagonist, recent positive intentions offset negative consequences. When asked to justify this decision, recent positive intentions were mentioned more frequently than negative consequences. Finally, when asked to award cookies, the children increased the amount awarded when the positive intentions were recent; they reduced the amount when the negative intentions were recent.

## Measuring Internal State Inferences
## Via Information Integration Approach

These evaluative inferences can be understood in terms of models for information integration (Anderson, 1971, 1974, Chapter 1, this volume; Lane & Anderson, 1976). Let $V_i$ be the value of the intentions on a scale of goodness and let $V_c$ be the value of the consequences on the scale. The effect on a judgment of these values is weighted by position factors. The integration of the weighted values into an overall, covert judgment is represented by an additive relation

$$j_A = w_1 V_i + w_2 V_c \qquad (1)$$

in which $j_A$ is the judgment on a scale for protagonist A and the $w_1$ and $w_2$ are the weights assigned to the values of the intentions and consequences, respectively. When two protagonists are compared, we suppose that the child makes a similar, covert judgment on protagonist B. After having differentially weighted and integrated the information from Story A and Story B, the judgment is mediated by a decision rule (for example, choose A if $j_A > j_B$). Equation (1) implies that various values of $V_i$ and $V_c$ add when combined in a story. Lane and Anderson (1976) tested Equation (1) on single-story judgments by adults and found that three levels of intentions added with three levels of consequences.

The information integration model promises us a way of disentangling the effect of an inferred value of an intention (or a consequence) from its location in a story. One could measure how children evaluate events separately, in which each event is a propositional statement containing only one intent or one act or one consequence. Then, knowing the scale value of each event in isolation, one could combine them to assess their joint effects. In the prior research, one does not know either the value or the weight of a location in the story. Piaget's (1932) finding could mean that the particular intentions portrayed held either low value for the children or low weight because of position in the story.

There have been two first attempts to apply the Anderson integration model to the problem of how children integrate or coordinate intention and consequent information in the making of moral judgments (Leon, Chapter 3, this volume; Surber, 1977).

The first of these by Leon had children from 6 to 13 years in age, as well as college students, judge protagonists in stories that were constructed with three levels of negative intentions and four levels of negative consequences. Leon examined individual rules for combining the information, the most predominant was to average the values of the intentions and the consequences. Several children used a "configural" rule in which consequences did not affect the judgments when the protagonist's intentions were neutral (accidental with respect to the consequences). Contrary to Piaget

(1932), very few younger children focused only on consequences—the vast majority used a multi-dimensional response strategy, and there were as many children who used an intention-only rule as there were who used a consequence-only rule.

Surber (1977) carried out two experiments on children, 5, 8, and 10 years of age, as well as college students. She asked for judgments of protagonists in single stories in which positive, neutral, or negative intentions were orthogonally paired with three levels of negative consequences. Surber found that all subjects at all ages used an averaging rule. However, unlike Leon, who examined individual subject data, Surber used only group data for each age group. Surber also obtained group estimates of the weights and scale values for intents and consequences. The weights of the intentions tended to remain the same with age; the weights of the consequences declined. While these data are consistent with Piaget (1932), they confound the order of intentions and consequences.

In a second study, Surber (1977) had subjects judge positive, neutral, or negative intentions combined orthogonally with two levels of positive or two levels of negative consequences. The group data showed integration at all age levels, but the nonlinear rule seemed to predominate. Again, weights of consequences declined dramatically with age, while the weights of intentions increased slightly with age.

In order to decide whether children can integrate intention and consequence information into a moral evaluation, which rule they use, and how much relative weight they assign to each source of information, one needs to have enough observations on individual children in order to test the information integration model. Analysis of variance or goodness-of-fit tests could be used to decide whether a child is focusing exclusively on intentions or consequences or using a multidimensional integration rule. One could then ask if the child is adding, averaging, multiplying, or discounting some levels, etc.—that is, what rule is he using to integrate. One also needs to address the problem of order of information. Because younger children remember best and use more recent information, the weight of consequences may be greater because of memory rather than moral value or other cognitive factors. Hence, the counterbalancing of intention–consequence information would allow assessment of order and weight effects, especially for children 5 to 8 years in age. Finally, one could explore the relationship between judgments made for single stories to that for story pairs.

## MEMORY AND TRANSITIVE INFERENCES

If a child can answer the question"Which is larger, A or C?" given the information that A is larger than B and that B is larger than C, he is assumed to be able to make a transitive inference. Transitive reasoning plays a central role in Piaget's general theory of cognitive development (Piaget, 1921, 1928, 1955, 1970; Piaget, Inhelder, & Szeminska, 1960), and in intelligence testing (Burt, 1919). The important aspect of such reasoning is that it requires the coordination of two terms, A and C, via a relationship to a third, common term, B. Making a transitive inference is thus but another case of information integration.

Memory, in the narrow sense of the term, meaning retention of the premises, would seem to be a necessary but not sufficient condition for answering an inference question. In most studies done on transitive inferences (cf. Smedslund, 1969), the premises are not present for the child to examine throughout the test. Rather, each comparison is demonstrated or told and is no longer available at the moment the transitive relationship is questioned. Consequently, a failure to retain the information from either premise may prevent the construction of a representation from the premises upon which the necessary operations for carrying out the inference would be made.

This problem led Bryant and Trabasso (1971) to reexamine the issue of transitive reasoning in children from 4 to 7 years of age. According to the Piagetian view, children in this age range are supposed to be "preoperational" and incapable of such reasoning.

Bryant and Trabasso (1971) had children learn color codes to relate differences in length between adjacent pairs of sticks in a series of five sticks. The children first learned the premises as a series of four pairwise comparisons: (1 vs. 2), (2 vs. 3), (3 vs. 4), and (4 vs. 5). The training on the premises continued until the child reached a criterion of six correct consecutive choices to each pair of sticks in a random series of all the adjacent pairs (premises). A test sequence followed in which the child was asked questions on all 10 possible pairs. Thus, information was obtained on the retention of the premises as well as on how well children performed on inferential pairs. (For a similar procedure, see Youniss & Murray, 1970, who, along with Bryant & Trabasso, 1971, devised the five-term series problems in order to satisfy the diagnostic criteria of Smedslund, 1969).

In the Bryant and Trabasso (1971) experiment, the performance of these children ranged above chance expectations, averaging from 78% to 92% correct answers on the critical inference test pair (2 vs. 4). More than one half of the 25 children in each of the age groups showed perfect performance on a series of four of these critical inference tests. In a subsequent experiment in which all the relations were stated verbally, performance was similar.

These data are better understood in a larger context involving several replications of the initial study. Trabasso (1975) describes some 29 different groups of children, adolescents, and adults, comprising some 379 subjects in all, who were trained and tested under similar conditions. For these 29 conditions, the correlation between retrieval of the premises and correct responding on the inference tests was very high and positive ($r = .80, p < .01$).

How do children succeed on these transitive test questions? The shortest answer is that they integrate the premises (1,2), (2,3), etc., into a serial order (1, 2, 3, . . . ) and then use this linear order representation to read off the desired relations. The most direct evidence for this generalization comes from studies by Trabasso, Riley, and Wilson (1975) and Riley (1976). Here, children 6 to 9 years in age were trained on five premises and given 15 tests after reaching criterion on training. The child's choice reaction time was obtained on each test trial. In the test series, six tests are of particular interest: three tests on the original premises, (2,3), (3,4), and (4,5); two inference tests involving a distance of one member apart, (2,4) and (3,5); and one test involving a distance of two members apart, (2,5). The tests vary in number of coordinations or premises involved. The first set involves no coordination. The second involves coordinating two premises. The third involves coordinating three premises. If the child stored the five premises in memory and coordinated them at the time of testing, the time to draw an inference should increase with the number of coordinations involved. On the other hand, if the child coordinates or integrates the members into a series during training and represents this integration as a linear order, then an opposite prediction follows, namely, that the further apart the two members are in the order, the faster the decision times (see Trabasso & Riley, 1975, for models on these processes). In the two studies cited above, this was exactly what was found.

The main developmental problem for the youngest children in these studies appears to be linguistic and memorial and not of a logical nature. When the relations are specified only in verbal terms and in the absence of external memory aids such as pictures of the members in the relationships, young children had difficulty in constructing the linear order. This difficulty is due, in part, to isolating the ends of the dimension. However, they had no such difficulty in mapping the codes onto physical displays or integrating them into orders when they had physical referents of the relationship or the members.

In performing transitive inferences, the central problem for the child lies in the construction of a representation that preserves the order information in the premises. A second problem lies in the limits of memory capacity of the child. A linear order or a simple seriation of the members on a dimension preserves order and reduces the load on memory. Because adults seem to use the same representation and mental operations as children, once they commit the premises to memory, it would appear that preschool children and adults are very much alike in the cognitive processes they use in these tasks.

The locus of the failure of the young child to perform transitive inferences is in the greater contextual dependency (MacNamara, 1972; Nelson, 1974) of language and a more limited memory capacity. Interpretation of the meaning of an utterance clearly depends upon the context in which it occurs (Bransford & Johnson, 1972; Bransford & McCarell, 1974). If the person has information in long-term memory that he can retrieve and use to interpret what is being said, he is more likely to comprehend the message. With young children, one cannot assume that they have the same information as adults. Rather, we suggest that they do depend more upon the external environment and the social context than do adults in order to interpret what is stated. If we provide examples, instances, or referents, we are more likely to succeed in our communication with the child.

### Inferences and the Constructivist Approach

Several recent studies by Bransford and his colleagues   (Bransford, Barclay, & Franks, 1972;  Bransford & Franks, 1972;  Bransford & McCarrell, 1974) have stressed the importance of context and inferences in language comprehension and have argued for a "constructive"—as opposed to an "interpretive"—approach to models of the compehension process.

The interpretive approach grew out of work in transformational linguistics (Katz & Fodor, 1963; Katz & Postal, 1964; see also Greene, 1972). This approach posits that a sentence is processed first by characterizing its surface structure. Then, transformational rules are used to produce a deep structure representation that is both necessary and sufficient to express the total meaning of the sentence. Interpretive models are generally unidirectional (sentence → surface structure → deep structure) and interact with memory primarily during the formation of the deep structure representation. The sentence is treated as a processing unit that can be characterized independently of other sentences.

The constructive approach derives from a renewal of interest in the pioneering work on memory of organized material by Bartlett (1932). A summary of the constructivist position may be found in a recent paper by Paris and Lindauer (1976). Here, it is assumed that exact recall of material is an exception rather than the rule. Memory usually involves a transformation of the original material presented. It is further assumed that these transformations involve omissions (simplifications) or additions (consolidation) of the information. In addition, constructive processes are influenced by the context, the person's abilities, and sociocultural background. Finally, memory structures are dynamic and changeable. Information may be retransformed and recomprehended. These changes may occur through the assimilation of new information into the existing memory structure or the merging of structures with one another.

The constructive approach is not itself a theory. Rather, it is a set of constraints or assumptions that suggests a class of theories. A constructive model typically stresses the role of context and world knowledge in language understanding and views a sentence as meaningful only in relation to the entire communication of which it is a part. Dewey's definition of meaning is certainly compatible with a constructivist position on memory. Memory interacts with every phase of processing, from the perception of the input signal to the final determination of the message's intended meaning.

An example of an experimental paradigm used to investigate constructive cognition in language comprehension by adults comes from Bransford, Barclay, and Franks (1972). They used a recognition task to demonstrate that subjects encode more information than was explicit in sentences to which they had been exposed. The example is one that entails a *spatial* inference and suggests that people do more than form a deep structural representation of each sentence. Consider the following sentences.

(4) Three turtles rested *on* a floating log, and a fish swam beneath *them*.
(5) Three turtles rested *beside* a floating log, and a fish swam beneath *them*.
(6) Three turtles rested *on* a floating log, and a fish swam beneath *it*.
(7) Three turtles rested *beside* a floating log, and a fish swam beneath *it*.

The adult subjects in the experiment were told that they would be asked questions about the sentence they heard and were told to listen carefully to sentences like (4) or (5) above. Those subjects who had heard (4) were later tested for recognition of (6) as well as (4); those who had heard (5) were tested later recognition of (7) and (5). The constructivist position predicts that subjects should encode a representation of the entire episode *implied* by each sentence. In (4) above, the fish who swam under the turtles must also have passed under the log upon which the turtles were resting (a spatial inference). Because the subjects represent the situation and not merely the sentence, it was assumed that they would mistakenly recognize, or at least accept as true, sentence (6) about as often as they would recognize (4). On the other hand, in the episode encoded by those who hear sentence (5), the fish did *not* necessarily swim under the log, and thus no significant tendency toward false recognition or acceptance of sentence (7) should occur. According to Bransford, Barclay, and Franks (1972), the interpretive model predicts that (6) and (7) should be recognized only as often as "filler" sentences that have not been heard before and that are not related to the sentences that were heard.

The constructive memory prediction was in fact realized. Information that could be inferred was falsely recognized almost exactly as often as the original sentences themselves. Bransford, Barclay and Franks (1972) ran control experiments to rule out the possibility that the adult subjects based their judgments upon recognition of pronouns or relational terms alone. Their procedures removed a possible confound in their initial experiment: Sentences that could be inferred from those originally presented contained the *same relational term:* those that could not be validly inferred contained a *different relational term.* Thus, true or yes responses might have depended upon identical relational terms; false or no responses might have depended upon different relational terms between the sentences tested and those originally presented.

In discussing their findings, Bransford, Barclay, and Franks (1972) reiterated their belief that

> a sentence (or set of sentences) is not merely a perceptual object which the listener may recall or recognize. If it were, a linguistic description might sufficiently characterize it as such. Rather a sentence is also a source of information which the listener assimilates to his existing source of cognitive knowledge... In a broader sense the constructive approach argues against the tacit assumption that sentences "carry meaning." People carry meanings, and linguistic inputs merely act as cues which people can use to recreate and modify their previous knowledge of the world. (pp. 206-207)

## The Constructivist Approach to Inferences by Children

The constructive memory approach to inferential ability by children has characterized the research of Paris and his colleagues and is a direct descendant of the Bransford et al. (1972) paradigm (Paris, 1975; Paris & Carter, 1973; Paris & Lindauer, 1976; Paris, Mahoney, & Buckhalt, 1974; Paris & Upton, 1976; Paris, Lindauer, & Cox, 1977; Liben & Posnansky, 1977; Posnansky & Liben, 1977; Thieman & Brown, 1977).

In this research, certain questions on the making of inferences by young children are of interest: Can young children draw inferences? If they make an inference, does it lead to better recall? Under what conditions do they draw inferences and/or use them to improve recall spontaneously? Does the ability to make inferences increase with age over and above an increase in memory capacity per se?

### Replication of Bransford et al. on Children

The paper by Paris and Carter (1973) is directly modeled after that of Bransford, Barclay, and Franks (1972). The same experimental procedure was used except that the subjects were 7 and 10 years in age rather than college students. The sentences in the acquistion list were grouped into "stories," and each "story" consisted of two premise statements and a filler sentence. For example:

(8) The bird is inside the cage. (premise)
(9) The cage is under the table. (premise)
(10) The bird is yellow. (filler)

There were seven such sets of three propositons in the acquisition list, and the recognition set contained four items for each acquisition list. The recognition items were of the following form:

(11) The bird is inside the cage. (true premise)
(12) The cage is over the table. (false premise)
(13) The bird is under the table. (true inference)
(14) The bird is on top of the table. (false inference)

In the data, children falsely "recognized" as true those sentences that could be inferred validly from the premises. In addition, the conditional probability that a child who recognized the original premise would report "true" for the implied sentence was .78, indicating that memory for the premises and the inferential sentences were highly correlated.

## Do Children Make Inferences at Time of Encoding?

Can we conclude that the children made inferences or that they did so spontaneously (Paris, 1975, pp. 226-227) or that they falsely thought that they had heard the implied sentences? The use of the false recognition paradigm casts doubt on a "yes" answer to these questions. As mentioned above, the paradigm used by Bransford et al. (1972) and adopted by Paris and Carter (1973) introduces possible confounds. In the Paris and Carter study (1973), the children could have attended only to the relational terms (e.g., "under," "over," "inside," etc.) in order to answer "true" or "false" to the test sentences. If so, then their false recognitions would be based on retention and recognition of specific lexical items and not on spontaneous inference during initial listening to the premises. The possible response rule is: If the relational item in the test item is the same as that in the premise (acquisition item), respond "true" (or "yes" or "old"); respond "false" (or "no" or "new") if they are different.

Paris, Mahoney, and Buckhalt (1974) carried out a study related to the one by Paris and Carter (1973) in which they looked at integration of information between sentences and pictures. The children were 8 to 10 years in age. In this experiment, the relational terms in the recognition tests were varied. This was done by preserving the meaning of the relation between the nouns but counterbalancing the spatial terms with the truth value of the test sentence. An example of the acquisition series was

(15) The box is to right of the tree. (premise)
(16) The chair is on top of the box. (premise)
(17) The tree is green and tall. (filler)

In testing, there were eight recognition items. The first four, (18)-(21) were syntactically equivalent and replicated Paris and Carter (1973). The second four, (22)-(25), were semantically equivalent and provided the counter-balance control for the spatial terms and the truth value of the sentence. An example of the set of recognition test items is

(18) The box is to the right of the tree. (true premise)
(19) The box is to the left of the tree. (false premise)
(20) The chair is to the right of the tree. (true inference)
(21) The chair is to the left of the tree. (false inference)
(22) The tree is to the left of the box. (true premise)
(23) The tree is to the right of the box. (false premise)
(24) The tree is to the left of the chair. (true inference)
(25) The tree is to the right of the chair. (false inference)

The data obtained on test sentences (18) through (21) replicated the Paris and Carter (1973) results. Sentence (20) was accepted as true or falsely recognized nearly as often as sentence (18) was recognized as old. When both the sentences and tests were verbal, the false alarm and hit rates were .73 and .73 for the 8-year-olds and .62 and .67 for the 10-year-olds, respectively. Sentence (21) and sentence (19) had lower rates, namely, .50 and .46 or .29 and .36 for the respective age groups, indicating that subjects recognized them as being invalid or a "new" set. In contrast, sentences (22) through (25) were responded to at nearly chance levels, respectively averaging .42, .46, .48, and .47 for the 8-year-olds and .40, .38, .48, and.46 for the 10-year-olds in the verbal–verbal condition. Because sentences (18)-(21) depend upon syntactic matches and sentences (22)-(25) depend upon semantic matches, the data indicate that the children operated on the surface properties and not on semantic representations. Responding to the spatial terms in (18)-(21), given a match on the nouns, thus remains as an alternative explanation of the data.

## Surface Versus Semantic Representations

For college students, Hayes–Roth and Hayes–Roth (1977) have shown that lexical, surface information may be retained as well as semantic or constructed representation and that the former may aid in discriminating new from old sentences. They tested college students on recognition and verification of old, synonymous, and false sentences. The synonymous sentences were nearly identical in meaning to those in the acquisition set except that the lexical verbs were changed. The data showed that old sentences were recognized with more confidence than the synonymous ones, that old sentences were verified faster than synonymous sentences, and that words identical to those in the acquisition set interfered with verification of test sentences. Hayes–Roth and Hayes–Roth argue that words rather than integrated constructions are stored and used in judgments of recognition and truth.

The reaction-time data are of interest because, if the students had spontaneously integrated the premise information and stored the resulting abstraction, then there should have been no difference in reaction time to verify or recognize sentences that were either presented originally or were synonymous implications. The fact that the reaction times for the implications were longer indicates that deductive processes occur at the time of testing (cf. Trabasso, Riley, & Wilson, 1975).

## Does Semantic Integration Occur?

Two recent studies have dealt with the issue of whether the children were making lexical recognition matches or false recognition based upon semantic integration.

The first of these, by Liben and Posnansky (1977), discusses several methodological problems with the false recognition paradigm. In particular, they focused on the lexical versus semantic problem as a basis for responding. The children were approximately 6 and 9 years in age and were trained and tested in a design similar to that of Paris, Mahoney, and Buckhalt (1974). An example of the acquisition sentences used is

(26) The surprise was in the box. (premise)
(27) The box was behind the door. (premise)
(28) The surprise was a birthday present. (filler)

The set of eight test sentences for this acquisition set was

(29) The surprise was in the box. (true premise)
(30) The box was in front of the door. (false premise)
(31) The surprise was a birthday present. (filler)
(32) The surprise was behind the door. (true inference)
(33) The door was in front of the surprise. (reversed, true inference)
(34) The surprise was in front of the door. (false inference)
(35) The door was behind the surprise. (reversed, false inference)

The main tests of interest are on sentences (32) and (34), which match the premises on both semantic and relational, lexical terms in comparison with sentences (33) and (35), which only match the premises semantically. If the children construct a semantic representation from the premises and match the tests to this representation, then the percentage of false recognitions should be the same for (32) and (33) and for (34) and (35). If the match is lexical, then the proportion of false recognition errors would be higher for (32) than (33) and for (34) than (35).

Liben and Posnansky (1977) tested the two age groups under two conditions of memory load in acquisition. For the 6-year-olds, with comparisons on true inferences, sentences (32) and (33) favored lexical recognition matching, regardless of the number of sentences in the original set. The proportions of false recognitions were .84 vs. .44 and .75 vs. .50 for the four- and eight-"story" acquisition sets, respectively. For the older, 10-year-old children, however, evidence was found for semantic integration but only when the number of "stories" was decreased from 12 to 8. Here the proportions were .64 vs. .64 for the eight-"story" set and .70 vs. .48 for the 12-"story" set. It is unclear why lexical memory would be better in the 12-rather than the eight-"story" set unless one assumes that sentences are retained better in the eight-"story" set and that the children were making semantically equivalent but consistent judgments *at the time* of testing between what was retained from the acquisition set with what is tested. We shall discuss this issue of recognition vs. semantic judgment below.

Liben and Posnansky (1977) conducted a second experiment on first-grade children (nearly 7 years in age) with eight stories in the acquisition set. They again found that these young children were basing their recognition judgments on relational terms and noun order rather than semantic integration. Here, the respective false recognition proportions for true inferences were .68 vs. .52. The false inference data were at chance (.49).

Thieman and Brown (1977) verified lexical and semantic matches for *false* test sentences by substituting a novel relational term. For example, if the premises were

(36) The telephone is on top of the book.
(37) The book is under the table.

then, the false inference tests would be

(38) The telephone is on top of the table.

which matches the lexical items in (36) and (37) while,

(39) The telephone is over the table.

does not match the relational term. Hence if the children match lexical items, they should make more false recognition errors to (38) than (39). This was indeed the case for both age groups. The proportion of errors were .30 vs. .15 for the 8-year-olds and .16 vs. .07 for the 11-year-olds.

On balance, one has to conclude that lexical memory occurs and complicates interpretation of data in the false recognition paradigm. Matching on the basis of semantic analysis would seem to occur for children about 10 years in age. However, this does not necessarily mean that the semantic interpretation occurred spontaneously at the time premises were first stated. Rather, it could have occurred at the time of testing.

## The Problem of Response Bias in Young Children

Another methodological problem of using the false recognition procedure with children is, as Paris and Upton (1976) report, the problem of response bias. Young children tend to say "yes" at greater-than-chance levels. In their study, Paris and Upton (1976) found that 5-year-old children made 72% "yes" responses compared with a (chance) level of 48% "yes" responses made by 10-year-old children. If the children respond "yes" more frequently than one would expect by chance, then the percentage of correct answers to the true premises and true inferences would increase; likewise, the percentage of errors to the false premises and false inferences would increase. This problem is not easily corrected by the use of signal detection procedures. Paris (1975, p. 231) has pointed out this problem in reviewing his work.

A second problem of interpretation has to do with a criterion the children set. It may be that they do not "falsely recognize," or believe that they heard, the inference statement in the acquisition series. Rather, their criterion of judgment may be to accept as "true" or valid any sentence, old or new, that is semantically consistent with the acquistion set.

## Recognition of New Versus
## Semantically Congruent Sentences

It is possible to separate out empirically the distinction between recognition of a sentence as "new" versus verification of a sentence as semantically consistent or "true." Lawson (1977) asked college students to do this, namely to make separate responses on the truth of a statement as well as whether a statement occurred in the acquisition set. It was found that they could make these distinctions, that is, they could correctly classify implication sentences as "true" but also as "new." This is an important finding because it calls into question a key assumption of the constructivist position, namely that the subjects falsely thought they heard the inference sentences in the acquisition set. That is, they constructed a semantic integration during encoding and confused this construction with the recognition test sentence. Rather, the data favor the idea that college students either use lexical information to decide old versus new sentences, having semantically integrated the sentences, or they make validity judgments at the time of testing along with recognition judgments based upon surface, lexical information. The Hayes–Roth and Hayes–Roth (1977) reaction-time data favor the latter alternative.

Posnansky and Liben (1977) have studied children's ability to distinguish between lexical matching and semantic consistency using Lawson's (1977) procedures. In their study, they had children 6, 9, and 11 years in age make two kinds of judgments. The children answered "right" if the test sentence contained information that was semantically consistent with the "stories" in acquisition and then judged whether they heard "exactly the same sentences as before." As in Liben and Posnansky (1977) study, tests were made on sentences that matched the premises on relational, noun order, and/or semantic content and gave immediate or delayed (2 hours) tests.

Of interest is the ability of children to distinguish exact recognition from semantic consistency. This was done by calculating the conditional probability of judging a test sentence as "old" given it was judged as "true." For tests on true premises, these were nearly perfect for all three age groups on immediate tests. For true, reversed premise tests, however, the 6-year-olds did not distinguish word order. Their conditional probability of judging reversed premises was 1.00. The older children made this distinction, although not perfectly because the 9- and 11-year-old conditional probabilities were .55 and .62, respectively. The differences between the conditional probabilities for tests on original true premises and reversed true premises were .00, .32, and .38 for the three age groups, respectively. Similar differences were found for immediate tests on true inferences that matched lexical items versus those that did not, namely, -.03, .38, and .36. With delayed premise tests, the respective age differences were .08, .05, and .25, showing that only the 11-year-olds remembered enough lexical information to make distinctions; on inference sentences, the rates declined and the differences were near zero.

These data indicate that when testing is done immediately, children 9 years and older use lexical information to recognize old information and can make semantically consistent judgments. However, these data indicate that all of those studies that have employed a single response measure confound recognition judgments based upon lexical with that based upon semantic consistency. On balance, the problems inherent in the false recognition test originally developed by Bransford, Barclay, and Franks (1972) cast doubts on its scientific merit as a procedure to evaluate the claims of the constructivist position.

## Free Recall and Inferences by Children

As an alternative, Paris and Lindauer (1976) developed a recall-probe procedure that appears to eliminate several of the problems of the false recognition method. They studied whether children encoded explicit and implicit instruments of verbs in sentences during acquisition. In one experiment, children 6 to 11 years in age listened to sentences of the following form:

(40) The workman dug a hole in the ground. (implied instrument)
(41) The workman dug a hole in the ground with a shovel. (explicit instrument)

The children heard eight sentences, half of which contained explicit instruments and half of which did not. After the sentences were heard, the children had to recall them under a probe-recall procedure in which the instrument, implied or explicit, was given as a probe. Recall of the sentences was better overall when the explicit instruments were given as probes. The percentages recalled correctly for the first-, third-, and fifth-grade children were 57%, 73% and 73% in this condition. When the implicit instrument served as a recall cue, the respective percentages were 31%, 48%, and 66%. Note that for the older children, the implicit and explicit cued recall was nearly the same. If the children generated the implied instruments and stored them with the actions during encoding, that is, if they made *lexical* inferences, then the two kinds of recall should look alike. The conclusion drawn by Paris and Lindauer (1976) was that the older children more spontaneously made these lexical inferences. The results did not depend upon the lack of knowledge about the instruments by the younger children, because Paris and Lindauer found that 5-year-old children could choose the appropriate instrument about 98% of the time in a subsequent test in which they were asked to pick out the appropriate instrument from a set of pictures containing four published alternatives for each structure.

Paris and Lindauer (1976) did a second experiment with children ranging in age from 5 to 10 years. In this experiment, the same eight sentences were used except that all of the instrument were implicit. In recall, the explicit subject, verb, or object, as well as the implicit instrument, were used as recall probes. When the children had an explicit instrument as a retrieval cue, the correct recall averaged 38%, 42%, and 61% for the kindergarten, second-, and fourth-grade children, respectively. The respective percentages correct for the implied instrument retrieval cues were 22%, 38%, and 69%. Thus, as in the first experiment, the implied instruments were as effective as explicit nouns or verbs in helping the children to retrieve the sentences for the older children. The disparity observed for the younger, 5-year-old children suggests that they did not infer the instrument when they heard the sentence.

This experiment would seem to correct a number of problems associated with the false recognition procedure. There is no response bias. There is no artifact of using syntactic matching rules. On the question of making the inference at the time of encoding, there still may be some problem of interpretation. When the child is given the instrument as a retrieval cue, the question is: Do they generate associations to the instruments? For example, given the cue "shovel," they might associate "dig" and then use this as a retrieval cue for the appropriate sentence. Thus, the task may not involve any inferences on the verbs but rather functional associations of instruments with their actions. This argument is plausible, because the verb probe data were nearly as high as the implicit instrument probe data. The developmental difference could be a result of the lower likelihood of the younger children having associated or learned the instrument with the appropriate verb.

We doubt this alternative explanation, because it is not likely that the associations could be generated perfectly by all children. Thus, if the association hypothesis were in effect, the implicit probed recall should have been less than explicitly probed recall for all age groups. This was not the case. A simple experiment could check this idea: Present the eight sentences and then present the eight instruments, asking the children to give a one-word association. If the appropriate verbs are given more often in the first than in the second condition, the associations are constrained by the acquisition set. This constraint, however, amounts to saying that the instruments were primed as associates at the time of acquisition, in line with Paris and Lindauer's hypothesis. As matters now stand, the issue of making the inference during listening or during retrieval is an open one.

In a clever, third experiment, Paris and Lindauer (1976) attempted to have the younger children process sentences to a deeper level of meaning (Craik & Lockhart, 1972) and to see if they were able to use implicit information to improve recall. Seven-year-old children were read 10 sentences like that illustrated in (40) above, five of which contained explicit instruments and five of which did not. The children were instructed to repeat the sentences aloud and then to *act out* the actions described in them. The explicit and implicit instruments were used as retrieval cues. When explicit cues were used, the recall averaged 72% correct on the sentences; when the implicit cue was used, the children averaged 70% correct. The conclusion was that young children can be required by the task demands to draw inferences (act out explicitly the implied instrument) and thus understand the sentences more fully (process them more deeply to the level of meaning).

Paris and Lindauer (1976) did not include certain controls in the latter study, and their interpretation is based upon an assertion of the null hypothesis. They did not compare the recall to children who *did not act out* the sentences. The omission of this control is serious because their data on 7-year-olds are inconsistent. In Experiment I, the 7-year-olds retrieved more information with explicit than with implicit cues (73% vs. 48%). In Experiment II, however, they did not (42% vs. 38%). If the control had been run concurrently on 7-year-old children with the same material, and if the overall recall was less, and if the explicit retrieval cues led to better recall than the implicit retrieval cues, then Paris and Lindauer (1976) would have been more justified in drawing the conclusions they did. Even then, the hypothesized superior recall may not depend upon depth of processing but upon the superiority of a motoric over a verbal representation in memory.

In a related study, Paris, Lindauer, and Cox (1977) extended the cued-recall technique to measure inferences about consequences from sentences. For example,

(42) My brother fell down on the playground.

has as an implication that

(43) He skinned his knee.

Paris, Lindauer, and Cox presented children nearly 8 and 12 years in age and college students with eight sentences like (42) with or without explicit consequences like (43). Then, after presentation of the sentences, they "cued" recall by presenting either cue. The cues were nouns such as "playground" or consequences as in (43). The percentage of sentences recalled for nouns and consequences did not differ within an age group when these cues were explicitly stated in presentation. However, the retrieval of the sentences was superior to explicit nouns as opposed to implicit consequences, suggesting that as the children became older, they derived the implications during the storage and could match these with implicit, consequence retrieval cues. The observed percentages for explicit nouns were 62%, 66%. and 69% for the three respective age groups. For implicit consequences, they were 24%, 48%, and 63%. Free recall controls showed no differences for noun versus consequence recall. An analysis of the conditional probabilities of recalling only with the explicit, only the implicit, or both cues showed that the latter increased with age. This results shows a correlation of memory and inferences.

In a second experiment, Paris, Lindauer, and Cox (1977) had children, 6 years in age, make up stories in an effort to induce spontaneous generation of inferences by younger children. They were successful in that about 50% of the stories contained implied consequences. Compared to the first experiment, recall of the implied consequences increased from 34% to 50%. This experiment apparently induced more active inferencing and better recall, analogous to Paris and Lindauer's (1976) acting-out condition of Experiment III. The conclusion is that the younger, 6-year-old children do not spontaneously generate as many inferences as do the older, 11-to 12-year-old children and college students, but can be induced to do so by activity or story telling.

The cued-recall experiments of Paris and Lindauer (1976) and Paris, Lindauer, and Cox (1977) may indicate that older children do encode sentences along with lexical or consequence implications. Then, in cued recall, retrieval is facilitated by presentation of a cue that matches the stored, inferential representation. However, it could be that at the time of retrieval, the older children are able to use the semantic information in the consequence cues to search for semantically consistent sentences in long-term memory, Paris, Lindauer, and Cox found that free recall improved with age (averaging 34%, 40%, and 48% for the respective age groups). If older children and adults retain more original sentences, then they have more information available to be searched and matched semantically by the implicit cues. There is the further, possibly developmental, problem that the older children are better able to derive the consequences of the sentences as well as use them as cues. This ability would help the older children, at retrieval, to find an association between the consequences and the sentences. Kobasigawa (1974) has shown such developmental differences in retrieval strategies.

The main argument against this retrieval interpretation comes from acceptance of the encoding specificity hypothesis of Tulving and Thompson (1973), who have argued and have support for the idea that retrieval is best when the same information is available at both encoding and retrieval. Paris, Lindauer, and Cox (1977) have evidence that college students do equally well when the cues were not available at encoding, suggesting that they were implicitly available or were inferentially derived at encoding. However, the evidence for children doing so is less clear. A comparison between their free recall groups with those who had cued recall shows that the implicit cues did not aid retrieval at all. For the 6-year-olds, the percent free recall was 34%; when implicitly cued, it was 24%. For the 11-year-olds, the respective percentages were 40% and 48%. These data indicate, then, no effect of implicit cueing over free recall and therefore no evidence for inferencing either at encoding and retrieval.

## Memory and Inferences

Better evidence that children can make inferences and that making inferences may lead to better recall comes from a recent study by Paris and Upton (1976). In one experiment, children ranging in age from 5 to 11 years heard "stories," 13 to 16 clauses in length. An example was

(44) Chris waited until he was alone in the house.
(45) The only sound he heard was his father chopping wood in the barn.
(46) Then he pushed the red chair over to the sink, which was full of dishes.
(47) Standing on the edge of the sink, he could just barely reach the heavy jar.
(48) The jar was behind the sugar and he stretched until his fingers could lift the lid.

(49) Just as he reached inside, the door swung open and there stood his little sister.

After hearing a story, the children were asked a series of eight questions, requiring yes/no answers. Half of the questions tested verbatim recall of either adjectives or prepositions. For example,

(50) Was the jar heavy?
(51) Was the jar in front of the sugar?

The other four tests were on inferences of different kinds. One kind was on what Paris and Upton call "presupposition" (actually, a motivational inference), as in

(52) Did Chris want his parents to know what he was doing?

Others tested "consequences," as in

(53) Did Chris catch his sister stealing cookies?
(54) Was there a girl standing by the door?

Finally, a fourth type tested implied instruments (lexical inferences), as in

(55) Did Chris's father use an axe?

Paris and Upton (1976) found that memory for the verbatim information and accuracy in answering the inferential questions covaried and increased with age. In an attempt to assess whether the ability to infer was greater than sheer memory ability, analyses of covariance were performed on the the inference data using verbatim recall as a covariate. Age was still found to be a significant factor in the covariate analysis on motivational and consequential inferences but not lexical inferences, leading to the conclusion that the child's inferential capacity increased with age

> This does not reflect the simple finding that older children recalled more of the original passages and also correctly answered contextual inference questions more often. The multiple regression analysis partialled out the successively better recall by older children and still revealed a significant correlation between recall and the ability to understand contextual inferences. Indeed, the functional utility of comprehending inferences in prose appears to increase with age and enhance recall. (Paris & Upton, 1976, p. 666)

This conclusion should be tempered by an alternative explanation. In the data, the verbatim and lexical inferences show linear relationships with age, while the other "contextual" inferences show a curvilinear relationship. Suppose that in fact the number of inferences one can make is a positively accelerated, curvilinear relation of the number of propositions one can retrieve. By analogy, if one retrieves only one proposition, one can create no combinations. If one retrieves two, one can create one combination. If one retrieves three propositions, one can generate three combinations, etc. The analogy is to taking combinations of $n$ things, two at a time. As $n$ increases, the number of combinations increases nonlinearly. Thus, the partialling out of memory for verbatim recall (a linear relationship with age) on inferences (a nonlinear one) would still leave an effect of age in the analysis but for reasons other than inferential ability per se. The older children may have made more inferences or may have been able to answer correctly more questions requiring inferences because they remembered the material better and not because they made more inferences to begin with. The question as to whether they made the inferences at the time of comprehension or at the time of testing and its relation to recall are still unresolved.

It is also unfortunate that Paris and Upton (1976) did not test for verbatim recall of the propositional information critical to making the inferences in question. A clearer idea of the functions of inferences and a taxonomy of inferences and appropriate questions would help (see chapter by Nicholas & Trabasso, this volume). It remains unclear as to why one would expect recall of propositions and adjectives to have any bearing on inferences.

Paris and Upton (1976), in a second experiment, tested for inferences prior to recall, using essentially the same design and materials of the first study. This allowed one to find a possible *correlation* between how well individual children answered inferential questions and how well they retained the stories. The constructivist assumption is that those children who made the inferences during encoding integrated the original information into a memory representation that "permitted a temporally ordered, logical, sequential unit that can be stored parsimoniously and accessed readily" (p. 667).

The causal connection between inferences and recall has been questioned by Omanson, Warren, and Trabasso (1978). They provide two kinds of evidence that indicates that recall may precede and be independent of comprehension. In one experiment with 8-year-olds, inferences about a protagonist's intentions and actions were increased by providing some children with setting and motive information (e.g., a girl, Nancy, wants to buy her brother, Fred, a birthday present, or she steals money from Fred's piggy bank to buy herself a present). In control condition, the children are told nothing about the protagonist's motivation. Then, children in all three conditions (positive, negative, and no intent) heard the same, core story and were tested on a variety of inferential questions and were asked to recall the story. For each condition, this was repeated over three different stories. The percentage of correct inferences averaged 69% for the positive and negative motive groups, compared to 42% for the control group. However, the three groups did not differ in recall. The positive and negative motive group averaged 57% correct propositions in recall, the control group averaged 62%. Thus, experimental variation that produced more inferences did *not* lead to better recall. The inference probes indicated that the positive and negative motive groups had different and far more detailed understanding of the stories than did the control groups. Yet, their recall was alike.

In a second experiment, 5-year-old children were compared to 8-year old children on recall and inferences in which the inferences were based upon critical premises in the story. When the children and inference questions were matched for retention of the premises, two result were found. First, as retention of the premises increased, so did the proportion of inferences. However, 8-year-old children made more inferences at every level of retention when matched for retention against the 5-year-olds. Thus, we have evidence that 8-year-olds are better able to integrate information than 5-year-olds, independent of memory. These data support Paris and Upton (1976) on the hypothesis that the ability to make inferences increases with age, independent of memory. They do not, however, support their assertion quoted above that inferences enhance recall.

## CONCLUSIONS

Returning to our opening comments in this section, we are led to the conclusion that young children can answer questions involving inferences and hence they can make them. They do not seem to make them spontaneously at the time of encoding. The making of inferences may not lead to better recall. The ability to make inferences appears to improve with age over and above memory per se.

If we are interested in whether children can make inferences, whether they make them at the time of hearing or reading a narrative, whether the making of such inferences leads to a memory representation that is better for long-term retention, and whether or not memory and inferences are independent, the above review suggests that the false recognition paradigm is inadequate and that direct procedures of questioning or on-line reaction-time methods might be profitably employed, such as having children read aloud, recording interword times, and looking for the effects of semantic, pronominal, presuppositional, and other violations on processing. The direct probe methods (e.g., Stein & Glenn, 1978; Omanson, Warren, & Trabasso, 1978) do not get at the spontaneous problem but they do address the other questions of competence, depth of understanding, memory, and inferences.

Finally, we need to address more explicitly the questions, "What is an inference?" because this has been quite intuitive, operationally defined, and limited (e.g., transitive, spatial, lexical, consequences). We need to know what role inferences play in a theory of memory representation and discourse processing. This job requires analysis of connected discourse, semantic and logical operations, as well as the role of world knowledge and context on comprehension. In our second paper (Nicholas & Trabasso, this volume), we begin by defining and analyzing functions and kinds of inferences.

## ACKNOWLEDGMENTS

The research was supported by National Institute of Education Grant No. NIE-G-77-0018 to T. Trabasso. This work was also supported by National Institute of Mental Health Grants, Nos. 19223 and 29365 to T. Trabasso, and by a National Institute of Child Health and Human Development program project grant (5 P01 HD05027) to the University of Minnesota's Institute of Child Development.

## REFERENCES

Anderson, N. H. Integration theory and attitude change. *Psychological Review*, 1971, *78*, 171–206.

Anderson, N. H. Information integration theory: A brief survey. In D. H. Krantz, R. C. Atkinson, R. D. Luce, & P. Suppes (Eds.), *Contemporary developments in mathematical psychology*. San Francisco: Freeman, 1974.

Austin, V. D., Ruble, D. N., & Trabasso, T. Recall and order effects as factors in children's moral judgements. *Child Development*, 1977, *48*, 470–474.

Bartlett, F. C. *Remembering: A study in experimental and social psychology*. Cambridge, England: Cambridge University Press, 1932.

Bearison, D. J., & Isaacs, L. Production deficiency in children's moral judgements. *Developmental Psychology*, 1975, *11*, 732–737.

Berndt, T.J., & Berndt, E.G. Children's use of motives and intentionality in person perception and moral judgement. *Child Development*, 1975, *46*, 904–912.

Bransford, J. D., Barclay, J. R., & Franks, J. J. Sentence memory: A constructive versus interpretive approach. *Cognitive Psychology*, 1972, *3*, 193–209.

Bransford, J. D., & Franks, J. J. The abstraction of linguistic ideas: A review. *Cognition: An International Journal of Cognitive Psychology*, 1972, *2*, 211–249

Bransford, J. D., & Johnson, M. K. Contextual prerequisites for understanding: Some investigations of comprehension and recall. *Journal of Verbal Learning and Verbal Behavior*, 1972, *11*, 717–726.

Bransford, J. D., & McCarrel, N. S. A sketch of a cognitive approach to comprehensions: Some thoughts about what it means to comprehend. In W. B. Weimer & D. S. Palermo (Eds.), *Cognition and the symbolic processes*. Hillsdale, N.J.: Lawrence Erlbaum Associates, 1974.

Brown, A. The development of memory: Knowing, knowing about knowing, and knowing how to know. In H. W. Reese (Ed.), *Advances in child development and behavior*. New York: Academic Press, 1975.

Bryant, P. E., & Trabasso, T. Transitive inferences and memory in young children. *Nature*, 1971, *232*, 456–458.

Burt, C. The development of reasoning in school children. *Journal of Experimental Pedagogy*, 1919, *5*, 68–77.

Craik, F. I. M., & Lockhart, R. S. Levels of processing: A framework for memory research. *Journal of Verbal Learning and Verbal Behavior*, 1972, *11*, 671–684

Dewey, J. How do we think? Portions published in R. M. Hutchins & M. J. Adler (Eds.), *Gateway to the great books* (Vol.10). Chicago: Encyclopedia Britannica, Inc. 1963. (Originally published by Heath, 1933, 1961).

Feldman, N. S., Klosson, E. C., Parsons, J. E., Rholes, W. S., & Ruble, D. N. Order of information presentation and children's moral judgements. *Child Development*, 1976, *47*, 556–559.

Flapan, D. *Children's understanding of social interaction.* New York: Teacher's College Press, 1968.

Greene, J. *Psycholinguistics: Chomsky and psychology.* Middlesex, England: Penguin Books, 1972.

Hayes-Roth, B., & Hayes-Roth, F. The prominence of lexical information in memory representation of meaning. *Journal of Verbal Learning and Verbal Behavior*, 1977, *16*, 119–136.

Katz, J. J., & Fodor, J. A. The structure of semantic theory. *Language*, 1963, *39*, 170–210.

Katz, J. J., & Postal, P. M. *An integrated theory of linguistic descriptions.* Cambridge, Mass.: MIT Press, 1964

Kobasigawa, A. Utilization of retrieval cues by children in recall. *Child Development*, 1974, *45*, 127–134.

Lane, J., & Anderson, N. H. Integration of intention and outcome in moral judgement. *Memory & Cognition*, 1976, *4*, 1–5.

Lawson, R. Representation of individual sentences and holistic ideas. *Journal of Experimental Psychology: Human Learning and Memory*, 1977, *3*, 1–9.

Liben, L. S., & Posnansky, C. J. Inferences on inference: The effects of age, transitive ability, memory load, and lexical factors. *Child Development*, 1977, *48*, 1490–14997.

Mandler, J. M., & Johnson, N. S. Remembrance of things passed: Story structure and recall. *Cognitive Psychology*, 1977, *9*, 111–151.

MacNamara, J. Cognitive basis of language learning in infants. *Psychological Review*, 1972, *79*, 1–13.

Nelson, K. Concept, word and sentence: Interrelations in acquisition and development. *Psychological Review*, 1974, *81*, 267–285.

Nummedal, S. G., & Bass, S. C. Effects of the salience of intention and consequences on children's moral judgments. *Developmental Psychology*, 1976, *12*, 475–476.

Omanson, R. C., Warren, W. H., & Trabasso, T. *Discourse processing, goals, themes, inferences, and memory: A developmental study.* 1978, *1*, 337–354.

Paris, S. G. Integration and inference in children's comprehension and memory. In F. Restle, R. M. Shiffrin, N. J. Castellan, H. R. Lindman, & D. B. Pisoni (Eds.), *Cognitive theory* (Vol. 1). Hillsdale, N.J.: Lawrence Erlbaum Associates, 1975.

Paris, S. G., & Carter, A. Y. Semantic and constructive aspects of sentence memory in children. *Developmental Psychology*, 1973, *9*, 109–113.

Paris, S. G., & Lindauer, B. K. The role of inference in children's comprehension and memory for sentences. *Cognitive Psychology*, 1976, *8*, 217–227.

Paris, S. G., Lindauer, B. K., & Cox, G. L. The development of inferential comprehension. *Child Development*, 1977, *48*, 1728–1733.

Paris, S. G., Mahoney, G. J., & Buckhalt, J. A. Facilitation of semantic integration in sentence memory of retarded children. *American Journal of Mental Deficiency*, 1974, *78*, 714–720.

Paris, S. G., & Upton, L. R. Children's memory for inferential relationships in prose. *Child Development*, 1976, *47*, 660–668.

Piaget, J. Une forme verbal de la comparison chez l'enfant. *Archives de Psychologie*, 1921, 141–172.

Piaget, J. *Judgement and reasoning in the child.* London: Routledge & Kegan Paul, 1928.

Piaget, J. *The moral judgment of the child.* London: Kegan Paul, Trench, & Trubner, 1932.

Piaget, J. *The language and thought of the child.* New York: Meridian Books, Inc., 1955.

Piaget, J. *Genetic Epistemology*. new York: Columbia University Press, 1970.

Piaget, J., Inhelder, B., & Szeminska, A. *The child's conception of geometry*. London: Routledge & Kegan Paul, 1960.

Posnansky, C. J., & Liben, L. S. Constructive and lexical aspects of children's memory for related sentences. Unpublished manuscript, 1977.

Riley, C. A. The representation of comparative relations and the transitive inference task. *Journal of Experimental Child Psychology*, 1976, *1*, 1–23.

Rumelhart, D. E. Notes on a schema for stories. In D. G. Bobrow & A. Collins (Eds.), *Representation and understanding: Studies in cognitive science*. New York: Academic Press, 1975.

Smedslund, J. Psychological diagnostics. *Psychological Bulletin*, 1969, *71*, 237–248.

Stein, N. L., & Glenn, C. G. An analysis of story comprehension in elementary school children. In R. Freedle (Eds.), *New Directions in discourse processing* (Vol.2). Norwood, N.J.: Ablex, 1979.

Surber, C. F. Developmental processes in social inferences: Averaging of intentions and consequences in moral judgement. *Developmental Psychology*, 1977, *13*, 654–655.

Thieman, T. J., & Brown, A. L. *The effects of semantic and formal similarity on recognition memory for sentences in children*. Technical Report No. 76. Center for the Study of Reading, University of Illinois at Urbana-Champaign, 1977.

Thorndyke, P. W. Cognitive structures in comprehension and memory of narrative discouse. *Cognitive Psychology*, 1977, *9*, 77–110.

Trabasso, T. Representation, memory and reasoning: How do we make transitive inferences? In A.D. Pick (Ed.), *Minnesota Symposia on Child Psychology* (Vol. 9). Minneapolis: University of Minnesota Press, 1975.

Trabasso, T., & Riley, C. A. On the construction and use of representations involving linear order. In R. L. Solso (Ed.), *Information processing and cognition: The Loyola Symposium*. Hillsdale, N.J.: Lawrence Erlbaum Associates, 1975.

Trabasso, T., Riley, C. A., & Wilson, E. G. The representation of linear order and spatial strategies in reasoning: A developmental study. In R. Falmagne ( Ed.), *Reasoning: Representation and process*. Hillsdale, N.J.: Lawrence Erlbaum Associates, 1975.

Tulving, E., & Thompson, D. M. Encoding specificity and retrieval processes in episodic memory. *Psychological Review*, 1973, *80*, 352–373.

Youniss, J., & Murray, J. Transitive inference with nontransitive solutions controlled. *Developmental Psychology*, 1970, *2*, 169–175.

# 10 Toward a Taxonomy of Inferences for Story Comprehension

David W. Nicholas
*Carnegie-Mellon University*

Tom Trabasso
*University of Chicago*

## TOWARD A TAXONOMY OF INFERENCES

Several difficulties plague virtually all research on inferences in cognition. First, no precise definitions of the terms "inference" and "context" are available. In colloquial usage, an "inference" may refer to the information implied in an expression, the data inferred from it, or the process of inferring those data. Thus, in discussions of inference, it is not clear whether the topic is a data structure or a process. Context is a similarly ill-defined term that may refer to a part of the input to be comprehended or to the world knowledge that the child has to bring to bear in comprehending it. It will remain a difficult problem to construct any model of processes in comprehension and making inferences as long as such confusions exist.

In this chapter, we would like to present a taxonomy of inferences that we have found to be useful in thinking about the above issues and in the construction of questions and materials to study the processes by which they occur. In any model of language understanding, inferences play numerous and diverse roles in comprehension. In order to begin, we first took upon ourselves the task of defining the functions of inferences and then categorized them into an overall taxonomy of inference types. Once we knew what kind of inferences we wished to probe, we could then develop questions or stories that exemplified them, assess a child's ability to draw such inferences, and then explore the mechanisms by which inferences are made.

## FUNCTIONS OF INFERENCES

There are several ways in which inferences contribute to the use of knowledge in language understanding, and these deserve to be mentioned.

### Lexical Ambiguity

First, inferences resolve lexical ambiguity. Many natural language words have more than one meaning, and so it is necessary to choose a single, appropriate interpretation from a field of several possibilities. In the "Mary had a little lamb" examples (Trabasso & Nicholas, this volume), the verb "had" means, respectively, "owned (as a pet)," "ate," and "gave birth to"; "lamb" in the first sentence is a living animal, while in the second sentence it refers to a prepared meal. The intended meanings of individual words in context must sometimes be arrived at inferentially.

### Nominal-Pronominal Reference

A second function of inferences is the resolution of nominal and pronominal references. Suppose it were observed that

(1) Joseph the carpenter hit Pontius on the head with his hammer. He dropped like a stone.

Are the "Joseph" and the "Pontius" referred to in (1) particular individuals with whom we are expected to be familiar? Is some specific association intended or do the names belong to two figures to whom we are just being (or have just been) introduced? Whose hammer was used to strike the blow? Who dropped like a stone? The answers to these questions (they are not explicitly answered in the text) are readily available if one can apply: (a) some familiarity with the life of a certain biblical figure (and with various names associated with his story), and (b) the knowledge that carpenters regularly carry hammers and that being struck on the head by a hammer may cause one to fall down.

### Identifying Context

Third, inferences aid in the identification of context. The events of the "Mary had a little lamb" example in the second sentence appear to take place within the context of a meal; in the third sentence, it describes the interaction of a veterinarian and a pregnant ewe, possibly in a barn (or in the vet's office). The setting, situation, or action being described must have some analog in the reader's experience for the message to fit into a meaningful framework.

## Establishing a Framework for Interpretation

Fourth, once such a framework (a data structure whose purpose is to represent the writers intended meaning) has been established, a great many facts unmentioned in the written text can be supplied inferentially. For example:

> (2) Bill stepped off the curb without looking either way. After an explosion of pain and blackness, he felt himself being lifted by gentle hands. He awoke to white walls and the smell of antiseptic, with a nurse at his side.

No mention is made in (2) of a street, an auto, a pedestrian being struck by a vehicle, an ambulance, an emergency room, doctors, or a hospital. Nonetheless, most adult users of the English language could readily supply these and other elements of the intended meaning of (2). As soon as some particular interpretation is chosen, however, a complete sequence of probable events can be derived inferentially from context.

## Recognition of Incongruent Events

Fifth, inferences contribute to the recognition of anomalous, abnormal, or surprising events. A slight variation on (2) above might read:

> (3) Bill stepped of the curb without looking either way. After an explosion of pain, and blackness, he arose unwrinkled from the pavement and continued on across the street.

The violent connotations of "an explosion of pain and blackness" are completely incompatible with the description of Bill rising "unwrinkled" and continuing on his way. The effects of violent events, especially those that occur on roadways, are rarely so transitory; the effects of violent pain never are. Conflicting expectations—that Bill has been seriously injured and that he is not only healthy but seemingly unaffected by what happened when he stepped off the curb—make it impossible to infer what has transpired. Thus, the detection of incongruity information or of some meaningful deviation from expected norms.

## Predicting Causes and Consequences of Events

Sixth and finally, inferences enable the prediction not only of the consequences of actions and events but also of their probable preconditions and causes; likewise, the motivations and goals of animate entities may be predicted. In the second sentence of the "Mary had a little lamb" example, the preparation of Mary's meal and its placement before her on a plate are probably necessary preconditions to her eating and spilling it. As a result of the spill, her new dress will be soiled and will require cleaning. She may express displeasure over what was happened. If she is a child, she may be punished. In (2) above, Bill may have been distracted, or simply careless, when he stepped off the curb without looking. He probably had some destination in mind that (unless he intended to go to the hospital) he did not reach. Some kind of vehicle, probably a car or a truck, must have been approaching on the street before it struck Bill. As a consequence of his accident, he will have to spend time in the hospital and (to the extent that his insurance fails to cover his expenses) pay large medical bills. His livelihood will probably be interrupted, and his family will worry. If he dies, funeral arrangements will be necessary. And so on.

The naturally redundant information structure of language and of the knowledge applied in language understanding contributes to the accuracy of predictive inferences. However, in anomalous or ambiguous situations such predictions are difficult to formulate and often prove unreliable; in (2) above, for example, it is not clear what events the text is intended to describe, and so it is nearly impossible to infer probable preconditions or consequences of the action depicted.

This discussion of some of the properties and functions of inferences constitutes only a preliminary working definition of several phenomena to which the term is commonly applied. It is not an attempt to propose a formal functional definition of inferences, but rather an introduction to the terms in which such a definition might be framed. We do not believe that we can define inferences rigorously or propose a specific psychological theory of their workings at this time, given the little that is known about the mechanisms underlying language understanding. Even if no final answers are forthcoming, one may still pose the relevant questions and suggest approaches to them that may be fruitful.

A precise, formal definition of inferences must inevitably derive from a particular model of language understanding. The value of such a definition lies in the fact that the model behind it can be tested experimentally. In this paper, a model of the representation—in some temporary storage medium—of story information (accumulated during the reading of short pieces of text and encoded into data structures that will be called "event chains") will be described and a precise definition of inferences presented. The "psychological reality" of these constructs will not be argued, although it is hoped that they may provide a framework for future research that *will* produce arguably valid models.

One fact that must be accounted for in any model of language understanding is that inferences play numerous and diverse roles in comprehension. Functionaly different kinds of inferences should be recognized as such and separated into different categories in an overall taxonomy of inference types, if their various underlying mechanisms are to be understood. In this paper such a taxonomy will be proposed, not to argue the necessity of a particular set of categories, but to examine the problem of constructing a taxonomy that will provide a useful framework for the future research.

The remainder of this chapter is divided into three parts. The first comprises a discussion of context and its role in language understanding, a description of the event chain formalism, and a definition of inferences in terms of their interaction with event chains. The second is devoted to the proposed inference taxonomy, followed by some concluding remarks.

The task domain in all cases is confined to the reading of short passages of text. The major theoretical focus is on the construction and representation of meaning in a temporary memory structure (as distinct from any permanent or long-term memory), a hypothetical "working area" in which information relevant to a story being understood is organized and temporily stored (either directly or by some sort of "pointer" to the appropriate permanent memory trace). No particular model of human memory is presupposed.

The primary goal of this paper is to approach problems involved in defining inferences and context, and in constructing an inference taxonomy, in a way that will serve as a useful model for future efforts in this area.


## CONTEXT AND INFERENCES

*Webster's New Twentieth Century Dictionary* defines "context" as

1. the parts of a sentence, paragraph, discourse etc., that occur just before and just after a specified word or passage, and determine its exact meaning.
2. the whole situation, background, or environment relevant to some happening or personality.

This definition captures several important characteristics of context.

First of all, any context is the context *of* some event or expression (what will be called here the *focal* event or expression, or the *focus* of the context). It is a relative term, and only for purposes of defintion (such as these) is it used without reference to a particular focus.

Secondly, the alternate defintions above suggest a distinction between what will be called *surface* and *deep* context, corresponding roughly to the surface and deep structures of language. Surface context refers to a group of sentences or paragraphs (the story surrounding the focus), whereas deep context can be thought of as a semantic framework built of facts that are relevant (meaningfully related) to a focal event, and the interrelationships among those facts. Surface context is of only passing interest in the study of inferences (the topic is more central to exercises in grammar of writing style), and so future references to "context" may be taken to mean "deep context."

Finally, the Webster's definition asserts that context aids in determining the precise meanings of expressions. It would seem that focus and context are mutually dependent upon one another, and further, that no clear line separates the two; to analyze the meaning conveyed by either the focus or the context alone would ultimately be self-defeating.

For purpose of discussion, language understanding is best treated as a process of constructing context—of continually building and modifying semantic frameworks to accomodate and assimilate new information. Context, considered as an information structure, will be represented using the event chain formalism.

## Event Chains as Story Representation

The most fundamental function of an event chain is, quite simply, to represent what happened in a given story. Each link in the chain corresponds to a single episode or action, which may be: (a) an act performed by a story character (Edgar had lunch; Pauline wrote a letter to her cousin; Kathie bought a pack of cigarettes in town), (b) a change in the state of the world (night fell; the temperature dropped; the milk froze), or (c) a change in the internal state of a character (Tom became impatient; David got a headache). The order of the links in the event chain matches the order of events in the story. To illustrate the structure of event chains, several episodes out of a typical day in the life of Charlie Brown (the "Peanuts" comic strip character created by Charles M. Schultz) will be fabricated and anlayzed, beginning with this brief and inauspicious sequence:

(4) Charlie Brown jumped out of bed as soon as he awoke. He dressed rapidly, and after wolfing down his own breakfast he hastily left food out for Snoopy. He missed his bus and was late for school again.

Among the events that take place in this story are:

(4.1) C. B. woke up.
(4.2) C. B. jumped out of bed.
(4.3) C. B. dressed (rapidly).
(4.4) C. B. wolfed down his (own) breakfast.
(4.5) C. B. left food out for Snoopy (hastily).
(4.6) C. B. missed his bus.
(4.7) C. B. was late for school again.

While (4.1)–(4.7) represent all the action explicitly described in (4) above, they make no mention of a number of events that must have transpired for (4) to have occurred. Charlie Brown's bed is almost certainly located in his bedroom, and, although he might be expected to awake and dress there, it probably is not where he ate breakfast and prepared Snoopy's food. No mention is made of his walking (or running) from his bedroom to any other part of the house, of where he ate breakfast, where he prepared Snoopy's food, or where he left it (out by Snoopy's celebrated doghouse, one might guess), of his trip to the school bus stop (if he made one), or what exactly transpired there (did he miss the bus by thirty seconds? thirty minutes?), or of how he finally managed to get to school (on foot? by cab? with his parents?). Furthermore, either something slowed him down while he was dressing, eating breakfast, feeding Snoopy, and so on, or he overslept for some reason. Did he exercise poor judgment in deciding the night before what time to set his alarm clock for? Did he sleep through his alarm? Perhaps he does not own a clock, or he forgot to set it. Clearly important elements of the chain of events described in (4) are missing from (4.1)-(4.7). Actions taken by Charlie Brown have been omitted, the timing of the whole chain is somewhat nebulous, and the physical setting of the story is barely mentioned at all. Any complete representation of (4) above must be far more versatile than the simple, unqualified chain of events (which does not even fully answer the question ("What happened") expressed in (4.1)-(4.7). Consider a further example.

(5)  In history class that morning, Charlie Brown's teacher asked him what a feudal lord was. He had not been paying attention and the question caught him off guard. He told her that it was either a Hatfield or a McCoy, whoever won the fight. She made him write "Nobody likes a smart aleck" on the blackboard 50 times, and then sent him to stand in the corner until lunch.

The basic sequence of events here is:

(5.1)  C. B. failed to pay attention in history class that morning.
(5.2)  The teacher asked C. B. what a feudal lord was.
(5.3)  The question caught C. B. off guard.
(5.4)  C. B. answered that it was either a Hatfield or a McCoy, whoever won the fight.
(5.5)  The teacher told C. B. to write "Nobody likes a smart aleck" on the blackboard 50 times.
(5.6)  C. B. wrote "Nobody likes a smart aleck" on the blackboard 50 times.
(5.7)  The teacher told C. B. to stand in the corner until lunch.
(5.8)  C. B. stood in the corner until lunch.

Example (5) begins with a reference to the approximate time and setting of the episode to follow; such reference points are needed in a representation of story information. Event chains are linked to several types of reference data, which establish not only the approximate time and location of the action, but also the state of the world (the precise setting, characters, and so on) before the story starts and after it is over and an evaluation of the significance of the story as a whole, as shown in the following display of qualified story information.

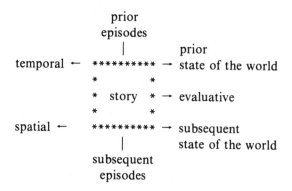

This qualifying information (related not to individual links, but rather to the chain itself) clarifies somewhat the overall meaning of the story, which certainly is not explicit in (5.1)-(5.8) above. Nonetheless, the full story has still not been accounted for. How can the event chain formalism capture the interaction and the points of view of the two major characters in (5)? There is a complex overlapping of events in this story that no simple temporal order will express. How is that to be represented? What of the motivations of the characters and their understanding of one another? Why and *exactly* how did these events take place? One answer to all these questions is to place further qualifying information at each link in the chain.

Much as the story is qualified by several kinds of data, each individual event (which is still the nucleus of the link, of course) is elaborated upon by information of five basic types: (1) temporal—the duration of the event and when it occurred, relative to other events in the chain; the overlap of this and other events in the chain; (2) spatial—the physical location of the action and the spatial scope of the event (whether it took place within one square meter of floor space or over an entire continent, for example), again relative to the other events in the chain; (3) the prior state of the world—a characterization of the environment and its contents prior to the occurrence of the event, especially (a) the history, internal state, and external state of every object and entity involved: human (feelings, goals, intentions, motivations, models of other characters, etc.), animate–nonhuman (drives, health, appearance, etc.), inanimate–concrete (function, state of repair or disrepair, etc.), and abstract; (b) those preconditions necessary for the occurrence of the event, and any discrepancies between them and the conditions that actually obtained; and (c) causal data associated with the event; (4) the subsequent state of the world—a characterization of changes wrought by the occurrence of the event, especially (a) the internal and external states of objects and entities involved; (b) the expected consequences of the event, and any discrepancies between them and the actual consequences (as revealed later in the event chain); and (c) causal data associated with future events; and (5) evaluative perspectives—an evaluation of the event itself; the degree to which it is interesting, significant, or anomalous; its moral value and whether or not it reflects events as they normally occur in the real world.

These relations are summarized in the following display as the structure of an event chain.

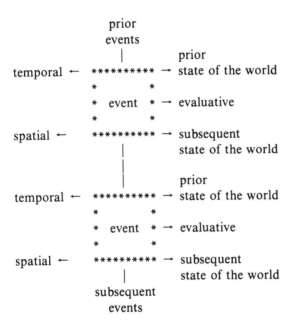

Logical and semantic relationships, captured in these five information classes, constitute most of the data in the framework. In fact, as the structural intricacies that the framework requires (if stories are to be represented effectively) are more closely examined, it becomes clear that the so-called "chain" looks more like a network or a directed graph. Although a central pathway—corresponding to the answer to the question "What happened?"— can be followed from one end of a story to another, many other paths can be followed as well. "What happened to character (or object) X?" "What caused the occurence of Y?" "How did Z perceive the action described in the story?" The answers to these questions define alternate pathways through the story, multiple chains that must be directly derivable from the information encoded in the framework.

The intricate structure of event chains, then, is dictated by the amount and variety of world knowledge that must be brought to bear in story understanding. Those who remain unconvinced of the need for such complexity of representation should consider (6) and (7) below.

(6) That afternoon Charlie Brown's team lost another baseball game.

(7) That afternoon at the baseball field, Charlie Brown's team was playing its usual unusual game. In the ninth inning, with two outs, a tie score (0-0), and one runner on base, Schroeder stalked angrily over to the pitcher's mound from his position at home plate to protest that Lucy, who was blowing kisses to him from the outfield, was distracting him and preventing him from reading Charlie Brown's pitching signals. Linus started over from second base to defend his sister's honor, but he was intercepted by Snoopy (at shortstop) who began dragging Linus' blanket—the owner still firmly attached to one end of it—off into the trees beyond right field. Pigpen, accompanied by his usual cloud of dust, wandered curiously over to the mound and reduced the visibility there to zero. Nobody, not even Lucy (who by this time was dreamily watching the clouds pass overhead), noticed Peppermint Patty stealing second base, third base, and home to give Charlie Brown's team its 410th consecutive defeat.

The greatest difficulty posed by these examples is that they are equivalent; they describe, at different levels of detail, the same sequence of events. The event chain formalism has not been developed to the point at which it can accommodate the interaction of different *levels* of representation. It is easy to understand that what is represented by a single node in one framework might be represented by an entire graph in another; to place the two in the same framework, however, creates the need not only for the acknowledgment of different levels of processing (similar to Craik & Lockhart, 1972), but also for an explanation of the links between levels. Perhaps some future treatment of event chains will be able to provide a clear picture of those links, which today are so poorly understood.

Event chains have been proposed as a representation of story context in a temporary storage medium, and an overview of their properties has been presented. Inferences can now be defined in terms of the formalism proposed.

During the language understanding process, information is drawn from two basic sources: What is not explicit in the natural language input must be inferred (as even the most informal definition of inferences asserts) from the knowledge of the world and of the context in question. Inferences form a whole class of mental operations, the mechanisms of which are unknown, but which are characterized by their interaction (in the present model) with event chains. Inferences build and restructure this contextual framework: adding data, corroborating facts, reevaluating the interrelationships between events.

Linguistic inferences are processes that increase the information content of event chains without copying data explicitly represented in the natural language input.

## TOWARD A TAXONOMY OF INFERENCES

Categories of inferences can be defined (a) in terms of their functional properties and (b) by the information structures with which they interact. Functional categories are more easily observed and manipulated in an experimental setting. Structural considerations, on the other hand, may contribute to more elegant theoretical models of the representation of knowledge. Ideally, an inference taxonomy should be made up of classes that differ from one another in both structural and functional respects. That goal is approached, if not completely achieved, by this taxonomy.

The basic inference categories are: Lexical, spatio-temporal, extrapolative, and evaluative. Extrapolative inferences are further subdivided along two dimensions: the temporal direction of the extrapolation (past or future), and the dominance of either preventive or facilitative factors (to be explained later). It should be noted that, strictly speaking, spatial and temporal inferences form *two* classes. Because of the striking structural and functional parallels between them, however, they will generally be discussed together. As a general rule, each inference class interacts principally with a different part of the event chain, and each is characterized by the unique role it plays in story understanding.

### Lexical and Spatio-Temporal Inferences

Lexical and spatio–temporal inferences might by called "protosemantic," in that virtually *none* of the meaning of an expression (except for purely syntactic relationships between words) is clear until these inferences have been drawn. Consider the plight of the one-time student of Latin upon encountering Aeneas' encouraging advice to his men: "forsan et haec olim meminisse iuvabit." This student can remember enough to distinguish between different parts of speech ("meminisse" and "iuvabit" are verb forms, "forsan" and "olim" adverbs, "et" a conjunction, and "haec" an adjective being used as a noun) but, even with a dictionary at his disposal, he cannot decide which meanings (out of several choices for each word) are appropriate in the current context. Moreover, while he can recognize verbs as such, he no longer remembers the rules for forming different tenses. In short, deprived of much lexical and all spatio-temporal information, the student is unlikely to understand Aeneas' hopeful prophecy (made in attempt to cheer his comrades during a moment of adversity) that "perhaps one day (we) will look back on this and laugh."

## Lexical Inferences

Lexical inferences resolve nominal pronominal references and facilitate the selection of appropriate interpretations of words that have more than one possible meaning. Often, lexical inferences provide information that appears at first glance to be explicit in the text, as this example first used by Charniak (1972) illustrates:

> (8) Today was Jack's birthday. Penny and Janet went to the store. They were going to get presents. Janet decided to get a top. "Don't do that," said Penny. "Jack has a top. He will make you take it back."

Most adult readers would consider it obvious that in (8) "they" refers to Penny and Janet, "he" to Jack, and "it" to the new top Janet was thinking of buying for Jack. When asked if that information is explicit in the text, many will reply that it is and that no inferences are necessary to establish the pronoun–referent connections. How does one know, however, that "they" does not refer to all three story characters?

To be *certain* that "they" are Penny and Janet, one must know that: (a) The birthday present is going to be for Jack, and if it is to be a surprise (as such presents typically are) Jack cannot be around when it is bought: (b) Penny and Janet appear to have gone to the store for the purpose of buying Jack a present, and the expectation is established that a subsequent reference to present-buying will probably involve Penny and Janet; and (c) people do not as rule buy themselves presents on their own birthdays. To know that "he" is Jack (a simple inference, because Jack is the only male, human entity described in the story), one must know that "Penny" and "Janet" are names usually given to girls and that "Jack" is a boy's name. Obvious? Yes. Explicit? Not at all. By the same token, to be certain that "it" is the new top to be given to Jack (and not the one he already owns), one must have a clear picture of the transactions involved: the purchase, giving, receiving, and returning of presents.

Lexical inferences also resolve nominal references. Are Jack, Janet, and Penny merely characters in a story, or are they particular individuals with whom the reader has had past experience and whom he is expected to recognize? In this case it would appear not. By contrast, in example (1) Joseph and Pontius are intended to suggest figures with whom most readers will be familiar. Every object and entity introduced in a story must be identified either as novel (and thus meaningful only within the framework of the story) or as evocative of particular knowledge on the reader's part.

The use of lexical inferences to choose between alternate meanings of words has already been discussed (in the "Mary had a little lamb" examples). In general, the role of lexical inferences in language understanding is to resolve ambiguities in the precise meanings (or referents) of words. The information they provide for the contextual framework is encoded in the *event* portion of the event chain link. Although lexical inferences could easily be thought of as the "simplest" and "most basic" inference class, it should be noted that, on many occasions, the data utilized by lexical inferences must be provided by the "more complex" extrapolative and evaluative inferences. No class of inferences can operate *in vacuo,* and there is no fixed hierarchy of classes.

Of the six famous questions reputedly posed by journalists—who, what, where when, how, and why—the answers to the first two in any story are obtained mainly through lexical inferences; the next two questions, where and when, are dealt with by spatial and temporal inferences, respectively.

## Spatial and Temporal Inferences

Spatial and temporal inferences anchor each event in a story to an appropriate locale and time-span. They encode the physical parameters within which specific actions must take place. The information they contribute to the contextual framework may be extremely complex when events have been described in terms of multiple spatial and temporal referents (Bruce, 1972).

Example (8) begins by establishing a time frame for the event in the story; it is daytime (apparently), and the day in question is an anniversary of Jack's birth. The action begins in some unspecified location (possibly one of the girls' homes) within traveling distance of the store and then moves (the trip taking no less than several minutes and no more than an hour, probably) to the store itself, the size and layout of which are indeterminate. How long Janet took to decide on a top for Jack is not clear (but again, probably on the order of minutes rather than hours). Penny's response to Janet's decision presumably took only a few seconds. While talking with one another the two girls must have been fairly close together (separated by less than a dozen feet or so), unless the store was very large, in which case they might have been able to call loudly back and forth from a distance of several dozen yards. These basic physical parameters constrain the action depicted in the story. An understanding of the approximate magnitudes of the spatial and temporal measures of that action is prerequisite to an understanding of the story itself.

The timing of any two events (call them A and B) in a story may never be explained in terms of their occurrence relative to one another; A and B may each be described relative only to some third event C, provided as a reference time-span to make possible an estimate of the temporal relationship between A and B. Moreover, the action of a story may be anchored to *multiple* reference time-spans. The relationship between A and B may depend upon a whole network of other relationships, involving events C, D, E, F, etc. If the notion of multiple temporal references spans is difficult to appreciate in the abstract, example (7) should be consulted. ("Points" of time do not exist in this formalism, because everthing that occurs has some duration; Bruce, 1972.) Did Peppermint Patty steal second base before or after Snoopy intercepted Linus? When did Lucy begin gazing at the clouds? Where was Linus when Pigpen arrived at the pitcher's mound? The reader who can answer these questions can appreciate just how complex the interaction and overlap of story events may be.

Multiple spatial referents—various features of the field, the loci of particular interactions between characters—can also be found in example (7). A single referent, the baseball field, delimits the scope of most of the action. However, there is always Linus, off in the trees beyond right field, to serve as a reminder that only rarely is all the action in a story representable relative to only one location.

Perhaps because time and motion are so closely related in most people's models of the world, there are striking parallels between the spatial and temporal properties of events. World knowledge about movement contains both spatial temporal information, and movement of one kind or another is central to virtually all stories. The spatial and temporal "maps" of events, appended to each individual link in the event chain and to the structure as a whole, are similar in their use of multiple referents and ( in an appropriate model) might be made structurally isomorphic to one another.

The addition of spatial and temporal information makes an event in the chain independently meaningful. Extrapolative inferences make events meaningful in relation to each other. By answering the last two of the journalist's question—how and why—they build complete models of the state of the world (and all its contents) prior and subsequent to the occurence of every event, linking each event to every other.

## Extrapolative Inferences

Extrapolative inferences are central to the taxonomy and meaning. They are subdivided—again, on both structural and functional grounds—in accordance with the world model (the prior state of the world, or the subsequent one) they service. They correlate facts and expectations about what must have happened in the past, what the effects of the focal event are, and what will probably happen in the future. Extrapolative inferences (both past and future) are further subdivided on logical grounds. They separate the world of the past into those factors or events that have contributed to the establishment of whatever conditions were necessary for the occurence of the focal event, and those that have interfered with or disrupted those conditions. Likewise, the world of the future is divided between conditions that the focal event is likely to produce and those it is likely to prevent. Extrapolative inferences, then, may deal with the past or the future, and with events related to the focus in either a facilitative or preventive role.

Returning once again to example (8) and Jack's birthday, several observations can be made about the beginning of this little story. The mention of Jack's birthday will invoke, through lexical inferences, everything known about Jack and about birthdays. In this case, because the story has just started and there is no indication that some particular Jack is being discussed, the only conclusion that can be drawn is that Jack is probably a male human being. The anticipatory aspect of extrapolative inferences comes into play at this point. Until some other human male is mentioned, it can be inferred that future references to an unspecified human male ("he" or "him") are intended to refer to Jack. It turns out that this expectation (reminiscent of one of Charniak's, 1972, "demons"), once established by (8) above, never needs to be modified or discarded because no other human male is ever mentioned.

Myriad expectations are derived from the information called forth from memory about birthdays: that gifts may be given (this fact in turn calls upon information about going to stores, picking out presents, exchanging money for them, etc.), funny hats worn, candles blown out on a cake (with atonal singing in the background), and so on. One might be tempted to assert that as all of this information constitutes a framework for the action to follow, a context has been established. However, no events have occurred yet and no action has been described. Information has been made available to qualify the event chain as a whole and the individual events in it (as necessary), but there is no chain yet. There is no focal event for the framework to be a context of.

Extrapolative inferences drawn by the reader have established a certain set: A tentative model of events to be described has already been formed, and future mention of any of the expected topics—parties, cakes, presents (or trips to stores to buy them)—will reinforce that model and produce contextual referents (or a first approximation of them) for the story. Of course, it is always possible that the story might continue with a second sentence like "He mixed fulminate of mercury with his bubble gum and blew his brains out." In that case, the earlier set would have to be replaced by one sensitive to some mention of despair, suicide, a knowledge of chemistry, and possibly an oddly perverse sense of humor.

Actually, the first sentence of (8) contains relatively little information for extrapolative inferences to work with. The second sentence describes the first event of the story, a trip to the store by Penny and Janet. Lexical inferences call up data about going places and about stores, and enable the conclusion that Penny and Janet are probably female human beings; spatio-temporal inferences provide some basic reference information about the event (as discussed previously). Extrapolative inferences then attempt to answer a series of questions. Why and how did Penny and Janet go to the store? What are the necessary preconditions for such a trip? What will probably happen as a result of it?

The activation of information about stores matches the expectation (informed while reading the first sentence) that such data would be referred to in the future. The fact that the expectation (generated from data about birthdays) has been satisfied should enable the generation of an entire sequence of hypothetical, birthday-related events: (a) Penny and Janet prepare for the trip (if they are adults they collect their purses, keys, etc.; if children, they get their money); they are planning to go to a store to buy a birthday present for Jack, which they will give to him; (b) Penny and Janet travel to the store (the means of conveyance is not known); (c) Penny and Janet pick out a present to give to Jack for his birthday; (d) they give money to the clerk at the cash register in exchange for the gift; (e) the clerk wraps the gift for them; (f) Penny and Janet leave the store; (g) Penny and Janet go to where Jack is; (h) Penny and Janet give Jack the gift and he thanks them; (i) Jack removes the wrapping of the gift.

Such a sequence would require considerable validation and would have to be modified more than once to account for incoming information. The first part of it receives that validation as the story progresses, both from information explicit in the story and from the fact that extrapolative inferences, seeking causes for each event and motivations for each action, repeatedly activate information that matches expectations formed during the reading of earlier sentences. It is the repeated satisfaction of expectations that makes one particular model of the meaning of a passage (out of any number of hypothetical sequences suggested by points touched upon in the story) stand out from the rest (Rieger, 1974). If extrapolative inferences are unable to validate any one model, the meaning of the text will be perceived as ambiguous.

The extrapolative inferences, both past and future, discussed previously are facilitative: They deal with preconditions, causes, postconditions, consequent events, and the like, attempting to find as many ways as possible in which events or conditions can contribute to other events or conditions. When Janet decides to get a top, facilitative, extrapolative inferences point out that: she must be in the store to buy one (she is, and so that expectation is fulfilled); she must have money (that information is not provided); that she must have some motivation or reason for buying the top (she does; it is to be a present for Jack, whom it would appear she likes); that her decision will have certain consequences (she will own the top, which is prerequisite to giving it as a present, and she will have less money); and so on.

Preventive extrapolative inferences are also a necessary of story understanding, because the significance of events sometimes lies in their *failure* to occur. For example, suppose Penny and Janet had been unable to go to the store, but the reader was not told why. What might have prevented them from making the trip? They might have lived too far away to walk and had no means of transportation; the weather might have been prohibitively bad; Penny and Janet might be children unable to gain parental permission to go out. It could easily be important to an understanding of the story to know what interfered with their plans and to know the effects that interference will have on Penny and Janet. It is also true that the significance of some events lies in what they prevent from happening in the future. Why did Penny tell Janet not to buy Jack a top? Her motivation was probably to avoid an embarassing situation for her friend.

One of the major functions of extrapolative inferences is to keep track of changes in the state of the world as the story progresses. If qualifying information were encoded precisely, as suggested previously—the state of the world described twice in its entirety at each link in the chain—the resulting representation of story context would be somewhat less than economical. Storage economy is a luxury, not an imperative, in a formalism for the representation of knowledge. Parsimony, however, *is* desirable, especially as opposed to a computationally unmanageable alternative. All that is absolutely necessary at each link in an event chain is some representation of *changes* in the state of the world (relative to some prior event, or to the basic state of the world referent that qualifies the entire event chain) that are relevant to the link. When, during the formation of the chain, a link is missing (i.e., the consequences of event N in the chain do not satisfy the necessary preconditions for event N + 1), the discrepancy must be detectable. But, for the most part, the basic model of the world and its contents corresponding to a given story can most conveniently be thought of as being stored in one place: the prior state-of-the-world story referent.

The state-of-the-world referent characterizes people, as well as places and things, and it is necessary to represent their internal states—feelings, drives, models of one another and of problems they are called upon to solve—in addition to their external attributes. Back in example (5), Charlie Brown was punished by his history teacher. The punishment (writing "Nobody likes a smart aleck" on the blackboard 50 times) indicates that the teacher was more concerned about what she misconstrued as impertinence than about the fact that Charlie Brown's answer was incorrect. An understanding of her model of Charlie Brown's behavior is necessary if her choice of punishments is to make sense.

### Evaluative Inferences

Working largely from the complex of patterns and potentialities, past and future, maintained in the event chain's world models are the evaluative inferences. They answer a question off-limits to most journalists (because it is reserved for the writers of editorials): So what?

Evaluative inferences assess: (a) the significance of an event (relative to other events in the story; (b) its normality (surprising or anomalous events must be recognized as such); and (c) its moral value, if any. Consider once more the second sentence of example (8), in which Penny and Janet are first introduced. Whereas lexical inferences suggest that they are female and probably human, evaluative inferences indicate that they are almost certainly human beings. Normally, going to stores (for the purpose of buying something, as extrapolative inferences assert in this case) is a behavior typical of people. Extrapolative inferences further support this hypothesis by being unable to produce a reason why any entity other than a human being would be inclined to visit a store and buy Jack a birthday present.

As might be expected, evaluative inferences are extremely sensitive to the contents of the reader's knowledge base and belief system. An event may seem unusual to a reader not because it is any way inconsistent with its context, but simply because its meaning is unfamiliar. Furthermore, what one reader considers significant (or surprising, or immoral), another may not even notice, depending upon the prior experience each has had with similar subject matter. It should be noted again that what are evaluated are not merely the events, but the events *in context* (i.e., the events as qualified by data about intentions, motivation, consequences, etc.). It is not clear how a mechanism to draw evaluative inferences might be designed; it is evident, though, that judgments made by such a mechanism must take into account the state of the world prior and subsequent to the focal event.

### Summary of Inference Classes and Functions

The following display gives a summary of the inference classes and their functions.

1. Lexical inferences: who, what
     Pronominal references
     Nominal references
     Ambiguous word meanings

2. Spatio–temporal inferences
   a. Spatial inferences: where
      Spatial scope of the action
      Location (relative to other events)
   b. Temporal inferences: when
      Duration of the action
      Time when (relative to other events)
3. Extrapolative inferences: how, why
   a. Past, facilitative
      Preconditions
      Causes (prior related events)
      Motivations, intentions, and goals
   b. Past, preventive
      Interfering preconditions
      Obstructions, counter-causes
      Preventive motivations, intentions, and goals
   c. Future, facilitative
      Postconditions
      Consequent events
      Expectations
   d. Future, preventive
      Obstructed postconditions
      Consequent non-events
      Negative expectation
4. Evaluative inferences: so what?
   Significance
   Normality
   Morality

By way of summary, then, consider the taxonomy of inferences in display above and the task of understanding this rhyme by Hughes Mearns (1976).

(9) As I was going up the stair
   I met a man who wasn't there.
   He wasn't there again today.
   I wish, I wish he'd go away.

The first line of (9) is straightforward. No lexical ambiguities require inferential resolution, and both nominal and pronominal referents are fairly explicit. Information about stairways and walking up them must be activated, of course. Spatio–temporal inferences delimit the physical event, and some representation of an individual climbing a stairway (perhaps 3 feet wide; no more than 15 or 20 steps, each 6 to 9 inches high; the trip up the stairs should take between 20 and 45 seconds, roughly), possibly one in his own house, is suggested. Extrapolative inferences establish the expectation that some event will occur *during* the climb, possibly a mental, vocal, or manual operation (there are definite limits to what can be done while climbing stairs).

The second line introduces a level of semantic ambiguity that is never completely resolved. Lexical inferences fail to resolve the riddle of meeting "a man who wasn't there." Strictly speaking, *no* literal sense of the verb "to meet" can be placed in a predicate with "a man who wasn't there" in a meaningful way. The spatio-temporal implications of "met" are uncomplicated, but again "a man who wasn't there" yields little useful information. Extrapolative inferences, attempting to expand (in terms of preconditions and consequences) on the ideas captured in the verb and direct object, produce contradictory expectations immediately. Evaluative inferences, noting the anomaly, may be able to bring to bear sufficient knowledge of language usage to suggest that: (1) some nonliteral or metaphorical interpretation of "met," "a man who wasn't there," or both is necessary; and (b) the contradictions themselves are so striking that they may have been included deliberately to convey some significant piece of information. It should be noted that a model of the author's intentions in writing the poem (as distinct from the information that can be derived "directly" from the text) has had to be constructed in order to process this heavily metaphorical material effectively.

The third line adds one significant piece of information—the recent recurrence of the event described in the second line—and bits of a pattern begin to emerge. Lexically, line 3 is just as puzzling as line 2. No new spatial or temporal data have been added, but the recurrence of the "encounter" causes the addition of another (very similar) link to the event chain. Extrapolative inferences yield the expectation that, if the event (whatever it was) occurred twice, it may possibly have occurred many times, a pattern could continue into the future. Evaluative inferences, in the light of the paucity of new information in this line, begin to investigate the possibility that the recurrence of the event is significant (something has to be).

The fourth line is processed with the reader prepared to look for metaphor, for the suggestion of significant facts by the juxtaposition of contradictory ideas, for clues as to the author's intentions in writing the poem, and for some indication of further recurrence of (and thus more significance in) the pattern of meeting "a man who wasn't there." The repetition of "I wish" is studied by both lexical and temporal inferences, which conclude that it may convey intense desire, desire over a long period of time, or some combination of the two. Extrapolative inferences further analyze the fourth line, looking for a reason why the protagonist might want the "man who wasn't there" to go away. Normally (evaluative inference), people seek to avoid unpleasant experiences or stimuli; therefore (extrapolative inference), meeting the "man who wasn't there" may be unpleasant. An evaluative hypothesis is generated, suggesting that the events depicted in lines two and three might be symbolic of some unspecified but unpleasant experience.

At this point the reader has finished the poem, having drawn a huge number of inferences along the way, and *failed* to understand the author's intended meaning. If he is persistent, the reader may return to the beginning of the poem armed with a rough representation of part of the meaning and a large number of unfulfilled expectations. The reader who finally *does* understand the rhyme will have to have access to the knowledge that poems often describe intensely subjective experiences, and that the author's goal may have been to convey such an experience.

The final solution to the problem of the meaning of Mearns' poem comes about through the integration of almost all the unfulfilled expectations with the facts that by this time have become available. The hypothetical recurrence of the unpleasant event suggests that it may be inescapable. The possibility that the whole poem is a metaphor for some subjective (emotional) experience—of the sort that typically is not under the control of the individual—produces the evaluative hypothesis that to search for a precise, concrete *meaning* for the poem may be inappropriate. This last hypothesis, when integrated with all the rest of the information brought to bear on the problem, provides the final insight necessary for a solution.

The poem is the lament of a man who in his daily life (suggested by the recurrence of the experience and the depiction of the stairway as one with which the protagonist may well be familiar) is unable to escape regular encounters with some unpleasant emotional experience (perhaps a memory, or a feeling of guilt). No more precise interpretation than this is necessary (or was intended by the author, in all probability).

This analysis of the processing of example (9) above is not intended to be a rigorously formal description of how inferences work; clearly only a few of the tens of thousands of inferences that must be drawn in the understanding of such a poem have been mentioned. Rather, this last example should be considered a demonstration of the power of a systematic inference taxonomy, applied to a carefully designed representation of context, in revealing some of the components of the understanding of connected discourse.

## CONCLUDING REMARKS

Although we have not been able to find conclusive evidence to support the idea, we still believe that *inferencing,* or the finding of relations among events in a narrative, is critical to good comprehension and retention of story material. Our review of the studies of inferences by children (Trabasso &

Nicholas, this volume) indicated that they can and do make inferences. It remains unclear as to when such inferences are made and whether the making of such inferences aids memory. In the work on natural understanding and artificial intelligence, from which much of our present work derives, some (Rieger, 1974, 1975) have voiced the opinion that most inferencing is automatic and that as many inferences as possible should be generated. Schank (1975a) has argued that a large number of unnecessary inferences obstruct the processing of relevant information and that inferencing should be curbed whenever possible. There must be limits, but how many and what kind remain unknown.

We hope that our taxonomy and related set of question forms prove useful in the construction of test probes to assess comprehension and the making of inferences. Comparisons of how different kind of inferences are made should lead to a better understanding of language comprehension. The promotion of inferencing during reading or listening via questions may promote deeper understanding and better retention. These kinds of experiments should be feasible, once one identifies the structure of a narrative via the event chain analysis and the kinds of relations one wishes to test or promote via the taxonomy.

## ACKNOWLEDGMENTS

This paper is based, in part, on a Junior Paper by the first author submitted in partial fulfillment of a Bachelor of Arts degree, Department of Psychology, Princeton University, 1976. The research was supported by National Institute of Education Grant No. NIE-G-77-0018 to T. Trabasso. This work was also supported by National Institute of Mental Health Grants, Nos. 19223 and 29365 to T. Trabasso, and by a National Institute of Child Health and Human Development program project grant (5 PO1 HD05027) to the University of Minnesota's Institute of Child Development.

In developing our taxonomy, current work on natural language processing and artificial intelligence was of considerable use and provides much discussion on inferences. Among, these, Schank's conceptual dependency theory (Schank, 1972, 1973, 1975a, 1975b, 1975c; Schank & Rieger, 1974)—and a case–structure formalism using a series of rich, semantic interconnections built up from a set of semantic primitives—was especially useful, particularly on how information is qualified and how events in discourse are linked. In addition, Bruce (1972) has examined the nature of temporal information contained in sentences. Rieger (1974, 1975) has developed a taxonomy of inferences quite different from the present one. We found his categories instructive but not systematic and not mutually exclusive. We also have found the work on the representation of connected discourse (Abelson, 1975; Schank & Abelson, 1975; Rumelhart, 1975) as well as Charniak's (1972, 1975) papers on children's story comprehension both stimulating and useful in our thinking about inferences and the making of inferences. Our final formulation did not seem to rely directly on any of these sources, but we wished to acknowledge the basis for our ideas, many of which can be found in the above works.

## REFERENCES

Abelson, R. P. Does a story understander need a point of view? In R. C. Schank and B. .L. Nash–Webber (Chairpersons), *Theoretical issues in natural language processing.* An interdisciplinary workshop in computational linguistics, psychology, linguistics, artificial intelligence. Cambridge, Mass., 1975.

Bruce, B. C. A model for temporal references and its application in a question anwering program. *Artificial Intelligence,* 1972, *3,* 1–25.

Charniak, E. *Towards a model of children's story understanding.* Unpublished dissertation, Massachusetts Institute of Technology, 1972.

Charniak, E. Organization and inference in a frame-like system of common knowledge. In R. C. Schank & B. L. Nash–Webber (Chairpersons), *Theoretical issues in natural language processing.* Cambridge, Mass., 1975.

Craik, R. I. M., & Lockhart, R. S. Levels of processing: A framework for memory research. *Journal of Verbal Learning and Verbal Behavior,* 1972. *11,* 671–684.

Mearns, H. Untitled poem reprinted in *The New York Times,* April 9, 1976.

Rieger, C. J., III. Conceptual memory: *A theory and computer program for processing the meaning content of natural language utterances.* Unpublished doctoral dissertation, Stanford University, 1974.

Rieger, C. J., III. The commonsense algorithm as a basis for computer models of human memory, inference, belief, and contextual language comprehension. In R. C. Schank & B. L. Nash–Webber (Chairpersons), *Theoretical issues in natural language processing.* Cambridge, Mass., 1975.

Rumelhart, D. E. Notes on a schema for stories. In D. G. Bobrow & A. Collins (Eds.), *Representation and understanding: Studies in cognitive science.* New York: Academic Press, 1975.

Schank, R. C. Conceptual dependency: A theory of natural language understanding. *Cognitive Psychology,* 1972, *3,* 552–631.

Schank, R. C. Identification of conceptualization underlying natural language. In R. C. Schank & K. M. Colby (Eds.), *Computer models of thought and language.* San Francisco: W. H. Freeman, 1973.

Schank, R. C. *Conceptual information processing.* Amsterdam: North-Holland, 1975. (a)

Schank, R. C. The primitive acts of conceptual dependency. In R. C. Schank & B. L. Nash–Webber (Chairpersons), *Theoretical issues in natural language processing.* Cambridge, Mass., 1975. (b)

Schank, R. C. Using knowledge to understand. In R. C. Schank & B. L. Nash–Webber (Chairpersons), *Theoretical issues in natural language processing.* Cambridge, Mass., 1975. (c)

Schank, R. C., & Abelson, R. P. Scripts, plans and knowledge. In *Advance Papers of the Fourth International Joint Conference on Artificial Intelligence.* Tbilisi, Georgia, USSR, 1975.

Schank, R. C., & Rieger, C. J., III. Inferences and the computer understanding of natural languages. *Artificial Intelligence,* 1974, *5,* 373–412.

# 11

# Children's Understanding of Stories: Assimilation by a General Schema for Actions or Coordination of Temporal Relations?

Heinz Wimmer
*University of Salzburg, Austria*

The goal of this study is to explore some developmental issues in the understanding of simple action-based stories. Stories are a certain kind of verbal description of coherent event sequences in a mentally possible world. The competent story teller has such an event sequence in his mind, and he describes this sequence in accordance with the rules of language, with the postulates of conversation, and in accordance with some specific conventions about story telling.

Several theoretical accounts have shown knowledge of the world to be of critical importance for the understanding of stories (e.g., Charniak, 1972; Schank & Abelson, 1977; Nicholas & Trabasso, Chapter 10, this volume). The importance of world knowledge arises partly from the fact that speakers leave out information that they feel can be inferred by the listener. Trying to meet the speaker's expectation, the listener fills the gaps in the story by knowledge-based inferences. The world knowledge necessary for this inferencing can be of a very specialized type, for example, knowledge about the guest's actions in a restaurant, but stories often relate the actions of people in nonstereotype situations and therefore general knowledge about the structure of action seems necessary for story understanding (see Rumelhart, 1977; Schank & Abelson, 1977). This latter kind of world knowledge will be called "action-schema" in the following.

The action-schema is defined here as the conceptual knowledge of the constituent parts of an affirmative action and their relations to one another. It can be represented by two rewrite-rules, which are given in Table 11.1.

The first rule says that an action consists of a goal, one or more attempts, and a final outcome. These constituent parts are causally related, that is, the

TABLE 11.1
Representation of Action-Knowledge in Two Rewrite-Rules

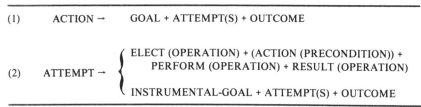

(1)    ACTION →    GOAL + ATTEMPT(S) + OUTCOME

(2)    ATTEMPT →    { ELECT (OPERATION) + (ACTION (PRECONDITION)) + PERFORM (OPERATION) + RESULT (OPERATION)

INSTRUMENTAL-GOAL + ATTEMPT(S) + OUTCOME

goal causes one or more attempts and the last attempt and/or external factors cause the final outcome. In the second rule—the attempt-subschema—a distinction is made between direct and indirect attempts. In a direct attempt, the person elects an operation that will transform the present state to the goal state. If preconditions of the operation are not given, they will be sought by actions that have the preconditions as goals. When the preconditions are given, the chosen operation is performed with a negative or positive result. An indirect attempt consists of an action, the goal of which is causally related to the goal of the original action.

The knowledge represented in the two rewrite-rules can be seen as a stereotype causal chain connecting certain abstract categories of mental and physical events. A further property of this knowledge is its recursiveness, which allows any degree of hierarchical complexity.

A simple story is commonly the verbal description of the more or less complex actions of a single person. A prototypical example of such a single person-oriented story is Rumelhart's (1977) version of an old English tale, given in Table 11.2, which is used in the experiments of this study.

How is the action-schema used when a listener understands the "Farmer Story?" A plausible possibility is that the schema gets activated by proposition (3), which instantiates the GOAL slot of the schema and an ATTEMPT is expected next. Proposition (4) is recognized as the performance of an operation and so instantiates the PERFORMANCE slot of the attempt-schema. The ELECT slot and the PRECONDITION slot of the attempt-schema, which are positioned before the PERFORMANCE slot, are not instantiated by story propositions but can easily be filled by schema-based inferences. The next expectation that a RESULT should occur is fulfilled by (5). Then the attempt-schema offers no further expectations and therefore control goes back to the action-schema that allows another ATTEMPT or a final (negative) OUTCOME to be expected. Propositions (6) and (7) fit into the attempt-schema in the same way as (4) and (5) did, and again control goes back to the action-schema. Propositions (8) and (9) state a new goal that is causally related to the original one. These two propositions, therefore, instantiate the GOAL slot of the indirect attempt-schema

TABLE 11.2
The Well-Structured Farmer Story

---

(1) Once upon a time there was an old farmer. (2) This old farmer had a naughty donkey. (3) One evening the farmer wanted to put his donkey into the stable. (4) First he tried to pull the donkey. (5) But the donkey didn't move. (6) Then he tried to push the donkey from behind. (7) Again the donkey didn't move. (8) Then the farmer had the idea (9) that he could frighten the donkey. (10) He went to his dog (11) and said to him: (12) "Dog, please bark at the donkey very loudly (13) then the donkey will be frightened (14) and run into the stable." (15) But the dog said: (16) "No farmer, I won't. (17) The donkey is my best friend." (18) So the farmer thought again, what he should do. (19) He went to his cat (20) and said: (21) "Dear pussy, please scratch the dog. (22) The dog will then bark (23) and frighten the donkey." (24) But the cat said: (25) "I'll only scratch the dog, (26) if you bring me some fresh milk to drink." (27) So the farmer went to his cow (28) and said: (29) "Cow, please give me some milk." (30) The cow said to the farmer: (31) "Yes farmer, you can have some milk. (32) But first you must bring me some hay to eat." (33) So the farmer went to the big pile of hay (34) and brought hay to the cow. (35) When the farmer gave the hay to the cow, (36) the cow gave the farmer the milk. (37) Then the farmer brought the milk to his cat. (38) When the cat had drunk the milk (39) she scratched the dog. (40) The dog then barked so loudly (41) that the donkey was frightened (42) and ran into the stable. (43) The farmer closed the heavy door (44) and was pleased.

---

according to which an attempt is expected next. Figure 11.1 shows how the rest of the story is assimilated by the action-schema.

The important characteristics of the above understanding process are the generation of plausible expectations that guide the information processing and the filling of the gaps in the story by schema-based inferences. The mental representation that might result from such a schema-based assimilation of the Farmer Story is depicted in Fig. 11.1. It can be seen that nearly all propositions of the story are placed in a coherent, hierarchically structured causal chain that leads from the initiating goal [proposition (3) in Table 11.2] to the final outcome of the main action [proposition (42)]. The initiating goal and the final outcome constitute the highest level of the hierarchy (see the right side of Fig. 11.1). Level 2 comprises the first two direct attempts. The goal of the first indirect attempt, which is repeated in the askings of the farmer, and the outcome of this attempt are classified as level 3. The next level includes the goal and the outcome of the second indirect attempt, and so on.

The mental representation of the Farmer Story that results from a schema-directed understanding process should be very efficient for story recall. The hierarchical nature of the representation allows the use of a top-down recall strategy, which starts recall with the highest level action and goes from there through the set of embedded actions. The causal connectedness of the representation allows the action-schema to serve as a network of retrieval cues for the propositions. If original story propositions cannot be recalled, the specification constraints of the schema constituents and of the relations between the constituents allow good guesses. From this reasoning, the prediction follows that the degree to which a story can be represented in a

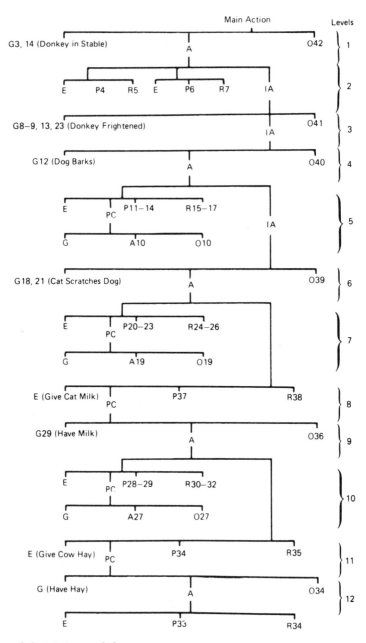

G=Goal, A=Attempt, O=Outcome
E=Elect (Operation), P=Perform (Operation), R=Result (Operation);
IA=Indirect Attempt; PC=Precondition.

FIG. 11.1.   Representation of the well-structured Farmer Story. The numbers refer to the propositions of the story (cf. Table 11.2).

coherent, hierarchical action structure should be a strong determinant of recall performance. This prediction was tested in several experiments by Thorndyke (1977). In one of his experiments he presented his subjects the Farmer Story (nearly identical to the one in Table 11.2) or destructured versions of this story for comprehensibility ratings and recall. It was found that the variation of the structuredness of the story had a strong effect on ratings and recall, and that a very high correlation existed between rated comprehensibility and the number of propositions recalled. It can be assumed that both the comprehensibility ratings and the recall performance reflect the degree to which the subjects were able to represent the story input in a coherent, hierarchical action structure. Strong evidence that the coherency of the mental representation of stories determines both comprehensibility ratings and recall comes from demonstrations by Bransford and Johnson (1973). The stories used in these experiments could not be given a coherent interpretation without the help of a picture or title that specified the situation. Comprehensibility ratings and recall depended on whether this aid to a coherent representation was provided before story presentation or not.

The dependency of recall performance upon the coherency with which a story is mentally represented was used in the first experiment to get information about how able children of different age levels are in building up a coherent, hierarchically structured representation of a story. Two stories were used: the Farmer Story of Table 11.2 as a prototype of a story that easily can be assimilated in a hierarchical, causally connected action structure (see Fig. 11.1), and a destructured version of this story as an example of a story that cannot be represented in such a way (see Table 11.3).

TABLE 11.3
The Destructured Farmer Story

(1) Once upon a time there was an old farmer. (2) This old farmer had a naughty donkey. (3) One evening the farmer went for a walk. (4) He walked across a meadow and (5) saw his donkey. (6) He went to his donkey quickly. (7) First the farmer tried to pull the donkey. (8) But the donkey didn't move. (9) Then he tried to push the donkey from behind. (10) Again the donkey didn't move. (11) Then the farmer went to his cow and (12) said to her: (13) "Cow, please give me some milk." (14) The cow said to the farmer: (15) "Yes farmer, you can have some milk, (16) but first you must bring me some hay to eat." (17) Then the farmer went to his dog and (18) said to him: (19) "Dog, please bark at the donkey very loudly." (20) But the dog said: (21) "No farmer, I won't, (22) the donkey is my best friend." (23) Then the farmer went to the big pile of hay and (24) brought hay to the cow. (25) When the farmer gave the hay to the cow (26) the cow gave the farmer the milk. (27) Then the farmer went to his cat and (28) said to her: (29) "Dear pussy, please scratch the dog." (30) But the cat said: (31) "I'll only scratch the dog, (32) if you bring me some fresh milk to drink." (33) So the farmer gave the cat his milk. (34) When the cat had drunk the milk (35) she scratched the dog. (36) Then the dog barked so loudly (37) that the donkey was frightened and (38) ran into the stable. (39) The farmer saw that the donkey was in the stable now. (40) He closed the heavy door. (41) The farmer built his stable all by himself and (42) when he had finished building (43) he bought the donkey.

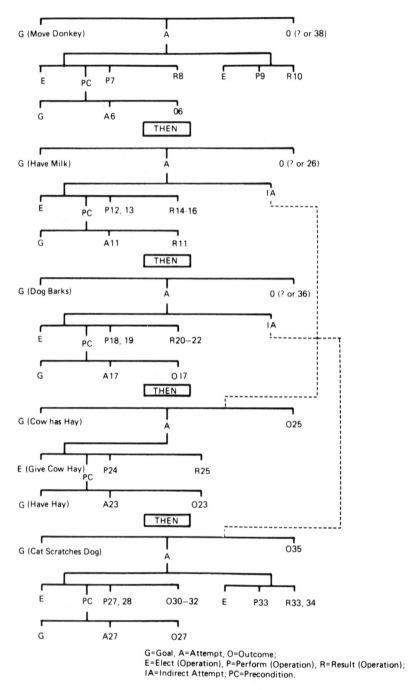

FIG. 11.2.  Representation of the destructured Farmer Story. The numbers
refer to the propositions of the story (cf. Table 11.3).

In the destructured story version, the overall goal of the farmer (putting the donkey in the stable) and the goal of the first indirect attempt (frightening the donkey) were deleted and the order of the farmer's actions was changed so that it is impossible or at least difficult to assimilate the destructured version in a hierarchical, causally connected action structure. Most of the farmer's actions can be connected by temporal links only, for example, ". . . the donkey didn't move. Then the farmer went to his cow," or ". . . The cow said to the farmer . . . you must bring me some hay to eat. Then the farmer went to his dog," or " . . . But the dog said . . . the donkey is my best friend. Then the farmer went to the big pile of hay." Figure 11.2 depicts some characteristics of the mental representation that might result from the understanding process. Instead of causal relations between the actions as in Fig. 11.1, most actions in Fig. 11.2 are connected by the relation THEN, which puts no constraints on its arguments. The broken lines between two temporally nonadjacent action pairs indicate that the subsequent action in each of the pairs might be recognized by some children as an indirect attempt in relation to the foregoing action, so that each of these action pairs might be mentally represented as just one hierarchical action.

The temporal connections between the important actions in the representation of the destructured story make the use of the effective top-down recall strategy impossible and also prevent the action-schema from providing retrieval cues that lead from one action to the other, as it is in the case of the causally related actions of the well-structured story. The recall of the destructured story should, therefore, be lower than the recall of the well-structured one.

The better recall of the well-structured version can only be expected if the story is actually assimilated in a hierarchical, causally connected action structure. If the young children do not assimilate the well-structured story version in such a way, then their recall of this version should be about the same as their recall of the destructured version. By having children of a wide age range (4-, 6-, 8-, 10-, and 14-year-olds) recall the well-structured or the destructured version in Experiment I, an attempt was made to determine the age level at which children do not assimilate well-structured stories in hierarchical, causally connected, action structures. The pattern of results one would expect is that for the youngest or maybe the two youngest age groups the recall of the well-structured version should be no better than the recall of the destructured version. For the older age groups, the well-structured version should be better recalled than the destructured version, and generally there should be a higher level of recall in the older than in the younger age groups.

These predictions follow from the action-schema approach and a plausible developmental hypothesis. They can be contrasted with predictions derivable from Piaget's (1969) theoretical approach to story comprehension. Piaget regards a story as being basically a description of a series of events and he assumes that the crucial problem in the assimilation of series of events is the mental coordination of the temporal relations between the events. This mental coordination of temporal relations depends on concrete operational thought, that is a stage in Piaget's theory of cognitive development that is entered by the child at about 7 to 8 years of age. A preoperational child lacking the ability to coordinate temporal relations should not be able to understand that event B is both after event A and before the other events in the series, and he or she should also not be able to infer that C is after A when being told that B is after A and C is after B. By this theorizing, Piaget explained the many violations of the original event order, which he observed in the story recall of preoperational children. According to this theoretical approach, both of our story versions are just descriptions of event series. The prediction would therefore be that preoperational children should show the same high amount of order violations in the recall of both the well-structured and the destructured version while concrete-operational children should show the same low amount of order violations for both versions. Experiment 1 allows to check the validity of this prediction by having preoperational as well as concrete-operational children recall the well-structured and the destructured story version.

## EXPERIMENT 1: STORY RECALL IN RELATION TO STORY— STRUCTUREDNESS AND CHILDREN'S AGE

### Method

*Subjects.* Twenty-four children from each of five age groups, that is, a total of 120 children, took part in the experiment. The median age in the five groups was 4 years-3 months (range 4-0 to 4-9), 6 years-3 months (range 5-10 to 6-7), 8 years-1 month (range 7-8 to 8-7), 10 years-3 months (range 9-7 to 10-7), and 14 years-1 month (range 13-6 to 14-5). The children were enrolled in a kindergarten, an elementary school, and a secondary school in a middle-class neighborhood. Two children of the youngest age group refused to cooperate and were replaced.

*Materials.* The well-structured story given in Table 11.2 and the destructured version given in Table 11.3 were rated by 10 students on a 1 (low) to 10 (high) scale for coherency. The raters were told that "1" means a passage consisting of independent events or actions and that "10" means a passage consisting of causally connected events or actions. The mean coherency for the destructured version was 4.5; the structured version was always given 10 (Wilcoxon-test, $T = 0$, $p < .01$).

*Procedure.*   Each child was tested individually in an unoccupied room of the kindergarten or school. After a warm-up period, the child was told that he or she would hear a story and should listen carefully so that he or she could retell the story afterwards. Then the experimenter recited the story, referring to a text in order to insure accuracy. Recordings were not used as they appeared to lead to lower levels of attention by the younger children. To minimize the effects of short-term memory and rehearsal, the children were asked to compare pictures for about 5 minutes, following story presentation, as to whether they were the same or different. Then they were given unlimited time to retell the story. Their reproductions were recorded.

*Design.*   The experimental design consisted of two between-subjects variables: story-condition (2) and age (5), with 12 subjects evenly divided according to sex in each of the 10 cells.

*Evaluation.*   The extent to which the propositions of the two stories were recalled was ascertained first ("propositions-recall"). A proposition was scored as recalled when that meaning of the original proposition that is relevant for the coherency of the story was properly reconstructed. For instance, a reconstruction like "The donkey jumped into the stable" was scored as a correct recall for "The donkey ran into the stable." All deletions of adjective and adverb modifiers were permitted too. Scoring was done independently by two scorers using the same general scoring criteria mentioned. The results given by the scorers were 96% in agreement.

Secondly, it was determined to what extent the content relevant to the action structure of both story versions ("action-recall") was recalled. Often a child would recall an action correctly but different in content from the original propositions. Frequently this represented a summary of the original propositions. Using only the original story propositions would underestimate the child's competence considerably, and it therefore seemed more appropriate to score recall performance with respect to the essential constituents of the action structure. To do this, just one relatively abstract proposition was generated for each major action-constituent of Fig. 11.1. The resulting set of 20 condensed propositions is given in Table 11.4. It is evident that a condensed proposition like "Farmer asked dog to bark" can be scored as recalled, given quite different formulations of the farmer's original asking. Again, scoring was done independently by two scorers. Interrater agreement was 95% for both versions. The comparison of action-recall between the two story versions was made without taking into account the propositions (1) and

TABLE 11.4
The Condensed Propositions of the Well-structured Farmer Story

---

(1) Farmer wanted to get donkey into the stable. (2) Farmer pulled donkey. (3) Two unsuccessful. (4) Farmer pushed the donkey. (5) Four unsuccessful. (6) Farmer wanted to frighten donkey. (7) Farmer asked dog to bark. (8) Seven unsuccessful. (9) Farmer asked cat to scratch the dog. (10) Cat made a condition. (11) Farmer asked cow for milk. (12) Cow made a condition. (13) Farmer fetched hay. (14) Cow got hay. (15) Cow gave milk. (16) Cat got milk. (17) Cat scratched dog. (18) Dog barked. (19) Donkey was frightened. (20) Donkey ran into the stable.

---

(6) of Table 11.4, as they were deleted in the presentation of the destructured story. These propositions were used to evaluate how often the deleted action-goals were reintroduced in the recall of the destructured version.

Thirdly, the condensed propositions of Table 11.4 were used to evaluate how well the order of actions in recall corresponded to that of the presentation. This was done by determining for each recall transcript the number of inversions, that is, the number of times an action from a later position in the story precedes an action from an earlier position. It was found that 85 of the 120 children recalled without inversion, 29 showed one inversion, 4 children had two inversions, and there was 1 child with three and 1 with five inversions. Because of this distribution, it was decided to classify each child as with or without inversion and to test the above predictions by using this two-valued score. For descriptive reasons, a proportion of inversions was determined for each experimental condition at each age level. This proportion of inversions indicates the number of inversions in the group relative to the maximum possible number of inversions in the group, i.e., the number of recalled actions minus number of subjects.

## Results and Discussion

*Recall of Action Order.*    Figure 11.3 shows the proportion of subjects in each group who produced at least one inversion and also gives the proportion of inversions for each group. Figure 11.3 shows that many (especially younger) children produced at least one inversion in the recall of the destructured version, but it is also evident that the proportion of inversions relative to the maximum possible is rather low. In the recall of the well-structured story, few of the younger children produced at least one inversion, and for the 8-, 10-, and 14-year-olds, inversions were absent.

To test the predictions derived from Piaget's theory, we classified the 4- and the 6-year-old children as "preoperational" and the 8-, 10-, and 14-year-olds as—at least—"concrete operational." The predictions were that there should be (1) equally poor order recall for both story versions in "preoperational" stage and (2) equally good order recall for both story versions in "concrete operational" stage. Both predictions are contradicted by the data. There were

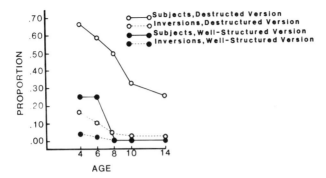

FIG. 11.3.   Action order recall in relation to story structuredness and age.

more children with at least one inversion in the destructured than in the well-structured condition, both in the "preoperational" stage, $\chi^2(1) = 5.4$, $p < .05$, and in the concrete operational stage, $\chi^2(1) = 15.9$, $p < .01$. Although the "preoperational" children showed instances of inversion more often than the "concrete operational" children, $\chi^2(1) = 10.8$, $p < .01$, there were only few preoperational children who produced an inversion in recalling the well-structured story, and the proportion of inversions for the preoperational group in this condition is close to zero.

    The result that, in the three older age groups, there were more subjects with inversions in the destructured story condition than in the well-structured one is consistent with the prediction derived from the action-schema approach. But, contrary to the expectations, the same result holds for the two youngest age groups. So one must conclude, that even 4-year-olds had at least partial success in the assimilation of the well-structured story.

    *Recall of Propositions and Actions.*    Figure 11.4 shows proposition- and action-recall in relation to story condition and children's age. Both story condition, $F(1, 110) = 16.7$, $p < .01$, and age, $F(4, 110) = 30.9$, $p < .01$, had a significant, but their interaction was not significant, $F(4, 110) = 1.6$, $p > .1$. The effect of story condition on recall is clearly limited to age levels older than 4-year-olds. For the 4-year-olds, the different structuredness of the stories had no effect on proposition- or action-recall, the means being identical The effect of story condition on recall is clearly limited to age levels older than 4-year-olds. For the 4-year-olds, the different structuredness of the stories had no effect on proposition-or action-recall, the means being identical (proposition-recall) or nearly identical (action-recall) for both conditions. These results are in accord with the expectation that the youngest age group would not be able to assimilate the well-structured story. So these recall measures lead to a different conclusion about the 4-year-olds ability to assimilate than the recall of action order. Experiment 2 will provide a

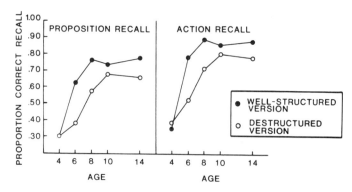

FIG. 11.4.   Proposition- and action-recall in relation to story structuredness and age.

clarification of this point. Here some further evidence for the role of the action-schema in the assimilation of the destructured story version will be presented.

*Intrusion of the Protagonist's Deleted Main Goal.*   If a child classifies "Farmer pulls (pushes) donkey" as attempts of an action, the goal of which is not instantiated, then the last story event, "Donkey runs into the stable," allows one to infer this goal as "Farmer wanted to get donkey into the stable." Maybe it is then also possible to classify "Farmer asks dog for barking" as an indirect attempt to reach the inferred main goal via the inferred instrumental goal "frightening the donkey." The results of this inference process being included in the mental representation of the story should also show up in story recall. These goal intrusions were indeed evident in 1, 1, 4, 7, and 8 children of the respective age groups, who included "Farmer wanted to get donkey into the stable" in their recall of the destructured version. One of the 10-and one of the 14-year-olds included "frightening the donkey" as a protagonist goal. The intrusion of the main goal was generally accompanied by very high action recall, the proportion of which was .72, .78, .90, .86, and .81 for the children who introduced goals in the respective age groups. These recall proportions are higher or about the same as the mean proportions of well-structured story recall in the respective age groups (see Fig. 11.4). One might interpret the high recall performance of these goal-introducing subjects as resulting from the causal connectedness of the story representation that was achieved by inferring the main goal.

*Reuniting Separated Parts of an Action.*   In the above characterization of the mental representation that might result from the action-schema based assimilation of the destructured story, it was pointed out that two pairs of separated actions might be assimilated as two hierarchical, complex actions (see dotted lines in Fig. 11.2). The first of these assimilations should occur when "Farmer fetches hay and gives it to the cow" is recognized as an indirect attempt of the farmer to get milk, although this attempt is separated from the first attempt to get milk by the farmer's first attempt to make the dog bark. If this assimilation occurs, one would expect that the indirect attempt to get milk should be recalled immediately subsequent to the direct attempt. The second case of such an assimilation depends on the recognition of "Farmer asks cat to scratch the dog" as an indirect attempt to make the dog bark. Again, this action is presented not immediately subsequent to the first direct attempt to make the dog bark, but it should be recalled immediately subsequent if the sketched assimilation process is carried out. This was indeed the case for 2 children of the 4-year-olds and for 2, 6, 5, and 4 children of the older age groups. The number of children in the respective age groups, who recalled the farmer's "hay"-actions immediately subsequent to the first attempt to get milk, was 3, 3, 2, 3, 1. Remarkably, there was no subject who showed both instances of reuniting, therefore the reuniting is not directly responsible for inversions. While the goal intrusions occurred more often in the older than the younger children's story recall, this developmental trend was not evident for the reuniting of separated action parts.

Experiment 2 was intended to clarify the interpretational problem posed by the incongruency of the 4-year-old's story recall in Experiment 1. Their proposition- and action-recall was the same for the well-structured and the destructured version, but their recall of action order was better for the well-structured than for the destructured story. Experiment 2 tried to check the generality of this finding by using stories with lower degrees of hierarchical complexity. Two new, well-structured Farmer Stories were constructed by systematically reducing the high degree of hierarchical embedding of actions that was characteristic for the original Farmer Story. For each of these versions with reduced degrees of hierarchical embedding, a corresponding destructured version was prepared (see Materials section following).

## EXPERIMENT 2: STORY RECALL IN RELATION TO STRUCTUREDNESS AND COMPLEXITY OF STORIES

### Method

*Subjects.* Sixty 4-year-old children from kindergartens in Salzburg participated in the experiment. The median age of the children was 4 years-6 months (range 4-1 to 4-11). Half of the children in each experimental condition were males and half were females.

*Materials.*   Six stories were used in this experiment. For the highest degree of hierarchical complexity, the Farmer Story of Experiment 1 was used (see Table 11.2 and Fig. 11.1). The stories with reduced degrees of hierarchical complexity were shorter versions of the original Farmer Story. The story with a "medium" degree of hierarchical complexity consisted of the hierarchical levels 1–7 of the original story, and the version with a "low" degree of hierarchical complexity consisted of the hierarchical levels 1–5 (see Fig. 11.1 and Tables 11.5 and 11.6). For each of these three well-structured stories there was a destructured version. The destructured version of the high complexity Farmer Story was already characterized in the Material section of Experiment 1 (see Table 11.3 and Fig. 11.2), and the destructured versions of the shorter Farmer Stories were constructed in the same way: The goal statements of the well-structured versions were deleted and the order of the events was changed so that causal relations between the events were difficult to infer. To keep the length of each destructured version approximately the same as the length of the corresponding well-structured version, some neutral filler sentences were included. The stories of Tables 11.5 and 11.6 were rated by 10 students for coherency in the same way as the story versions of

TABLE 11.5
The Farmer Stories of Medium Complexity

| *Well-Structured Version* |
| --- |
| Once upon a time there was an old farmer. This old farmer had a naughty donkey. One evening the farmer wanted to put the donkey into the stable. First he tried to pull the donkey. But the donkey didn't move. Then he tried to push the donkey from behind. Again the donkey didn't move. Then the farmer had the idea that he could frighten the donkey. He went to his dog and said to him: "Dog, please bark at the donkey very loudly, then the donkey will be frightened and run into the stable." But the dog said: No farmer, I won't. The donkey is my best friend." So the farmer thought again what he should do. He went to his cat and said: Dear pussy, please scratch the dog. The dog will then bark and frighten the donkey." The cat said: "Yes farmer, I would like to do that." Then the cat scratched the dog. The dog then barked so loudly that the donkey was frightened and ran into the stable. The farmer closed the heavy door and was pleased. |

| *Destructured Version* |
| --- |
| Once upon a time there was an old farmer. This old farmer had a naughty donkey. He also had a dog and a cat. One evening the farmer went for a walk. He walked across a meadow and saw his donkey. He went to his donkey quickly. The farmer tried to pull the donkey. But the donkey didn't move. Then the farmer went to his cat and said to her: Dear pussy, please scratch the dog." The cat said : "Yes farmer, I would like to do that." Then the farmer tried to move the donkey from behind. But the donkey didn't move. So the farmer went to his dog and said: "Dog, please bark at the donkey very loudly." But the dog said: No farmer, I won't. The donkey is my best friend." Then the cat scratched the dog and the dog barked so loudly that the donkey was frightened and ran into the stable. The farmer saw, that the donkey was in the stable now. He closed the heavy door. The farmer built his stable all by himself and when he had finished building he bought the donkey. |

TABLE 11.6
The Farmer Stories of Low Complexity

---

*Well-Structured Version*

---

Once upon a time there was an old farmer. This old farmer had a naughty donkey. One evening the farmer wanted to put the donkey into the stable. First he tried to pull the donkey. But the donkey didn't move. Then he tried to push the donkey from behind. Again the donkey didn't move. Then the farmer had the idea that he could frighten the donkey. He went to his dog and said to him: "Dog, please bark at the donkey very loudly then the donkey will be frightened and run into the stable." The dog said: "Yes farmer, I would like to do that." Then the dog barked so loudly that the donkey was frightened and ran into the stable. The farmer closed the heavy door and was pleased.

---

*Destructured Version*

---

Once upon a time there was an old farmer. This old farmer had a naughty donkey. He also had a dog and a cat. One evening the farmer went for a walk. He walked across a meadow and saw his donkey. He went to his donkey quickly. The farmer tried to pull the donkey. But the donkey didn't move. So the farmer went to his dog and said: "Dog, please bark at the donkey very loudly." The dog said: "Yes farmer, I would like to do that." Then the farmer tried to push the donkey from behind. But the donkey didn't move. Then the dog barked so loudly that the donkey was frightened and ran into the stable. The farmer saw that the donkey was in the stable now. He closed the heavy door.

---

Experiment 1. The well-structured versions were always given the highest coherency rating (10 on the 10-point scale). The destructured version of the medium complexity story had a mean coherency of 3.7, and the destructured version of the low complexity story had one of 5.7. The difference in the rated coherency between the structured and the destructured version was for both complexity levels significant (Wilcoxon-test, $T = 0$, $p < .01$).

*Procedures.* The procedure of Experiment 2 corresponded to that of Experiment 1. The only modification was that, instead of the informal warming up period of Experiment 1, the children had to recall two short episodes to make them familiar with the recall task.

*Design.* The design included two between-subjects variables: hierarchical complexity (3 levels) and structuredness (2 levels), with the data of 10 children in each of the six cells.

*Evaluation.* The assessment of recall performance was carried out in the same way as in Experiment 1. Only in the evaluation of the action-recall was a slight modification necessary. For the Farmer Story with medium hierarchical complexity, proposition (10) in Table 11.4 was changed from "Cat made a condition" to "Cat agreed" and the propositions (11)–(16) were deleted. For the Farmer Story with low hierarchical complexity, proposition

(8) was changed from "Seven unsuccessful" to "Dog agreed" and the propositions (9)–(17) were deleted.

## Results and Discussion

*Recall of Action Order.*   While there was not one instance of order inversion evident in the recalls of the three well-structured stories, some inversions occurred in each of the destructured versions. The proportion of children showing at least one inversion was .20 for the high complexity condition and .30 and .10 for the medium and the low complexity condition. These differences were not significant, $\chi^2(1) = 1.2, p > .1$, but the difference between the combined well-structured and the combined destructured versions was highly significant, $\chi^2(1) = 6.7$, $p < .01$. The proportion of inversions relative to maximum was .11 for the combined destructured versions.

*Recall of Propositions and Actions.*   Figure 11.5 shows these recall measures in relation to structuredness and hierarchical complexity of the stories. Only the variation in structuredness had a significant effect both on proposition-recall, $F(1, 54) = 8.3$, $p < .01$, and on action-recall, $F(1, 54) = 4.8$, $p < .05$. The hierarchical complexity had no significant effect on recall and neither did the interaction of the two factors. The differences between the recall of the well-structured and the destructured versions were checked by the Newman–Keuls procedure. Both proposition-and action-recall was significantly higher ($p < .01$) for the well-structured versions of the medium and low level of hierarchical complexity while for the high level of hierarchical complexity this difference was in the same direction but not significant.

In contrast to the findings in Experiment 1, there is no incongruency between recall of action order and recall of propositions and actions. On both

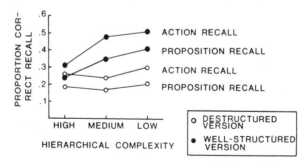

FIG. 11.5.   Proposition- and action-recall in relation to structuredness and complexity of the stories.

of these recall measures, the 4-year-olds show higher performance with well-structured than with destructured versions, thereby giving clear indication of at least partial success in the assimilation of the well-structured versions into hierarchical, causally connected action structures. Most impressive is the *complete absence* of order inversions in the recall of the well-structured versions, a finding which will be given further consideration below.

Both Experiments 1 and 2 relied on the superior recall of well-structured stories as compared to destructured ones, to make inferences about the nature of the assimilation process and about the resulting mental representation in different age groups. In particular, the superior recall of the well-structured version was taken as an indication of successful assimilation into hierarchical, causally connected structures via the use of the general action-schema. Experiment 3 was intended to provide direct evidence for the effect of such an assimilation process on recall by using why-questions *during* story presentation as a direct indicator for successful assimilation into hierarchical, causally connected action structures. A why-question was asked after each of the major attempts of the farmer, for example, "Why did the farmer ask the dog to bark at the donkey?" If a child has successfully assimilated the farmer's asking as an attempt to frighten the donkey and this in turn as an attempt to get the donkey into the stable, then the child should have no difficulty to answer the why-question with one of these goals. If the recall of the well-structured stories does indeed indicate the children's ability to assimilate story information in a causally connected action structure, then there should be a high correlation between the answering of goal-questions and recall. To control for possible alternative explanations of such a correlation, a second group of children was asked different questions. The questions in the control conditions were asked at the same positions during story presentation as the goal-questions, but these questions referred to one of the arguments of a before mentioned proposition, for example, "Whom has the dog to bark at?" Correct answers to these latter questions depend on the understanding of the sentences and not on the assimilation of the story in a causally connected action structure. They should not correlate as high with recall as the goal-questions if the assumed effect of successful assimilation on recall is given.

## EXPERIMENT 3: GOAL-QUESTION ANSWERING
## AND STORY RECALL

### Method

*Subjects.* Forty kindergarten children and 20 8-year-olds participated in the experiment. The median ages were 4 years-6 months (range 4-0 to 4-11) and 8 years-3 months (range 7-9 to 8-7). Each group was evenly divided according to sex. Four 4-year-olds had to be replaced because they refused to cooperate. Half of the 40 4-year-olds were asked goal-questions and the other half was asked proposition-related questions. The 8-year-olds were only asked goal-questions.

*Materials.* The well-structured story (Table 11.2) was used, and according to the condition, either the goal-related or the proposition-related question of the following pairs was asked: (1) Why did the farmer pull the donkey? or Who tried to pull the donkey? [After proposition (4), Table 11.2]. (2) Why did he do that? Who did that? [After proposition (6)]. (3) Why did the farmer want to frighten the donkey? or Who had the idea that he could frighten the donkey? [After proposition (9)]. (4) Why did the farmer want the dog to bark at the donkey? or Whom did the dog have to bark at? [After proposition (14)]. (5) Why did the farmer want the cat to scratch the dog? or Whom did the cat have to scratch? [After (23)]. (6) Why did the farmer want the cow to give him milk? or Who went to the cow? [After (29)]. (7) Why did the farmer bring the cow hay? or What did the farmer bring to the cow? [After (34)].

*Procedure.* The procedure corresponded to that of Experiment 1. As in Experiment 2, the children were given two short episodes to recall before the Farmer Story was told. After each question was asked, the child had about 7 seconds to begin the answer. Immediately after the answer, the experimenter continued the story. Both presentation and recall were tape-recorded.

*Evaluation.* The evaluation of recall performance in regard to action-and proposition-recall was done in the same way as in Experiment 1 except that all 20 propositions of Table 11.4 were considered in the evaluation of action-recall. The children's answers to the why-questions were scored as correct when a direct or a hierarchically supraordinate action goal was expressed. Answers in which the goal of the protagonist's main action were only indirectly expressed, such as "Because the donkey didn't want to go into the stable," were considered correct. All answers to the proposition-related questions were accepted as correct if they specified the argument referred to.

## Results and Discussion

First, question answering and recall for the two groups of 4-year-olds with different question-types will be compared. The seven proposition-related questions were more often correctly answered by 4-year-olds than the goal-questions. The mean number correct was 6.0 for proposition-related and 4.2 for goal-questions, $t(38) = 4.4$; $p < .01$. In regard to the why-question answers, a distinction was made between reference to direct or to supraordinated action-goals. Only the first two why-questions elicited direct goals; the other five questions were always answered by supraordinated goals. The 4-year-olds had a slightly higher percentage of supraordinated (65%) than of direct action goals (53%). For the 8-year-olds, the corresponding percentages were 92% and 95%. Wilcoxon-tests declared these differences between types of answers insignificant.

The recall performance of the two 4-year-olds groups was about the same. The action-recall of the goal-question group was 38%; the proposition-recall of this group was 26%. The corresponding percentages for the group with proposition-related questions were 39% and 30%. There were 4% inversions for both groups.

Next, the correlations between question-answering and recall performance were examined. The correlation between goal-question answering and action-recall was $r(18) = .77$, $p < .01$ and significantly higher ($p < .05$ one-tailed) than the correlation between proposition-related question answering and action-recall, $r(18) = .40$, $p > .05$. The correlation between goal-question answering and proposition recall, $r(18) = .63$, $p < .01$, was also higher than that between proposition-related question answering and proposition-recall, $r(18) = .42$, $p > .05$, but this latter difference was not significant.

Individual differences in the ability to answer questions and to recall were examined further. Of special interest was the recall performance of four 4-year-old children in the goal-question group who answered all questions correctly and so can be ascribed a complete assimilation of the action structure of the story. The action-recall of these children was 80% and their proposition-recall, $U = 7$, $p < .01$ one-tailed, was significant. The recall children who did not answer all action-related questions correctly was 28% and 20%. The difference for action-recall, $U = 0$, $p < .001$ one-tailed, and for propostion-recall, $U = 7$, $p < .01$ one-tailed, was significant. The recall performance of the four 4-year-olds with complete assimilation of the action structure was also better than that of the eight 4-year-olds who answered all proposition-related questions correctly. The latter had an action-recall of 46% and a proposition-recall of 37%. Only the difference in action-recall was significant, $U = 5$, $p < .05$ one-tailed.

The 8-year-old children answered nearly all of the seven goal-questions correctly. The mean number correct for the 8-year-olds was 6.6, which was significantly higher than the corresponding number of 4.2 for the 4-year-olds, $t(38) = 4.4$, $p < .01$. The recall performance of the 8-year-olds was 87% for action-recall and 69% for proposition-recall. The differences with respect to the corresponding numbers of the 4-year-olds, 38% and 26%, was significant for action-recall, $t(38) = 5.6$, $p < .01$, and for proposition-recall, $t(38) = 7.0$, $p < .01$.

Next, the four 4-year-old children who answered all goal-questions correctly were compared on recall performance with the 17 8-year-olds who also answered all questions correctly. It was found that the high action-recall of the 4-year-olds was still lower than that of the 8-year-olds; the respective percentages were 80% and 93%, $U = 7$, $p < .01$. The same was the case for proposition-recall; the respective percentages were 49% and 74%, $U = 3$, $p < .01$.

The high correlation between goal-question answering and recall for well-structured stories substantiates the initial assumption that it is indeed the successful assimilation into hierarchical, causally connected action structures that is critical for the recall of the well-structured stories. In fact, such an assimilation of the *whole* story seems to be decisive, at least for 4-year-olds. This is indicated by the finding that the recall of the few 4-year-olds who answered *all* goal questions correctly is between two and three times higher than the recall performance of the 4-year-olds without such perfect goal-question answering. The result that only 20% of the 4-year-olds but 85% of the 8-year-olds were able to make such a complete assimilation of the well-structured story indicates important developmental differences.

A developmental trend in the ability to answer story-related why-questions was also found by Stein and Glenn (1979, Experiment 2) between 6- and 10-year-olds. Stein and Glenn concluded, from the many goals given as answers to the why-questions, that the goals of the protagonist are perceived and represented as the principle locus of causality in a story even when the goals do not occur in recall. This is in agreement with the observation that most often the main goal of the farmer was given as an answer to the why-questions.

## GENERAL DISCUSSION

First, I want to discuss some findings in relation to the two main propositions that characterize Piaget's theorizing about the development of story understanding. These two propositions are: (1) The crucial problem in story understanding is the mental coordination of the temporal relations between the events described by the story. (2) Concerning this mental coordination, there exist two qualitatively different stages in development, that is general inability for the coordination of relations in the preoperational stage and a general ability for this coordination in the concrete operational stage. If we regard as "preoperational" just the 4-year-olds, then we have 82 "preoperational" children who recalled a well-structured story version in the three reported experiments. Eleven of these 82 children, that is 13%, produced inversions in their story recall but mostly not more than one. The proportion of inversions in relation to the maximal possible number is .03. All the inversions occurred in the recall of the highly complex Farmer Story and none occurred in the recall of the less complex ones. So the "preoperational" children's poor recall of event order, which was the phenomenon Piaget's theorizing tried to explain, does simply not exist for well-structured stories. As Mandler and Johnson (1977) pointed out, Piaget's observation of such a poor recall of preoperational children may have been caused by the "destructuredness" and by the difficult wording of his stories. Mandler and Johnson as well as Stein and Glenn (1978) found nearly perfect order in 6-year-olds' recall of well-structured and coherent stories. Poulson, Kintsch, Kintsch, and Premack (1979) assessed recall order, when 4- and 6-year-olds had to recall their own descriptions of well-structured or of scrambled picture stories. Poulson et al. found better recall of event order for the description of the well-ordered than of the scrambled picture stories. It is evident that the results of the studies mentioned are in complete accord with the present findings on order recall.

Piaget's general characterization of the preoperational child as being unable to coordinate relations is not only refuted in the domain of story understanding. There are convincing demonstrations that "preoperational" children are able to coordinate relations in transitive inferencing, if they manage to represent the premises correctly (see Trabasso & Nicholas, Chapter 9 this volume, for a review of this work).

Piaget's theoretical account of the development of story understanding does not only lead to wrong predictions about young children's recall of event order, it is also of very limited scope. So it does not allow to explicate notions like coherence, structuredness, or hierarchical action embedding, and it is silent about the effects of these story characteristics on understanding and recall. It also has nothing to say about question answering, about the occurrence of intrusions and of order changes in recall, about different importance of story parts, about summarizing, etc. I indicated how some of these phenomena can be dealt with if story understanding is conceived as assimilation by a general action-schema. But a more thorough theoretical treatment of story understanding would have to show how world knowledge of different domains and of different abstractness has to be used in the comprehension process (see Charniak, 1972; Kintsch, 1977; Nicholas & Trabasso, this volume; Schank & Abelson, 1977; Van Dijk, 1977; Winograd, 1977 for such theoretical accounts).

Now I want to return to the developmental issue and ask specifically, what develops in the observed age range if story understanding is conceived as assimilation by a general action schema? Two interesting answers, concerning (1) the development of the conception of a story, and (2) the acquisition of the general action-schema, can be ruled out immediately.

The first answer would assume that age differences in story understanding and adults do. This was suggested by Piaget (1969), who reported that, in the generation of stories, young children prefer to line up short disparate episodes than to tell just one coherent story. Stein and Glenn (1977) also found that generation of stories, young children prefer to line up short disparate episodes than to tell just one coherent story. Stein and Glenn (1977) also found that kindergarteners quite often generated simple descriptions of characters and of typical activities instead of causal episodes. If young children do not conceive stories as coherent wholes, then they cannot be expected to assimilate stories in causally connected action structures. The well-structured stories should therefore be assimilated and represented as series of disparate actions, similar to the assimilation and representation of the destructured stories. That this characterization of young children's story understanding cannot be valid is evidenced by the finding that even 4-year-olds showed better recall of the well-structured than of the destructured versions. It is also contradicted by the finding that 4-year-olds answered a high percentage of why-questions with distant goals. These findings also contradict the second plausible answer to the "what develops" question, namely, that the younger children do not yet have a general action-schema as older children and adults do. But if the 4-year-olds do not have such a schema, then they should not be able to recall the well-structured versions better than the destructured ones and they should not be able to answer why-questions with distant goals as they actually do.

The clearest evidence for developmental differences in understanding stories of the type used here is provided by the goal-question answering in Experiment 3. Because of the striking recall differences between 4-year-olds who answered all goal-questions and those who did not answer all goal-questions, "all goal-questions answered" can be considered as indicator for full comprehension. Only 25% of the 4-, but 85% of the 8-year-olds showed such a comprehension.

The question is, then, what prevents the 4-year-olds from full comprehension. Several factors seem possible. One could be a lack of relevant world knowledge. So, for instance, if a child could not imagine that "pushing the donkey" can cause "donkey is in the stable," she or he would be reluctant to recognize the former as an attempt. In other words, the child must have the knowledge to figure out the *specific* causal connections between the states, actions, and events of the story.

Another factor preventing full comprehension might be a basic limitation in 4-year-olds information processing capacity. The story used in Experiment 3 had a high degree of hierarchical action embedding. The successful assimilation of such a story requires that the structurally important parts of the already assimilated story information must be mentally present so that the incoming information can be connected with the already built up action structure. If this "keeping-present capacity" gets overloaded, then the integration of new information in the already existing structure would break down. Pascual–Leone (1970) proposed a systematic increase of this capacity in the course of children's development (but see Trabasso & Foellinger, 1978.) Another possibility is that the children of the different ages had the same amount of this mental capacity, but the older children were able to circumvent capacity problems by a continuing process of summarizing *during* story assimilation, thereby preventing information overload. How this summarizing might be accomplished is treated in some first theoretical accounts by Rumelhart (1977), Schank and Abelson (1977), and Kintsch & van Dijk (1978). Which one or which combination of the discussed or of the nonmentioned factors is responsible for the development of story understanding has yet to be found out. The theoretical and experimental study of story understanding seen as a certain type of heavily knowledge-based information processing has just begun.

## ACKNOWLEDGMENTS

This research was supported by the Austrian Fonds zur Förderung der wissenschaftlichen Forschung and by the Stiftungs- und Förderungsverein der Universität Salzburg. The manuscript was prepared while the author was at the Institute of Child Development, University of Minnesota, as a visiting postdoctoral associate, which was made possibly by a grant from the Stiftung Volkswagenwerk. The author wants to express his appreciation to the Amt der Salzburger Landesregierung and to the Magistrat der Stadt Salzburg as well as to the staff and the children of various kindergartens in Salzburg. Thanks are also due to the editors of this volume for helpful comments on earlier versions of the manuscript. I am especially grateful to Liselotte Grässle who took part in the planning of Experiment 1, which she also executed.

## REFERENCES

Bransford, J. D., & Johnson, M. K. Considerations of some problems of comprehension. In W. G. Chase (Eds.), *Visual information processing.* New York: Academic Press, 1973.

Charniak, E. *Toward a model of children's story comprehension.* (AI Memo TR-266) Cambridge, Mass.: M.I.T. Press, 1972.

Kintsch, W. On comprehending stories. In M. A. Just & P. Carpenter (Eds.), *Cognitive processes in comprehension.* Hillsdale, N. J.: Lawrence Erlbaum Associates, 1977.

Kintsch, W. & van Dijk, T. A. Toward a model of text comprehension and production. *Psychological Review,* 1978, *85,* 363–394.

Mandler, J. M. & Johnson, N. S. Remembrance of things parsed: story structure and recall. *Cognitive Psychology,* 1977, *9,* 111–151.

Pascual-Leone, J. A. A mathematical model for the transition rule in Piaget's developmental stages. *Acta Psychologica,* 1970, *63,* 301–345.

Piaget, J. *The child's conception of time.* London: Routledge & Kegan Paul, 1969.

Poulson, D., Kintsch, E., Kintsch, W., & Premack, D. Children's comprehension and memory for stories. *Journal of Experimental Child Psychology,* 1979.

Rumelhart, D. E. Understanding and summarizing brief stories. In D. LaBerge & J. Samuels (Eds.), *Basic processes in reading: Perception and comprehension.* Hillsdale, N. J.: Lawrence Erlbaum Associates, 1977.

Schank, R. C., & Abelson, R. P. *Scripts, plans, goals and understanding.* Hillsdale, N. J.: Lawrence Erlbaum Associates, 1977.

Stein, N. L., & Glenn, C. G. *A developmental study of children's construction of stories.* Paper presented at the SRCD Meetings, New Orleans, 1977.

Stein, N. L., & Glenn, C. G. An analysis of story comprehension in elementary school children. In R. Freedle (Ed.), *Multidisciplinary approaches to discourse comprehension.* Norwood, N.J.: Ablex, 1979.

Thorndyke, P. W. Cognitive structures in comprehension and memory of narrative discourse. *Cognitive Psychology,* 1977, *9,* 77–110.

Trabasso, T., & Foellinger, D. B. Information processing capacity in children: A test of Pasqual-Leone's model. *Journal of Experimental Child Psychology,* 1978, *26,* 1–17.

van Dijk, T. A. Semantic macro-strucures and knowledge frames in discourse comprehension. In M. A. Just & P. Carpenter (Eds.), *Cognitive processes in comprehension.* Hillsdale, N. J.: Lawrence Erlbaum Associates, 1977.

Winograd, P. A framework for understanding discourse. In M. A. Just & P. Carpenter (Eds.), *Cognitive processes in comprehension.* Hillsdale, N.J.: Lawrence Erlbaum Associates, 1977.

# Author Index

*Numbers in italis indicate the page on which the complete reference appears*

## A

Abelson, R. P., 264, *265,* 267, 287, 289, *290*
Adams, J. S., 35, *42*
Adams, M. J., 114, *142, 144*
Anderson, D. R., 113, *144*
Anderson, N. H., 2, 3, 4, 5, 6, 7, 8, 9, 10, 11, 12, 13, 14, 15, 19, 20, 21, 22, 23, 25, 26, 27, 28, 29, 30, 32, 34, 35, 36, 37, 38, 39, 40, *42, 43, 44,* 48, 51, 58, 62, 67, 68, 78, *69,* 92, *96, 97,* 101, *112,* 114, 132, 133, 139, 140, 142, *142,* 220, *240, 241*
Andrews, J. 16, *44*
Aronfreed, J., 113, 120, *144*
Astor, E. C., 172, 173, *181*
Astor-Stetson, E., 171, 173, *181*
Austin, V. C., 72, *96,* 219, *240*

## B

Barclay, J. R., 224, 225, 226, 227, 232, *240*
Barenboim, C. 72, 74, *96*
Bartlett, F. C., 215, 224, *240*
Bass, S. C., 219, *241*
Bearison, D. J., 218, *240*

Berch, D. B., 183, 184, 199, 200, 202, 211, *214*
Berndt, E. G., 218, *240*
Berndt, T. J., 218, *240*
Berscheid, E., 22, 35, *43, 45*
Bever, T. G., 29, *44*
Biederman, I., 122, *142*
Bogratz, R. A., 193, 202, *214*
Bogartz, R. S., 13, 15, *43,* 57, *69*
Bourne, L. E., Jr., 184, 189, *214*
Bower, G. H., 160, 161, *168*
Boyes-Braem, P., 167, *168*
Brainerd, C. J., 40, *43*
Bransford, J. D., 223, 224, 225, 226, 227, 232, *240,* 271, *289*
Brooks, W. N., 35, *43*
Brown, A. L., 215, 226, 230, *240, 242*
Bruce, B. C., 255, 256, 264, *265*
Bruner, J. S. 113, 117, *142*
Bryant, P. E., 222, *240*
Buchanan, J. P. 17, *43,* 72, 75, 77, 93, *96*
Buckhalt, J. A., 226, 227, 229, *241*
Burns, B., 123, 134, *142*
Burt, C., 222, *240*
Butzin, C. A., 3, 4, 5, 6, 7, 11, 19, 20, 21, 23, 24, 27, 36, 40, *43,* 132, *142*

### C

Carter, A. Y., 226, 227, 228, *241*
Chandler, M. J., 72, 74, *96*
Charniak, E., 254, 257, 264, *265*, 267, 287, *289*
Checkosky, S. F., 122, *142*
Coie, J. D., 17, *43*, 75, 76, 77, *96*
Cole, M., 117, 118, *144*
Corbin, D. W., 172, *181*
Costanzo, P. R., 17, *43*, 75, 76, 77, *96*
Cox, G. L., 226, 235, 236, *241*
Craik, F. I. M., 234, *240*, 252, *265*
Crowley, P. M., 74, *96*
Cuneo, D. O., 5, 9, 10, 11, 12, 13, 14, 15, 16, 25, 27, 28, 29, 34, 40, *42*, 48, 51, 58, 62, 68, *69*, 114, 132, 133, 139, 140, 142 *142*
Cunningham, J. D., 38, *44*
Cunningham, J. G., 171, 172, 173, 176, *181*

### D

Dewey, J., 215, *241*
Dion, K. K., 22, *43*
Doob, A. N., 35, *43*
Doyle, A., 113, *142*

### E

Eimas, P. D., 114, *143*
Eisen, S. V., 26, *44*
Elkind, D., 132, *143*, 148, 150, *168*

### F

Farkas, A. J., 36, *42*
Farnhill, D., 17, *43*, 75, 76, 77, *96*
Feldman, N. S., 26, *44*, 72, *96*, 219, *241*
Felfoldy, G. L., 115, 116, 120, 121, 122, 133, *143*
Fellows, B. J., 190, 196, *214*
Fisher, M. A., 113, *143*
Flapan, D., 217, *241*
Flavell, J. H., 28, *43*
Fodor, J. A., 224, *241*
Foellinger, D. B., 288, *290*
Foote, K. E., 113, *143*
Fraisse, P., 65, *69*
Frankel, G. W., 113, 114, *144*

Franks, J. J., 224, 225, 226, 227, 232, *240*
Franz, C. M., 6, *43*
Friedman, W. J., 63, *69*

### G

Garner, W. R., 114, 115, 116, 117, 119, 120, 121, 122, 123, 124, 138, 139, 141, *143*
Gelman, R., 29, 39, *43*
Gibson, E. J., 113, 117, 119, 120, 122, *143*, 171 *181*
Gibson, J. J., 171, *181*
Ginsburg, H., 132, *143*
Glass, A. L., 160, 161, *168*
Glenn, C. G., 216, 218, 219, 239, *242*, 286, 287, *290*
Glick, J., 117, 118, *144*
Gloth, J., 100, *112*
Go, G., 148, 150, *168*
Goldfarb, J. L., 65, *69*
Goldstone, S., 65, *69*
Gottwald, R. L., 122, *143*
Gray, W. D., 167, *168*
Greene, J., 224, *241*
Greenfield, P. M., 113, 117, *142*
Greenspan, S., 72, 74, *96*
Grumet, J. F., 17, *43*, 75, 76, 77, *96*
Gutkin, D. C., 25, *44*, 74, *96*
Guzman, R. D., 171, 173, *181*

### H

Hagen, J. W., 113, 114, *143*, 170, *181*
Haggbloom, S. J., 122, *144*
Hale, G. A., 114, *143*, 170, *181*
Hale, G. H., 113, 114, *143*
Halmos, P. R., 39, *43*
Handel, S., 115, 116, 120, 123, *143*
Harlow, H., 207, *214*
Hartshorne, H., 41, *43*, 95, *96*
Hartup, W. H., 23, *43*
Hayes-Roth, B., 228, 232, *241*
Hayes-Roth, F., 228, 232, *241*
Haygood, R. C., 184, *214*
Hebble, P. W., 17, *43*, 75, 76, *96*
Hendrick, C., 6, *43*
Holt, J. R., 117, *143*
Hommers, W., 100, 110, *112*
Hoving, K. L., 6, *43*
Hyman, R., 115, *143*

Lockhart, R. S., 234, *240*, 252, *265*
Lockhead, G. R., 119, 120, 133, 139, *144*
Lopes, L. L. 22, *43*

Imai, S., 115, 116, 121, 123, *143*
Inhelder, B., 28, *44,* 169, 170, *181,* 222, *242*
Isaacs, L., 218, *240*
Israel, M., 183, 184, 199, 200, 202, 211, *214*

**J**

Johnson, D. M., 167, *168*
Johnson, M. K., 223, *240,* 271, *289*
Johnson, N. S., 216, 218, *241,* 287, *289*
Johnson, P. J., 117, *144*

**K**

Karniol, R., 95, *96*
Katz, J. J., 224, *241*
Keasey, C. B.. 95. *96*
Kelley, H. H., 37, 38, *43*
Kemler, D. G., 113, 120, 121, 122, 123, 124, 125, 131, *143, 144*
King, W. L., 117, *143*
Kintsch, E., 287, *289*
Kintsch, W., 287, 289, *289*
Klahr, D., 113, *143*
Kleber, E. W., 100, *112*
Klosson, E. C., 72, *96,* 219, *241*
Kobasingawa, A., 236, *241*
Koegler, R. R., 148, 150, *168*
Kohlberg, L., 41, *43,* 72, *96*
Kosslyn, S. M., 147, 168, *168*
Krantz, D. H., 133, *143*
Kun, A., 24, 25, 27, 40, *44*

**L**

LaBerge, D., 142, *144*
Lane, J., 35, *44,* 92, *97,* 220, *241*
Laurendeau, M., 40, *44*
Lawson, R., 231, 232, *241*
Lemond, C. M., 171, *181*
Leon, M., 8, 11, 17, 18, 27, 40, *44,* 78, 82, *97*
Levy, R. M., 122, *144*
Liben, L. S., 226, 229, 230, 232, *241, 242*
Lidner, R., 22, *43*
Lindauer, B. K., 224, 226, 232, 233, 234, 235, 236, *241*

**M**

Maccoby, E. E., 113, *144*
MacNamara, J., 223, *241*
Mahoney, G. J., 226, 227, 229, *241*
Mandler, J. M., 216, 218, *241,* 287, *289*
May, M. A., 41, *43,* 95, *96*
McArthur, L. Z., 26, *44*
McCarrel, N. S., 223, 224, *240*
McDonough, D., 123, 134, *142*
Mearns, H., 261, *265*
Mehler, J., 29, *44*
Mervis, C. B., 167, *168*
Miller, S. A., 117, 125, *144*
Monahan, J. S., 133, *144*
Morgan, J. S., 114, *143*
Murray, J., 222, *242*

**N**

Nelson, K., 223, *241*
Nickerson, R. S., 117, *144*
Nummendal, S. G., 219, *241*

**O**

Oden, G. C., 8, *44,* 78, *97*
Odom, R. D., 171, 172, 176, 179, *181*
Olum, V., 117, *143*
Olver, R. R., 113, 117, *142*
Omanson, R. C., 238, 239, *241*
Opper, S., 132, *143*
Orvis, B. R., 38, *44*

**P**

Parducci, A., 11, *44*
Paris, S. G., 224, 226, 227, 228, 229, 231, 232, 233, 234, 235, 236, 237, 238, 239, *241*
Parsons, J. E., 24, 27, 40, *44,* 72, *96,* 219, *241*
Pascual-Leone, J. A., 288, *289*

Piaget, J., 17, 20, 21, 28, 29, *44,* 47, 63, 67, *69,* 71, 73, *97,* 113, 114, 125, 132, 133, 142, *144,* 169, 170, *181,* 212, *214,* 217, 219, 220, 221, 222, *241, 242,* 273, 287, *289*
Pick, A. D., 113, 114, *144*
Pinard, A., 40, *44*
Posnansky, C. J., 226, 229, 230, 232, *241, 242*
Postal, P. M., 224, *241*
Poulson, D., 287, *289*
Premack, D., 287, *289*
Pringle, R., 16, *44*
Pufall, P. B., 29, *44*

**Q**

Quine, W. V. O., 187, *214*

**R**

Rachlin, H. C., 30, *44*
Rest, J. R., 41, *44*
Rholes, W. S., 72, *96,* 219, *241*
Rieger, C. J., III, 258, 264, *265*
Riley, C. A., 223, 229, *242*
Rogers, J. C., 117, *144*
Rosch, E., 167, *168*
Ruble, D. N., 24, 26, 27, 40, *44,* 72, *96,* 219, *240, 241*
Rumelhart, D. E., 216, *242,* 264, *265,* 267, 268, 289, *289*

**S**

Saluja, S. K., 22, *44*
Schank, R. C., 264, *265,* 267, 287, 289, *290*
Schmidt, H. D., 100, 101, 102, 104, 110, *112*
Shanteau, J., 16, *44*
Shanteau, J. C., 32, *43,* 101, *112*
Shaw, R. E., 29, *44*
Shepard, R. N., 115, *144*
Shepp, B. E., 113, 114, 119, 120, 121, 122, 123, 125, 130, 132, 134, 141, *142, 143, 144*
Shwartz, S. P., 147, 168, *168*
Sidana, U. R., 22, *44*
Siegler, R. S., 67, *69*
Singh, R., 22, *44*

Smedslund, J., 222, *242*
Smith, L. B., 113, 120, 121, 123, 124, 125, 131, *144*
Spence, K. W., 183, 199, *214*
Srivastava, P., 22, *44*
Stein, N. L., 216, 218, 219, 239, *242,* 286, 287, *290*
Strutt, G. F., 113, *144*
Suls, J. M., 25, *44*
Surber, C. F., 19, *45,* 74, 78, *97,* 220, 221, *242*
Svenson, O. A., 31, *45*
Swartz, K. B., 120, 121, 122, 123, 125, 141, *144*
Szeminska, A., 28, *44,* 222, *242*

**T**

Tarski, A., 187, *214*
Taweel, S. S., 114, *143*
Thieman, T. J., 226, 230, *242*
Thompson, D. M., 236, *242*
Thompson, S. K., 17, *43,* 72, 75, 77, 93, *96*
Thorndyke, P. W., 216, *242,* 271, *290*
Tighe, L. S., 117, 118, 119, *144*
Tighe, T. J., 117, 118, 119, *144*
Trabasso, T., 72, *96,* 219, 222, 223, 229, 238, 239, *240, 241, 242,* 288, *290*
Tulving, E., 236, *242*
Turiel, E., 41, *45,* 74, *97*
Turrisi, F. D., 132, *144*
Tversky, A., 104, 107, 108, *112,* 133, *143*

**U**

Upton, L. R., 226, 231, 236, 237, 238, 239, *241*

**V**

van Dijk, T. A., 287, 289, *289, 290*
Verge, C. G., 15, *45,* 57, *69*

**W**

Wallace, J. G., 113, *143*
Walster, E., 35, *45*
Walster, G. W., 35, *45*

Warren, W. H., 238, 239, *241*
Weintraub, D. J., 133, *145*
Weiss, D. J., 62, *69*
Well, A. D., 113, 115, *143, 144*
Wender, L., 133, *145*
Wendt, D., 111, *112*
Werner, H., 117, *145*
Wertheimer, M., 160, *168*
Wiener-Erlich, W. K., 123, 134, *142*
Wilkening, F., 48, 51, 67, *69, 145*
Wilkening, R., 11, 12, 14, 27, *45,*

Wilson, E. G., 223, 229, *242*
Winograd, P., 287, *290*
Wohlwill, J. F., 28, *45,* 113, 114, 120, *145*
Wolff, J. L., 132, *145*


**XYZ**

Youniss, J., 222, *242*
Zeaman, D., 113, *143*

# Subject Index

## A

Abstraction, 117, 122
  reflective, 212
  structural, 183–213
Action schema, 267
Adding-type model, *see also* Integration rules
  parallelism theorem for, 5, 12
Additive integration, *see* Integration rules, adding-type
Analysis of information, 170, 176–181
Area, judgment of, 11–15, 48–58, 133, 139–142
Artificial intelligence, 264
Attention,
  developmental differences, 113
  limited processing, 26–28
    test for, 13, 28
  selective, 116, 120, 132, 139, 170
  and stimulus structure, 114–117
Attribution, 84
  social, 24–26
  theory, 37
Averaging model, 6–8, 75, *see also* Integration rules
  test for, 7, 75, 85

## C

Centering, *see* Centration
Centration, 27, 57, 67, 125, 132, 139, 147, 169
Choices among bets, 99–112
  and similarity of alternatives, 108–110
Choice tasks, Piagetian, 78–80
  critique of, 67, 71–75, 95
Classification, restricted, 116
Concept identification, 184–188
Conceptual-change theories, 170, 179
Conservation,
  definition of, 33
  measurement of, 34
  of quantity, 132, 139
Context, in language understanding, 224, 243–248, 253, 260, 263

## D

Décalage, 179
Decision making, 100–112
  probabilistic, 106
Deservingness, 19–21
  cognitive algebra of, 34

Discourse, understanding of, *see* Story
    understanding
Discrimination,
    conditional, 183–199
        form of solution in, 189–194
        structural transfer in, 194–199
    simple, 183, 196
    simultaneous, 117
Discrimination learning, 183–213
    information integration in, 183, 212
Disintegration of information, *see* Analysis
    of information


E

Equity,
    integration, 21, 36
    theory, 35
Ergodic heuristic, 39
Event chains, 248–253, 264
    structure of, 251


F

False-recognition paradigm, 225–231
    confounds in, 227
Functional measurement, 2–11


G

Gestalt principles,
    in perceptual parsing, 160
Groups, perception of, 22


I

Inferences, 215–240, 243–264
    causal, 38
    evaluative, 218, 260–262
    extrapolative, 256–262
        facilitative, 258
        preventive, 259
    functions of, 244–247
    implicit, 85, 89, 94
    about internal states, 217
        measurement of 220
    lexical, 233, 237, 253–255, 262

Inferences *(contd.)*
    and memory, 215–239
    about missing information, 84, 89
    motivational, 237
    spatial, 255
    spontaneous, generation of, 235
    taxonomy of, 253–263
    temporal, 255, 262
    transitive, 221–223
Information integration theory, 1–41, 47,
    71, 101, 132, 140, 220
Integral dimensions, properties of, 114–116
Integration rules,
    adding type, 12–16, 18, 24–26, 32, 48–62,
        83, 103
        general-purpose, 14, 18, 24, 68
    "as-if" models, 62, 66, 68
    averaging, 20, 22, 88
    configural, 18, 89–91
    multiplicative, 16, 25, 32, 48–62, 65, 91
Integration theory, *see* Information
    integration theory


L

Language understanding, *see also* Story
    understanding
    constructivist approach to, 224
    as context construction, 248
    contextual dependency of, 223
    natural, 264
Learning, structural, 211
Linear order, construction of, 223
Linear scale, 3–10


M

Matrix problems, 169, 173
Memory, *see also* Story recall
    in comprehension of narratives, 215–240
    and transitive inferences, 221–223
Moral judgment, 17–19, 24, 41, 71–97,
    217–221
    recency effects in, 219
Multiplicative integration, *see* Integration
    rules
Multiplying model, *see also* Integration
    rules
    linear fan theorem for, 8, 12

**N**

Narratives, comprehension of, *see* Story
understanding
Nonreversal shift, *see* Reversal shift

**P**

Paper-rock-scissors game, 199, 211
Perceptual learning, 117, 131
Perceptual parsing, 147–168
bottom-up processes, 150, 167
Person perception, 36
Picture Integration Test, 148
Probability,
and payoff integration, 101–104
subjective, 31–33
Problem solving, 169–181

**R**

Rating scale, *see also* Linear scale
methodology, 9–11
Rectangles, *see also* Area, judgment of
perception of, 132–141
Reversal shift, 118
Rewrite rules, 267
Rule Learning, 184

**S**

Salience, perceptual,
in perceptual parsing, 152–160, 167
in problem solving, 171–180
Scaling, functional, 6
Semantic integration, 229–231
Separable dimensions, properties of,
114–116
Similarity, perceived,
in choices among bets, 109
of multidimensional stimuli, 119
changes with age, 123–142
Social judgment, research prospects, 34–41

**Speed**, *see also* Velocity
judgment of, 30
Stage theories, alternative to, 41
Stimulus structure, 114–142
and processing options, 114–117
Story recall, 236–239, 269–288
and goal-question answering, 283–286,
288
order of categories in, 218
and story coherency, 271
and story complexity, 279–283
and story structuredness, 274–283
Story understanding, 215–240, 243–265,
267–289

**T**

Temporal relations, coordination of, 274,
286
Time,
concept, development of, 63
and velocity integration, 62–66
processes in, 66
Transitive inferences, 221–223
Transfer, structural, 194–211
in conditional discrimination, 194–199
in transverse patterning, 199–211
Transformational linguistics, 224
Transverse patterning, 183, 199–213

**V**

Velocity, *see also* Speed
concept, development of, 63
and time integration, 62–66
Visual memory, model of, 147
Volume, judgment of, 58–62

**W**

Wholistic perception, 117, 141
World knowledge, in story comprehension,
243, 252, 267, 287